4

Hitma matsuri

Masao Ohtake

D0111693

HINA MATSURI Vol.4

CONTENTS

CHAPTER 17

AN OFFERING TO THE GOD OF ROCK 'N' ROLL

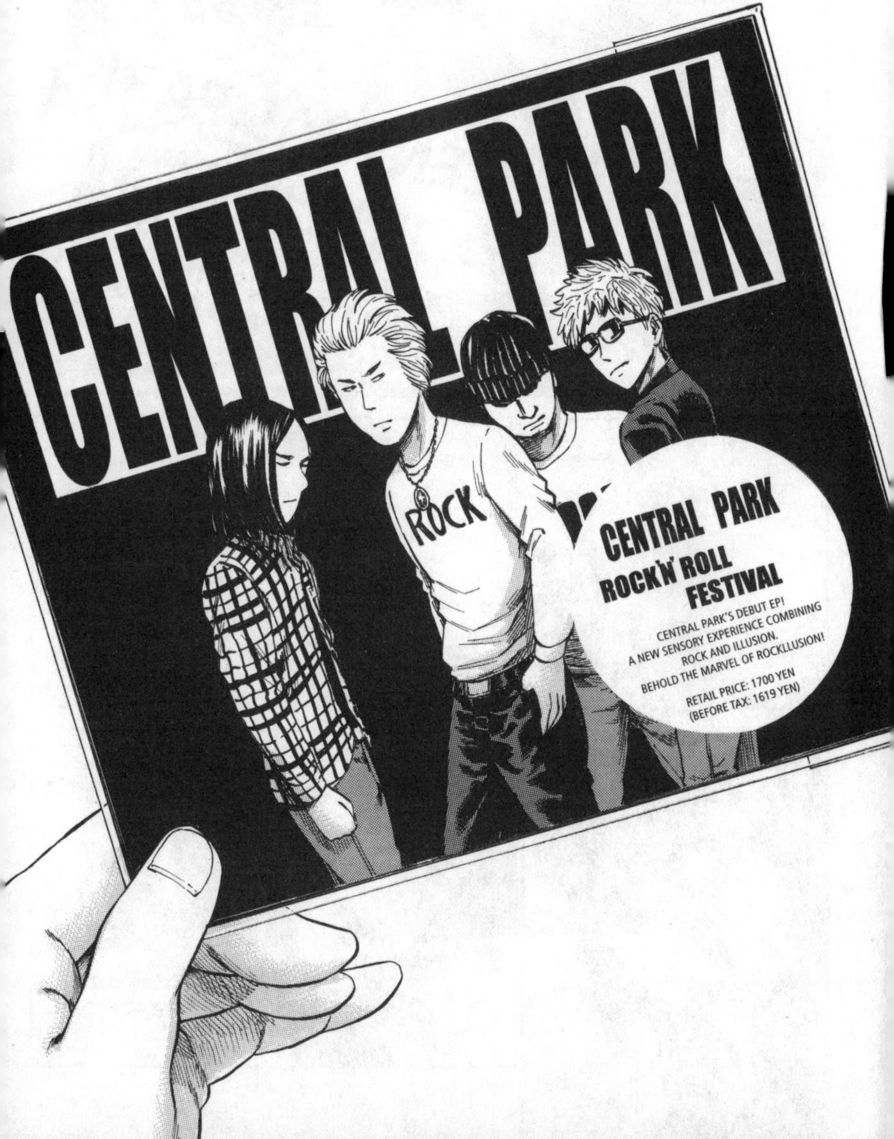
CENTRAL PARK
ROCK
CENTRAL PARK
ROCK'N' ROLL
FESTIVAL
CENTRAL PARK'S DEBUT EP!
A NEW SENSORY EXPERIENCE COMBINING
ROCK AND ILLUSION.
BEHOLD THE MARVEL OF ROCKLLUSION!
RETAIL PRICE: 1700 YEN
(BEFORE TAX: 1619 YEN)

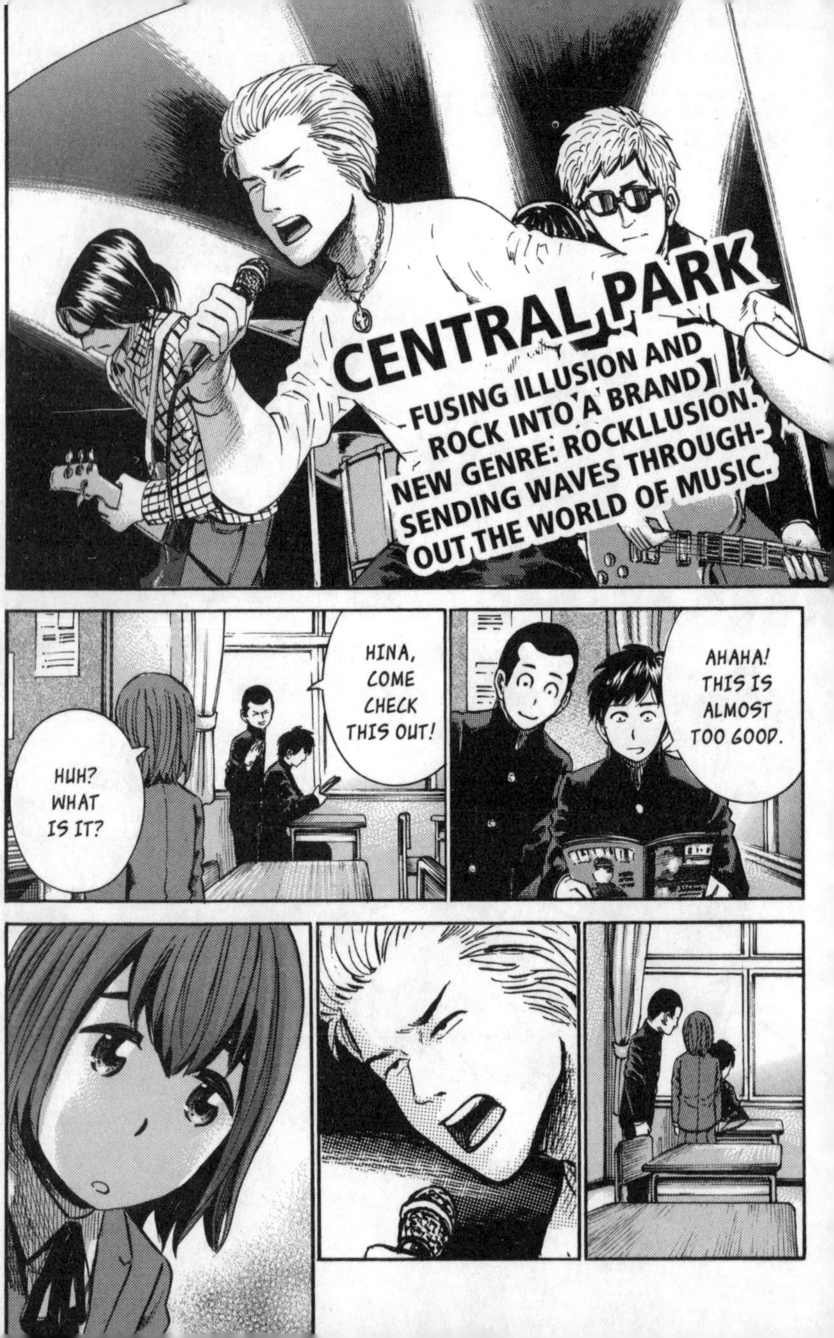
CENTRAL PARK
FUSING ILLUSION AND ROCK INTO A BRAND NEW GENRE: ROCKLLUSION. SENDING WAVES THROUGH-OUT THE WORLD OF MUSIC.
AHAHA! THIS IS ALMOST TOO GOOD.
HINA, COME CHECK THIS OUT!
HUH? WHAT IS IT?

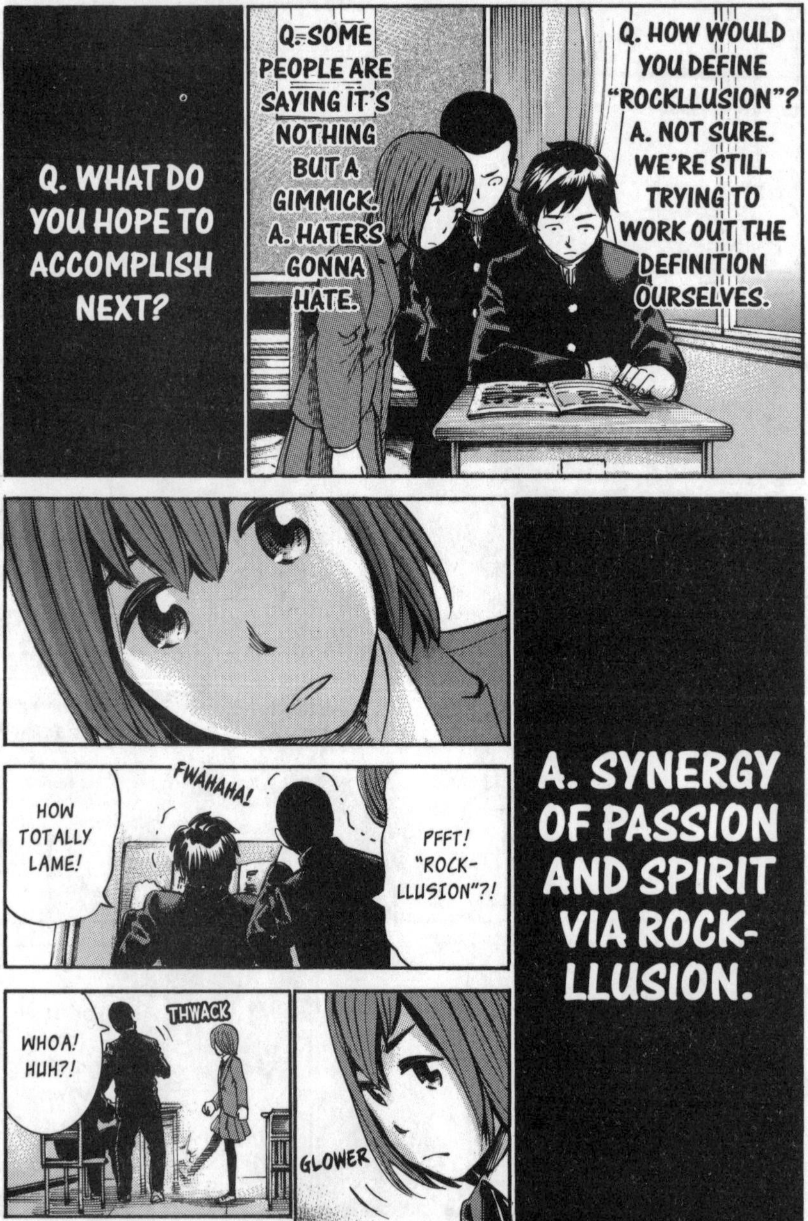
Q. HOW WOULD YOU DEFINE "ROCKLLUSION"? A. NOT SURE. WE'RE STILL TRYING TO WORK OUT THE DEFINITION OURSELVES.
Q. SOME PEOPLE ARE SAYING IT'S NOTHING BUT A GIMMICK. A. HATERS GONNA HATE.
Q. WHAT DO YOU HOPE TO ACCOMPLISH NEXT?
A. SYNERGY OF PASSION AND SPIRIT VIA ROCK-LLUSION.
PFFT! "ROCK-LLUSION"?!
FWAHAHA!
HOW TOTALLY LAME!
GLOWER
THWACK
WHOA! HUH?!

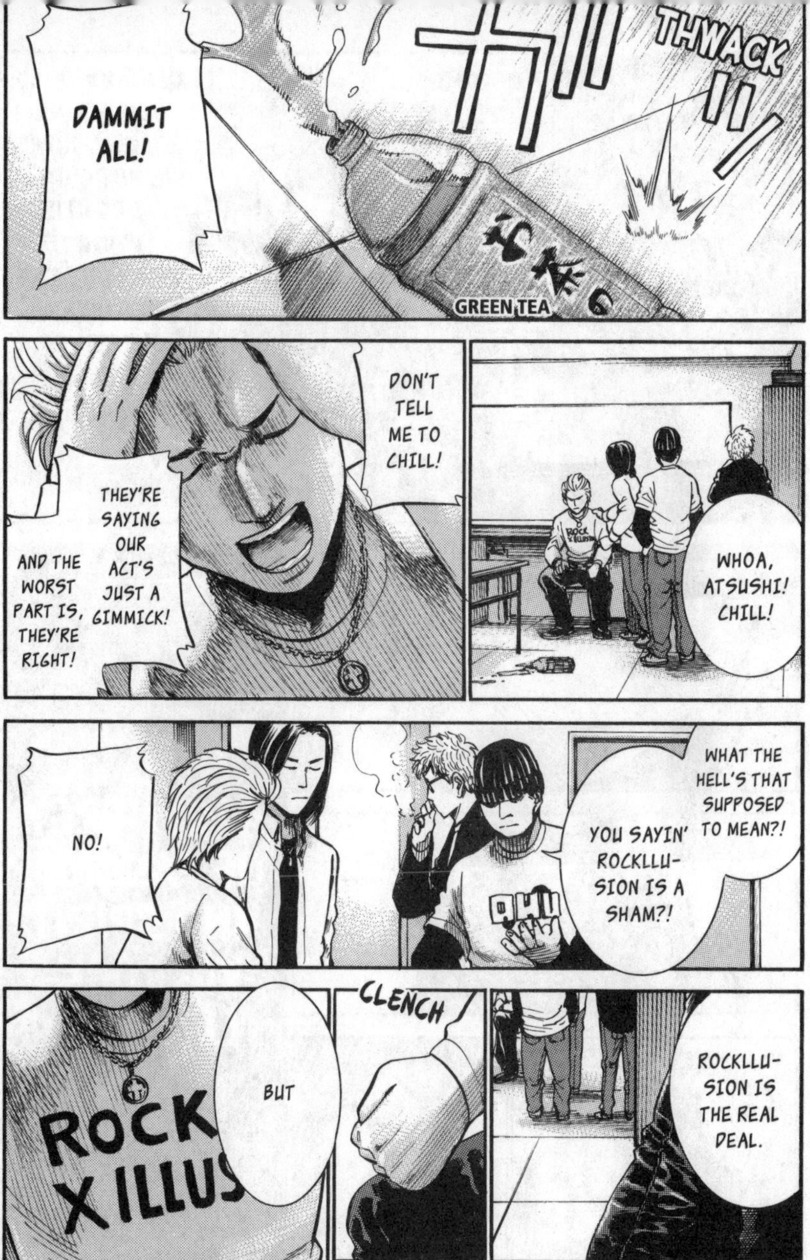
THWACK
DAMMIT ALL!
GREEN TEA
WHOA, ATSUSHI! CHILL!
DON'T TELL ME TO CHILL!
THEY'RE SAYING OUR ACT'S JUST A GIMMICK!
AND THE WORST PART IS, THEY'RE RIGHT!
WHAT THE HELL'S THAT SUPPOSED TO MEAN?!
YOU SAYIN' ROCKLLUSION IS A SHAM?!
NO!
ROCKLLUSION IS THE REAL DEAL.
CLENCH
BUT
ROCK X ILLUS

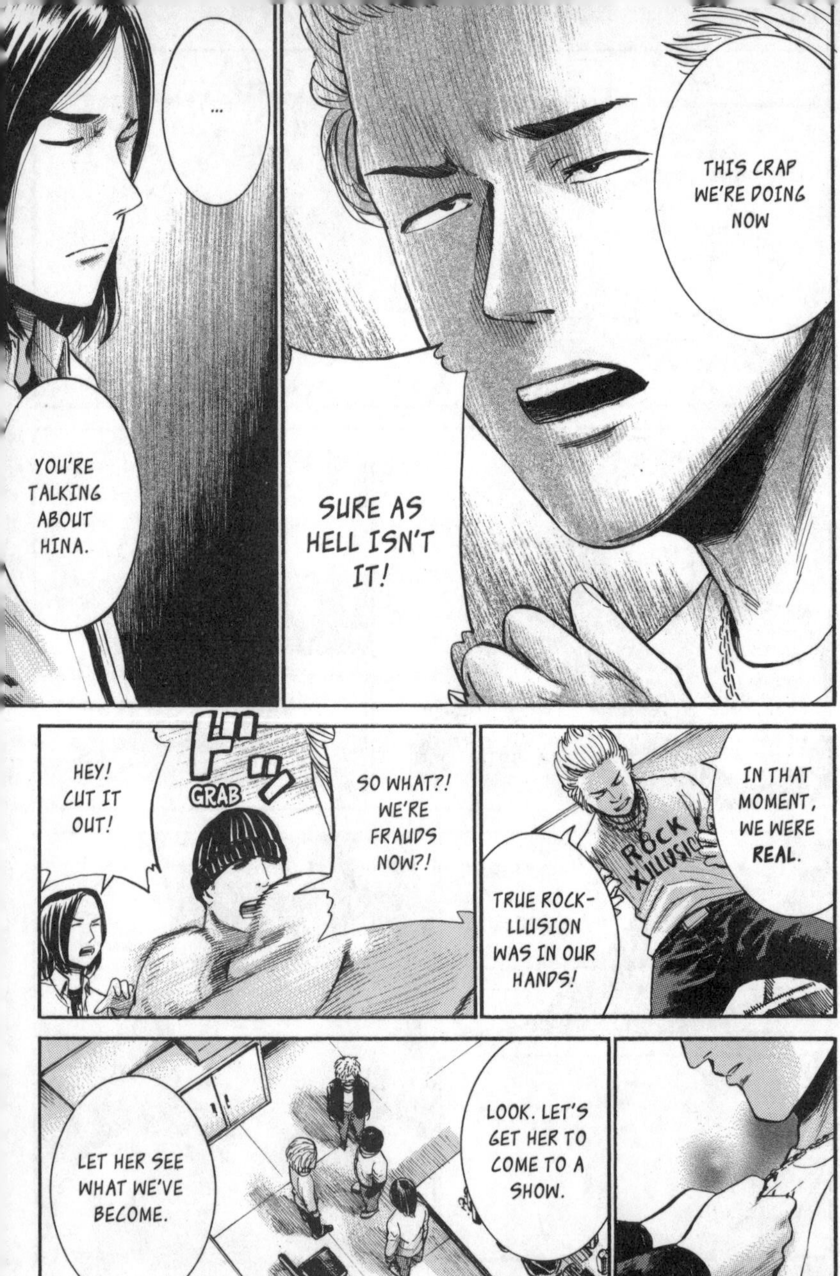
THIS CRAP WE'RE DOING NOW
SURE AS HELL ISN'T IT!
...
YOU'RE TALKING ABOUT HINA.
IN THAT MOMENT, WE WERE **REAL**.
TRUE ROCK-LLUSION WAS IN OUR HANDS!
SO WHAT?! WE'RE FRAUDS NOW?!
GRAB
HEY! CUT IT OUT!
LOOK. LET'S GET HER TO COME TO A SHOW.
LET HER SEE WHAT WE'VE BECOME.

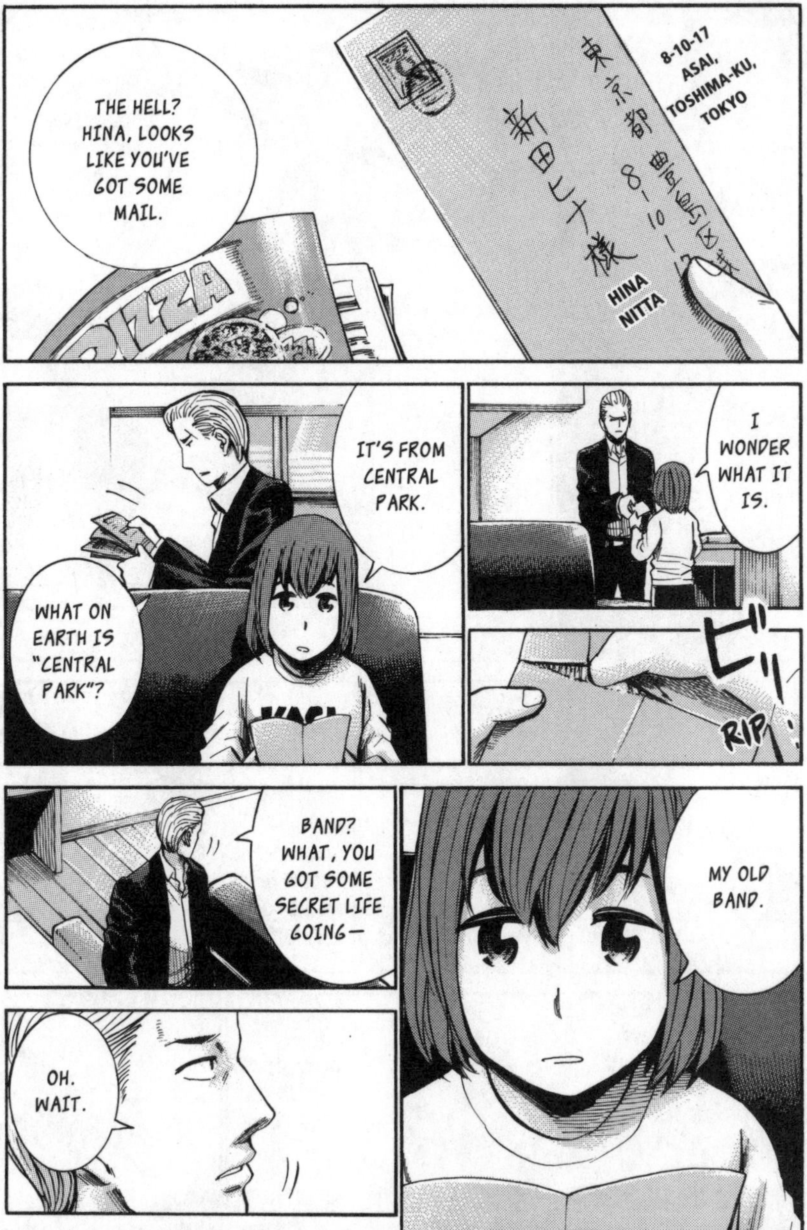
8-10-17 ASAI, TOSHIMA-KU, TOKYO
HINA NITTA
THE HELL? HINA, LOOKS LIKE YOU'VE GOT SOME MAIL.
I WONDER WHAT IT IS.
RIP
IT'S FROM CENTRAL PARK.
WHAT ON EARTH IS "CENTRAL PARK"?
MY OLD BAND.
BAND? WHAT, YOU GOT SOME SECRET LIFE GOING—
OH. WAIT.

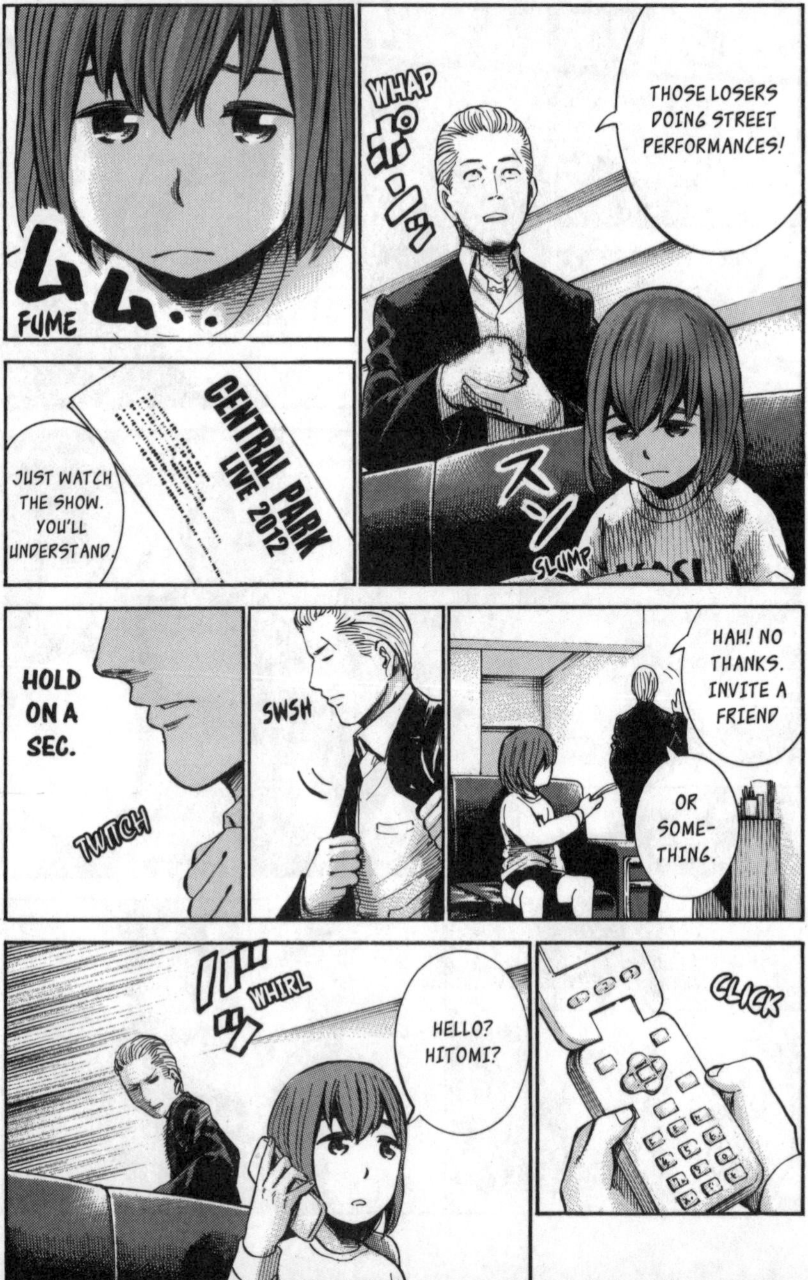
WHAP
THOSE LOSERS DOING STREET PERFORMANCES!
SLUMP
ムム…
FUME
JUST WATCH THE SHOW. YOU'LL UNDERSTAND.
CENTRAL PARK LIVE 2012
HAH! NO THANKS. INVITE A FRIEND
OR SOME-THING.
SWSH
HOLD ON A SEC.
TWITCH
CLICK
WHIRL
HELLO? HITOMI?

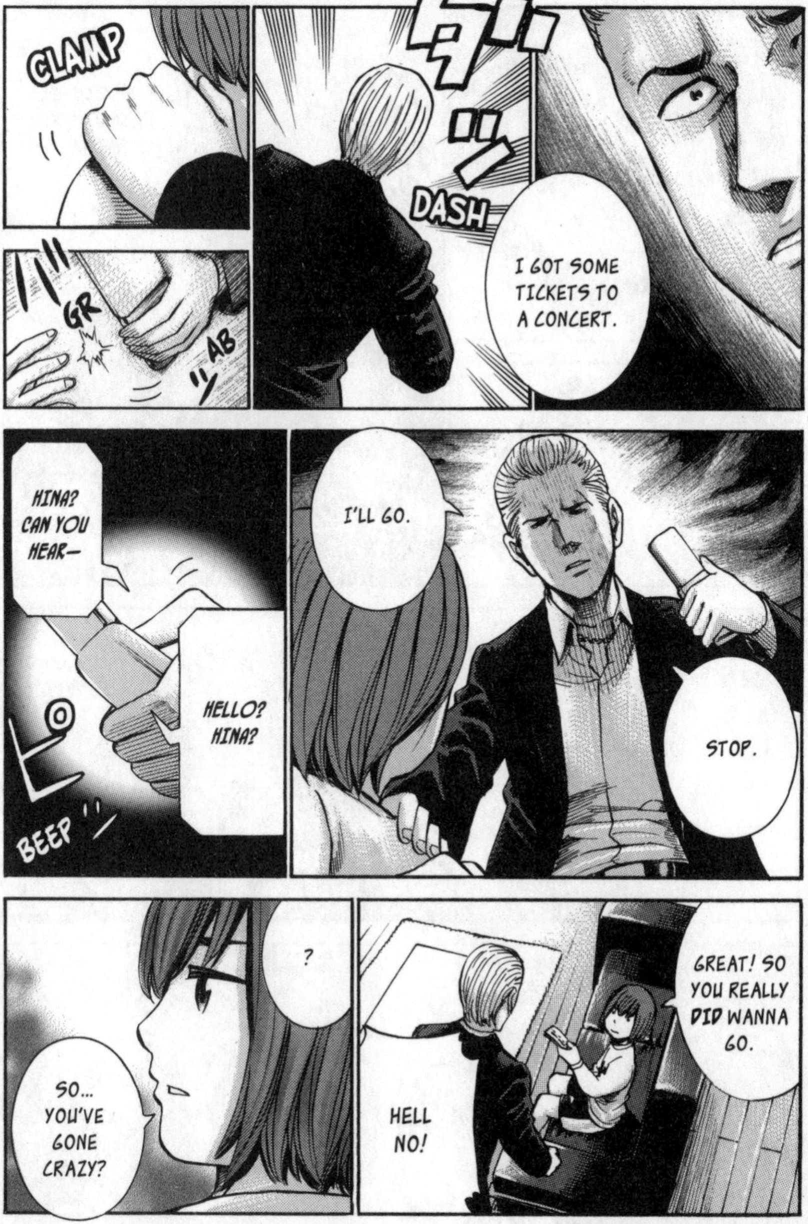
I GOT SOME TICKETS TO A CONCERT.
DASH
CLAMP
GR
AB
I'LL GO.
STOP.
HINA? CAN YOU HEAR—
HELLO? HINA?
BEEP
GREAT! SO YOU REALLY DID WANNA GO.
HELL NO!
?
SO... YOU'VE GONE CRAZY?

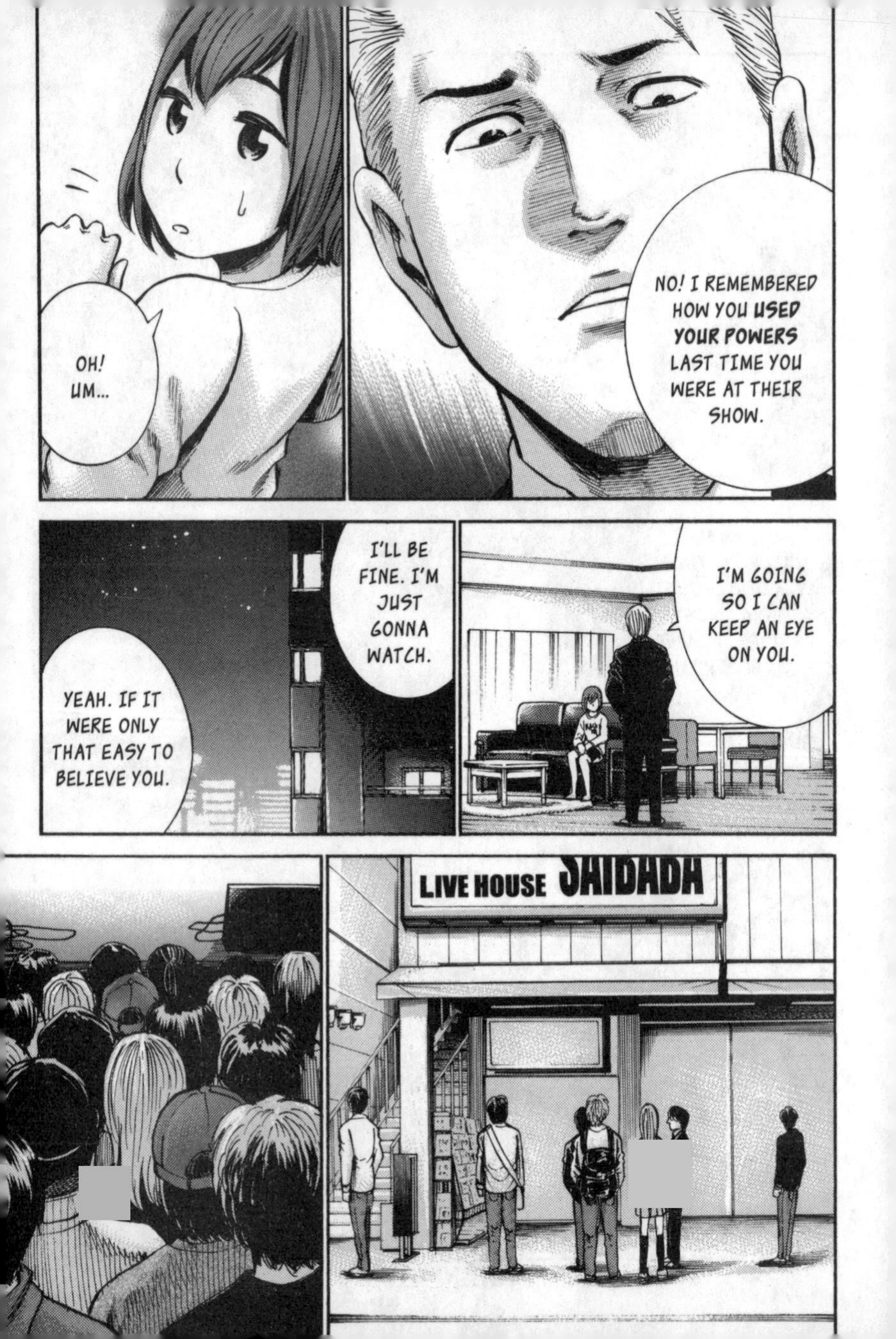
NO! I REMEMBERED HOW YOU **USED YOUR POWERS** LAST TIME YOU WERE AT THEIR SHOW.
OH! UM...
I'M GOING SO I CAN KEEP AN EYE ON YOU.
I'LL BE FINE. I'M JUST GONNA WATCH.
YEAH. IF IT WERE ONLY THAT EASY TO BELIEVE YOU.
LIVE HOUSE

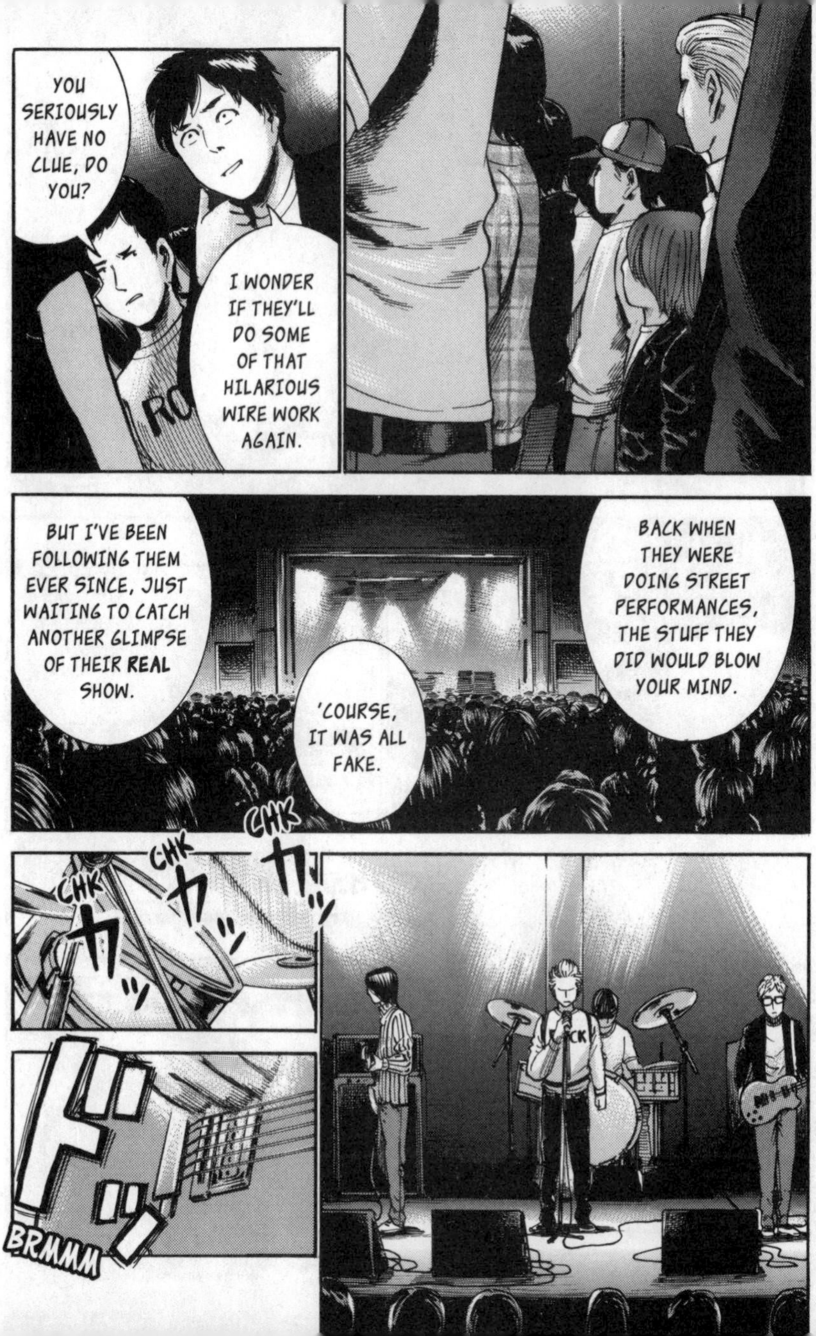
I WONDER IF THEY'LL DO SOME OF THAT HILARIOUS WIRE WORK AGAIN.
YOU SERIOUSLY HAVE NO CLUE, DO YOU?
BACK WHEN THEY WERE DOING STREET PERFORMANCES, THE STUFF THEY DID WOULD BLOW YOUR MIND.
'COURSE, IT WAS ALL FAKE.
BUT I'VE BEEN FOLLOWING THEM EVER SINCE, JUST WAITING TO CATCH ANOTHER GLIMPSE OF THEIR **REAL** SHOW.
CHK
CHK
CHK
BRMMM

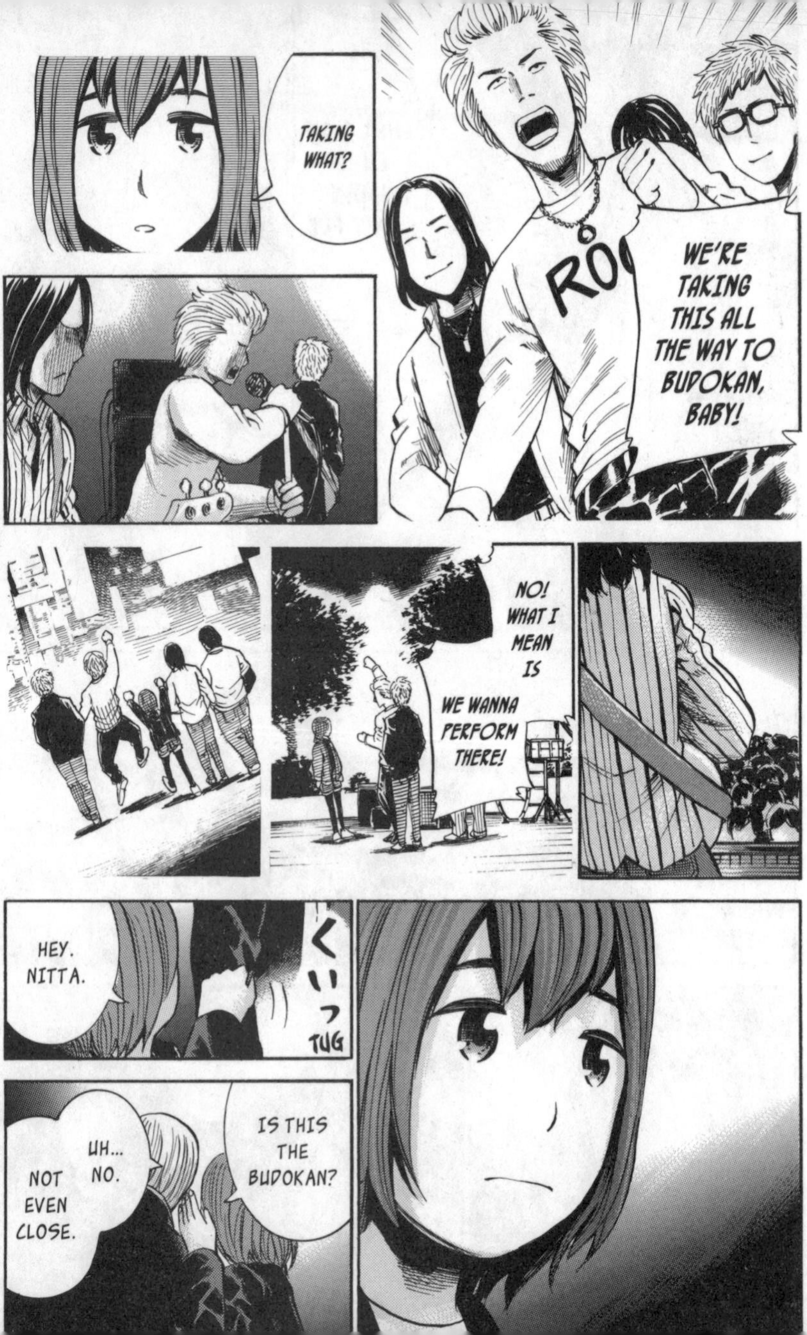
WE'RE TAKING THIS ALL THE WAY TO BUDOKAN, BABY!
TAKING WHAT?
NO! WHAT I MEAN IS
WE WANNA PERFORM THERE!
くいっ
TUG
HEY. NITTA.
IS THIS THE BUDOKAN?
UH... NO.
NOT EVEN CLOSE.

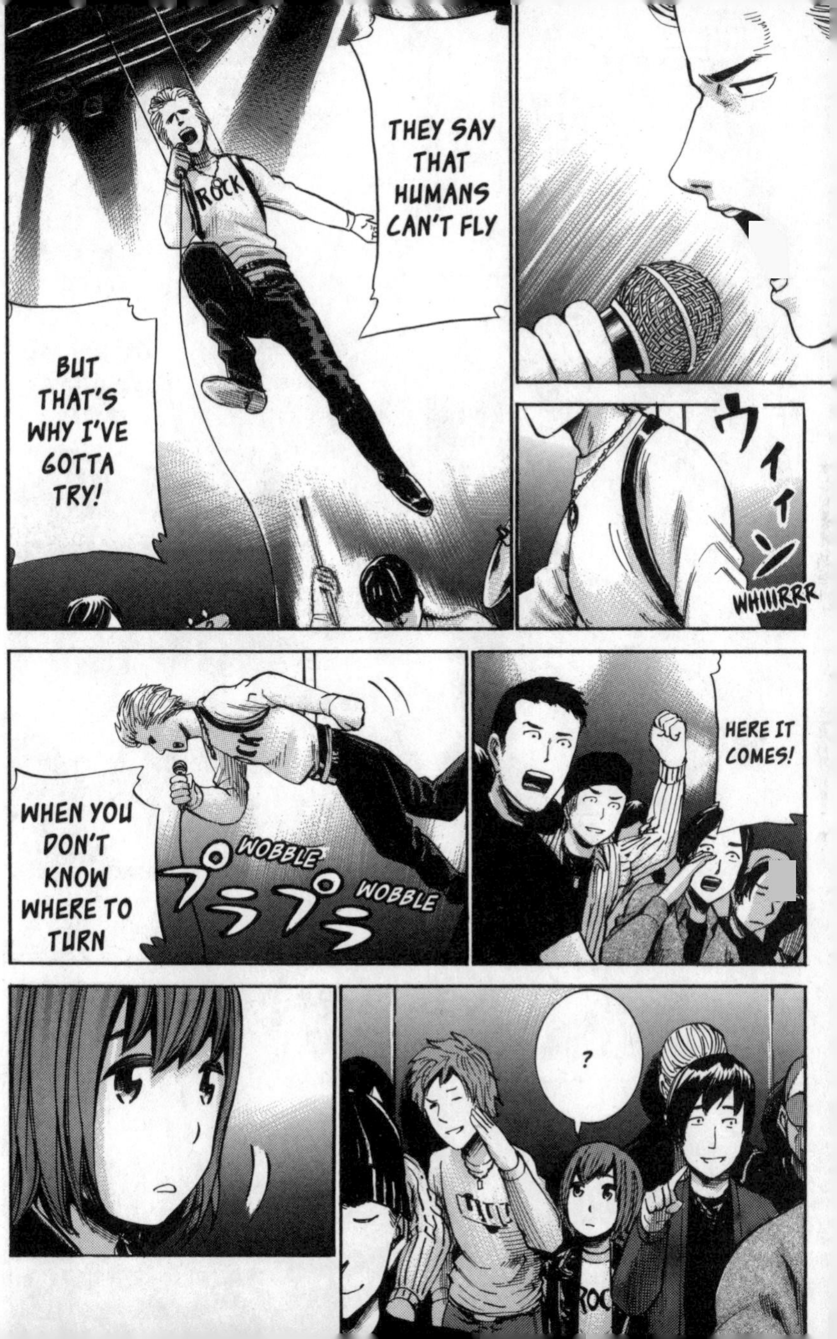
ウィィン
WHIIIRRR
THEY SAY THAT HUMANS CAN'T FLY
BUT THAT'S WHY I'VE GOTTA TRY!
HERE IT COMES!
WHEN YOU DON'T KNOW WHERE TO TURN
プラ WOBBLE
プラ WOBBLE
?

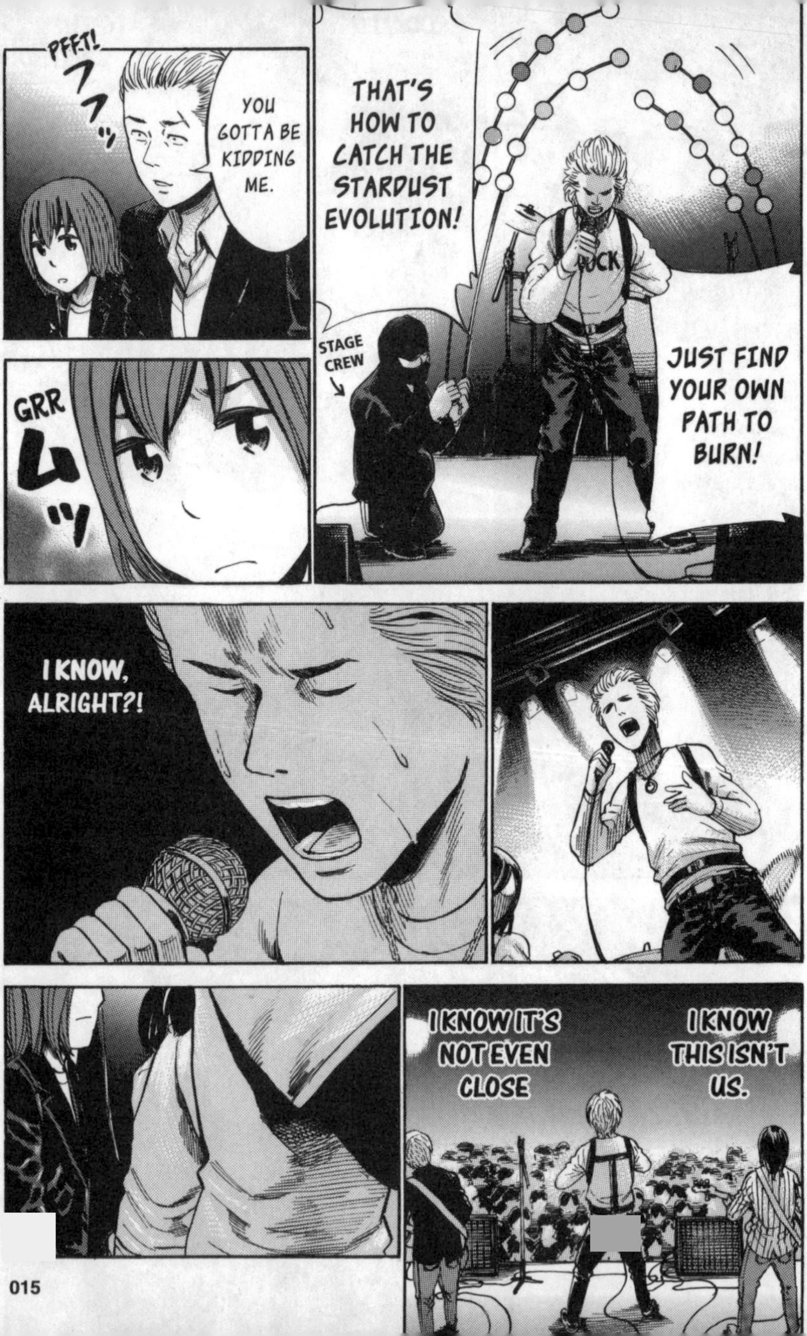
THAT'S HOW TO CATCH THE STARDUST EVOLUTION!
STAGE CREW
JUST FIND YOUR OWN PATH TO BURN!
PFFT!
フフッ
YOU GOTTA BE KIDDING ME.
GRR
ムッ
I KNOW, ALRIGHT?!
I KNOW THIS ISN'T US.
I KNOW IT'S NOT EVEN CLOSE

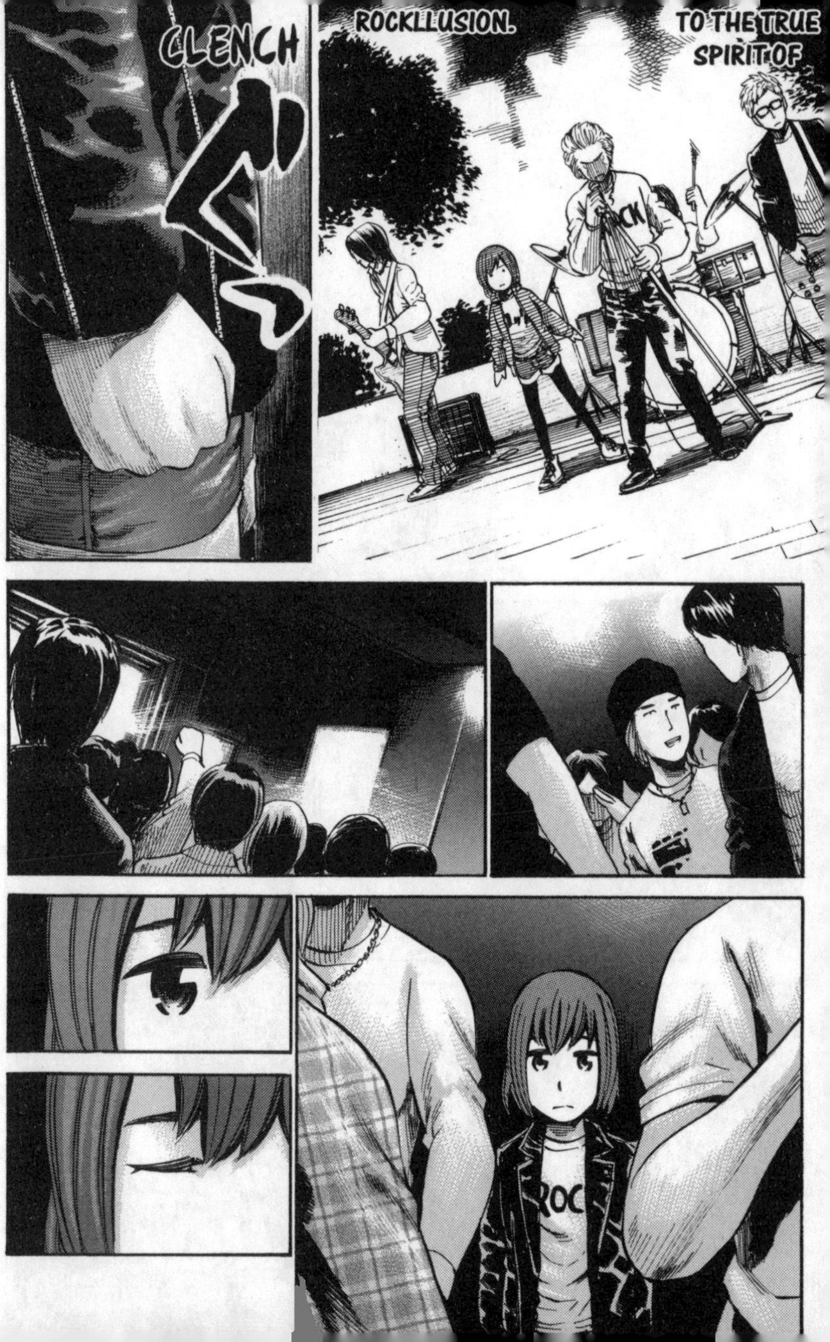
TO THE TRUE SPIRIT OF
ROCKLLUSION.
CLENCH

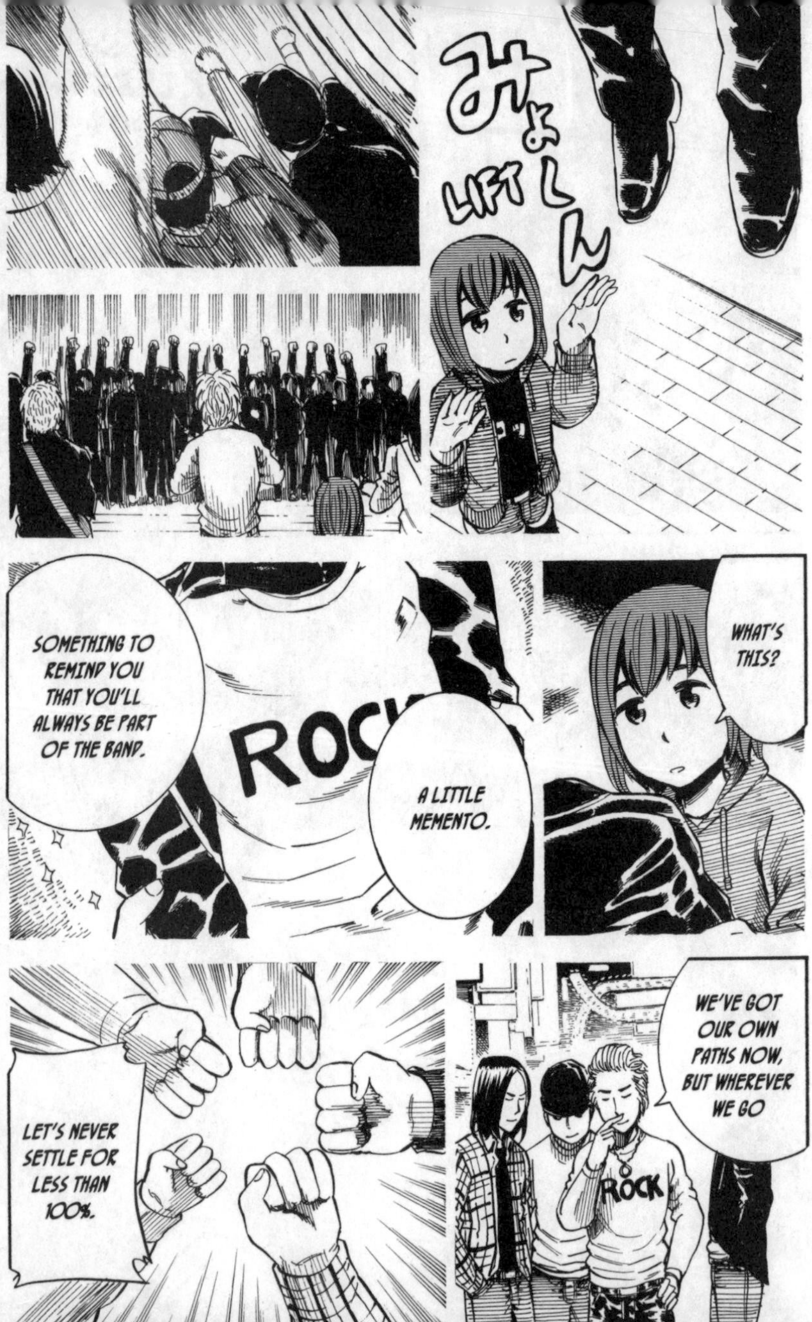
みよしん
LIFT
WHAT'S THIS?
A LITTLE MEMENTO.
SOMETHING TO REMIND YOU THAT YOU'LL ALWAYS BE PART OF THE BAND.
ROCK
WE'VE GOT OUR OWN PATHS NOW, BUT WHEREVER WE GO
LET'S NEVER SETTLE FOR LESS THAN 100%.
ROCK

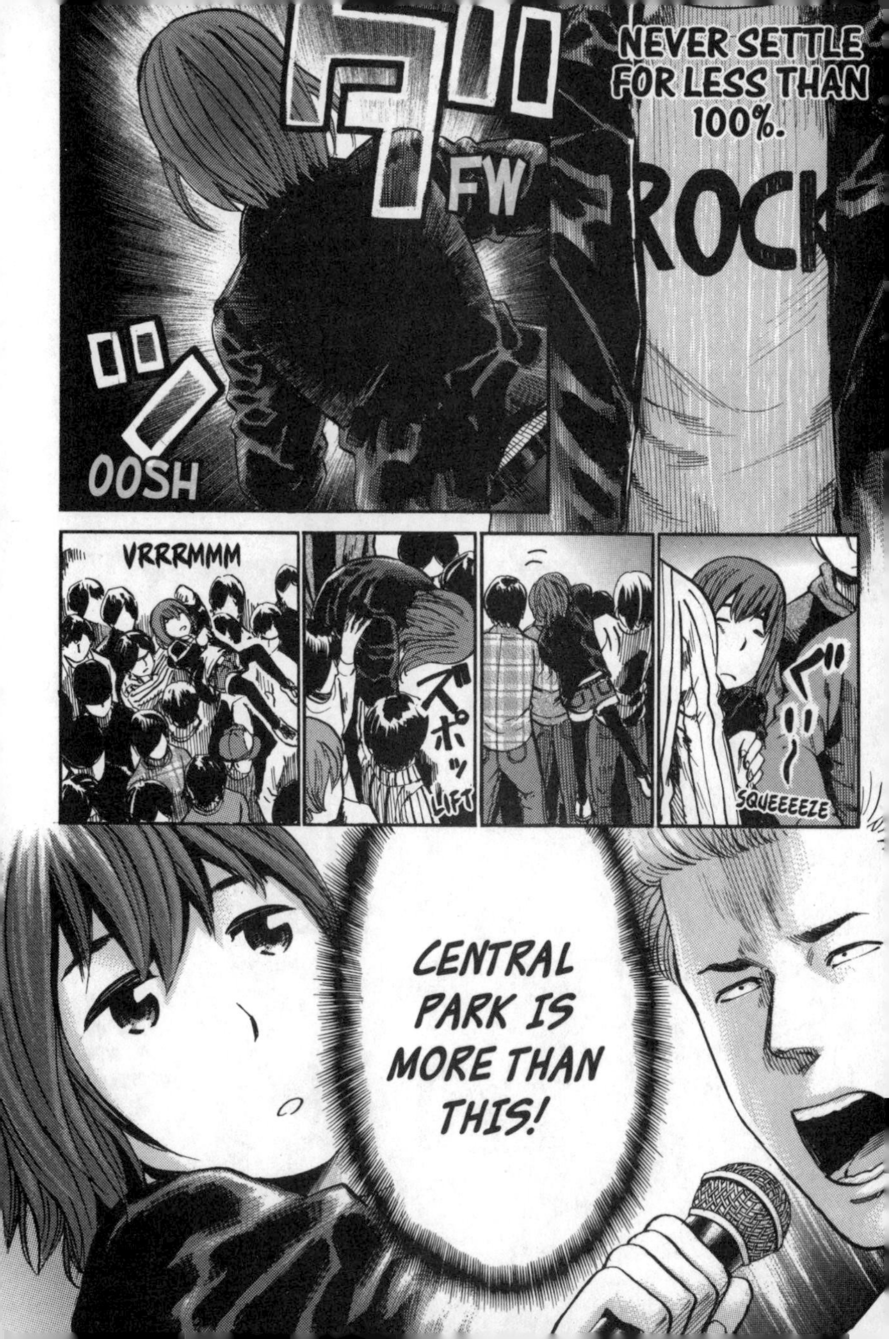
NEVER SETTLE FOR LESS THAN 100%.
ROCK
FW
OOSH
SQUEEEEEZE
ズポッ
LIFT
VRRRMMM
CENTRAL PARK IS MORE THAN THIS!

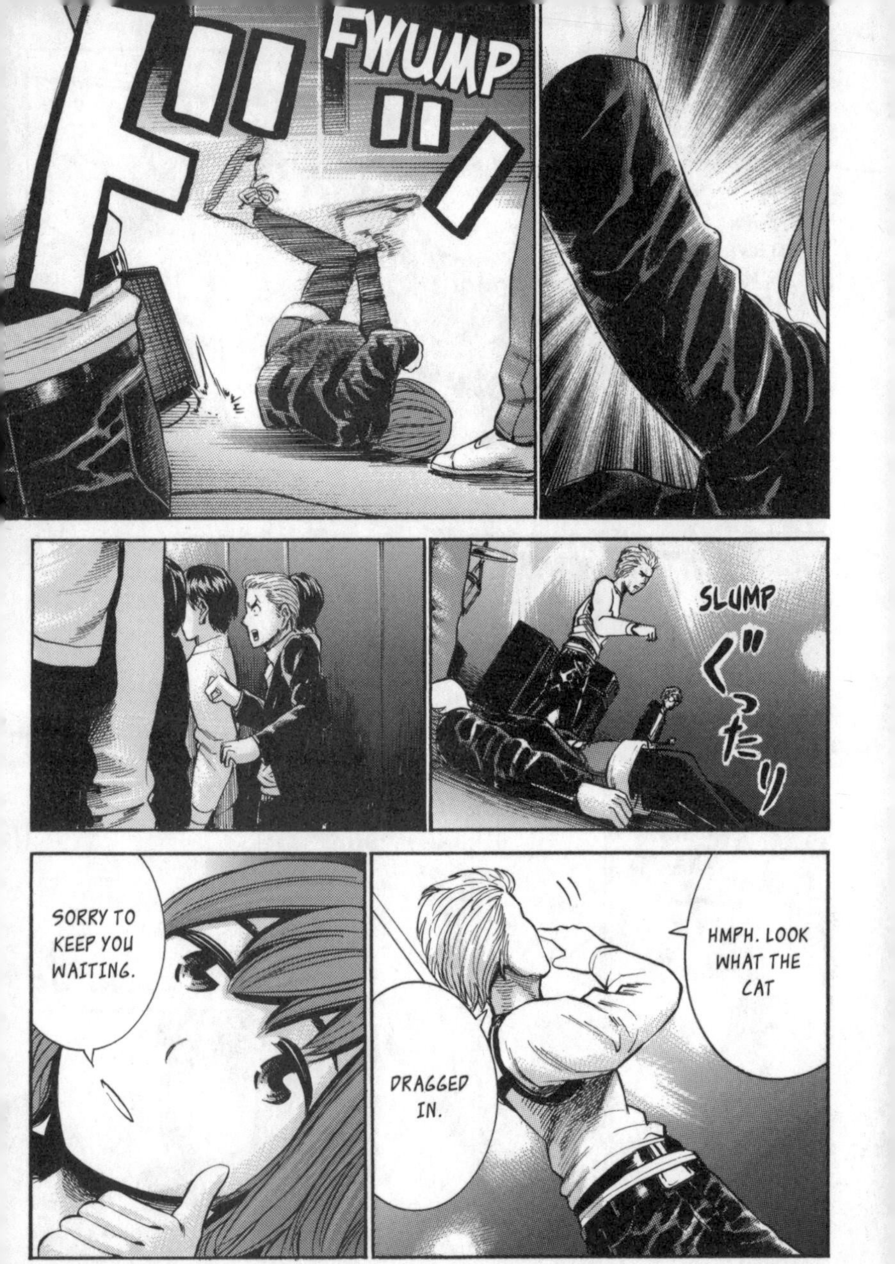
FWUMP
SLUMP
ぐったり
HMPH. LOOK WHAT THE CAT
DRAGGED IN.
SORRY TO KEEP YOU WAITING.

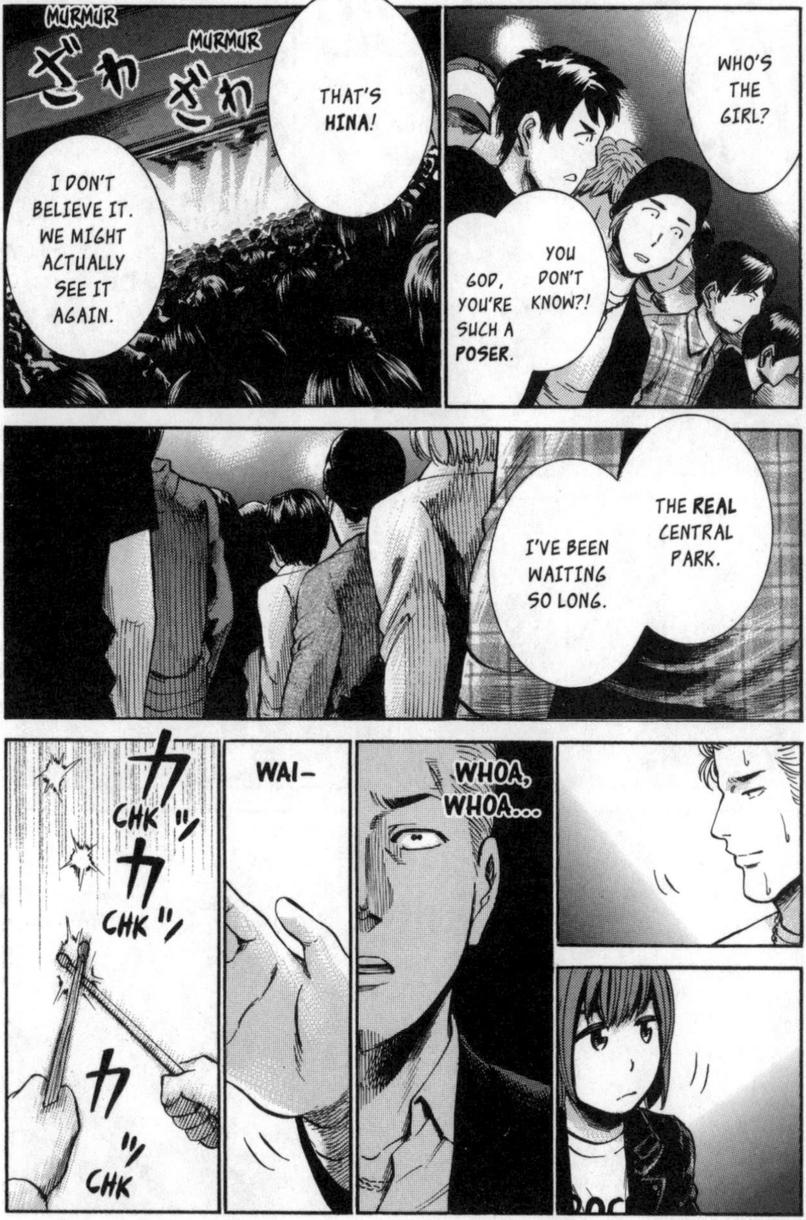
WHO'S THE GIRL?
YOU DON'T KNOW?!
GOD, YOU'RE SUCH A POSER.
THAT'S HINA!
MURMUR
MURMUR
ざわざわ
I DON'T BELIEVE IT. WE MIGHT ACTUALLY SEE IT AGAIN.
THE REAL CENTRAL PARK.
I'VE BEEN WAITING SO LONG.
WHOA, WHOA...
WAI-
カッ
CHK
カッ
CHK
カッ
CHK

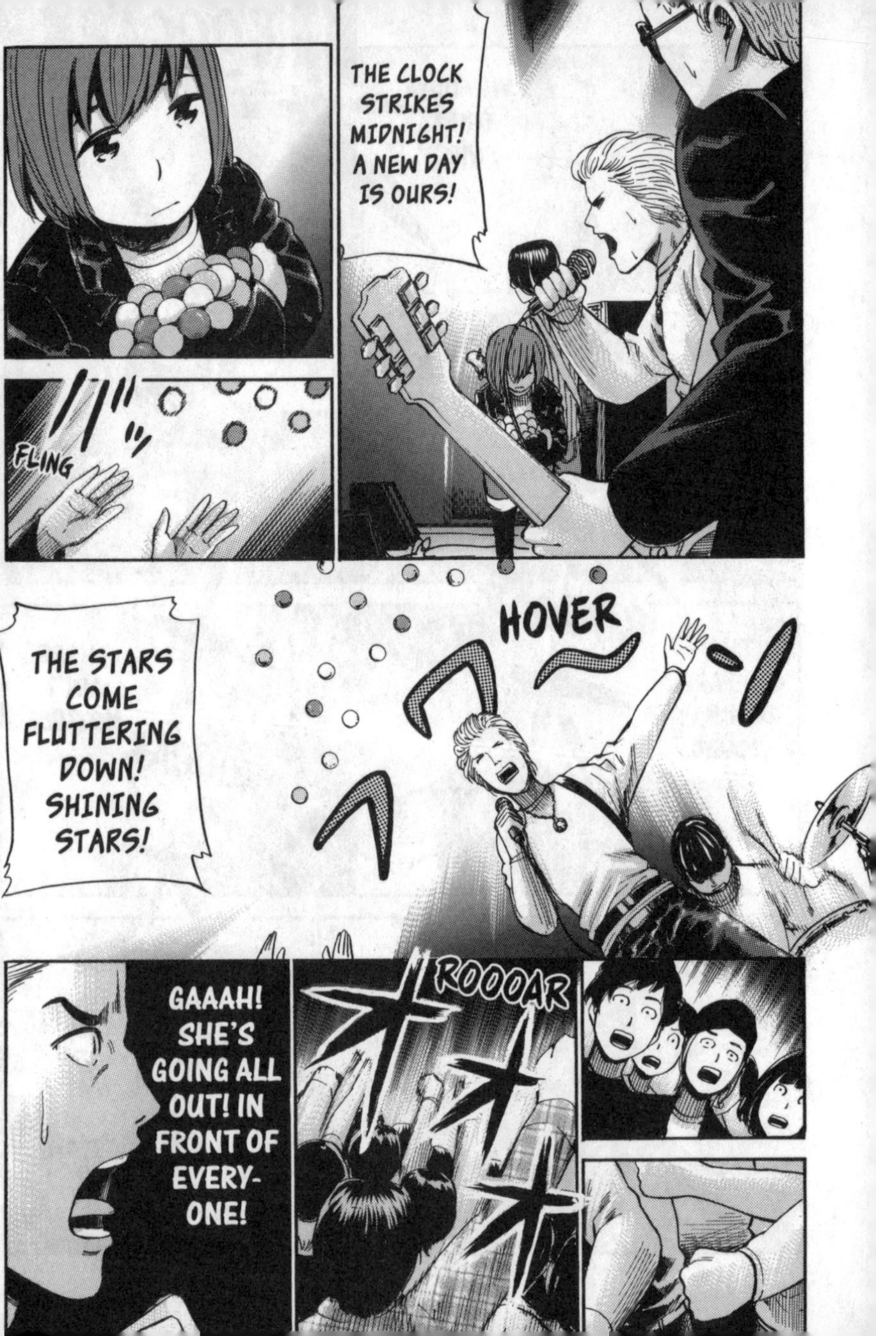
THE CLOCK STRIKES MIDNIGHT! A NEW DAY IS OURS!
FLING
HOVER
THE STARS COME FLUTTERING DOWN! SHINING STARS!
ROOOAR
GAAAH! SHE'S GOING ALL OUT! IN FRONT OF EVERY-ONE!

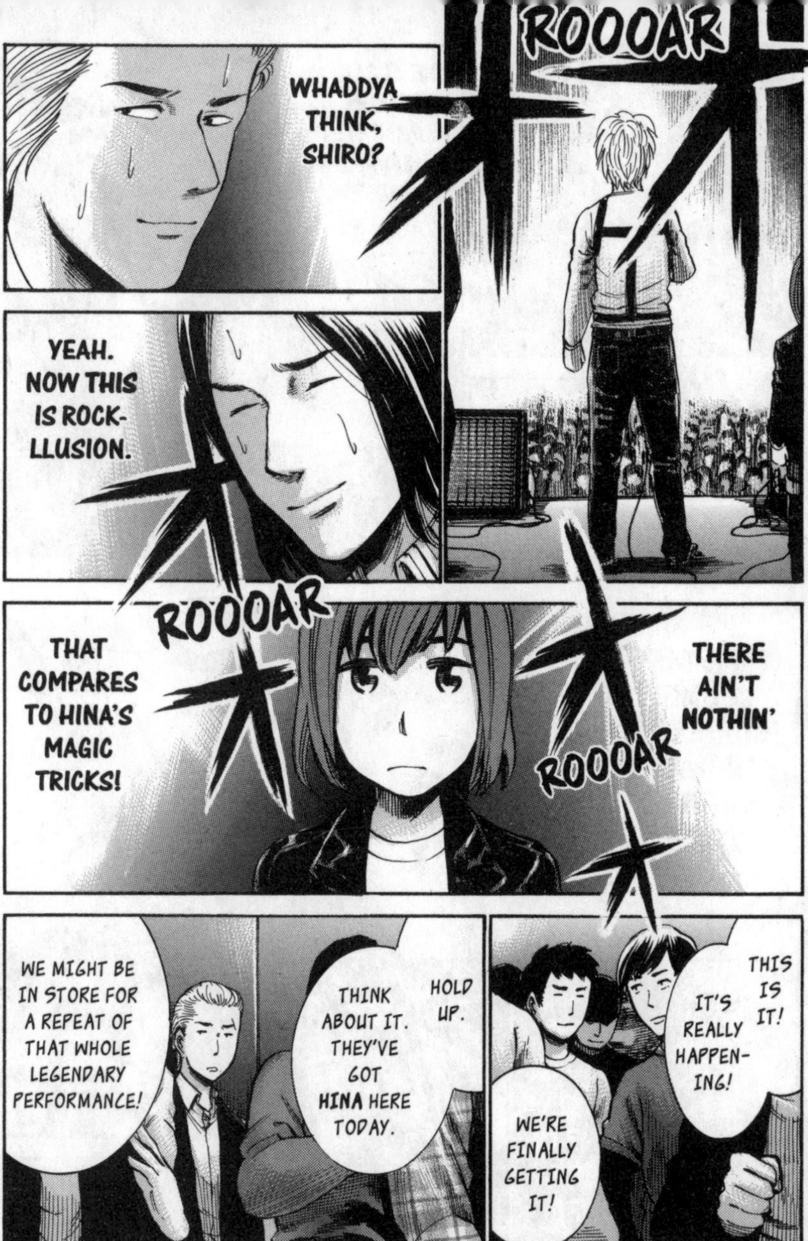
ROOOAR
WHADDYA THINK, SHIRO?
YEAH. NOW THIS IS ROCK-LLUSION.
ROOOAR
THERE AIN'T NOTHIN'
ROOOAR
THAT COMPARES TO HINA'S MAGIC TRICKS!
THIS IS IT!
IT'S REALLY HAPPEN-ING!
WE'RE FINALLY GETTING IT!
HOLD UP.
THINK ABOUT IT. THEY'VE GOT HINA HERE TODAY.
WE MIGHT BE IN STORE FOR A REPEAT OF THAT WHOLE LEGENDARY PERFORMANCE!

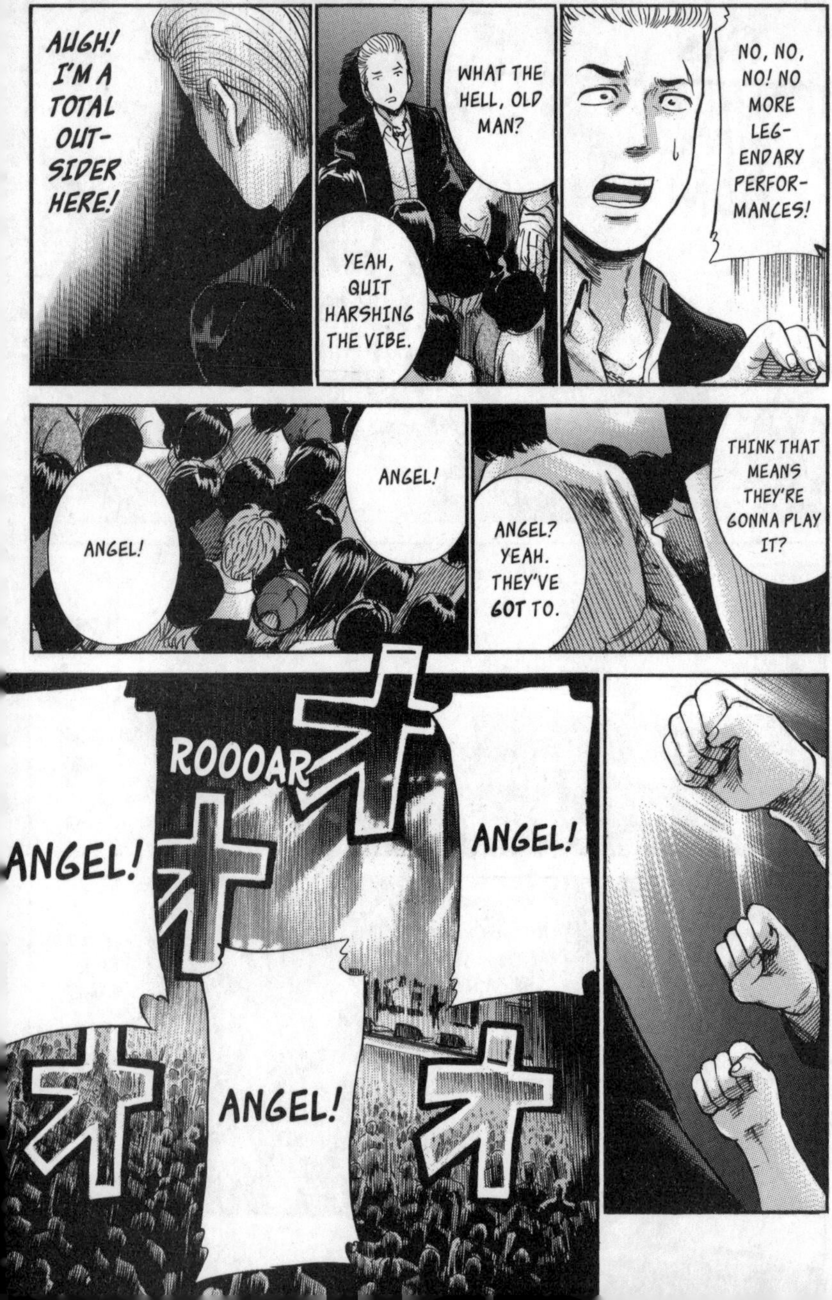
NO, NO, NO! NO MORE LEG-ENDARY PERFOR-MANCES!
WHAT THE HELL, OLD MAN?
YEAH, QUIT HARSHING THE VIBE.
AUGH! I'M A TOTAL OUT-SIDER HERE!
THINK THAT MEANS THEY'RE GONNA PLAY IT?
ANGEL? YEAH. THEY'VE GOT TO.
ANGEL!
ANGEL!
ANGEL!
ROOOAR
ANGEL!
ANGEL!

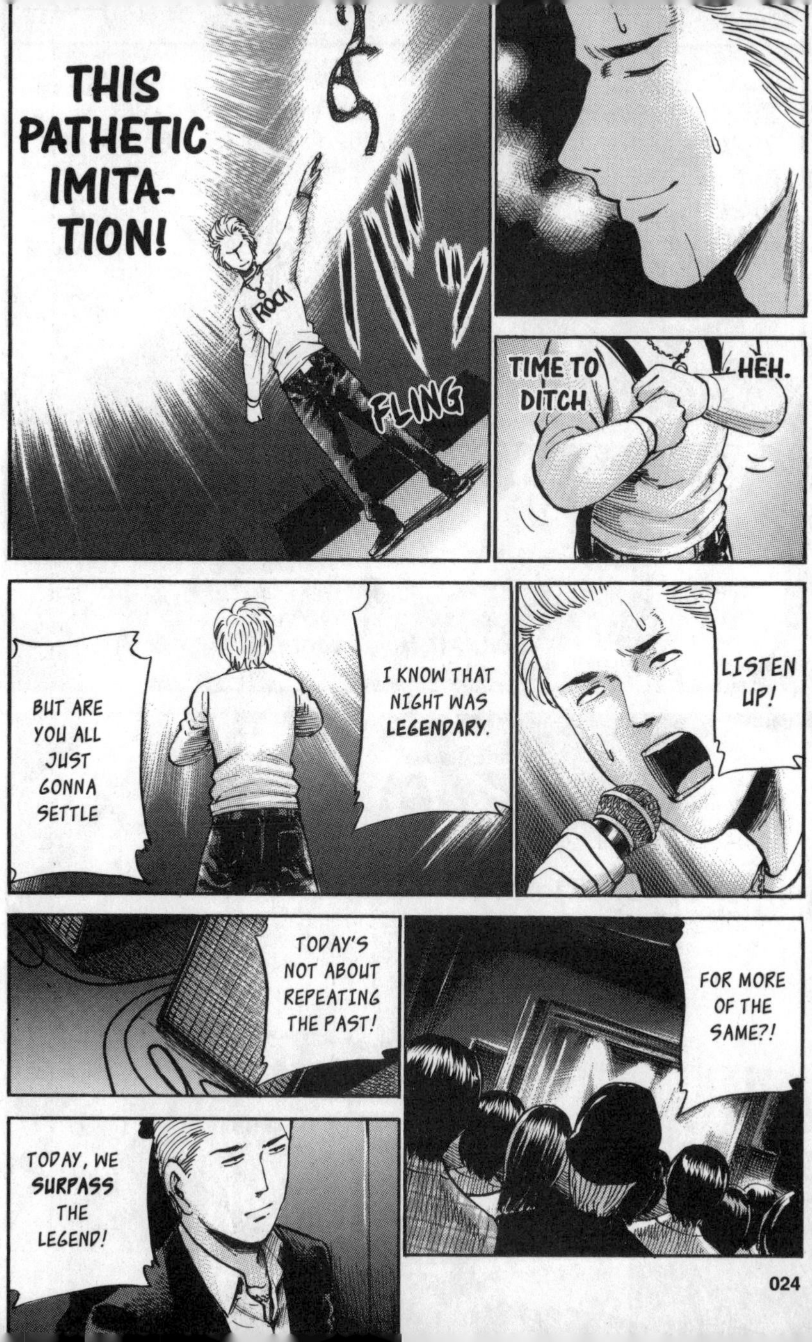
HEH.
TIME TO DITCH
FLING
THIS PATHETIC IMITA-TION!
LISTEN UP!
I KNOW THAT NIGHT WAS LEGENDARY.
BUT ARE YOU ALL JUST GONNA SETTLE
FOR MORE OF THE SAME?!
TODAY'S NOT ABOUT REPEATING THE PAST!
TODAY, WE SURPASS THE LEGEND!

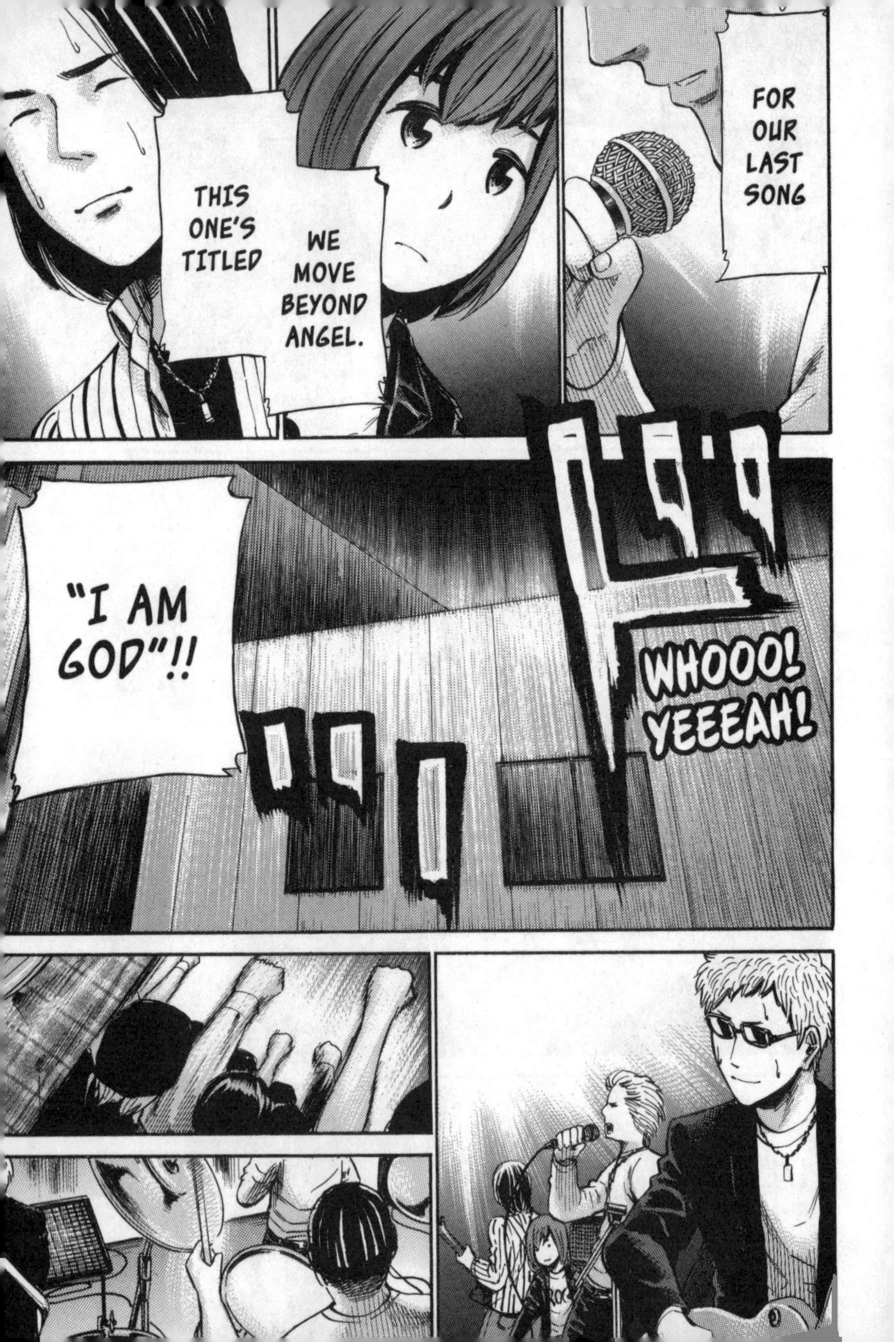

FOR OUR LAST SONG
WE MOVE BEYOND ANGEL.
THIS ONE'S TITLED
"I AM GOD"!!
WHOOO! YEEEAH!

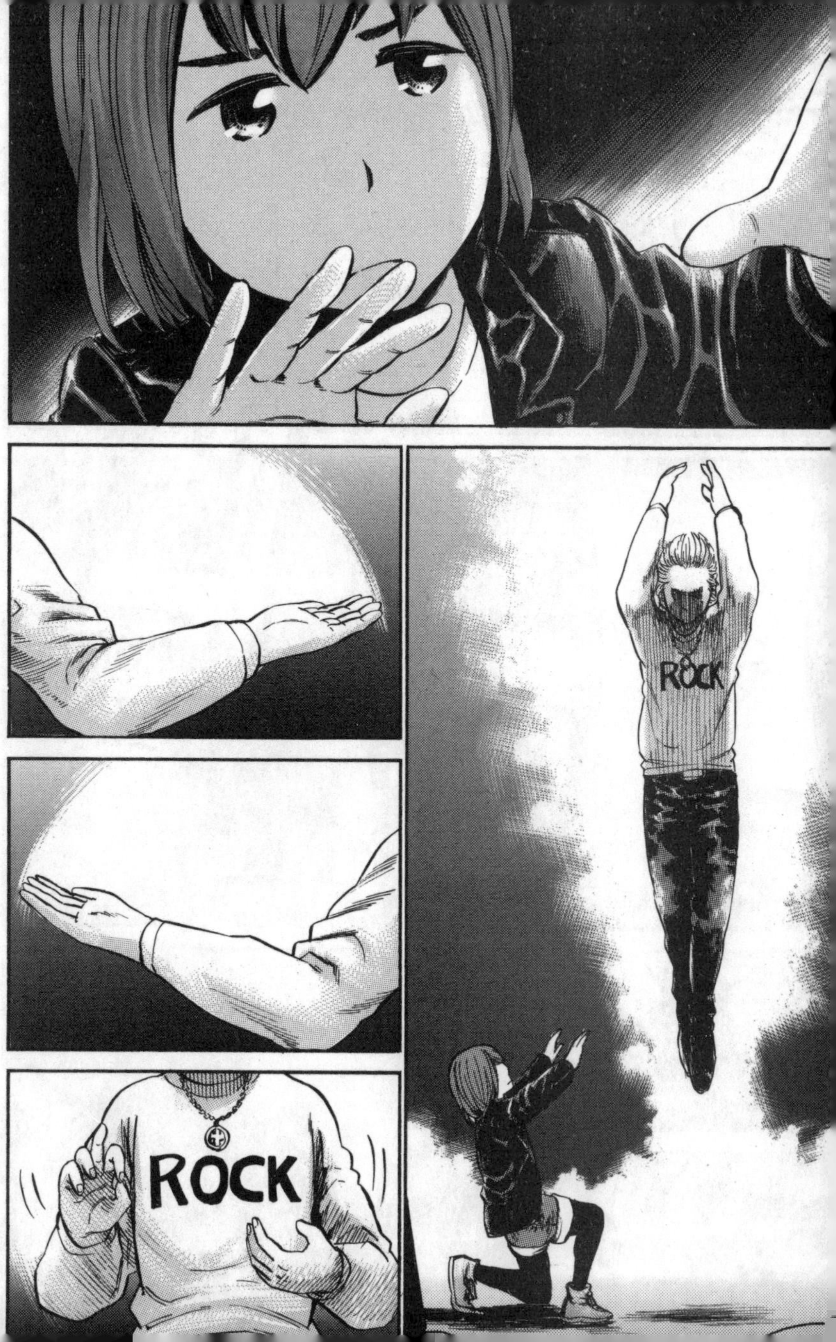
ROCK
ROCK

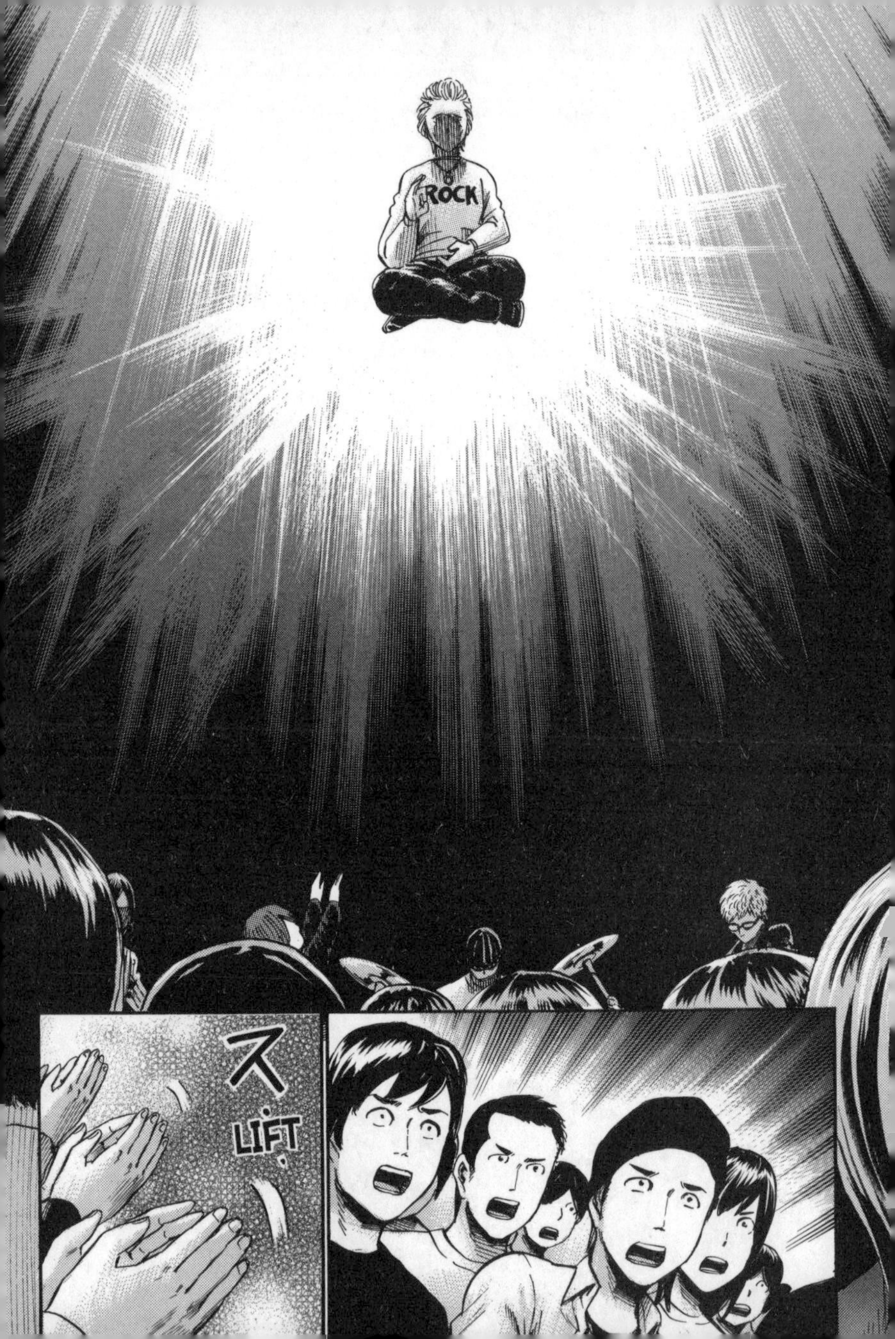
ROCK
ス
LIFT

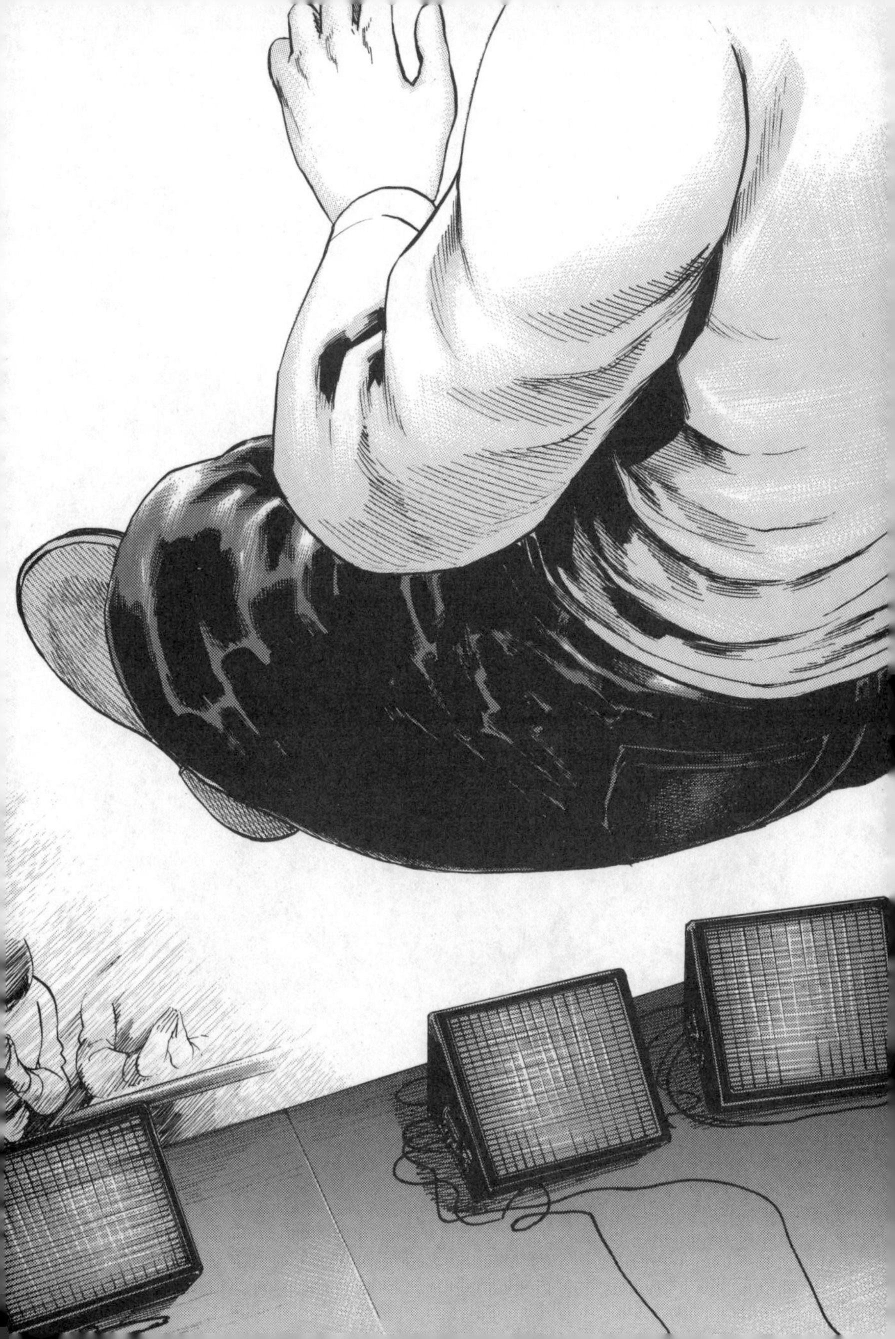

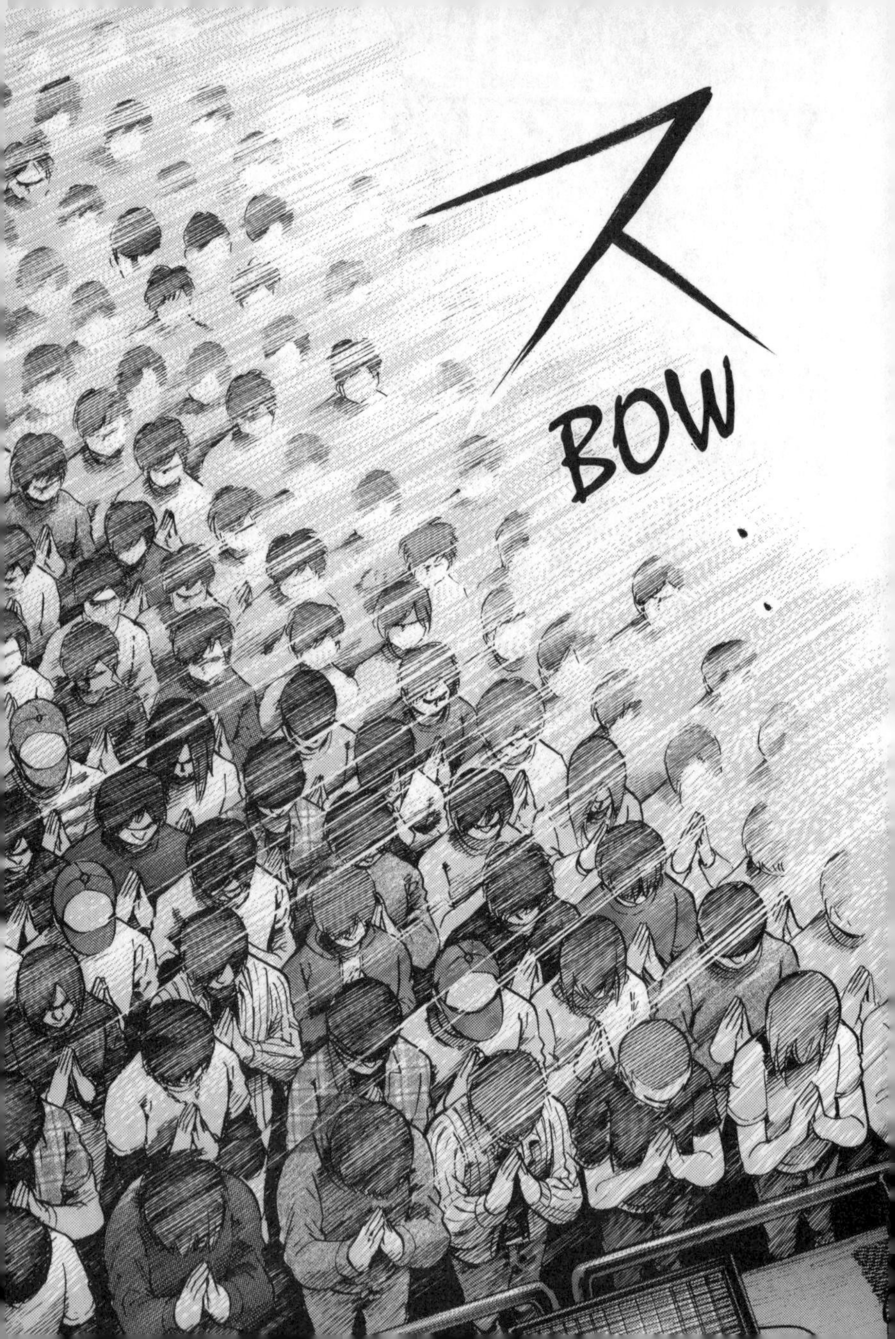
BOW

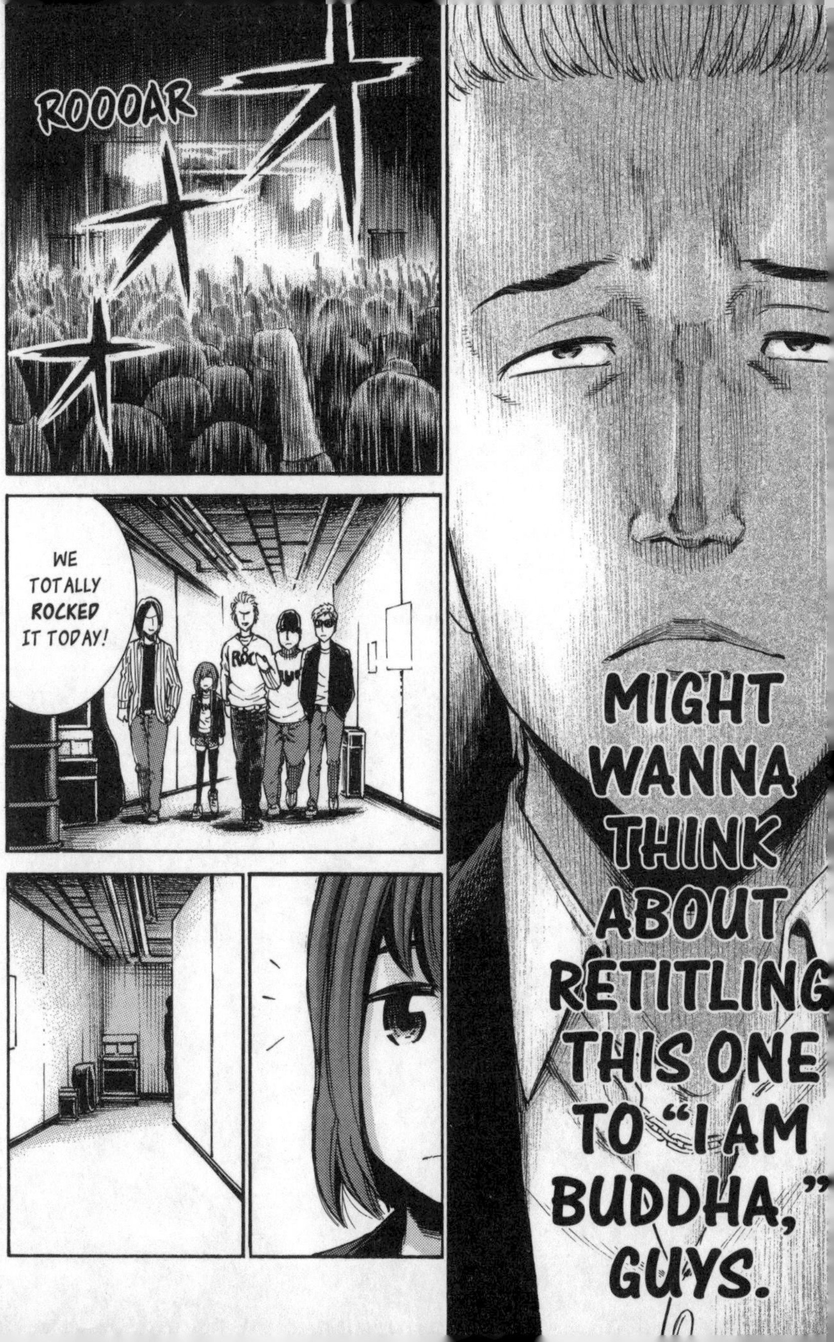
MIGHT WANNA THINK ABOUT RETITLING THIS ONE TO "I AM BUDDHA," GUYS.
ROOOAR
WE TOTALLY ROCKED IT TODAY!

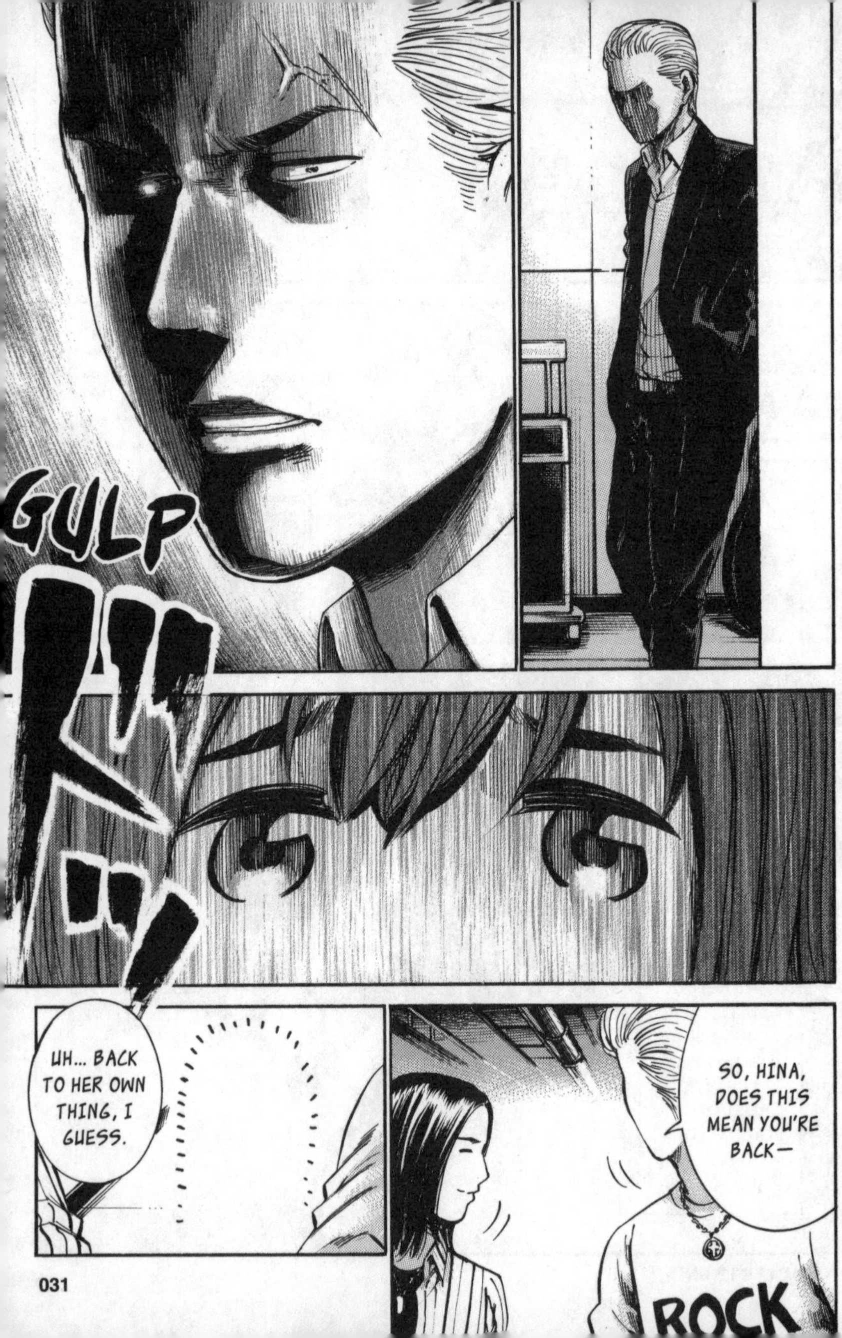
GULP
SO, HINA, DOES THIS MEAN YOU'RE BACK—
ROCK
UH... BACK TO HER OWN THING, I GUESS.

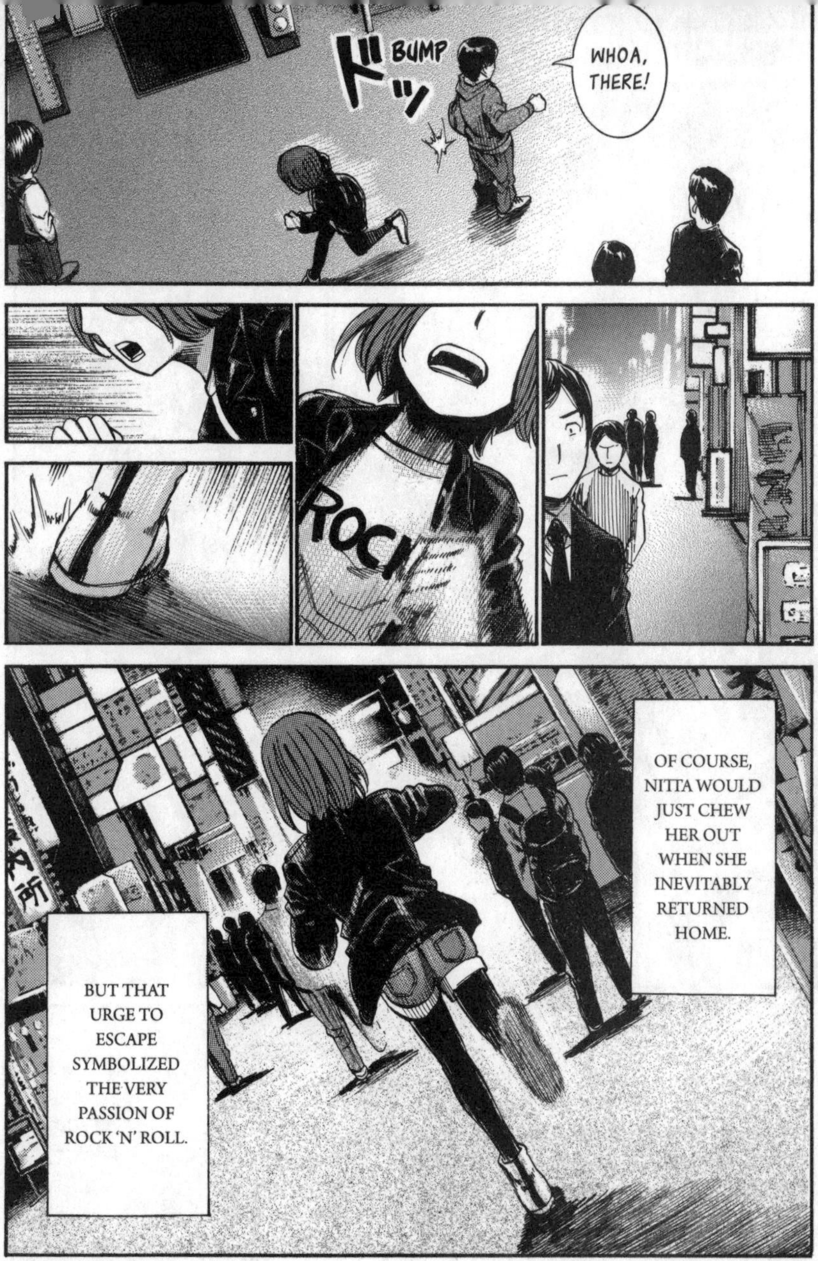
WHOA, THERE!
ドッ
BUMP
OF COURSE, NITTA WOULD JUST CHEW HER OUT WHEN SHE INEVITABLY RETURNED HOME.
BUT THAT URGE TO ESCAPE SYMBOLIZED THE VERY PASSION OF ROCK 'N' ROLL.

CHAPTER 17 END

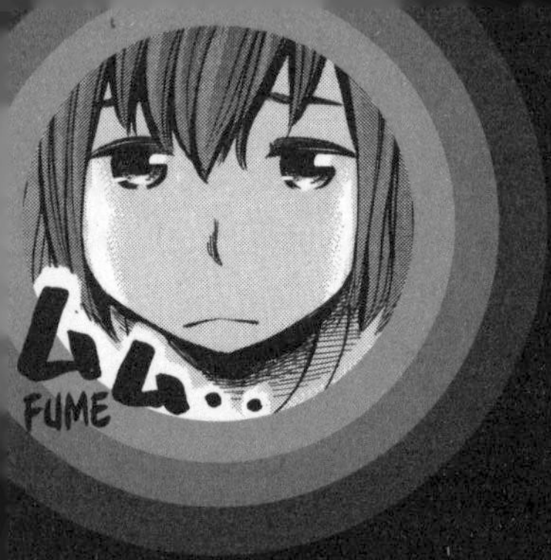
ムム..
FUME

CHAPTER 18
DEBT COLLECTION RHAPSODY

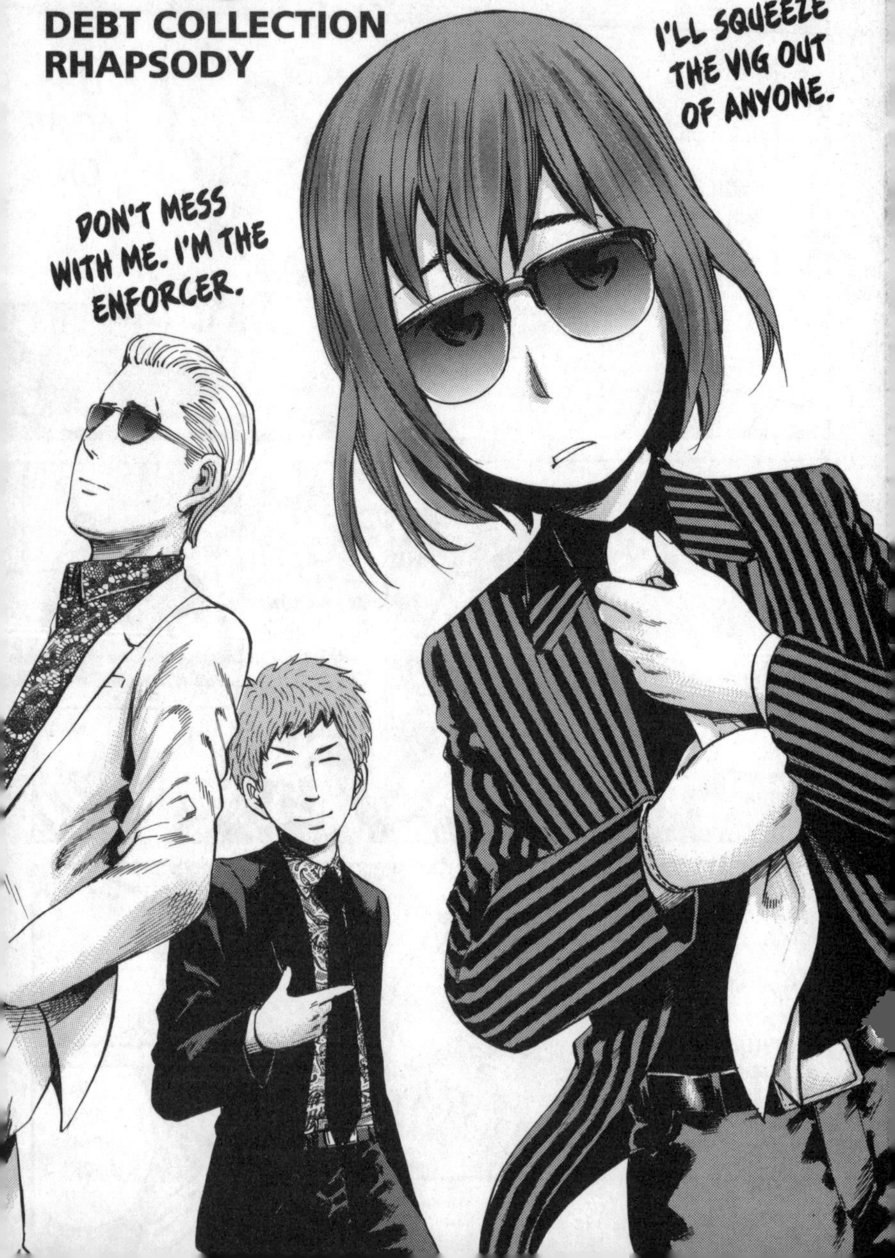
I'LL SQUEEZE THE VIG OUT OF ANYONE.
DON'T MESS WITH ME. I'M THE ENFORCER.

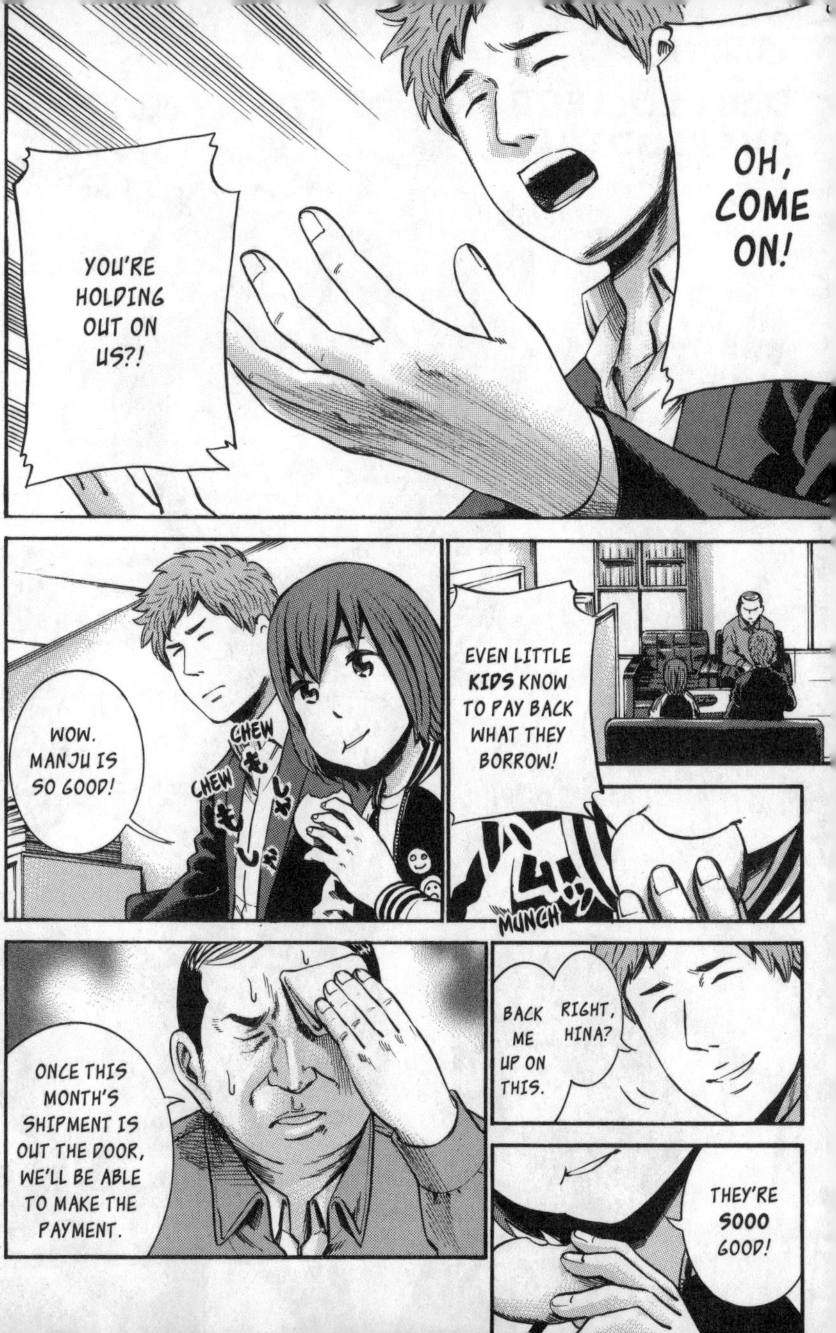
OH, COME ON!
YOU'RE HOLDING OUT ON US?!
EVEN LITTLE KIDS KNOW TO PAY BACK WHAT THEY BORROW!
MUNCH
CHEW
CHEW
WOW. MANJU IS SO GOOD!
RIGHT, HINA?
BACK ME UP ON THIS.
THEY'RE SOOO GOOD!
ONCE THIS MONTH'S SHIPMENT IS OUT THE DOOR, WE'LL BE ABLE TO MAKE THE PAYMENT.

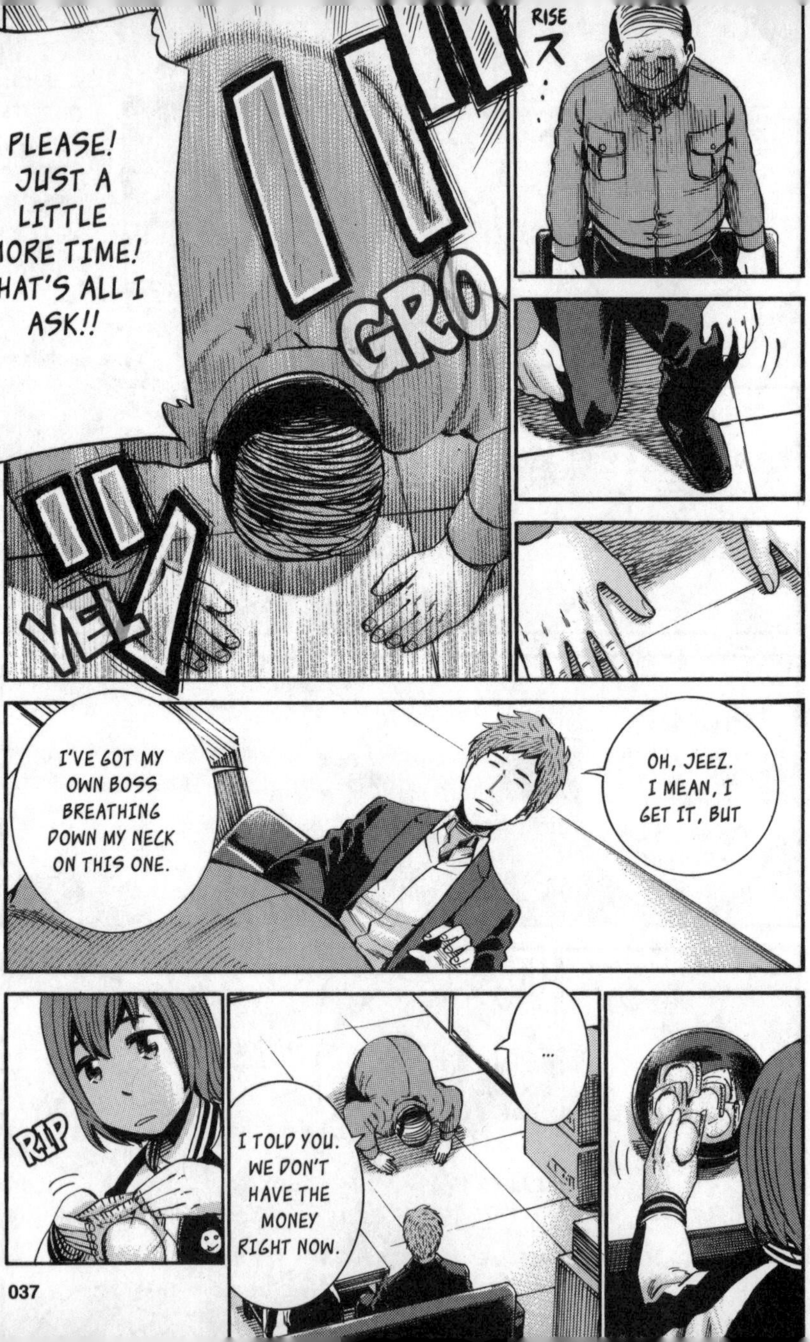
RISE
ス
PLEASE! JUST A LITTLE MORE TIME! THAT'S ALL I ASK!!
GRO
VEL
OH, JEEZ. I MEAN, I GET IT, BUT
I'VE GOT MY OWN BOSS BREATHING DOWN MY NECK ON THIS ONE.
...
I TOLD YOU. WE DON'T HAVE THE MONEY RIGHT NOW.
RIP

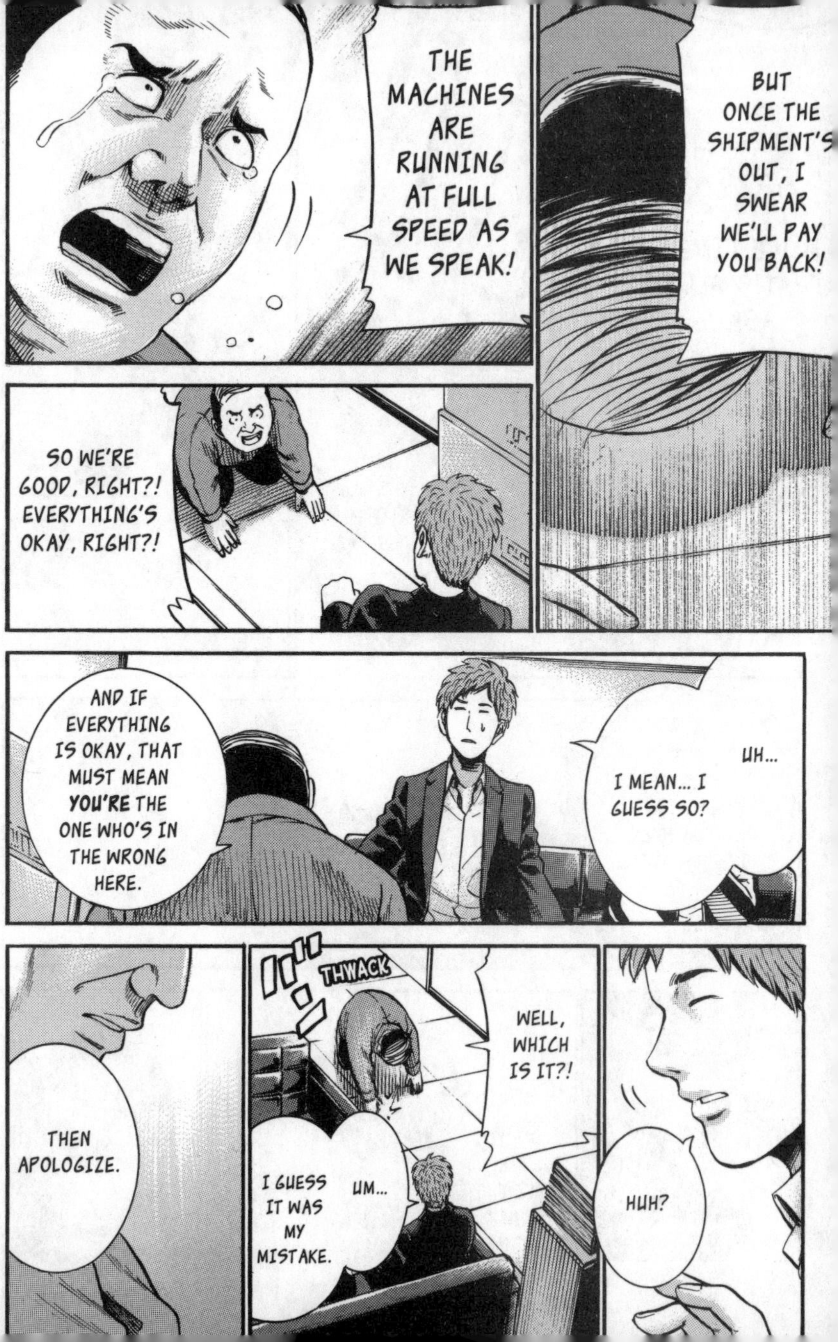

BUT ONCE THE SHIPMENT'S OUT, I SWEAR WE'LL PAY YOU BACK!
THE MACHINES ARE RUNNING AT FULL SPEED AS WE SPEAK!
SO WE'RE GOOD, RIGHT?! EVERYTHING'S OKAY, RIGHT?!
UH...
I MEAN... I GUESS SO?
AND IF EVERYTHING IS OKAY, THAT MUST MEAN YOU'RE THE ONE WHO'S IN THE WRONG HERE.
HUH?
WELL, WHICH IS IT?!
THWACK
UM...
I GUESS IT WAS MY MISTAKE.
THEN APOLOGIZE.

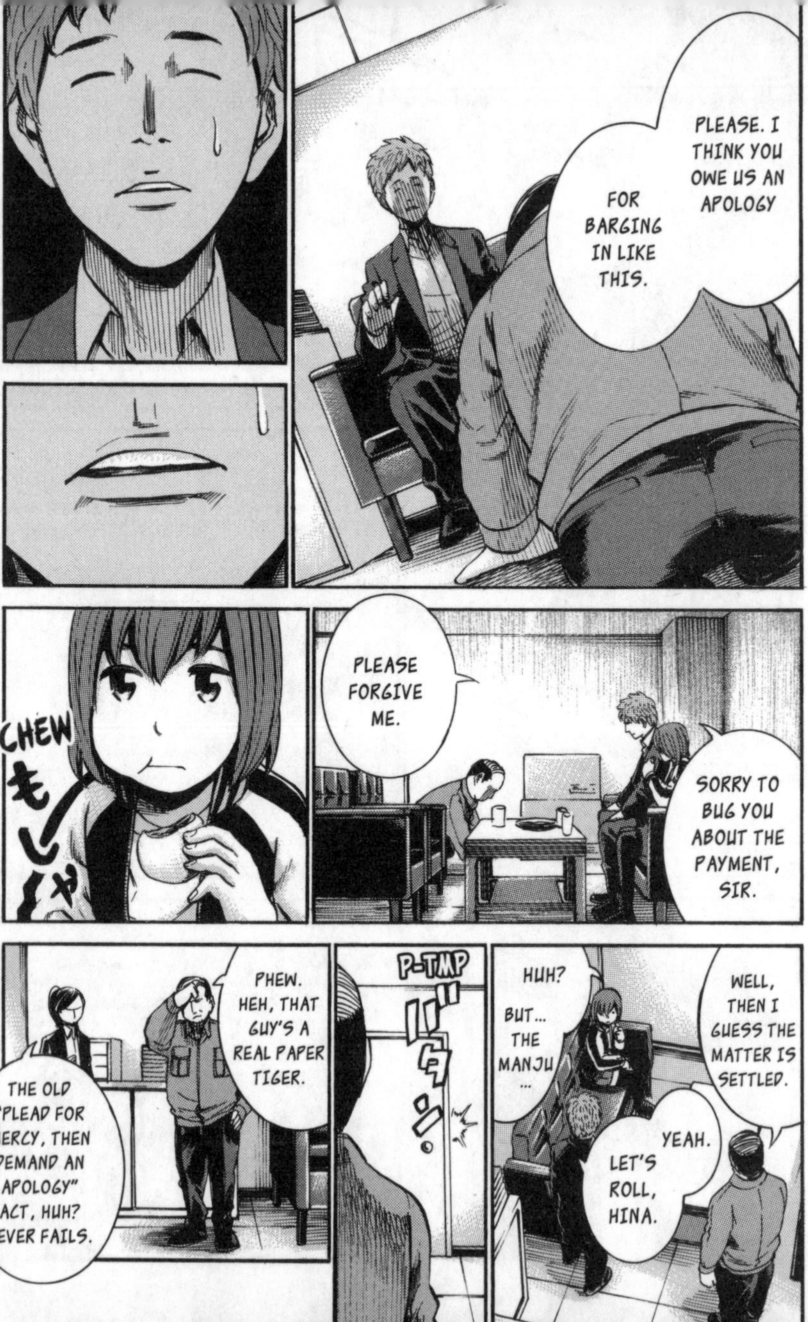
PLEASE. I THINK YOU OWE US AN APOLOGY
FOR BARGING IN LIKE THIS.
PLEASE FORGIVE ME.
SORRY TO BUG YOU ABOUT THE PAYMENT, SIR.
CHEW
もしゃ
WELL, THEN I GUESS THE MATTER IS SETTLED.
HUH?
BUT... THE MANJU...
YEAH.
LET'S ROLL, HINA.
P-TMP
バタン
PHEW. HEH, THAT GUY'S A REAL PAPER TIGER.
THE OLD "PLEAD FOR MERCY, THEN DEMAND AN APOLOGY" ACT, HUH? NEVER FAILS.

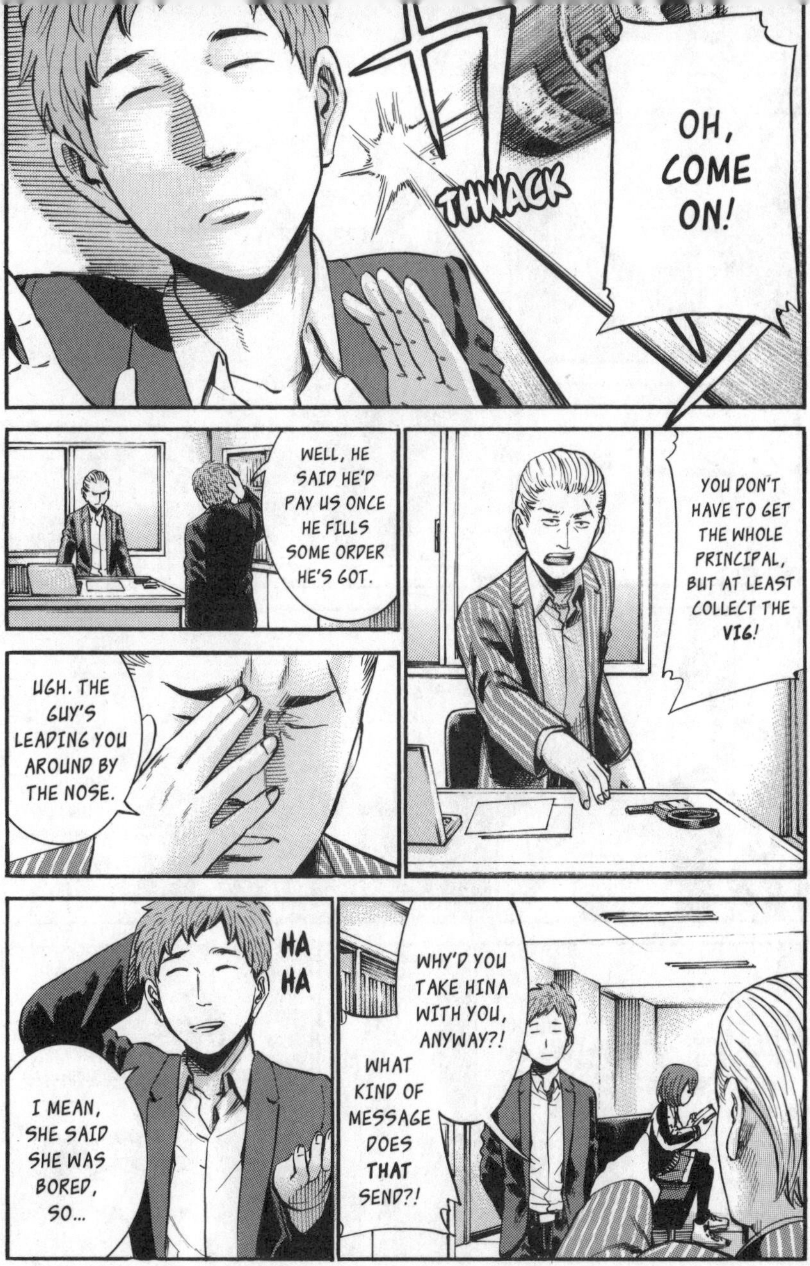
OH, COME ON!
THWACK
YOU DON'T HAVE TO GET THE WHOLE PRINCIPAL, BUT AT LEAST COLLECT THE VIG!
WELL, HE SAID HE'D PAY US ONCE HE FILLS SOME ORDER HE'S GOT.
UGH. THE GUY'S LEADING YOU AROUND BY THE NOSE.
WHY'D YOU TAKE HINA WITH YOU, ANYWAY?!
WHAT KIND OF MESSAGE DOES THAT SEND?!
HA HA
I MEAN, SHE SAID SHE WAS BORED, SO...

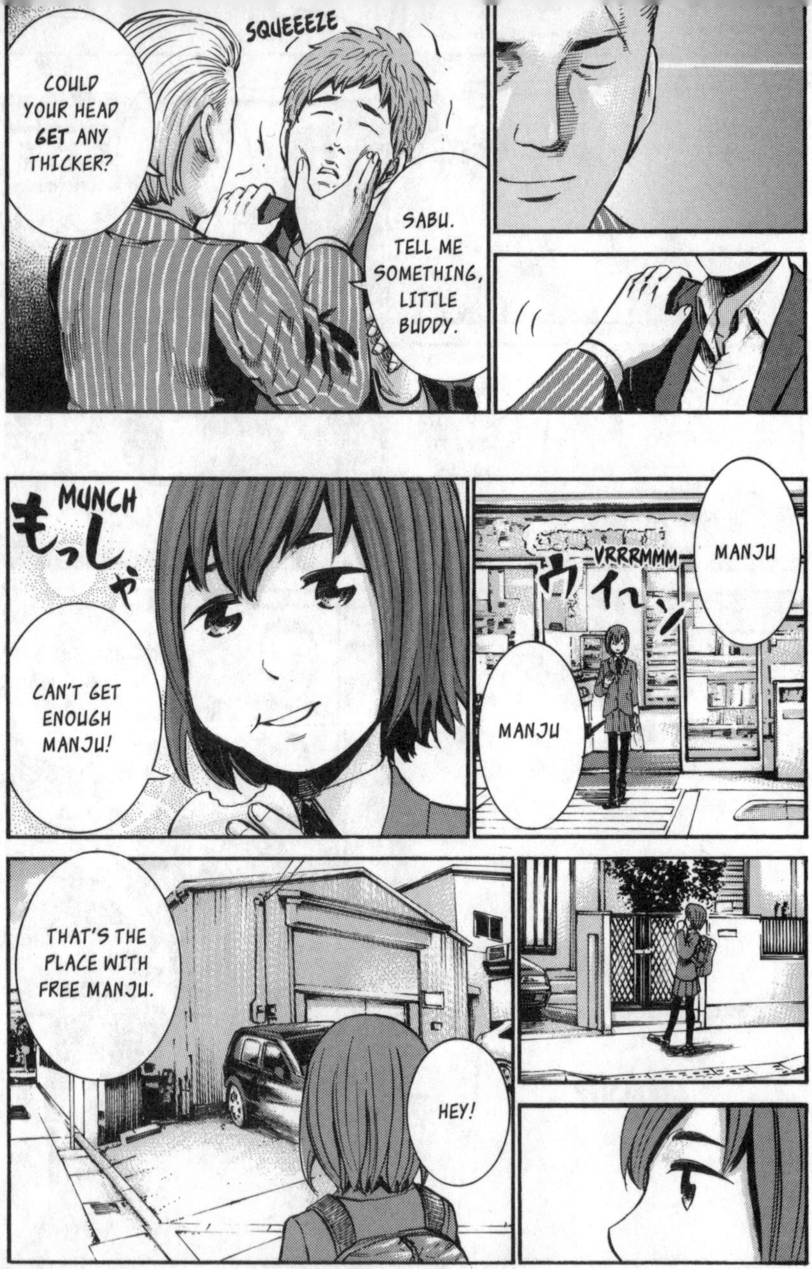
SQUEEEZE
SABU. TELL ME SOMETHING, LITTLE BUDDY.
COULD YOUR HEAD GET ANY THICKER?
MANJU
VRRRMMM
ウイ〜ン
MANJU
MUNCH
もっしゃ
CAN'T GET ENOUGH MANJU!
THAT'S THE PLACE WITH FREE MANJU.
HEY!

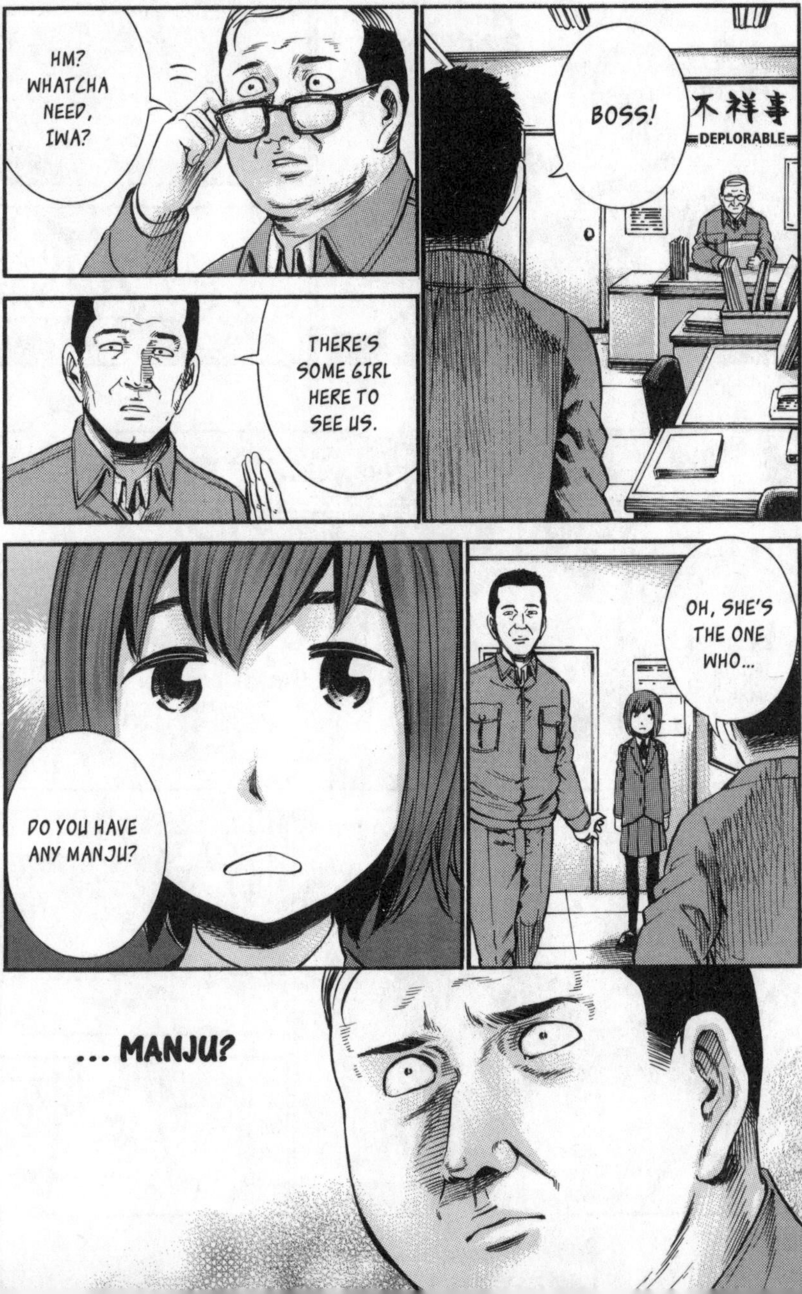
BOSS!
不祥事
DEPLORABLE
HM? WHATCHA NEED, IWA?
THERE'S SOME GIRL HERE TO SEE US.
OH, SHE'S THE ONE WHO...
DO YOU HAVE ANY MANJU?
... MANJU?

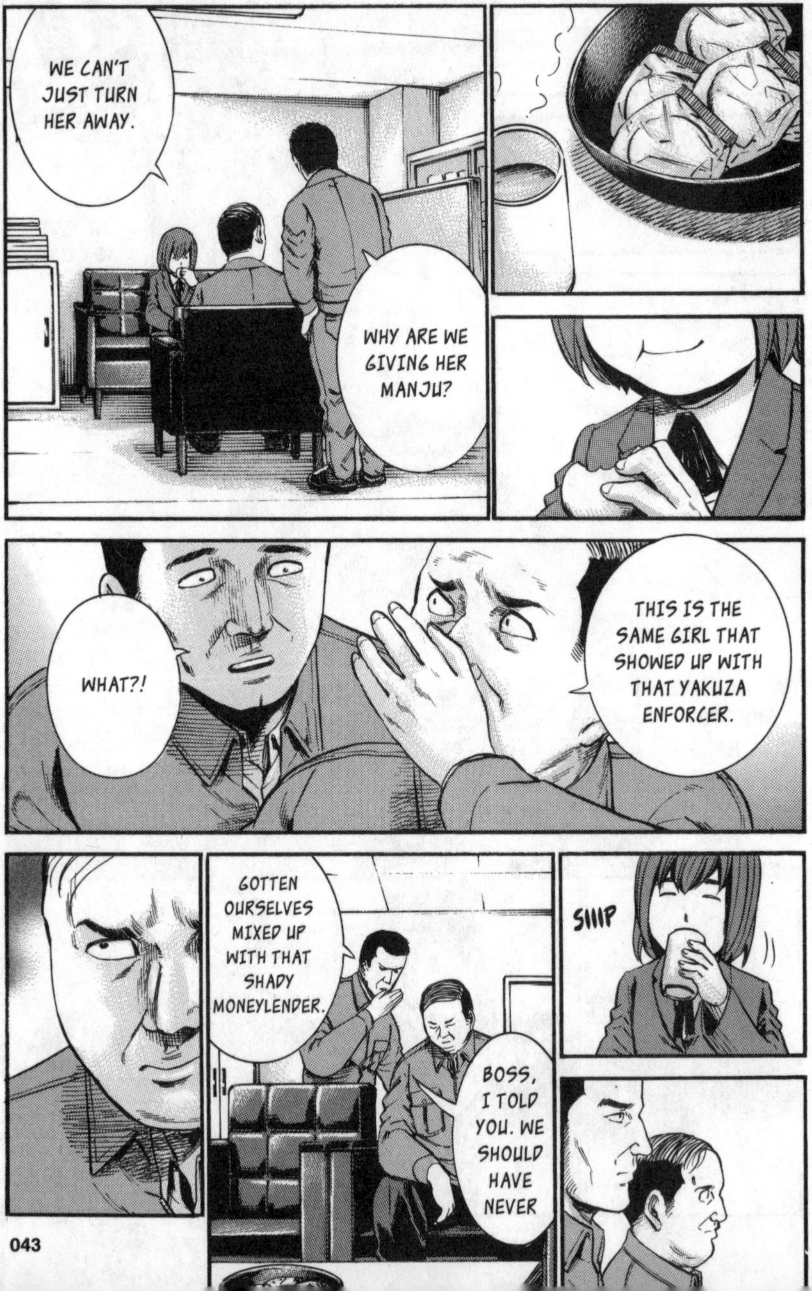
WHY ARE WE GIVING HER MANJU?
WE CAN'T JUST TURN HER AWAY.
THIS IS THE SAME GIRL THAT SHOWED UP WITH THAT YAKUZA ENFORCER.
WHAT?!
SIIIP
BOSS, I TOLD YOU. WE SHOULD HAVE NEVER
GOTTEN OURSELVES MIXED UP WITH THAT SHADY MONEYLENDER.

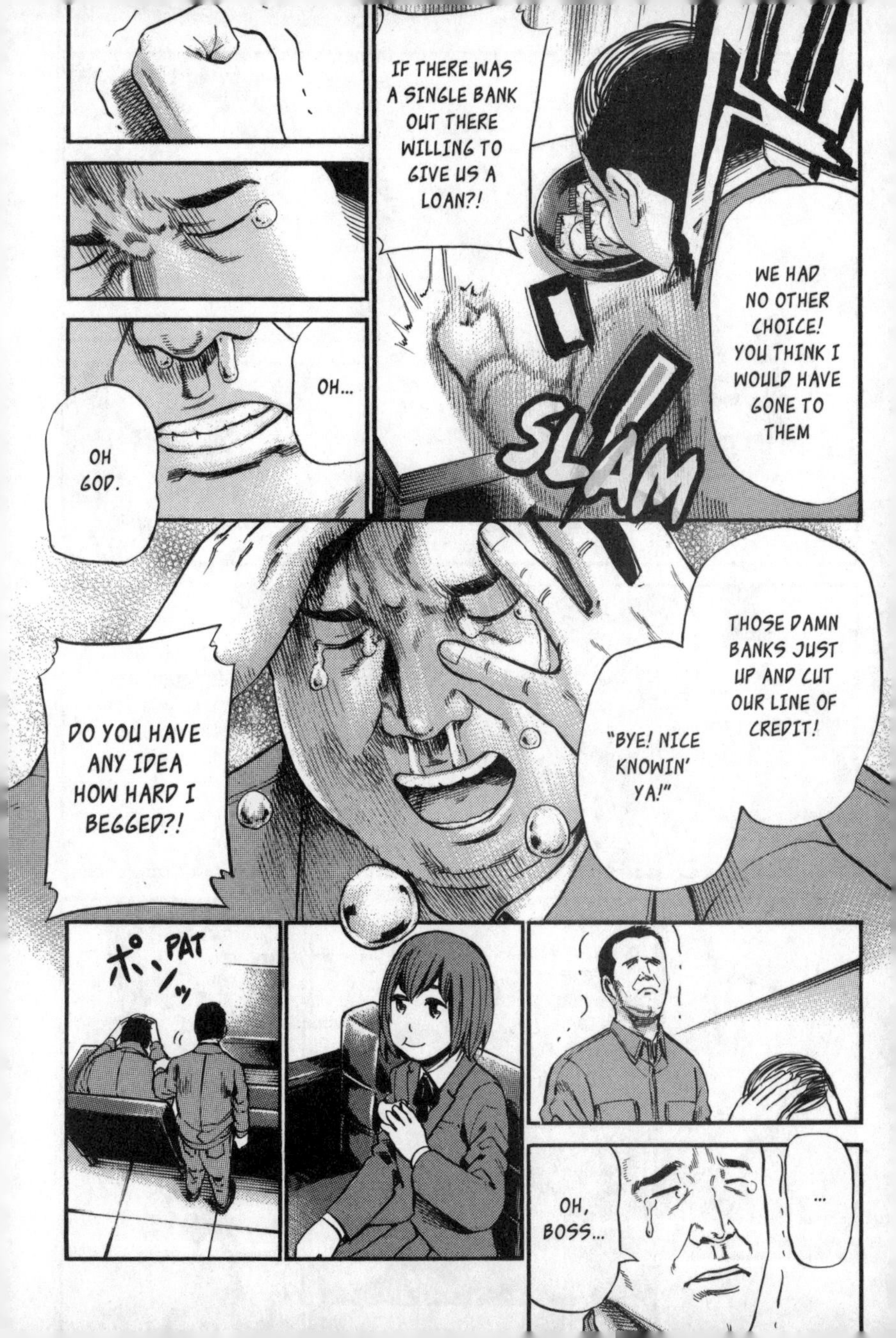
WE HAD NO OTHER CHOICE! YOU THINK I WOULD HAVE GONE TO THEM
IF THERE WAS A SINGLE BANK OUT THERE WILLING TO GIVE US A LOAN?!
SLAM
OH...
OH GOD.
THOSE DAMN BANKS JUST UP AND CUT OUR LINE OF CREDIT!
"BYE! NICE KNOWIN' YA!"
DO YOU HAVE ANY IDEA HOW HARD I BEGGED?!
...
OH, BOSS...
ポンッ PAT

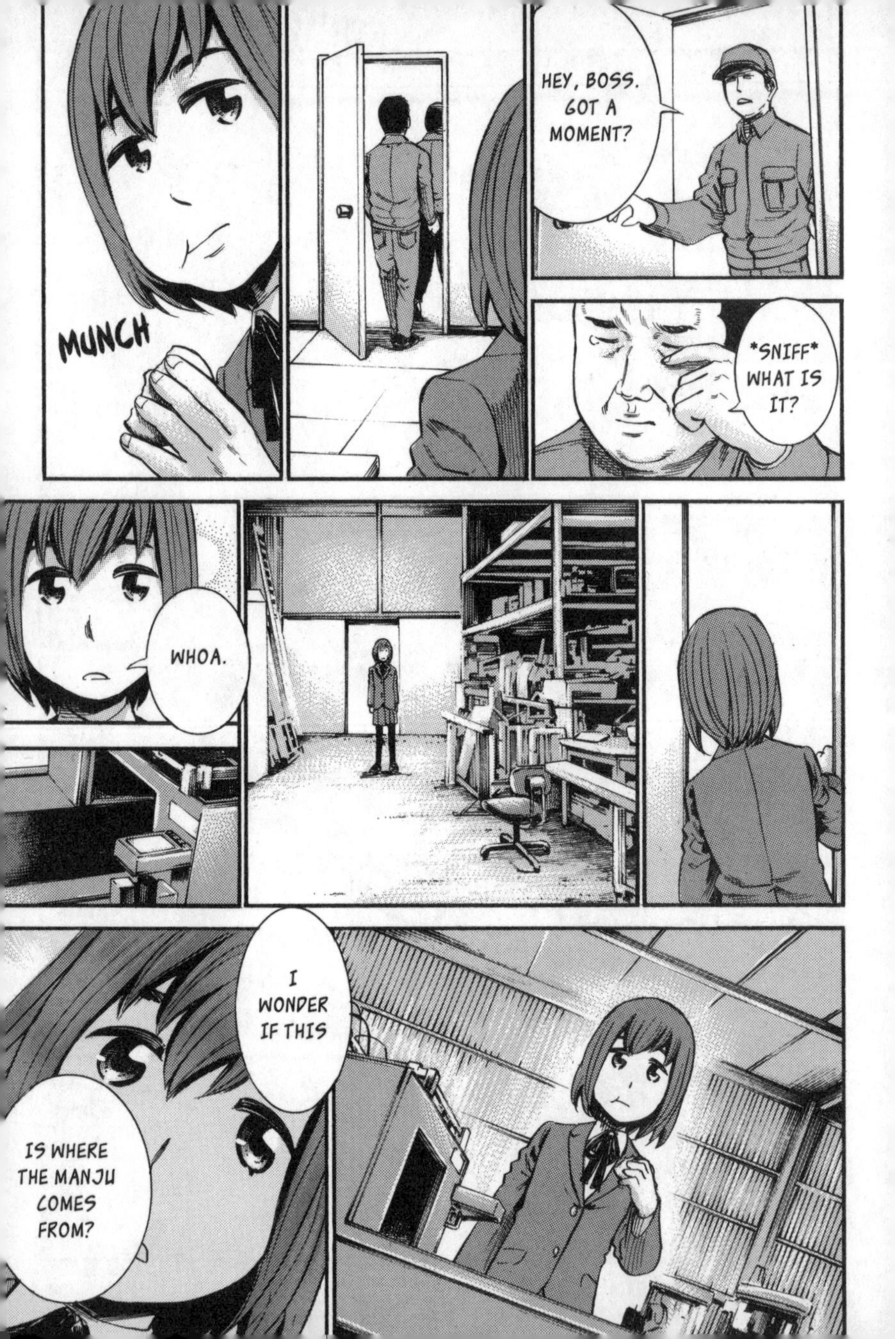
HEY, BOSS. GOT A MOMENT?
SNIFF WHAT IS IT?
MUNCH
WHOA.
I WONDER IF THIS
IS WHERE THE MANJU COMES FROM?

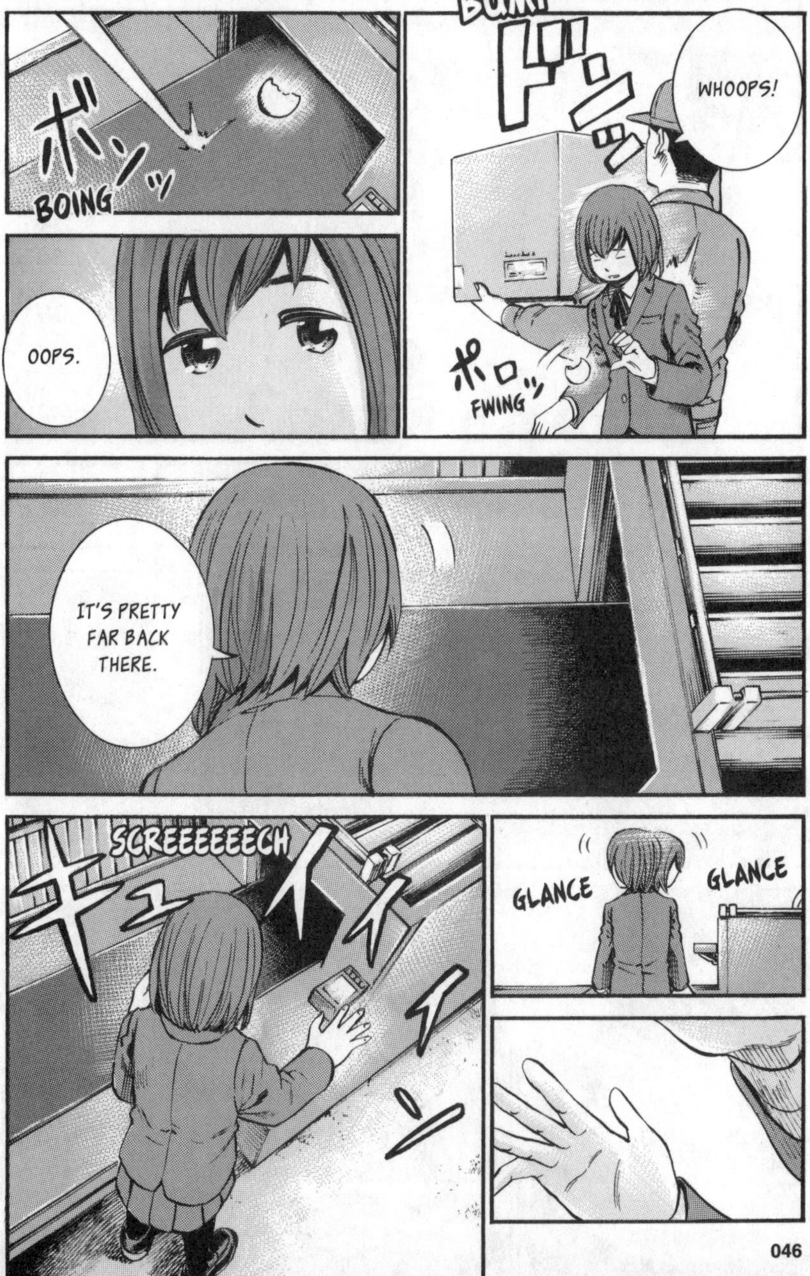
BUMP
ドンッ
WHOOPS!
ポロッ
FWING
ボンッ
BOING
OOPS.
IT'S PRETTY FAR BACK THERE.
GLANCE
GLANCE
SCREEEEEEECH
キュイイイー

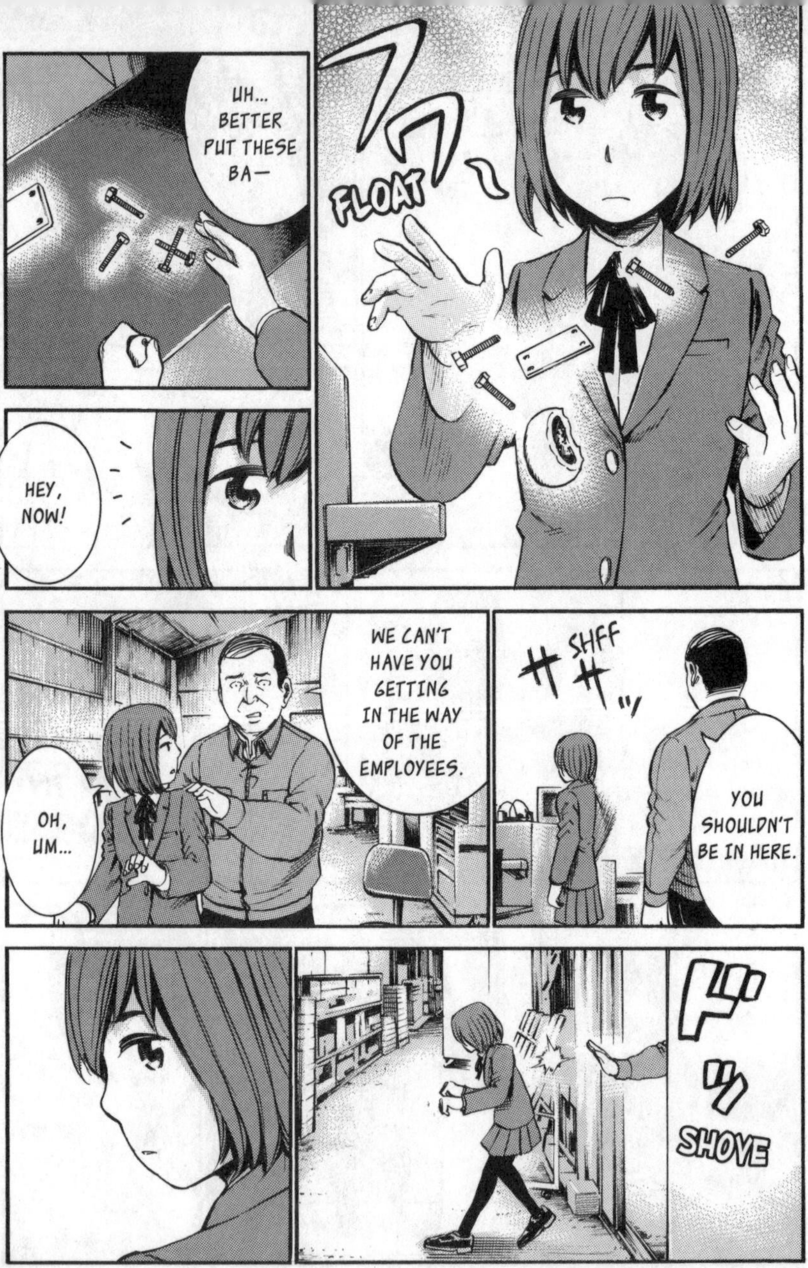
FLOAT
UH... BETTER PUT THESE BA—
HEY, NOW!
SHFF
YOU SHOULDN'T BE IN HERE.
WE CAN'T HAVE YOU GETTING IN THE WAY OF THE EMPLOYEES.
OH, UM...
SHOVE

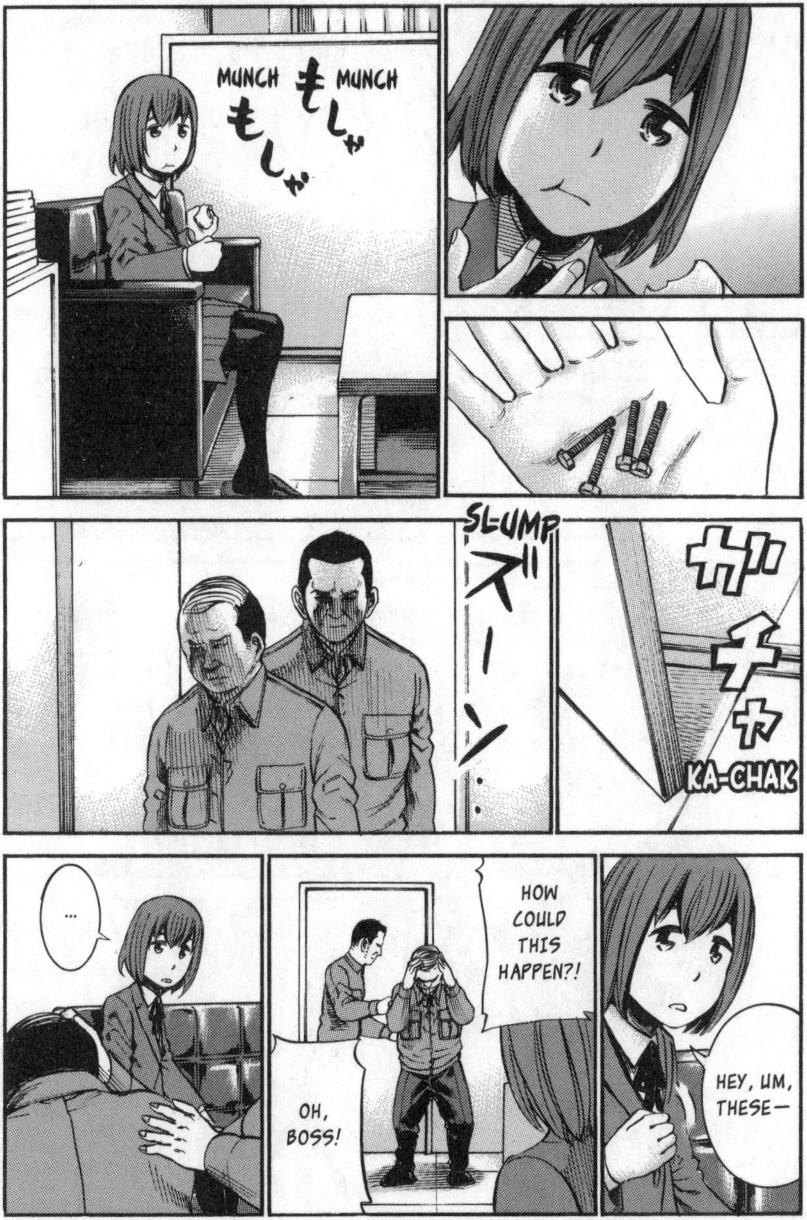
MUNCH MUNCH
もしゃ もしゃ
ガチャ
KA-CHAK
SLUMP
ズーン…
HEY, UM, THESE—
HOW COULD THIS HAPPEN?!
OH, BOSS!
...

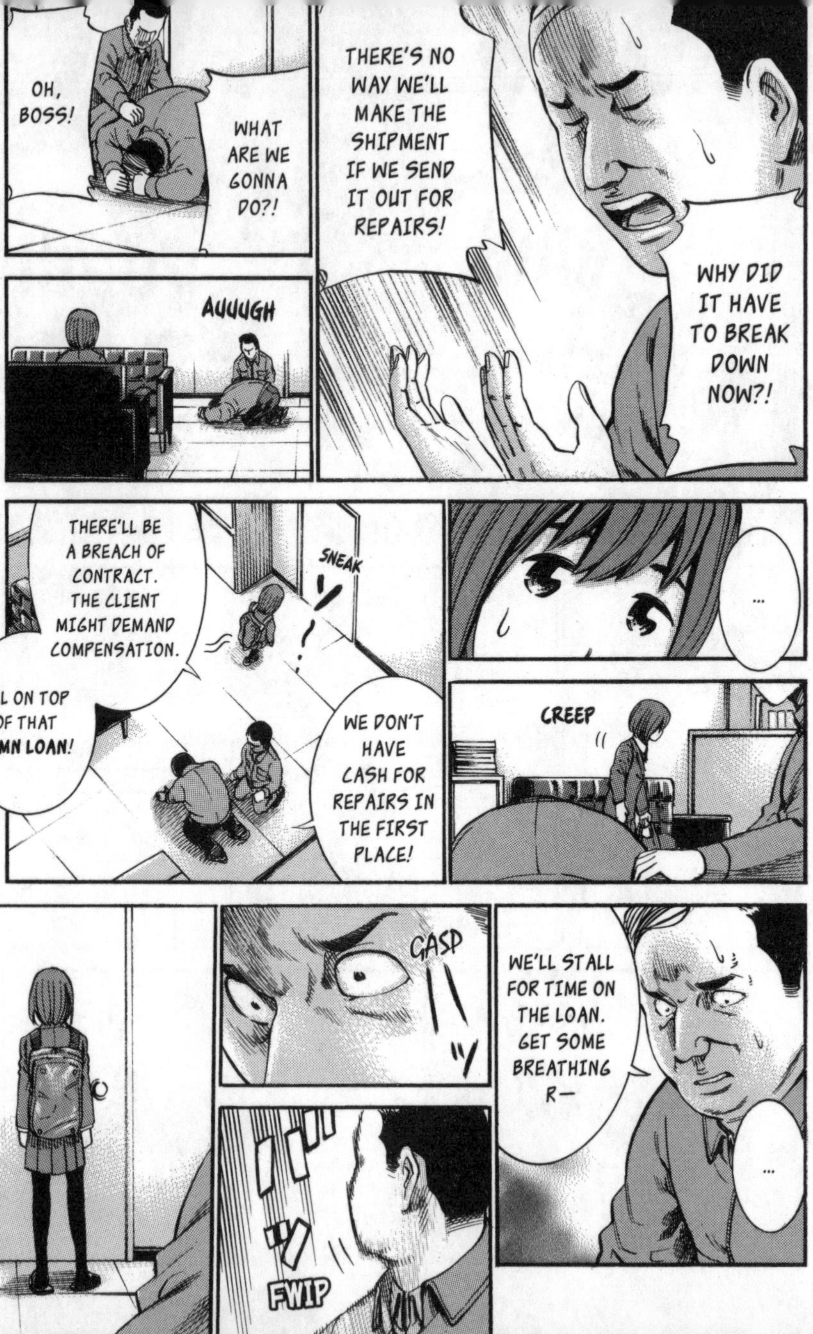
THERE'S NO WAY WE'LL MAKE THE SHIPMENT IF WE SEND IT OUT FOR REPAIRS!
WHY DID IT HAVE TO BREAK DOWN NOW?!
OH, BOSS!
WHAT ARE WE GONNA DO?!
AUUUGH
...
CREEP
THERE'LL BE A BREACH OF CONTRACT. THE CLIENT MIGHT DEMAND COMPENSATION.
SNEAK
ALL ON TOP OF THAT **DAMN LOAN**!
WE DON'T HAVE CASH FOR REPAIRS IN THE FIRST PLACE!
WE'LL STALL FOR TIME ON THE LOAN. GET SOME BREATHING R—
...
GASP
FWIP

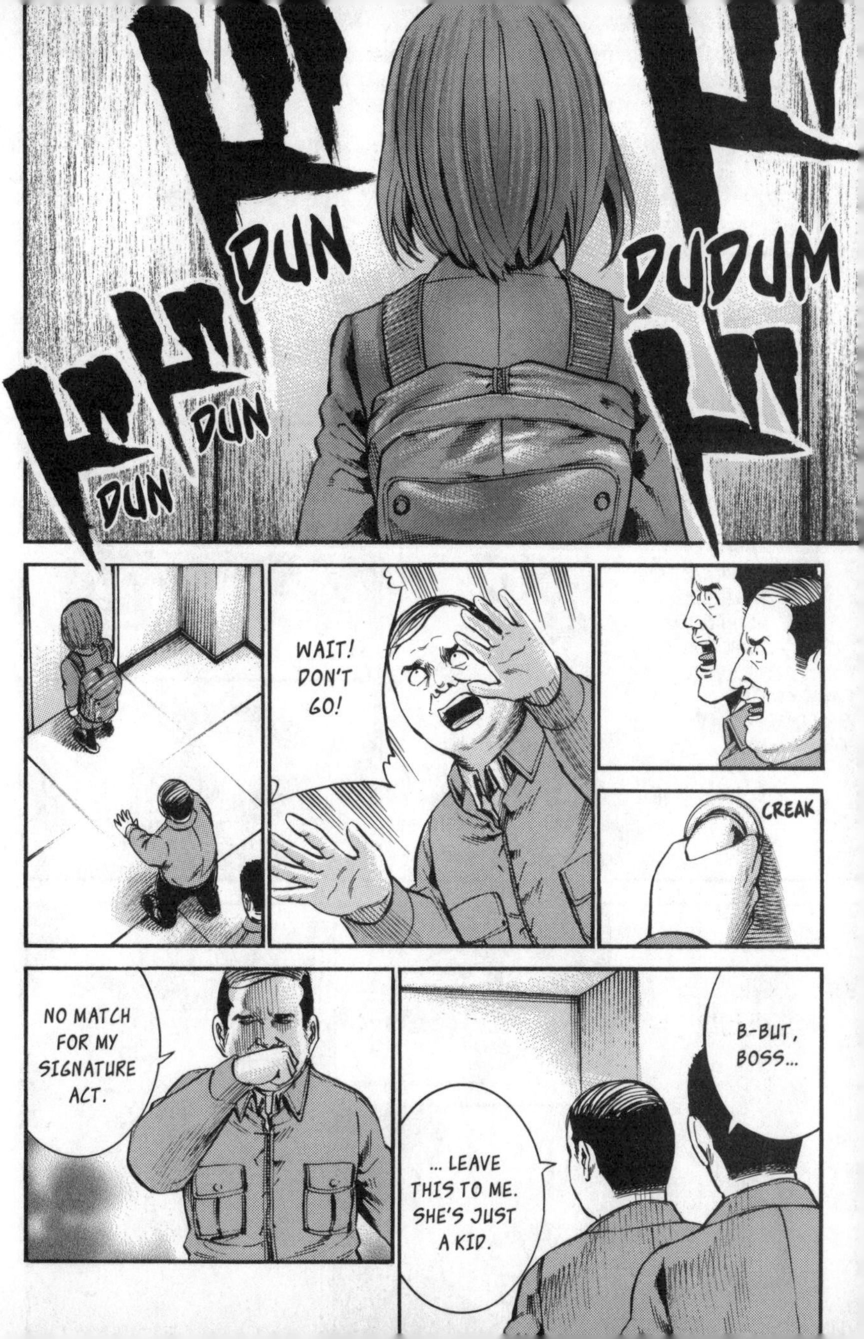
DUDUM
DUN
DUN
DUN
CREAK
WAIT! DON'T GO!
B-BUT, BOSS...
... LEAVE THIS TO ME. SHE'S JUST A KID.
NO MATCH FOR MY SIGNATURE ACT.

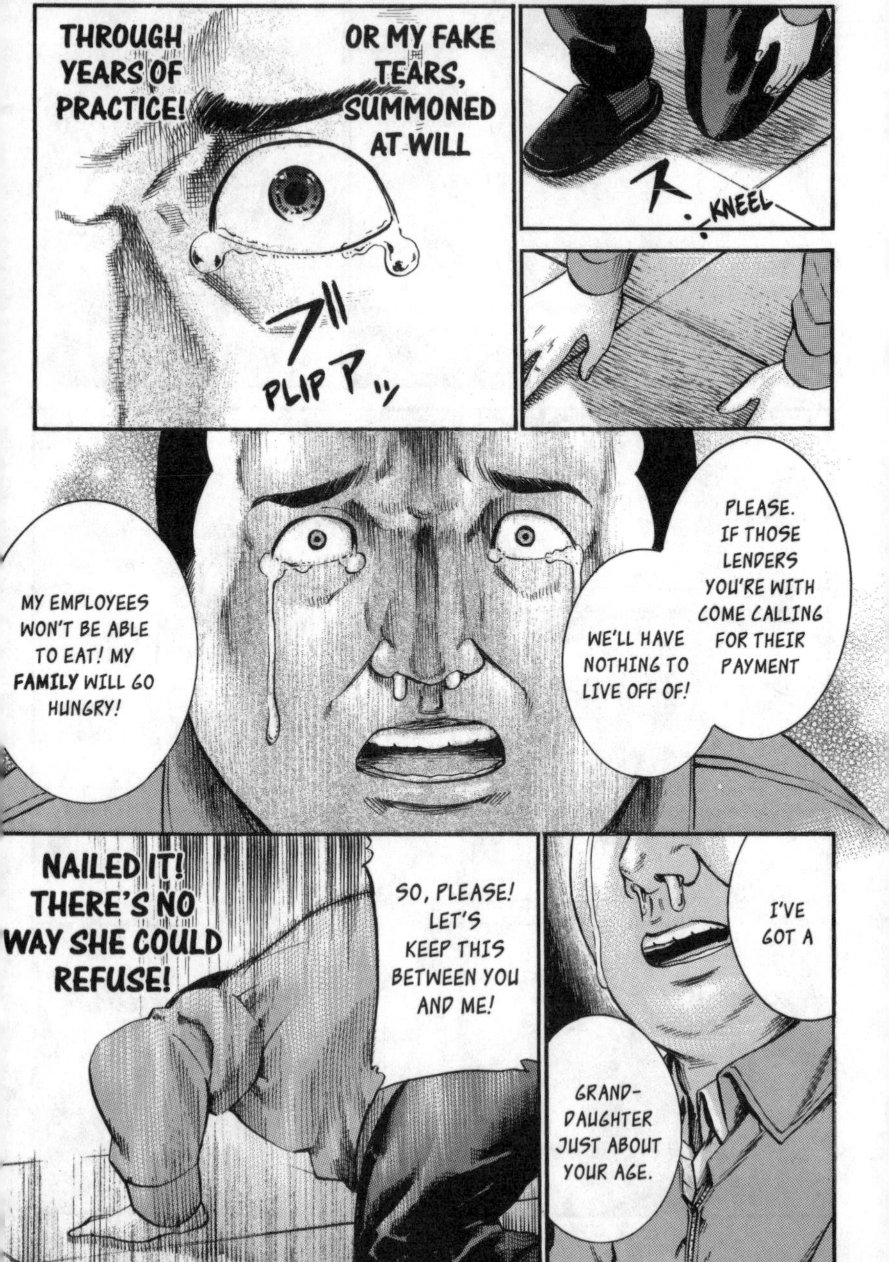
KNEEL
OR MY FAKE TEARS, SUMMONED AT WILL
THROUGH YEARS OF PRACTICE!
PLIP
PLEASE. IF THOSE LENDERS YOU'RE WITH COME CALLING FOR THEIR PAYMENT
WE'LL HAVE NOTHING TO LIVE OFF OF!
MY EMPLOYEES WON'T BE ABLE TO EAT! MY FAMILY WILL GO HUNGRY!
I'VE GOT A
GRAND-DAUGHTER JUST ABOUT YOUR AGE.
SO, PLEASE! LET'S KEEP THIS BETWEEN YOU AND ME!
NAILED IT! THERE'S NO WAY SHE COULD REFUSE!

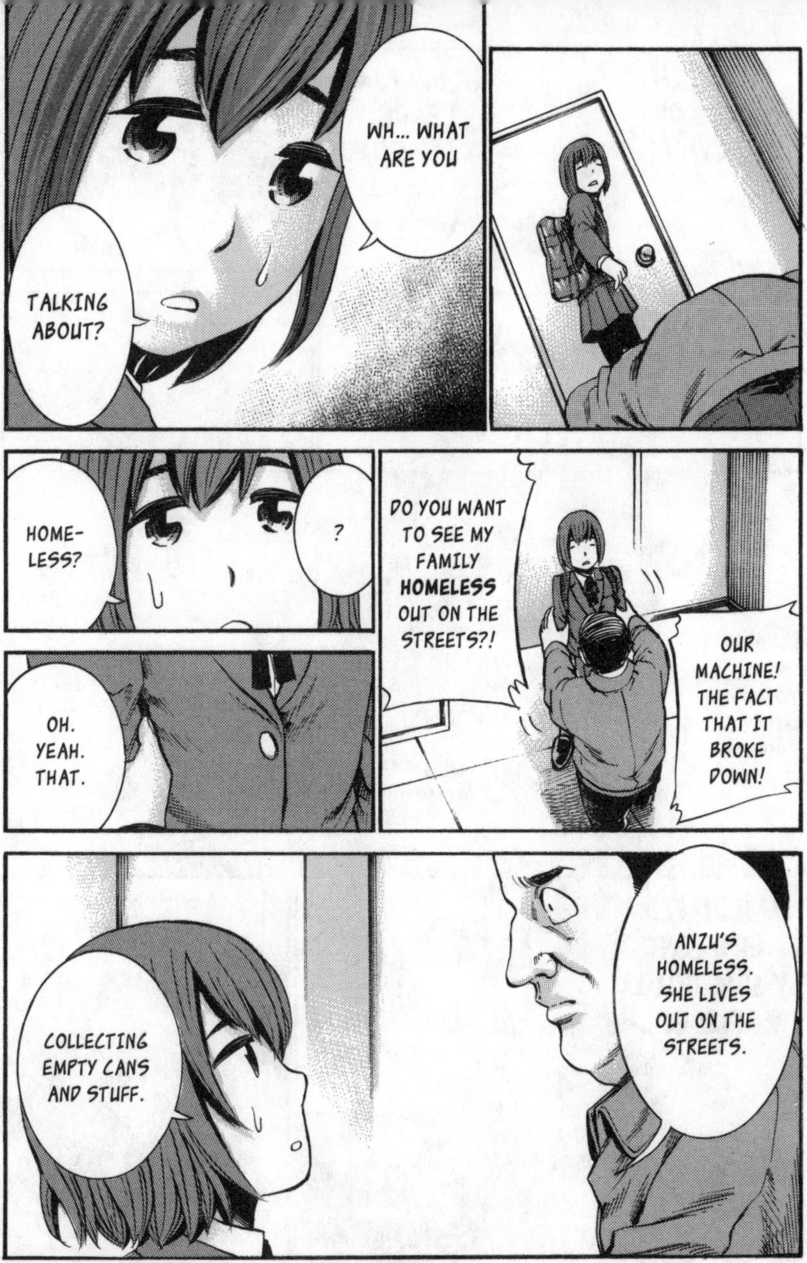
WH... WHAT ARE YOU
TALKING ABOUT?
OUR MACHINE! THE FACT THAT IT BROKE DOWN!
DO YOU WANT TO SEE MY FAMILY **HOMELESS** OUT ON THE STREETS?!
?
HOME-LESS?
OH. YEAH. THAT.
ANZU'S HOMELESS. SHE LIVES OUT ON THE STREETS.
COLLECTING EMPTY CANS AND STUFF.

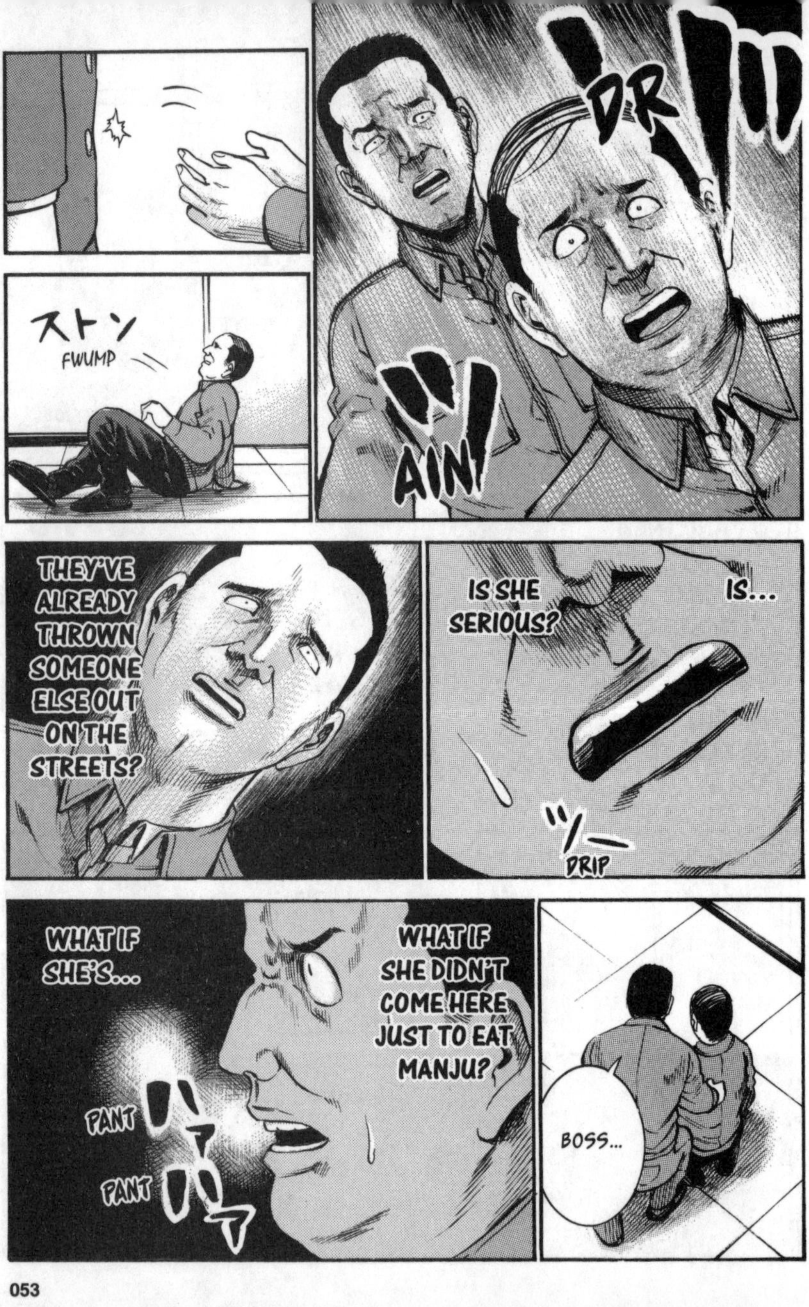
DR
AIN
ストン
FWUMP
IS...
IS SHE SERIOUS?
DRIP
THEY'VE ALREADY THROWN SOMEONE ELSE OUT ON THE STREETS?
BOSS...
WHAT IF SHE DIDN'T COME HERE JUST TO EAT MANJU?
WHAT IF SHE'S...
PANT
PANT

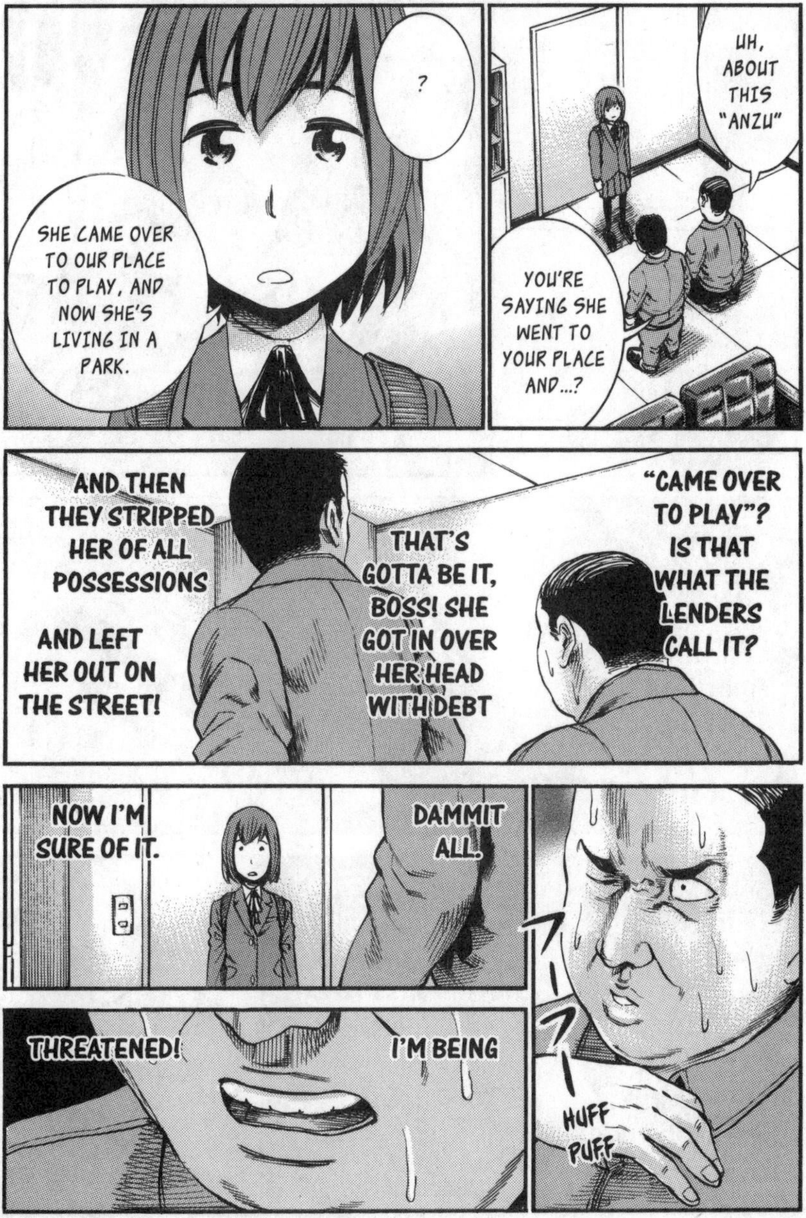
UH, ABOUT THIS "ANZU"
YOU'RE SAYING SHE WENT TO YOUR PLACE AND...?
?
SHE CAME OVER TO OUR PLACE TO PLAY, AND NOW SHE'S LIVING IN A PARK.
"CAME OVER TO PLAY"? IS THAT WHAT THE LENDERS CALL IT?
THAT'S GOTTA BE IT, BOSS! SHE GOT IN OVER HER HEAD WITH DEBT
AND THEN THEY STRIPPED HER OF ALL POSSESSIONS
AND LEFT HER OUT ON THE STREET!
HUFF
PUFF
DAMMIT ALL.
NOW I'M SURE OF IT.
I'M BEING
THREATENED!

HAVE BEEN SO BLIND?!

HOW COULD I

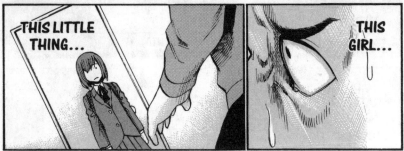

THIS LITTLE THING...

THIS GIRL...

WAS SENT HERE TO COLLECT ON THE DEBT!

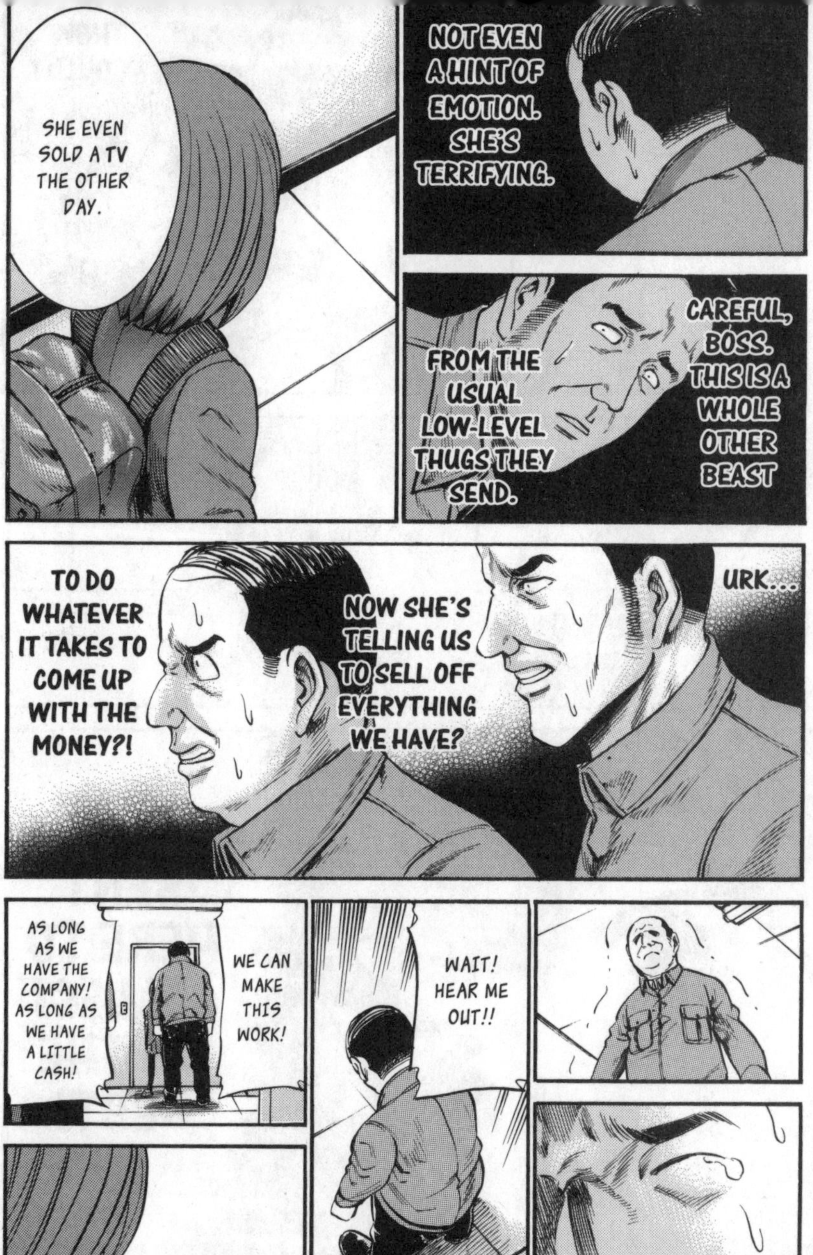
NOT EVEN A HINT OF EMOTION. SHE'S TERRIFYING.
CAREFUL, BOSS. THIS IS A WHOLE OTHER BEAST
FROM THE USUAL LOW-LEVEL THUGS THEY SEND.
SHE EVEN SOLD A TV THE OTHER DAY.
URK...
NOW SHE'S TELLING US TO SELL OFF EVERYTHING WE HAVE?
TO DO WHATEVER IT TAKES TO COME UP WITH THE MONEY?!
WAIT! HEAR ME OUT!!
WE CAN MAKE THIS WORK!
AS LONG AS WE HAVE THE COMPANY! AS LONG AS WE HAVE A LITTLE CASH!

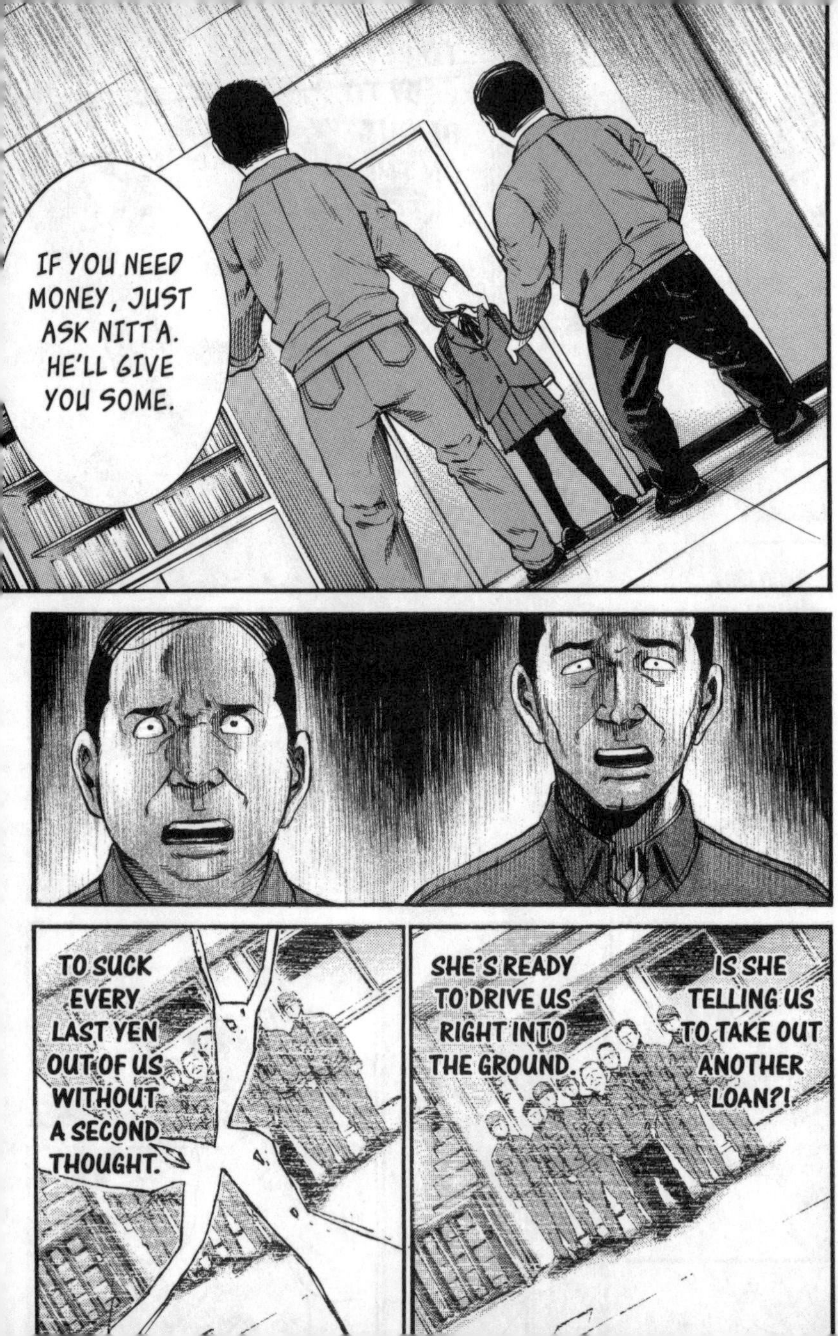
IF YOU NEED MONEY, JUST ASK NITTA. HE'LL GIVE YOU SOME.
IS SHE TELLING US TO TAKE OUT ANOTHER LOAN?!
SHE'S READY TO DRIVE US RIGHT INTO THE GROUND.
TO SUCK EVERY LAST YEN OUT OF US WITHOUT A SECOND THOUGHT.

SHE'S TELLING US

TO GET READY TO BE OUT ON THE STREETS!

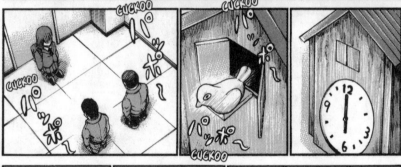

CUCKOO

CUCKOO

CUCKOO

CUCKOO

I'M GONNA GO NOW.

OKAY, THEN.

UH!

WAIT!

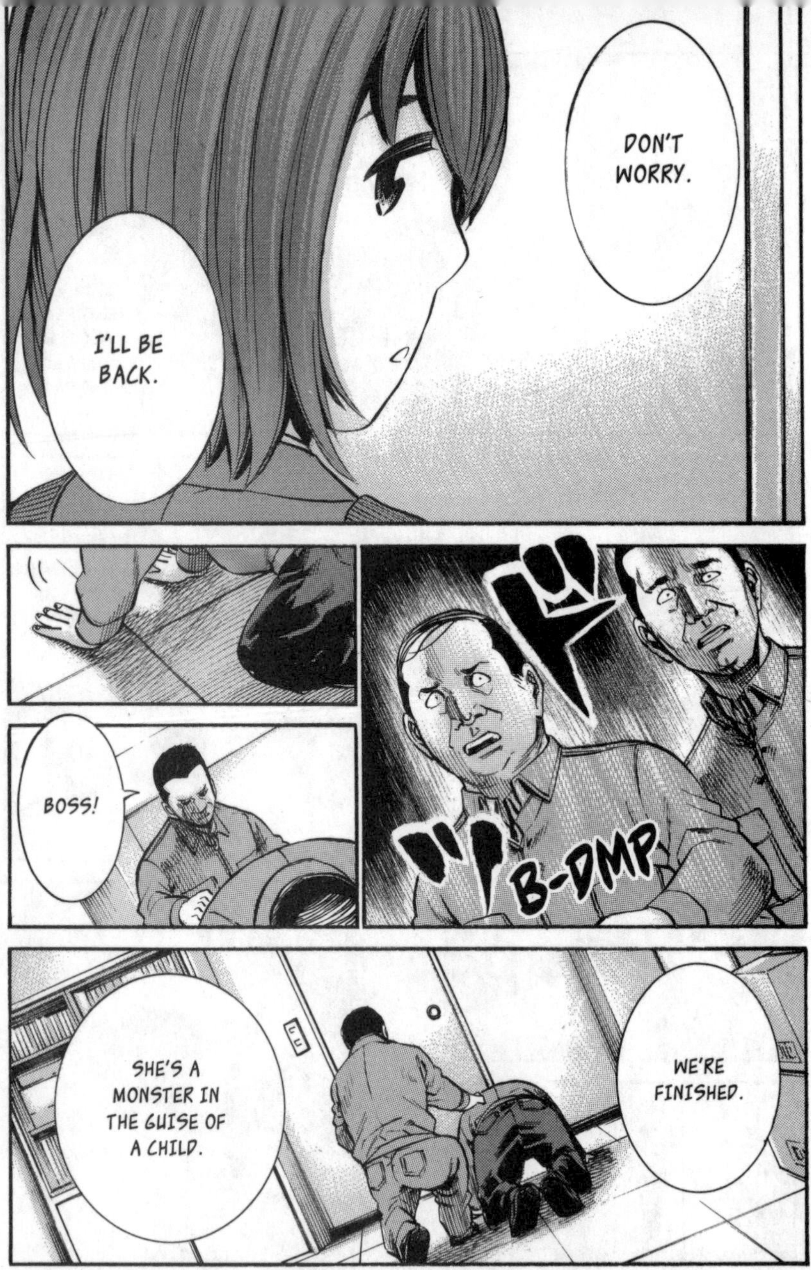
DON'T WORRY.
I'LL BE BACK.
B-DMP
BOSS!
WE'RE FINISHED.
SHE'S A MONSTER IN THE GUISE OF A CHILD.

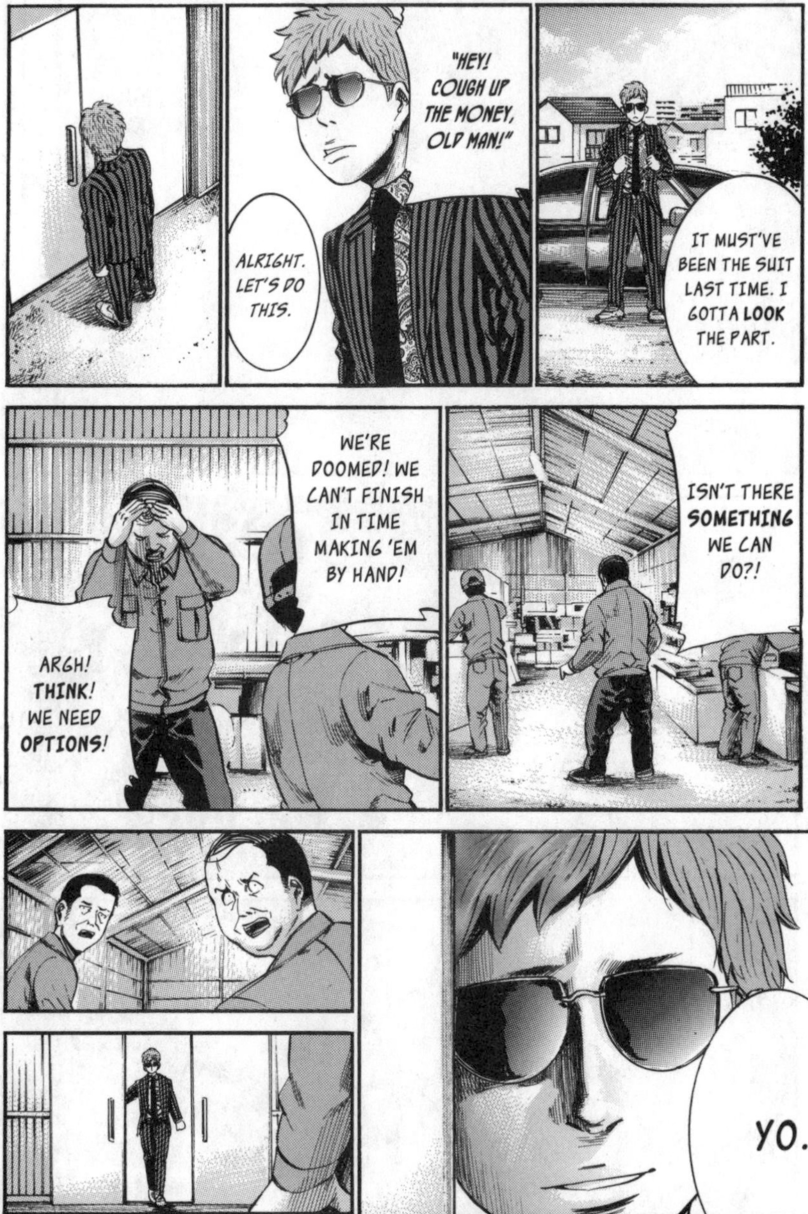
IT MUST'VE BEEN THE SUIT LAST TIME. I GOTTA LOOK THE PART.
"HEY! COUGH UP THE MONEY, OLD MAN!"
ALRIGHT. LET'S DO THIS.
ISN'T THERE SOMETHING WE CAN DO?!
WE'RE DOOMED! WE CAN'T FINISH IN TIME MAKING 'EM BY HAND!
ARGH! THINK! WE NEED OPTIONS!
YO.

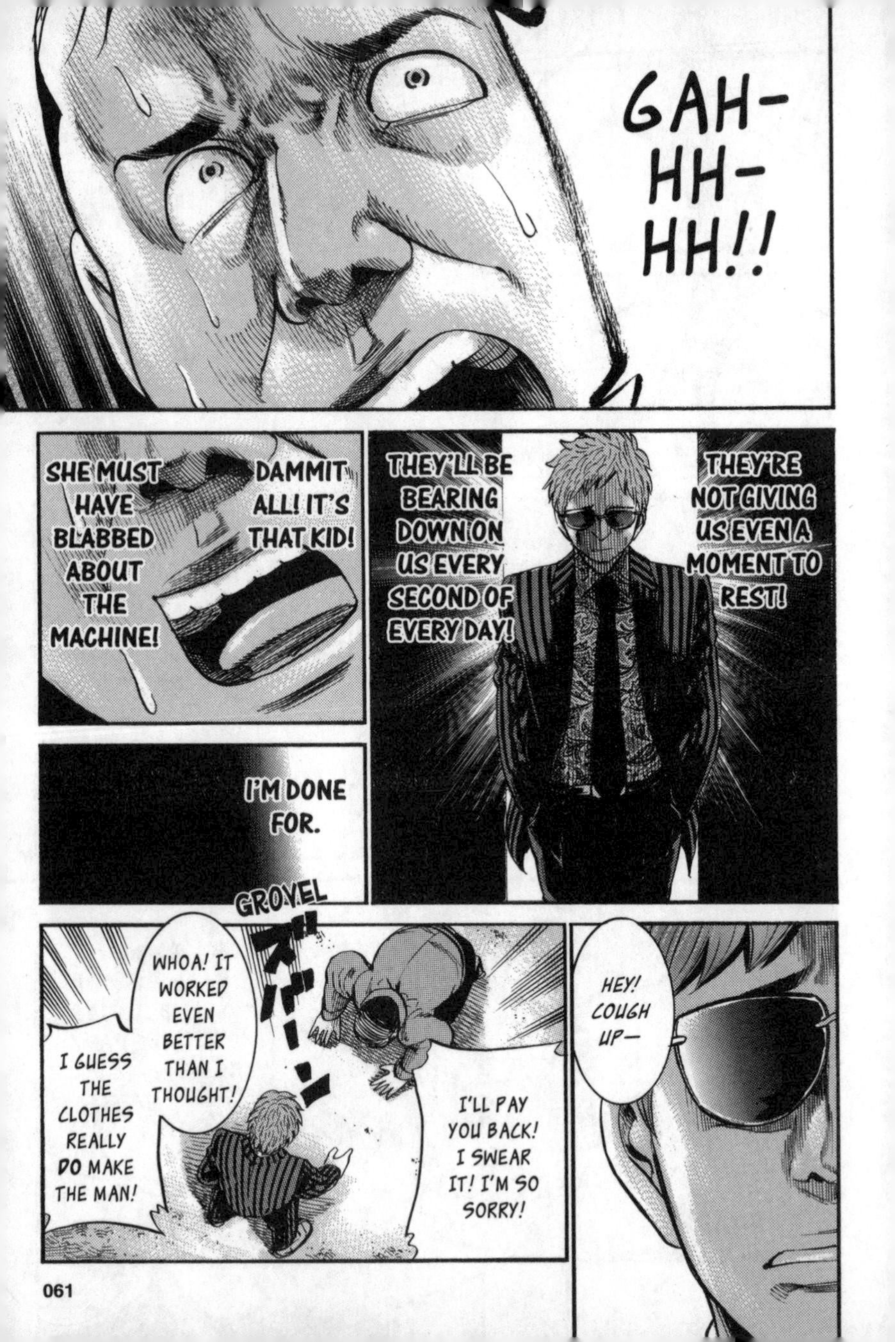
GAH-HH-HH!!
THEY'RE NOT GIVING US EVEN A MOMENT TO REST!
THEY'LL BE BEARING DOWN ON US EVERY SECOND OF EVERY DAY!
DAMMIT ALL! IT'S THAT KID!
SHE MUST HAVE BLABBED ABOUT THE MACHINE!
I'M DONE FOR.
HEY! COUGH UP—
GROVEL
I'LL PAY YOU BACK! I SWEAR IT! I'M SO SORRY!
WHOA! IT WORKED EVEN BETTER THAN I THOUGHT!
I GUESS THE CLOTHES REALLY DO MAKE THE MAN!

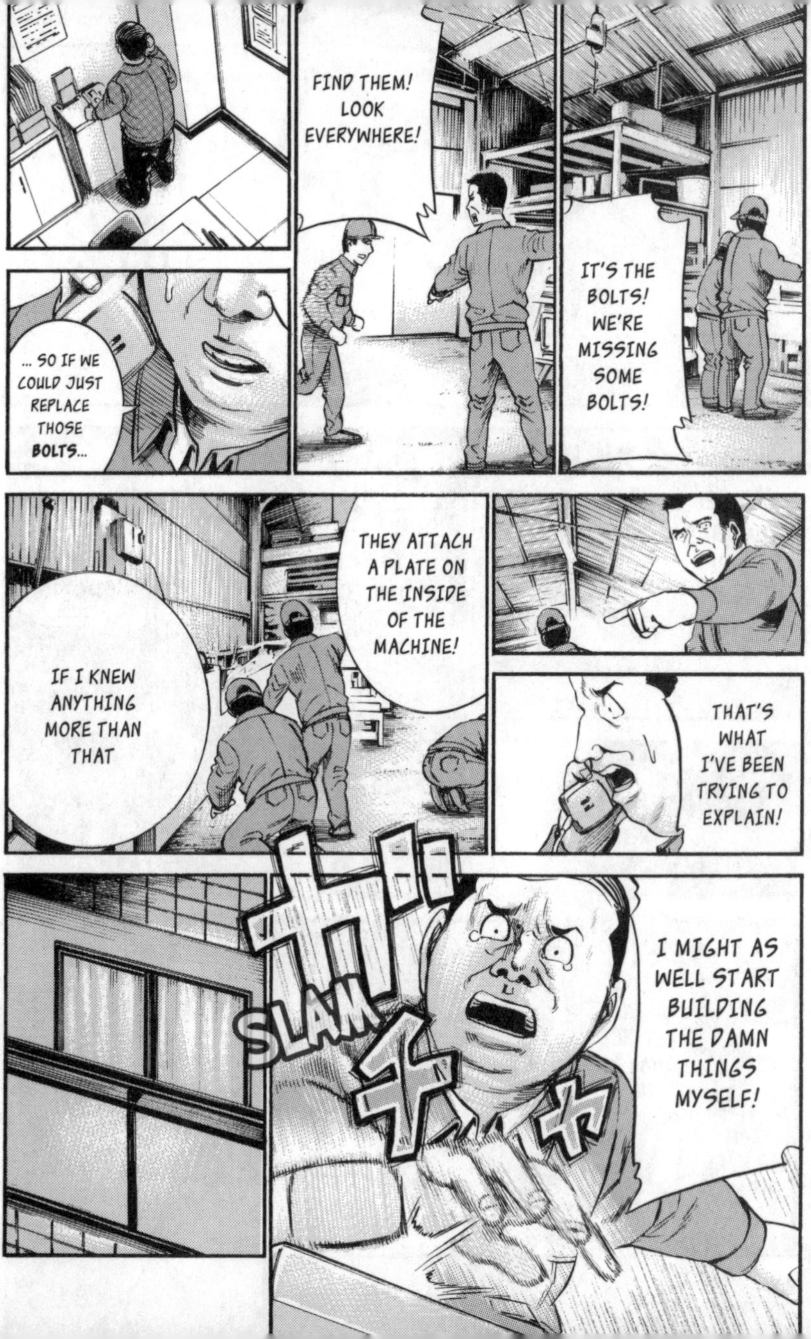
IT'S THE BOLTS! WE'RE MISSING SOME BOLTS!
FIND THEM! LOOK EVERYWHERE!
... SO IF WE COULD JUST REPLACE THOSE BOLTS...
THAT'S WHAT I'VE BEEN TRYING TO EXPLAIN!
THEY ATTACH A PLATE ON THE INSIDE OF THE MACHINE!
IF I KNEW ANYTHING MORE THAN THAT
I MIGHT AS WELL START BUILDING THE DAMN THINGS MYSELF!
SLAM

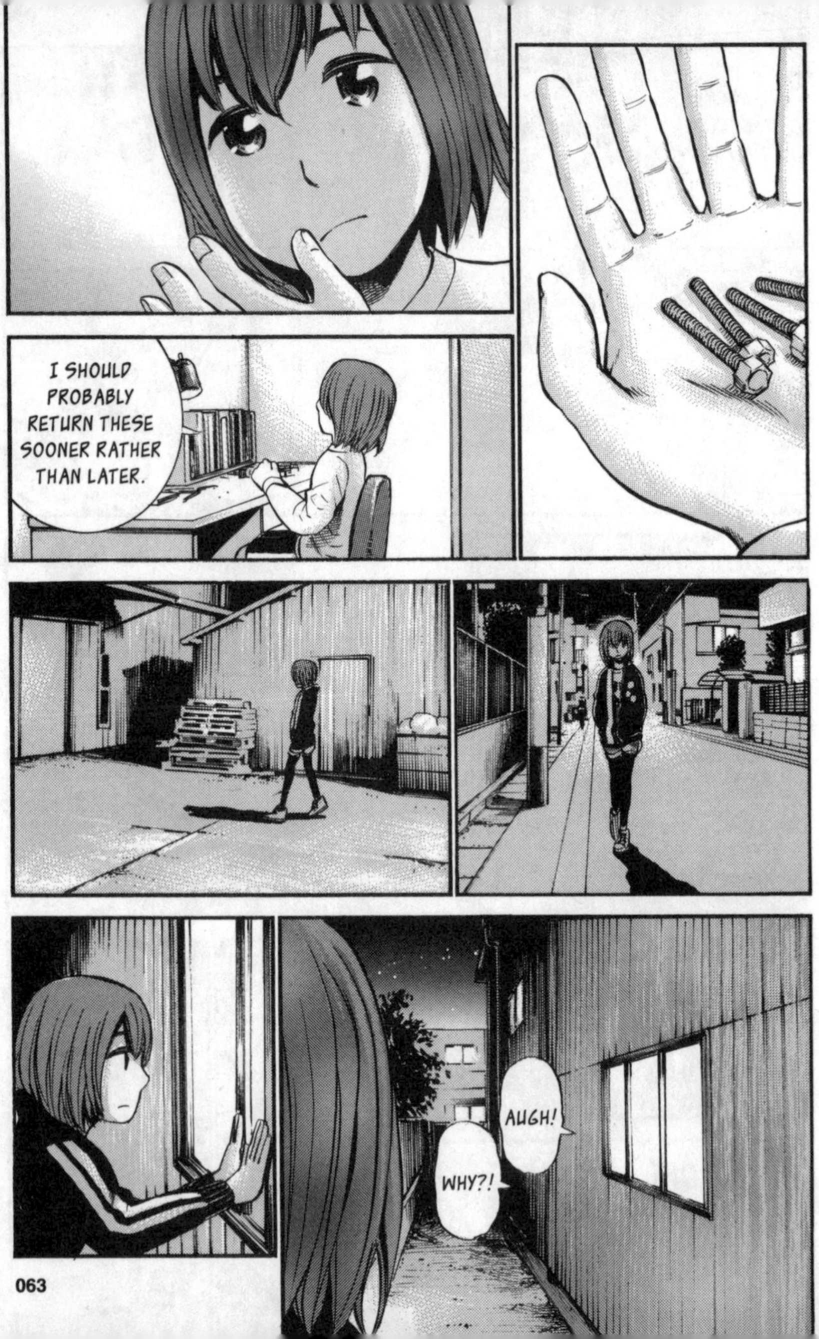
I SHOULD PROBABLY RETURN THESE SOONER RATHER THAN LATER.
AUGH!
WHY?!

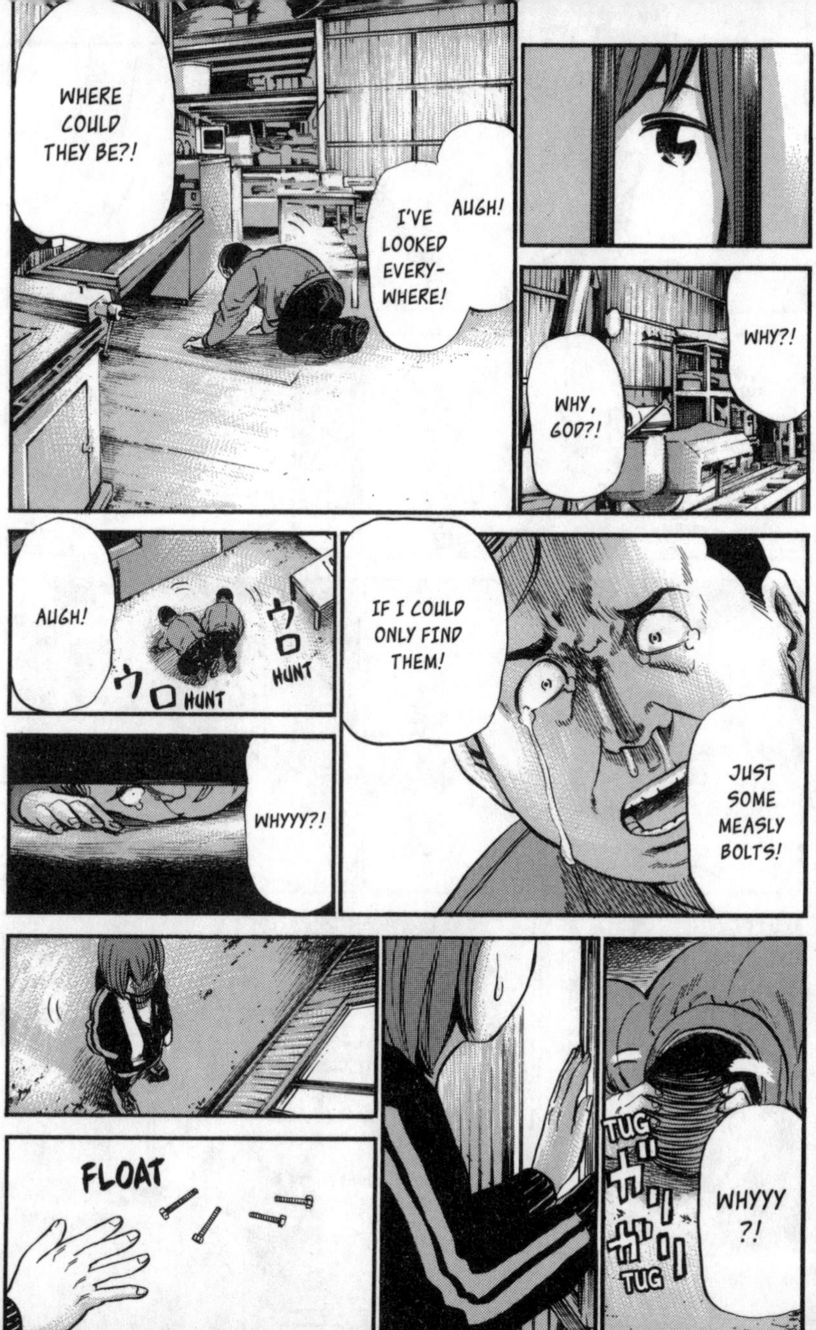
WHY?!
WHY, GOD?!
AUGH!
I'VE LOOKED EVERY-WHERE!
WHERE COULD THEY BE?!
IF I COULD ONLY FIND THEM!
JUST SOME MEASLY BOLTS!
AUGH!
ウロ HUNT
ウロ HUNT
WHYYY?!
TUG ガッ
ガッ TUG
WHYYY ?!
FLOAT

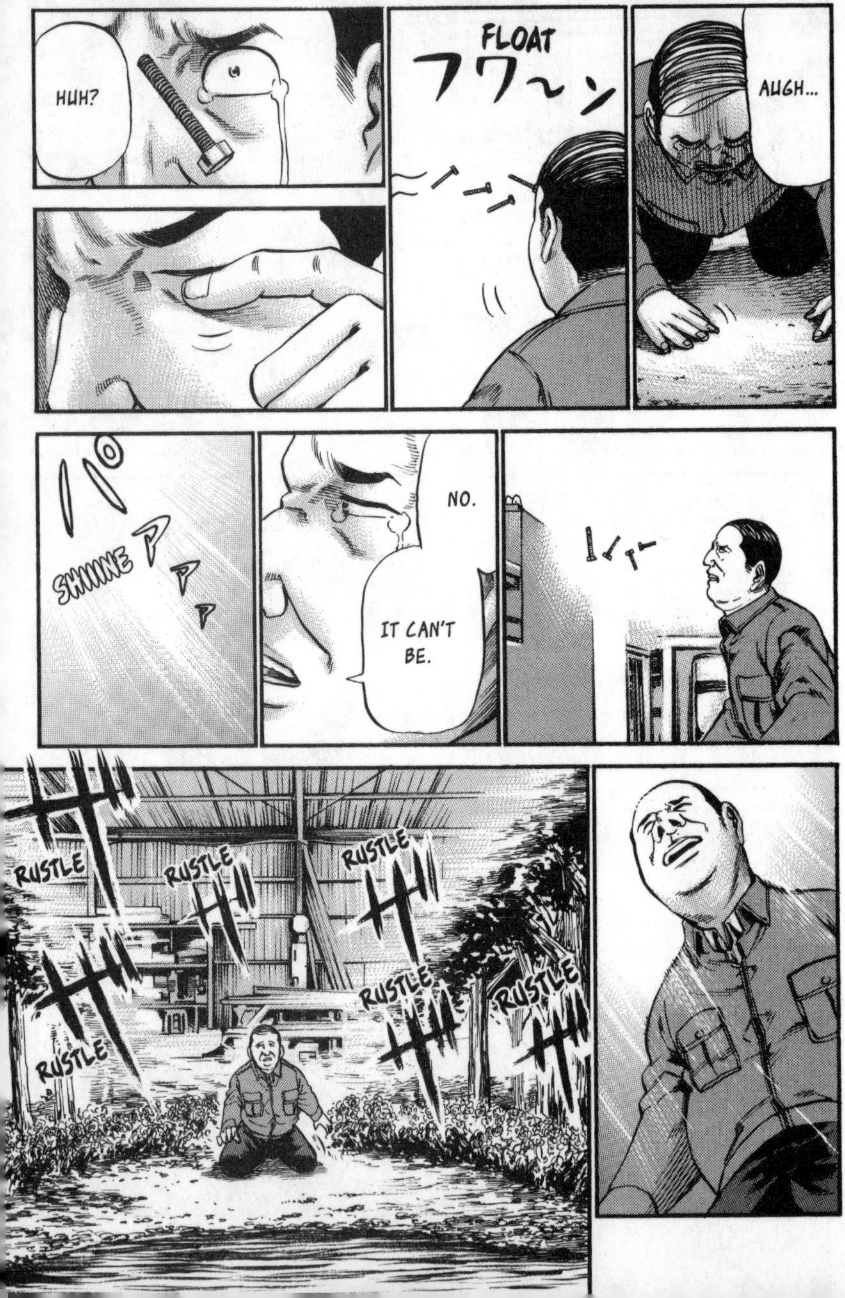
AUGH...
FLOAT
フワ〜ン
HUH?
NO.
IT CAN'T BE.
SHIIINE
パァァァ
RUSTLE
RUSTLE
RUSTLE
RUSTLE
RUSTLE
RUSTLE

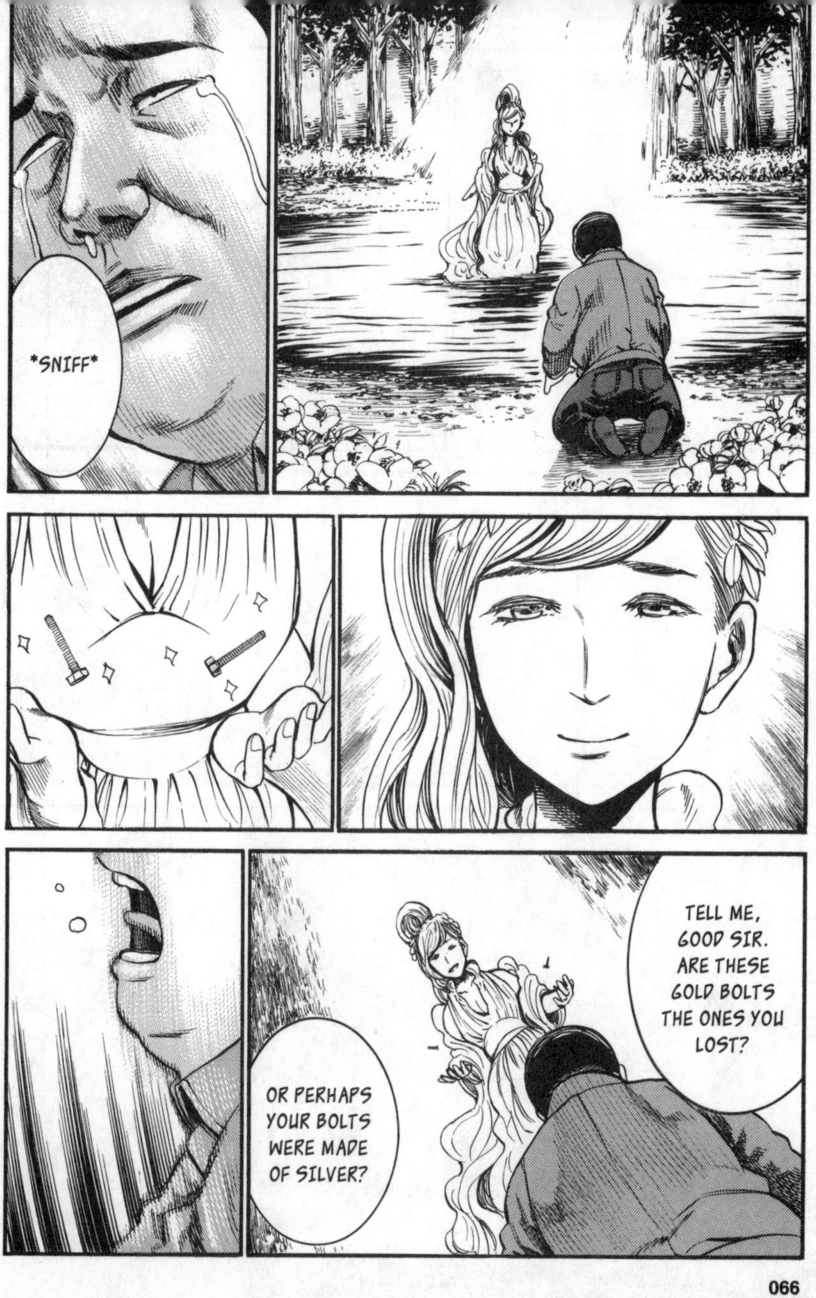
SNIFF
TELL ME, GOOD SIR. ARE THESE GOLD BOLTS THE ONES YOU LOST?
OR PERHAPS YOUR BOLTS WERE MADE OF SILVER?

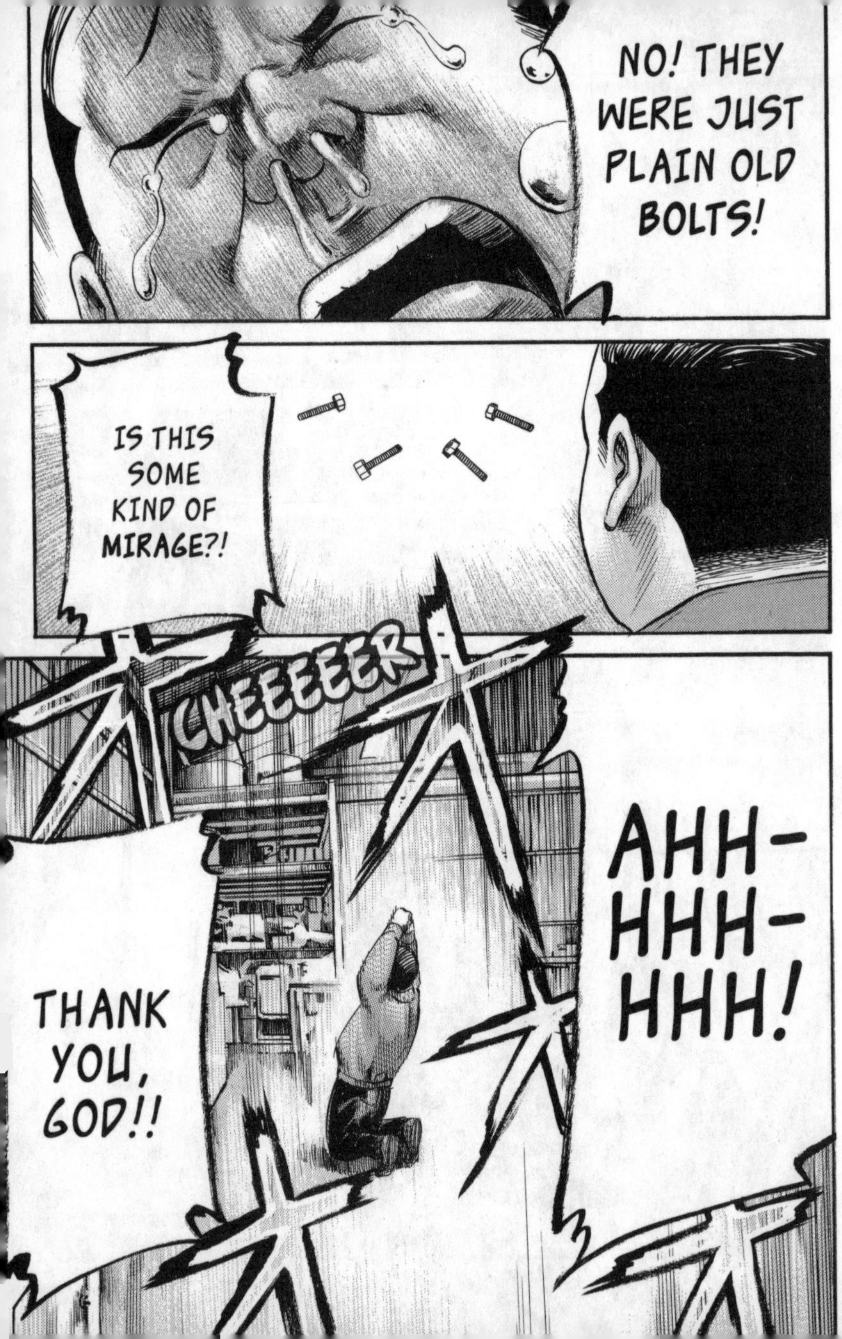
NO! THEY WERE JUST PLAIN OLD BOLTS!
IS THIS SOME KIND OF MIRAGE?!
CHEEEEER
AHH-HHH-HHH!
THANK YOU, GOD!!

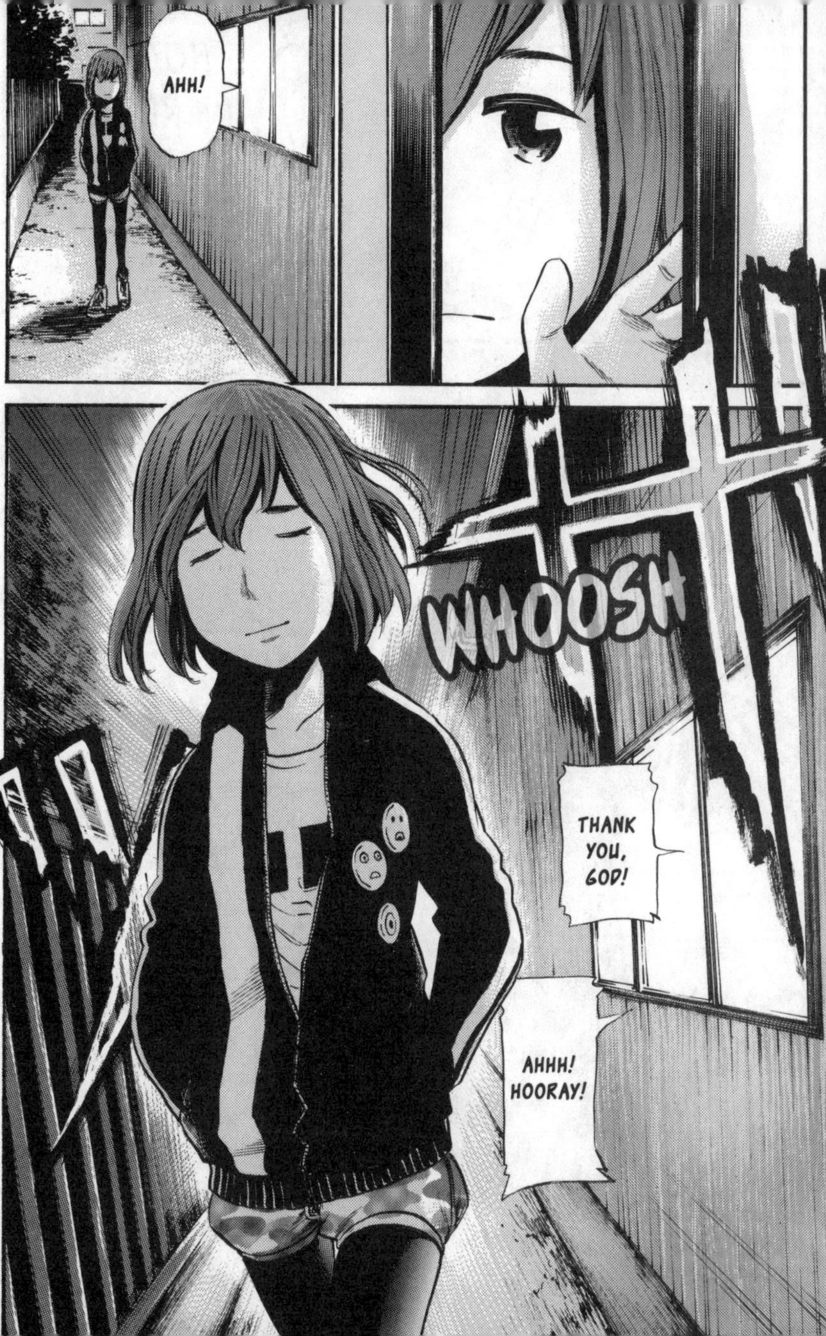
AHH!
WHOOSH
THANK YOU, GOD!
AHHH! HOORAY!

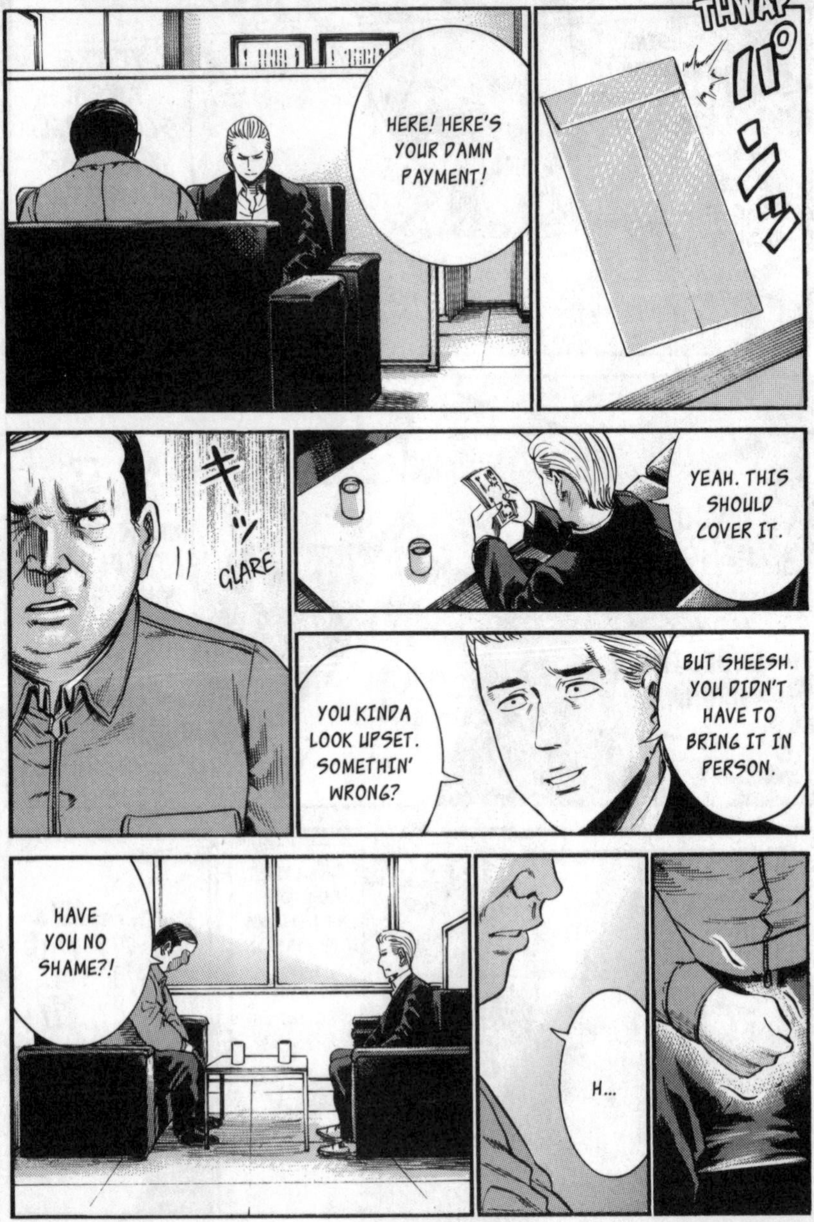
THWAP
HERE! HERE'S YOUR DAMN PAYMENT!
YEAH. THIS SHOULD COVER IT.
BUT SHEESH. YOU DIDN'T HAVE TO BRING IT IN PERSON.
YOU KINDA LOOK UPSET. SOMETHIN' WRONG?
GLARE
H...
HAVE YOU NO SHAME?!

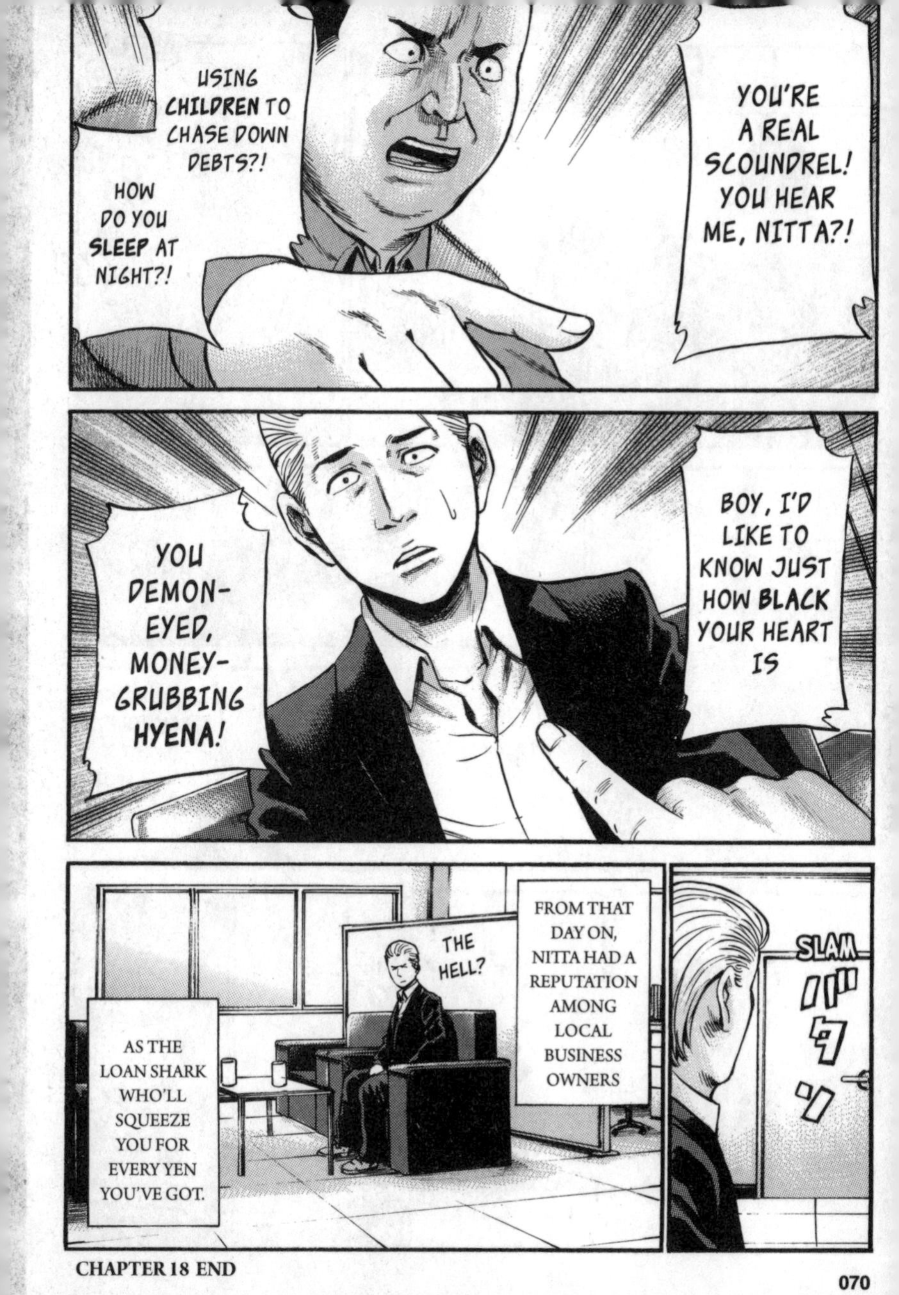
YOU'RE A REAL SCOUNDREL! YOU HEAR ME, NITTA?!
USING CHILDREN TO CHASE DOWN DEBTS?!
HOW DO YOU SLEEP AT NIGHT?!
BOY, I'D LIKE TO KNOW JUST HOW BLACK YOUR HEART IS
YOU DEMON-EYED, MONEY-GRUBBING HYENA!
SLAM
バタン
FROM THAT DAY ON, NITTA HAD A REPUTATION AMONG LOCAL BUSINESS OWNERS
THE HELL?
AS THE LOAN SHARK WHO'LL SQUEEZE YOU FOR EVERY YEN YOU'VE GOT.

CHAPTER 18 END

SLUMP
ズーン

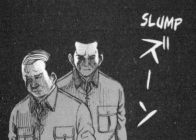

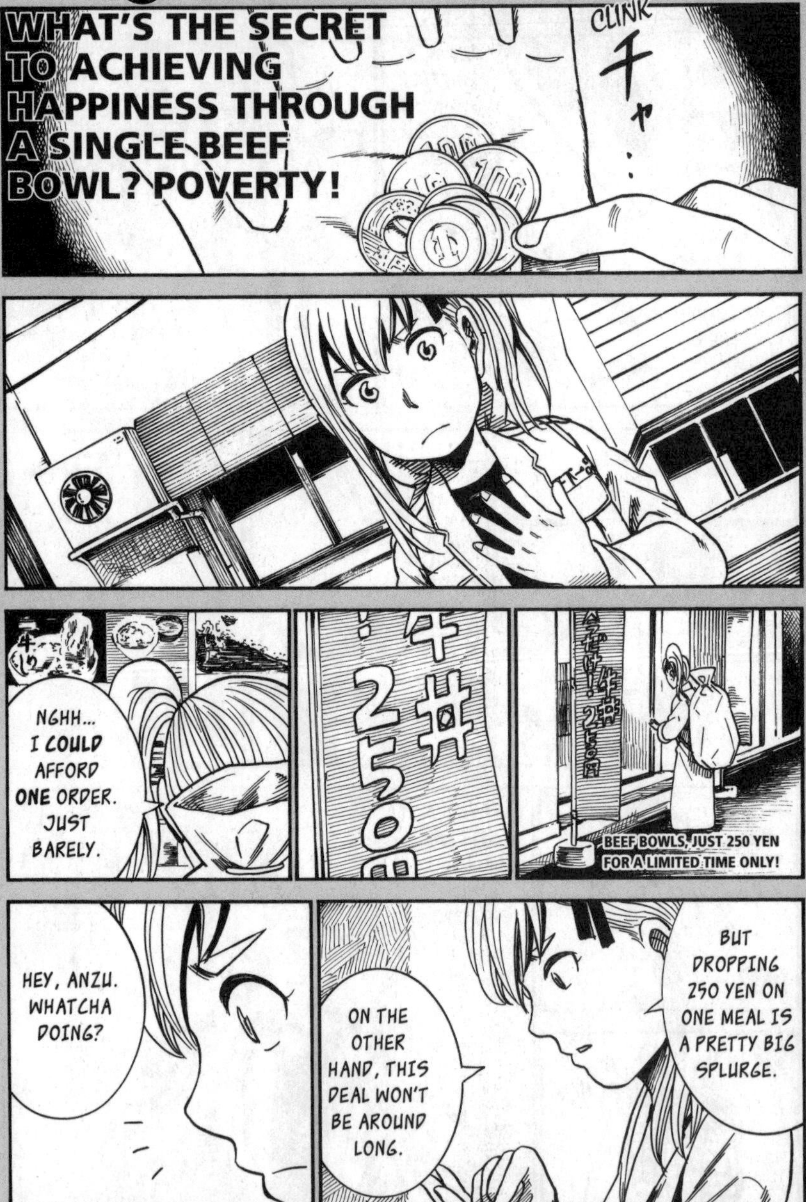
WHAT'S THE SECRET TO ACHIEVING HAPPINESS THROUGH A SINGLE BEEF BOWL? POVERTY!
CLINK
チャ…
BEEF BOWLS, JUST 250 YEN FOR A LIMITED TIME ONLY!
NGHH... I COULD AFFORD ONE ORDER. JUST BARELY.
BUT DROPPING 250 YEN ON ONE MEAL IS A PRETTY BIG SPLURGE.
ON THE OTHER HAND, THIS DEAL WON'T BE AROUND LONG.
HEY, ANZU. WHATCHA DOING?

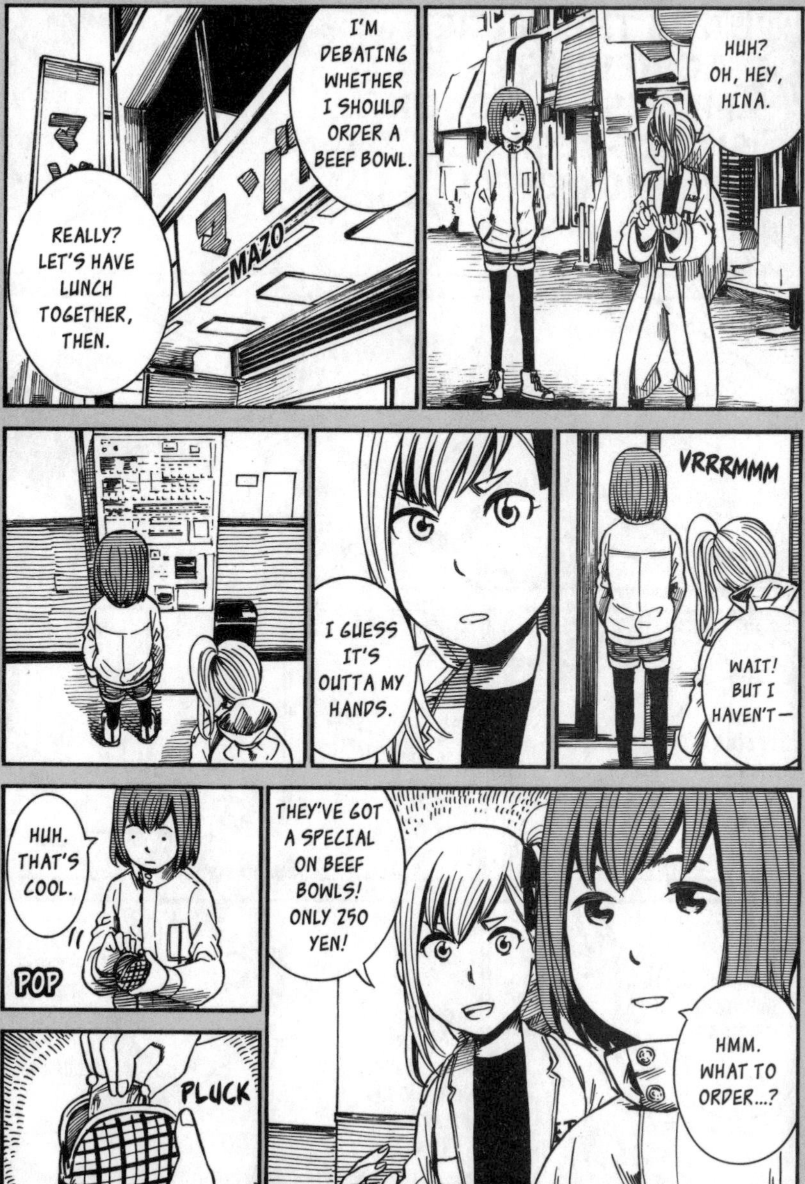
HUH? OH, HEY, HINA.
I'M DEBATING WHETHER I SHOULD ORDER A BEEF BOWL.
MAZO
REALLY? LET'S HAVE LUNCH TOGETHER, THEN.
VRRRMMM
WAIT! BUT I HAVEN'T—
I GUESS IT'S OUTTA MY HANDS.
THEY'VE GOT A SPECIAL ON BEEF BOWLS! ONLY 250 YEN!
HMM. WHAT TO ORDER...?
HUH. THAT'S COOL.
POP
PLUCK

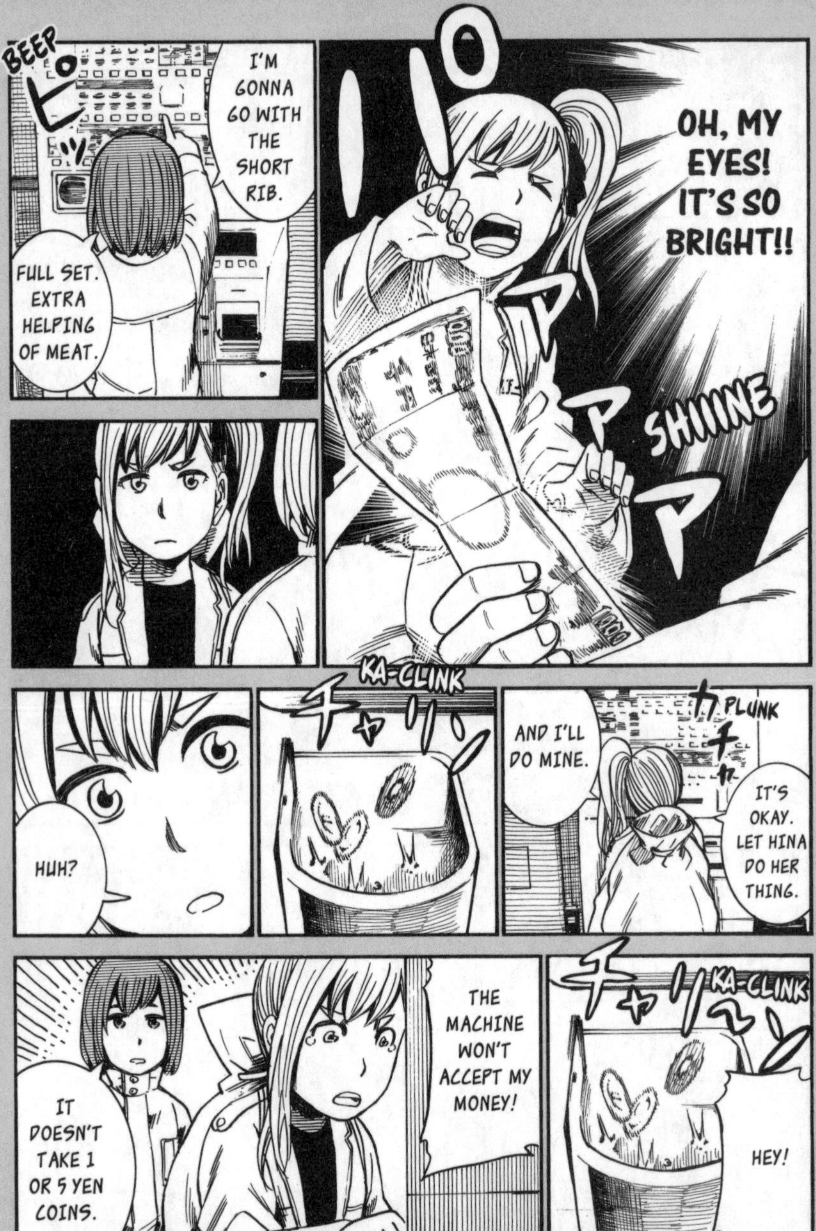
OH, MY EYES! IT'S SO BRIGHT!!
SHIIINE
BEEP
I'M GONNA GO WITH THE SHORT RIB.
FULL SET. EXTRA HELPING OF MEAT.
PLUNK
AND I'LL DO MINE.
IT'S OKAY. LET HINA DO HER THING.
KA-CLINK
HUH?
KA-CLINK
HEY!
THE MACHINE WON'T ACCEPT MY MONEY!
IT DOESN'T TAKE 1 OR 5 YEN COINS.

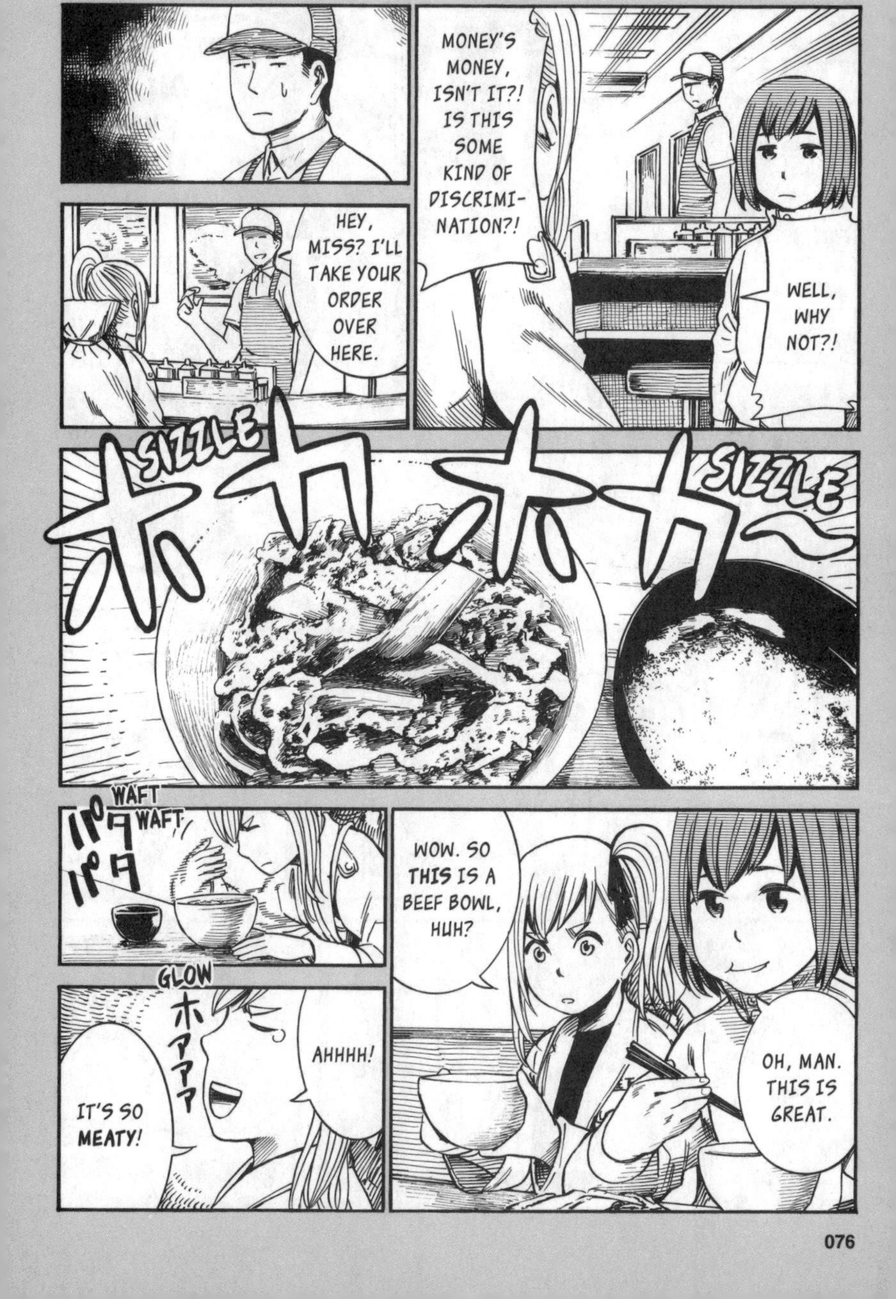
MONEY'S MONEY, ISN'T IT?! IS THIS SOME KIND OF DISCRIMINATION?!
WELL, WHY NOT?!
HEY, MISS? I'LL TAKE YOUR ORDER OVER HERE.
SIZZLE
ホカホカ～
SIZZLE
WOW. SO THIS IS A BEEF BOWL, HUH?
OH, MAN. THIS IS GREAT.
WAFT WAFT
パタパタ
GLOW
ホアアア
AHHHH!
IT'S SO MEATY!

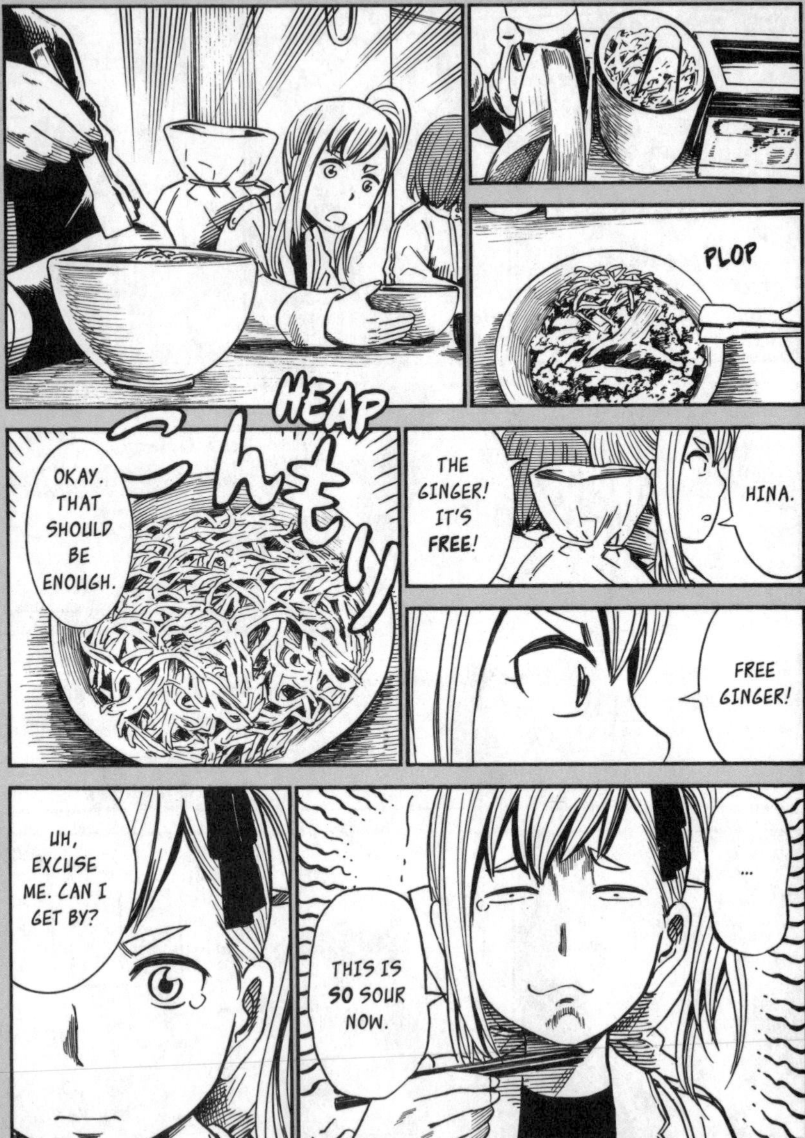
PLOP
HINA.
THE GINGER! IT'S FREE!
FREE GINGER!
HEAP
こんもり
OKAY. THAT SHOULD BE ENOUGH.
...
THIS IS SO SOUR NOW.
UH, EXCUSE ME. CAN I GET BY?

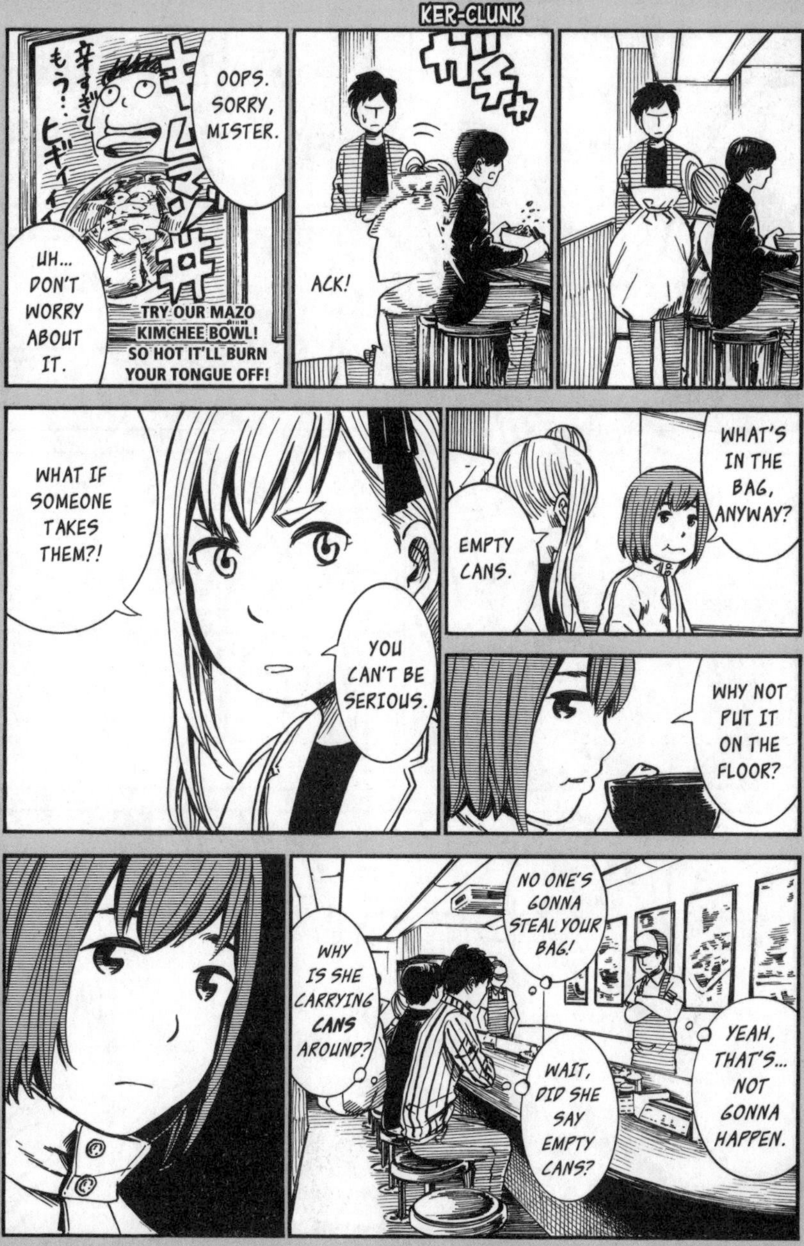
KER-CLUNK
ガチャ
ACK!
OOPS. SORRY, MISTER.
UH... DON'T WORRY ABOUT IT.
TRY OUR MAZO KIMCHEE BOWL! SO HOT IT'LL BURN YOUR TONGUE OFF!
WHAT'S IN THE BAG, ANYWAY?
EMPTY CANS.
WHY NOT PUT IT ON THE FLOOR?
WHAT IF SOMEONE TAKES THEM?!
YOU CAN'T BE SERIOUS.
NO ONE'S GONNA STEAL YOUR BAG!
YEAH, THAT'S... NOT GONNA HAPPEN.
WAIT, DID SHE SAY EMPTY CANS?
WHY IS SHE CARRYING CANS AROUND?

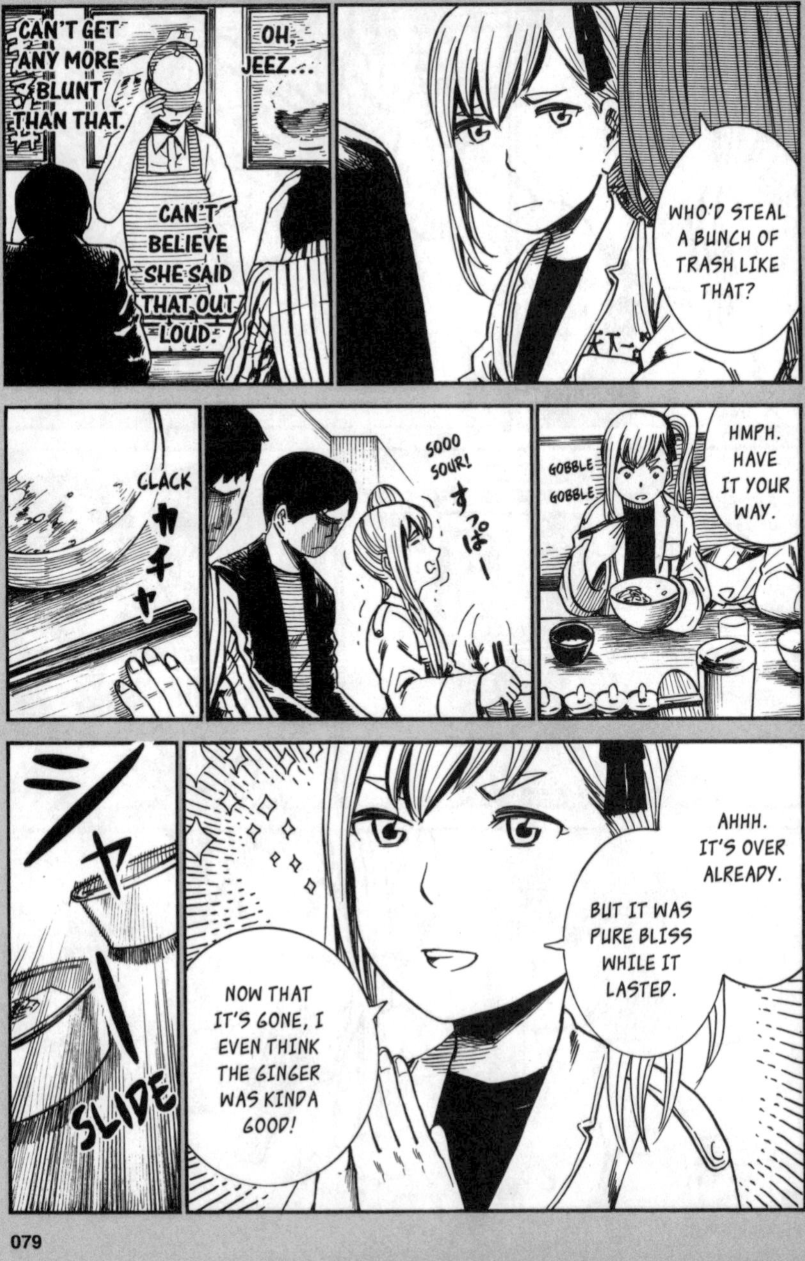
WHO'D STEAL A BUNCH OF TRASH LIKE THAT?
OH, JEEZ...
CAN'T GET ANY MORE BLUNT THAN THAT.
CAN'T BELIEVE SHE SAID THAT OUT LOUD.
HMPH. HAVE IT YOUR WAY.
GOBBLE GOBBLE
SOOO SOUR!
すっぱー
CLACK
カチャ
AHHH. IT'S OVER ALREADY.
BUT IT WAS PURE BLISS WHILE IT LASTED.
NOW THAT IT'S GONE, I EVEN THINK THE GINGER WAS KINDA GOOD!
シャー
SLIDE

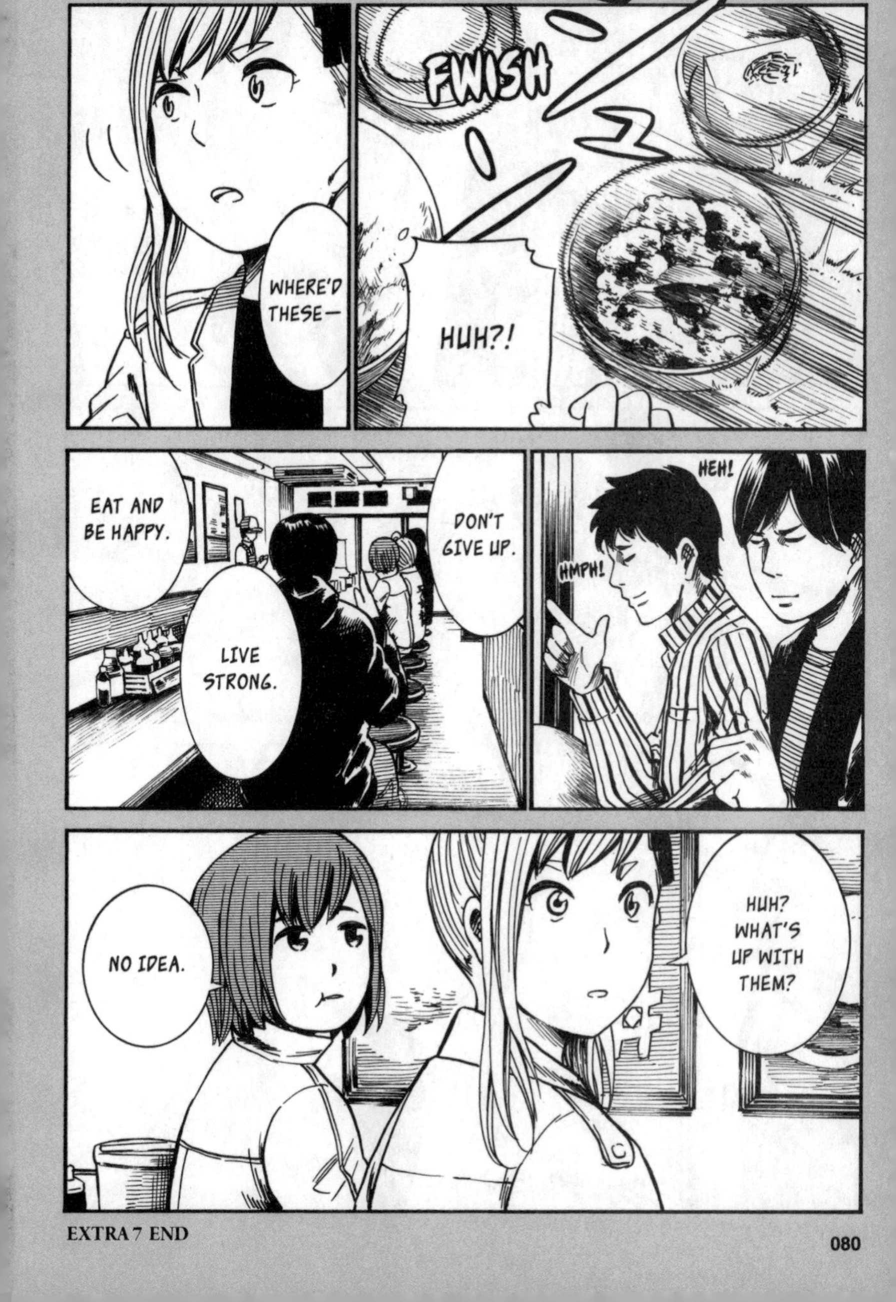
FWISH
HUH?!
WHERE'D THESE—
HEH!
HMPH!
DON'T GIVE UP.
EAT AND BE HAPPY.
LIVE STRONG.
HUH? WHAT'S UP WITH THEM?
NO IDEA.

EXTRA 7 END

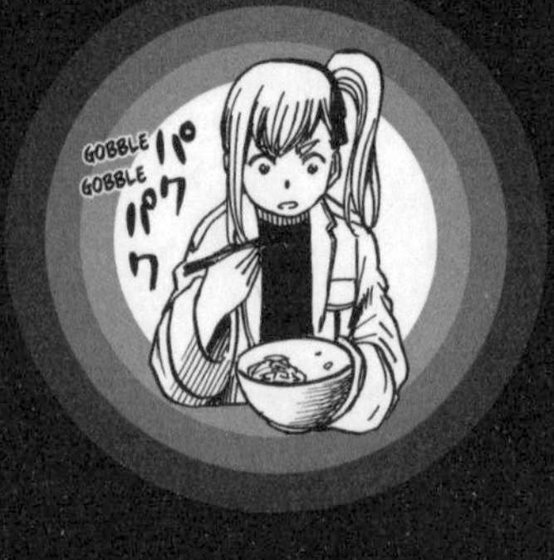
GOBBLE GOBBLE
パクパク

CHAPTER 19

INSPECTOR! IT'S GONNA BE A TOUGH CASE TO CRACK!

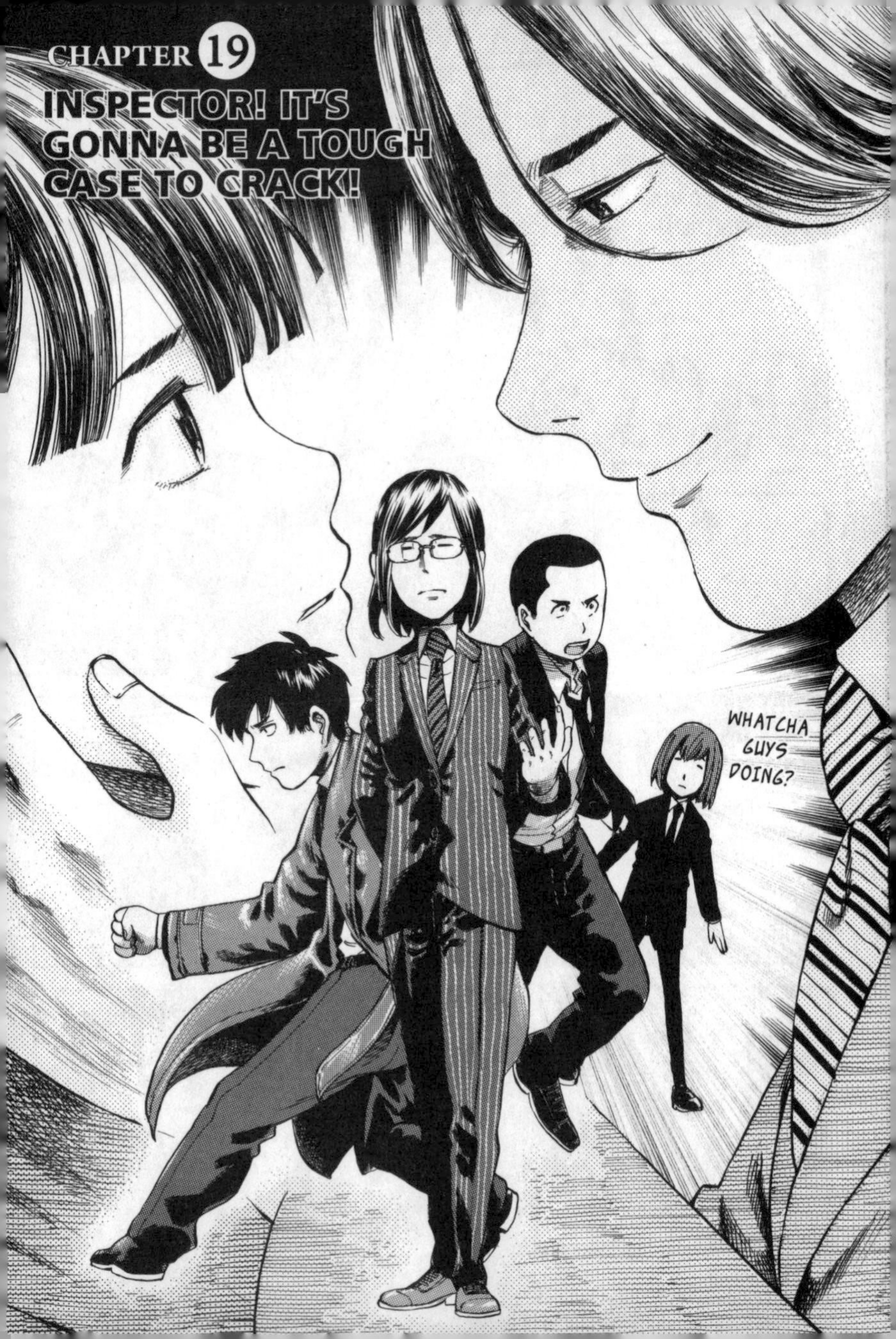
WHATCHA GUYS DOING?

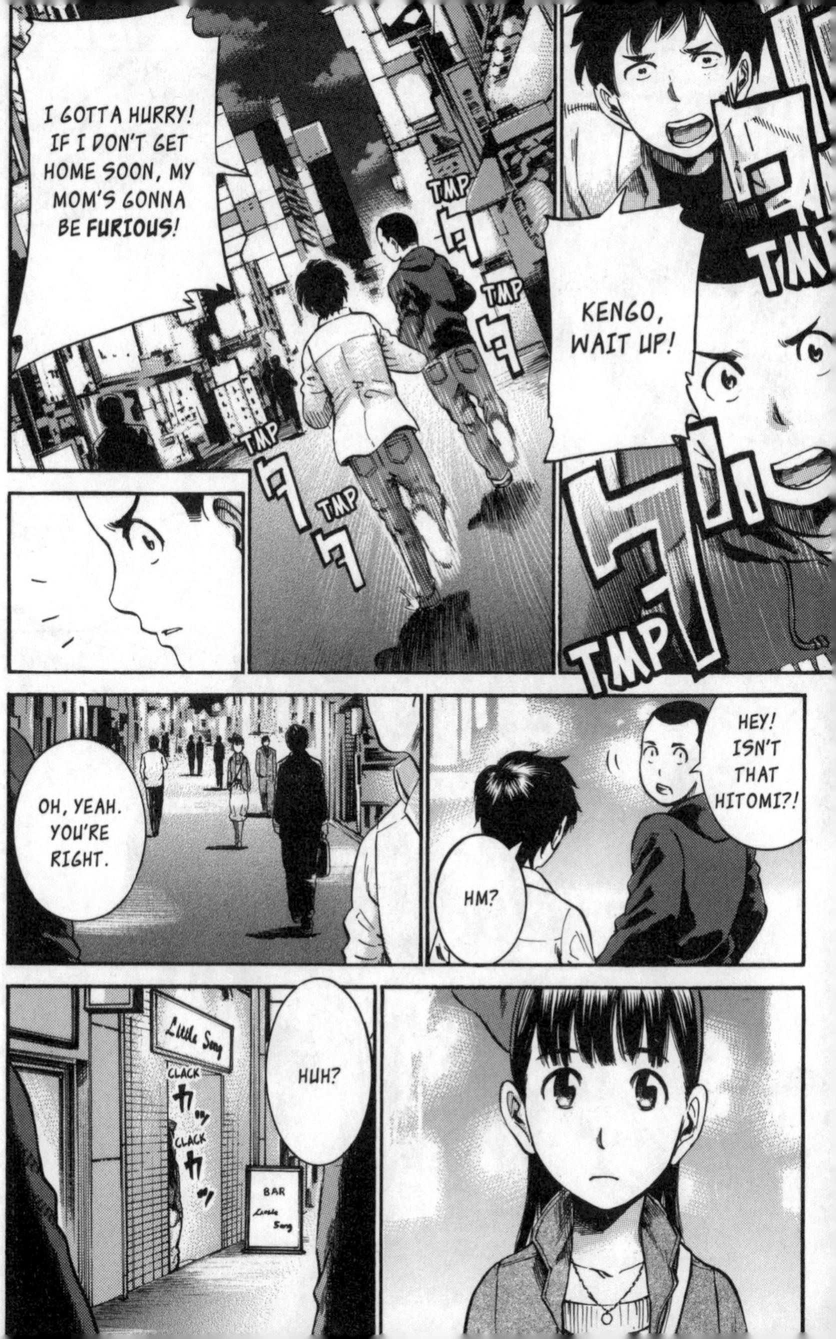
KENGO, WAIT UP!
TMP
TMP
I GOTTA HURRY! IF I DON'T GET HOME SOON, MY MOM'S GONNA BE FURIOUS!
TMP
TMP
TMP
TMP
HEY! ISN'T THAT HITOMI?!
HM?
OH, YEAH. YOU'RE RIGHT.
HUH?
Little Song
CLACK
CLACK
BAR
Little Song

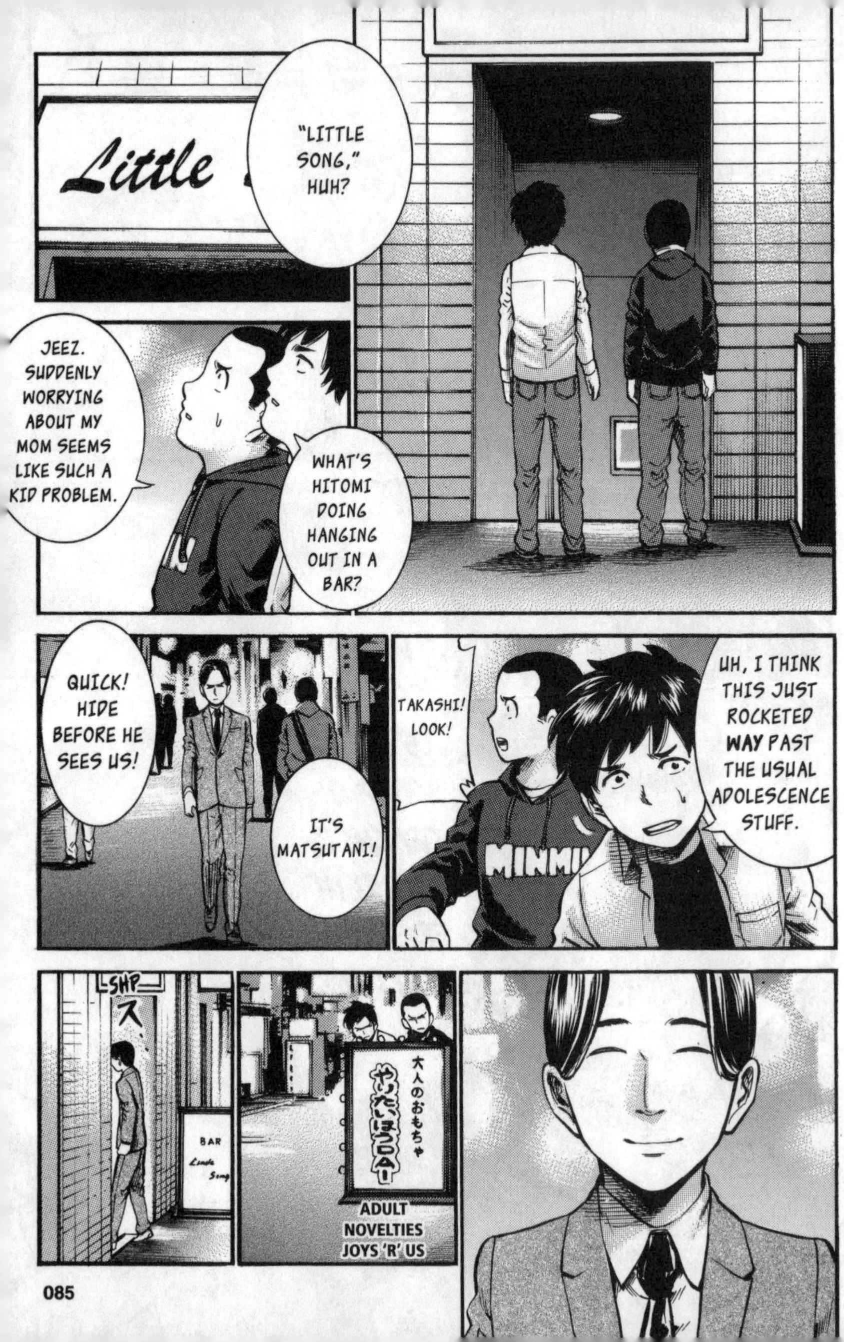
"LITTLE SONG," HUH?
Little
WHAT'S HITOMI DOING HANGING OUT IN A BAR?
JEEZ. SUDDENLY WORRYING ABOUT MY MOM SEEMS LIKE SUCH A KID PROBLEM.
UH, I THINK THIS JUST ROCKETED **WAY** PAST THE USUAL ADOLESCENCE STUFF.
TAKASHI! LOOK!
IT'S MATSUTANI!
QUICK! HIDE BEFORE HE SEES US!
MINMIN
大人のおもちゃ
やりたいほうだい
ADULT NOVELTIES JOYS 'R' US
BAR
SHP
ス

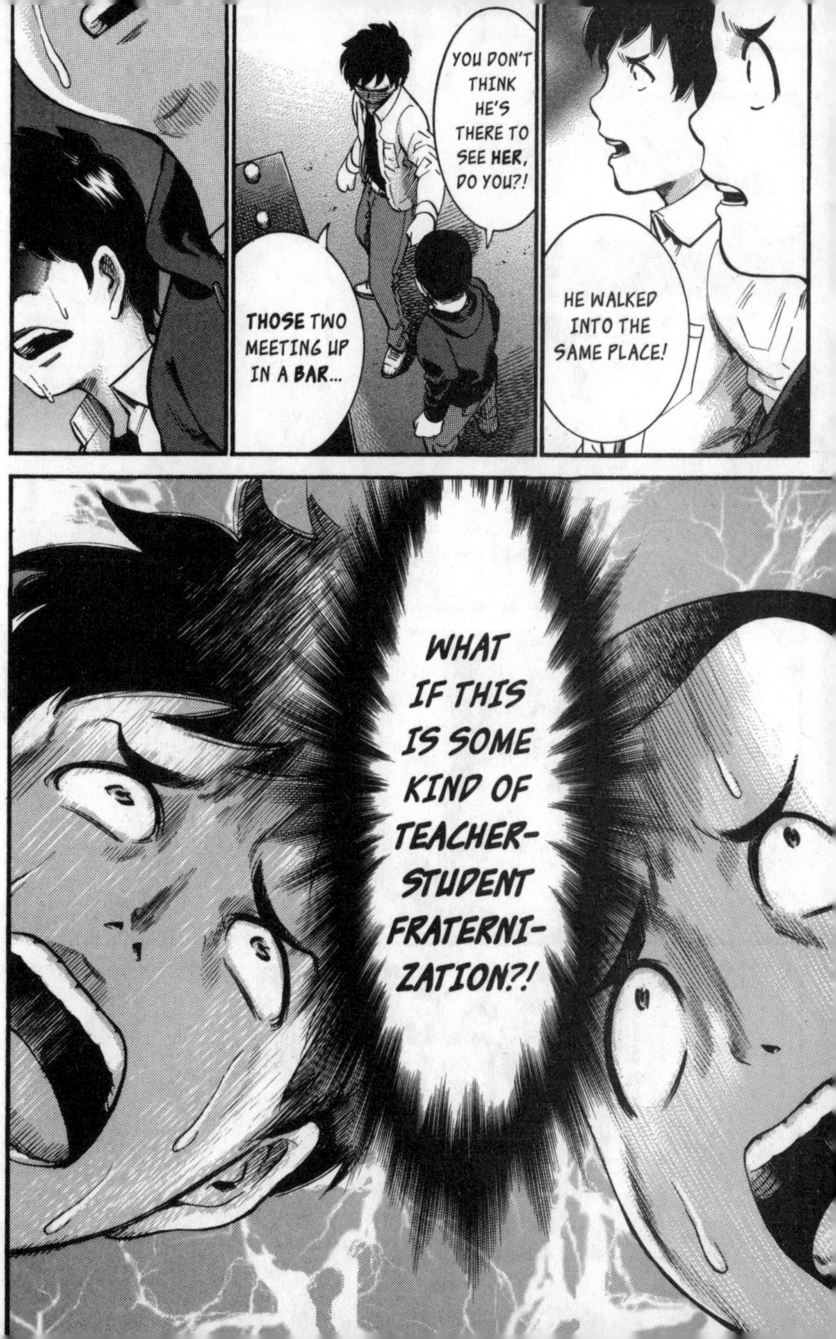
HE WALKED INTO THE SAME PLACE!
YOU DON'T THINK HE'S THERE TO SEE HER, DO YOU?!
THOSE TWO MEETING UP IN A BAR...
WHAT IF THIS IS SOME KIND OF TEACHER-STUDENT FRATERNIZATION?!

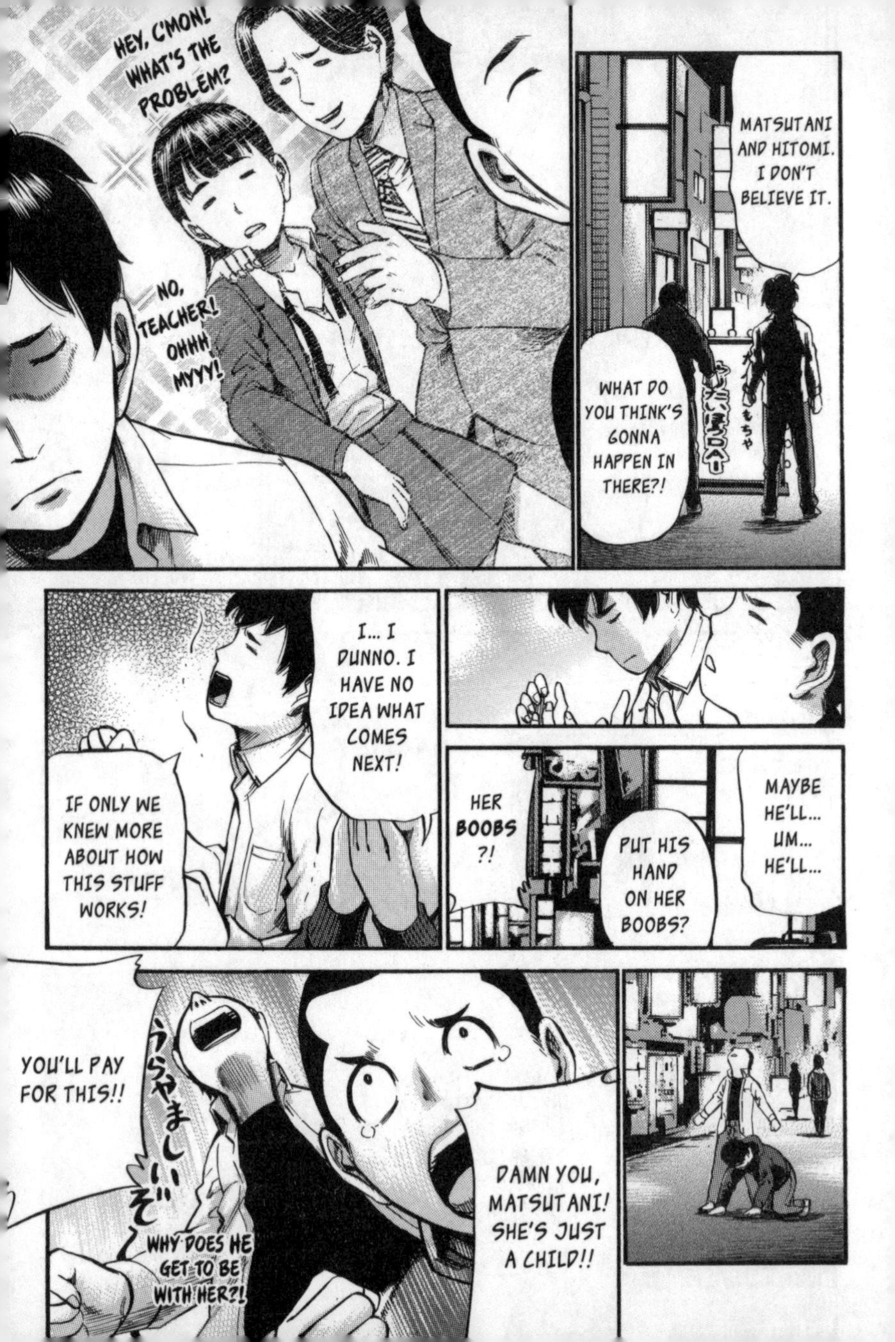

MATSUTANI AND HITOMI. I DON'T BELIEVE IT.
WHAT DO YOU THINK'S GONNA HAPPEN IN THERE?!
HEY, C'MON! WHAT'S THE PROBLEM?
NO, TEACHER! OHHH MYYY!
MAYBE HE'LL... UM... HE'LL...
PUT HIS HAND ON HER BOOBS?
HER **BOOBS**?!
I... I DUNNO. I HAVE NO IDEA WHAT COMES NEXT!
IF ONLY WE KNEW MORE ABOUT HOW THIS STUFF WORKS!
DAMN YOU, MATSUTANI! SHE'S JUST A CHILD!!
うらやましいぞ〜
WHY DOES HE GET TO BE WITH HER?!
YOU'LL PAY FOR THIS!!

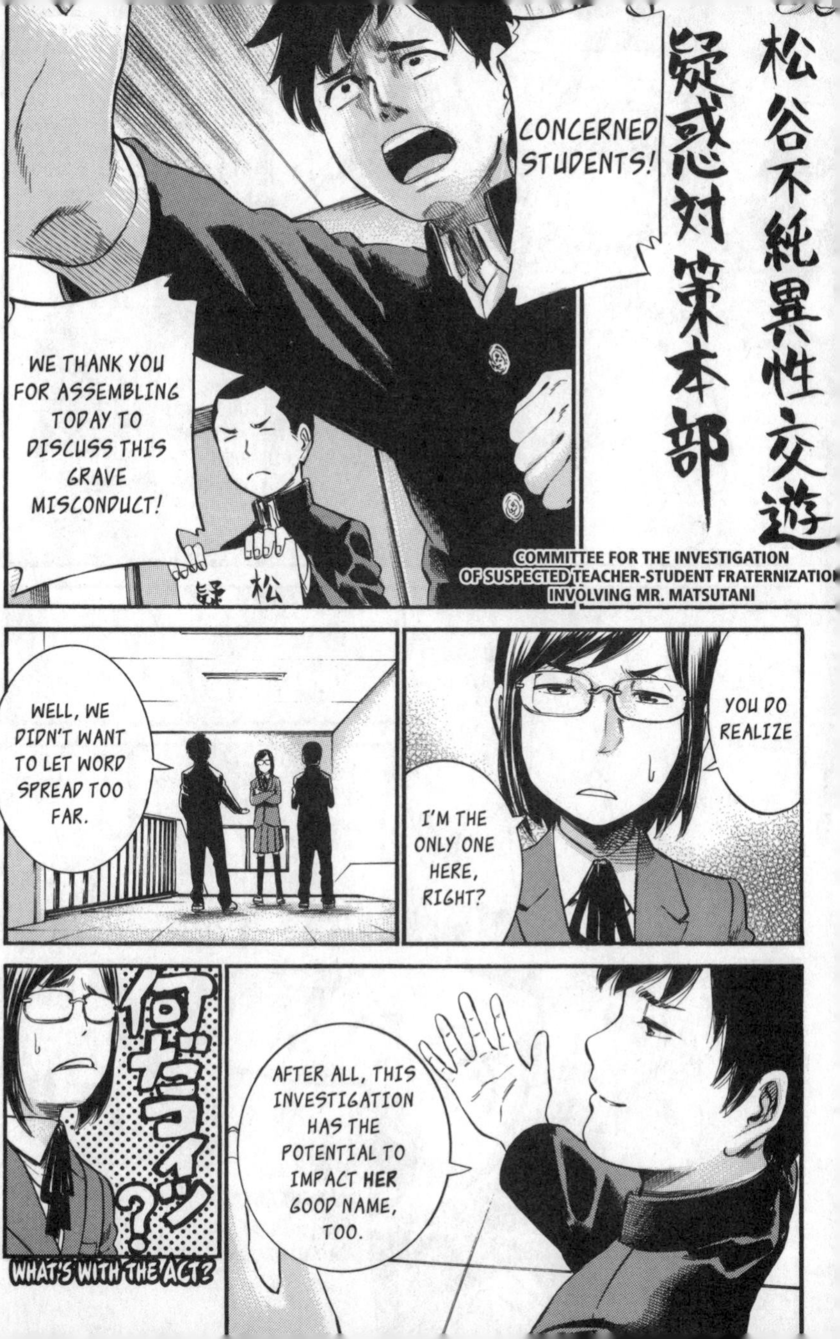
松谷不純異性交遊疑惑対策本部
COMMITTEE FOR THE INVESTIGATION OF SUSPECTED TEACHER-STUDENT FRATERNIZATION INVOLVING MR. MATSUTANI
CONCERNED STUDENTS!
WE THANK YOU FOR ASSEMBLING TODAY TO DISCUSS THIS GRAVE MISCONDUCT!
YOU DO REALIZE
I'M THE ONLY ONE HERE, RIGHT?
WELL, WE DIDN'T WANT TO LET WORD SPREAD TOO FAR.
AFTER ALL, THIS INVESTIGATION HAS THE POTENTIAL TO IMPACT HER GOOD NAME, TOO.
何だコイツ?
WHAT'S WITH THE ACT?

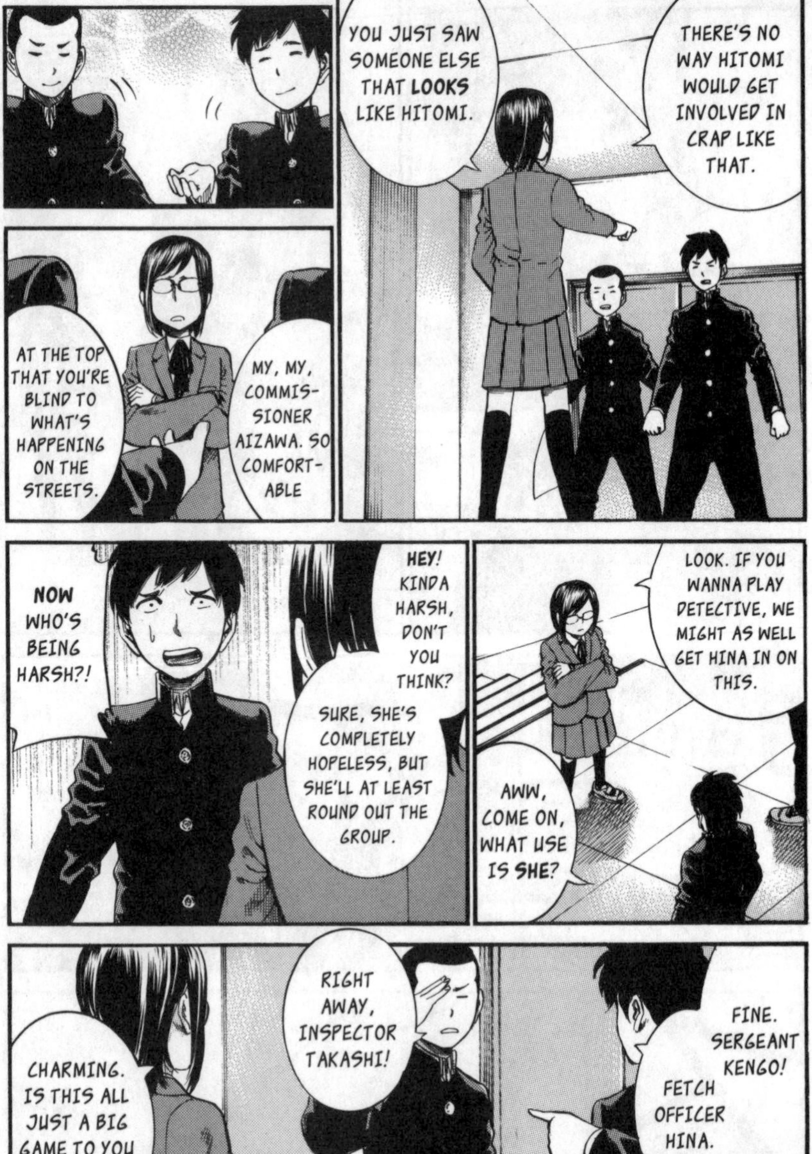
THERE'S NO WAY HITOMI WOULD GET INVOLVED IN CRAP LIKE THAT.
YOU JUST SAW SOMEONE ELSE THAT **LOOKS** LIKE HITOMI.
MY, MY, COMMIS-SIONER AIZAWA. SO COMFORT-ABLE
AT THE TOP THAT YOU'RE BLIND TO WHAT'S HAPPENING ON THE STREETS.
LOOK. IF YOU WANNA PLAY DETECTIVE, WE MIGHT AS WELL GET HINA IN ON THIS.
AWW, COME ON, WHAT USE IS **SHE**?
HEY! KINDA HARSH, DON'T YOU THINK?
SURE, SHE'S COMPLETELY HOPELESS, BUT SHE'LL AT LEAST ROUND OUT THE GROUP.
NOW WHO'S BEING HARSH?!
FINE. SERGEANT KENGO!
FETCH OFFICER HINA.
RIGHT AWAY, INSPECTOR TAKASHI!
CHARMING. IS THIS ALL JUST A BIG GAME TO YOU TWO?

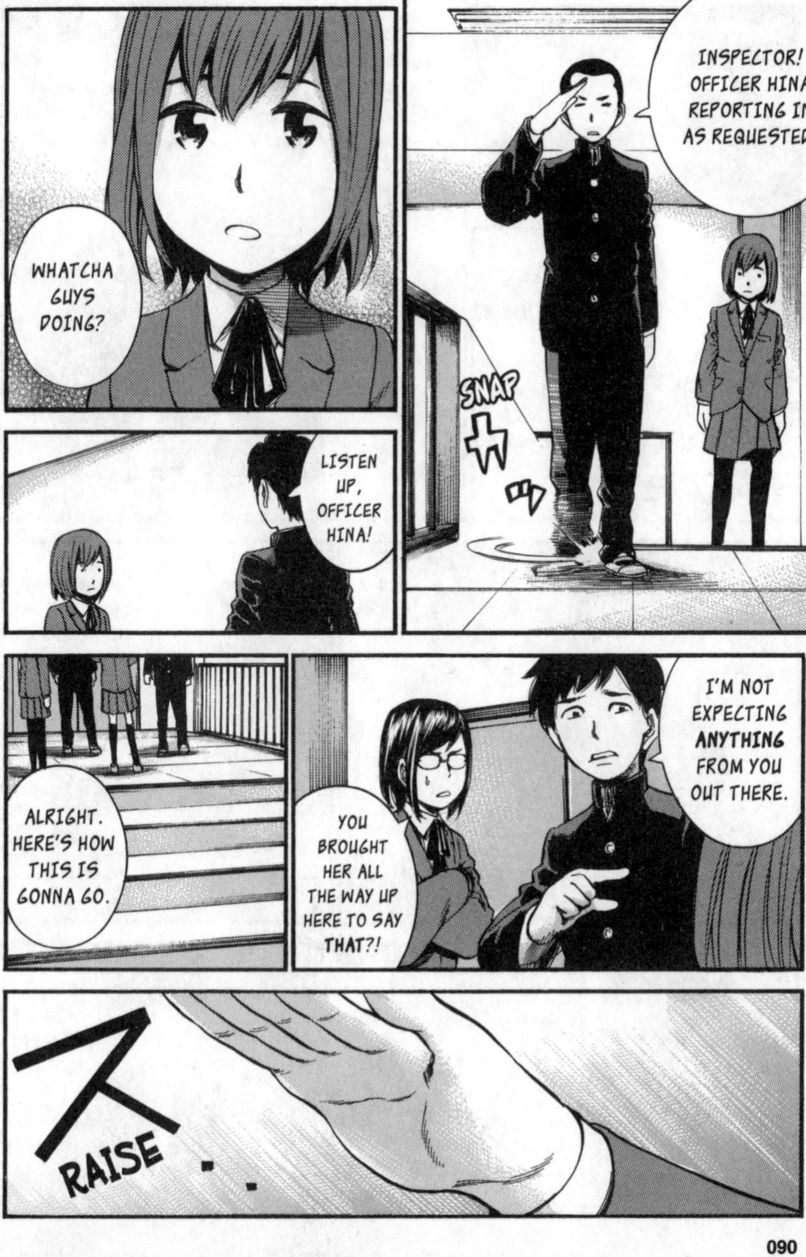
INSPECTOR! OFFICER HINA REPORTING IN AS REQUESTED!
SNAP
WHATCHA GUYS DOING?
LISTEN UP, OFFICER HINA!
I'M NOT EXPECTING **ANYTHING** FROM YOU OUT THERE.
YOU BROUGHT HER ALL THE WAY UP HERE TO SAY **THAT?!**
ALRIGHT. HERE'S HOW THIS IS GONNA GO.
RAISE

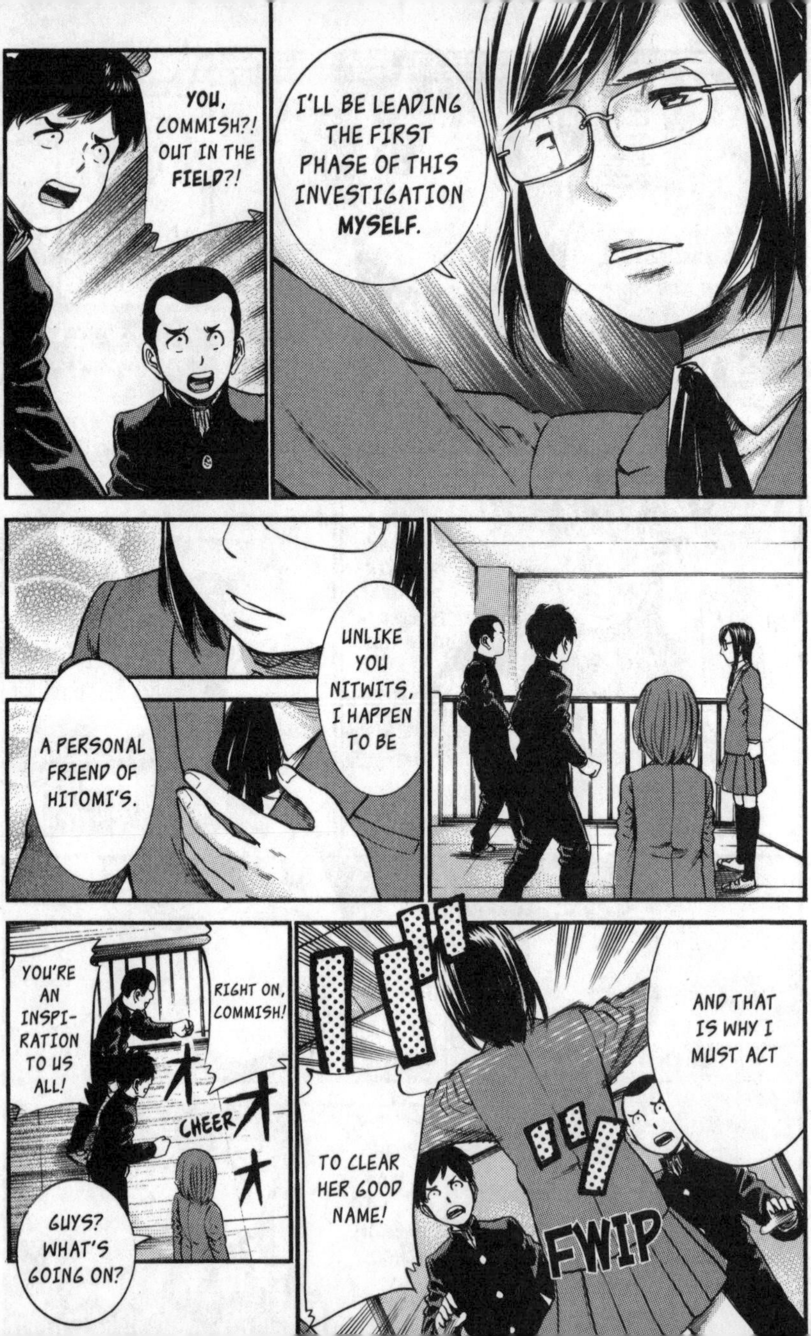
I'LL BE LEADING THE FIRST PHASE OF THIS INVESTIGATION MYSELF.
YOU, COMMISH?! OUT IN THE FIELD?!
UNLIKE YOU NITWITS, I HAPPEN TO BE
A PERSONAL FRIEND OF HITOMI'S.
AND THAT IS WHY I MUST ACT
TO CLEAR HER GOOD NAME!
FWIP
RIGHT ON, COMMISH!
YOU'RE AN INSPI-RATION TO US ALL!
CHEER
GUYS? WHAT'S GOING ON?

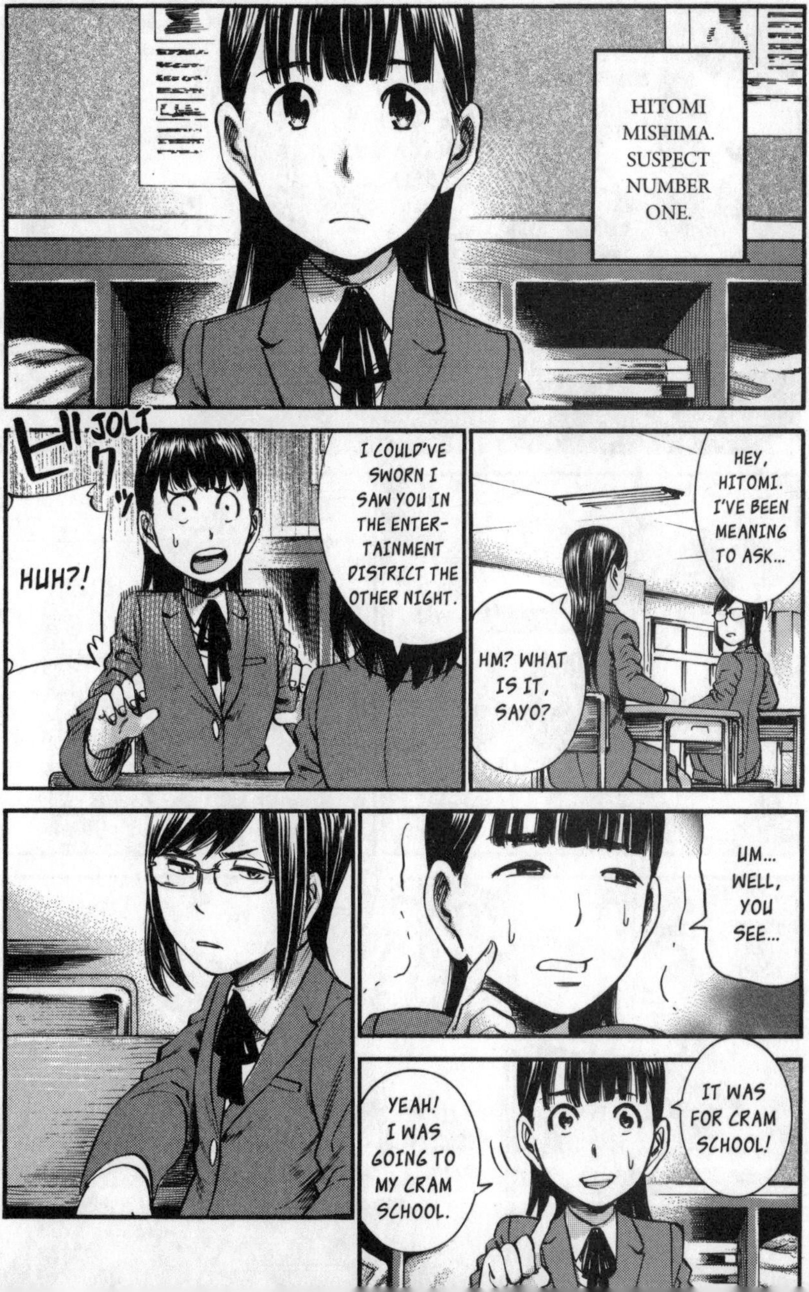
HITOMI MISHIMA. SUSPECT NUMBER ONE.
HEY, HITOMI. I'VE BEEN MEANING TO ASK...
HM? WHAT IS IT, SAYO?
I COULD'VE SWORN I SAW YOU IN THE ENTER-TAINMENT DISTRICT THE OTHER NIGHT.
JOLT
HUH?!
UM... WELL, YOU SEE...
IT WAS FOR CRAM SCHOOL!
YEAH! I WAS GOING TO MY CRAM SCHOOL.

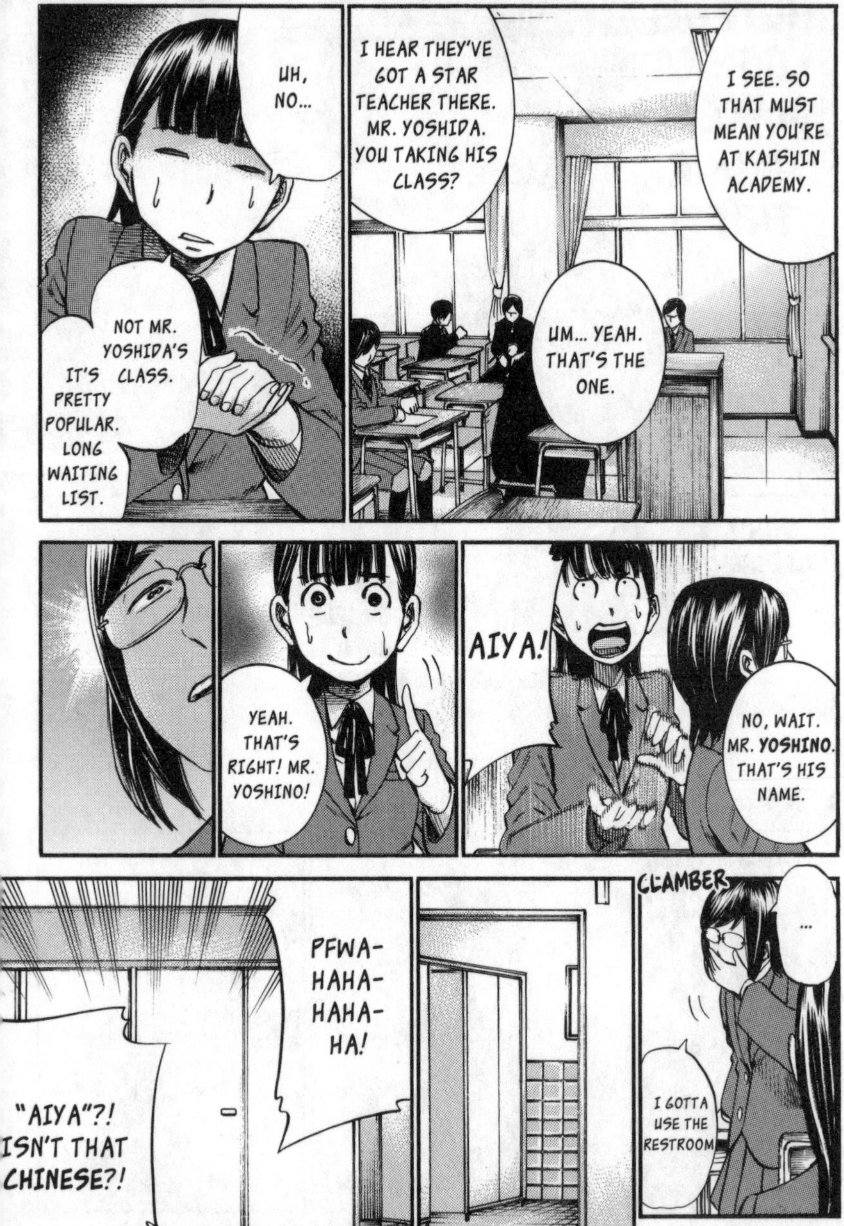
I SEE. SO THAT MUST MEAN YOU'RE AT KAISHIN ACADEMY.
UM... YEAH. THAT'S THE ONE.
I HEAR THEY'VE GOT A STAR TEACHER THERE. MR. YOSHIDA. YOU TAKING HIS CLASS?
UH, NO...
NOT MR. YOSHIDA'S CLASS. IT'S PRETTY POPULAR. LONG WAITING LIST.
NO, WAIT. MR. YOSHINO. THAT'S HIS NAME.
AIYA!
YEAH. THAT'S RIGHT! MR. YOSHINO!
CLAMBER
...
I GOTTA USE THE RESTROOM
PFWA-HAHA-HAHA-HA!
"AIYA"?! ISN'T THAT CHINESE?!

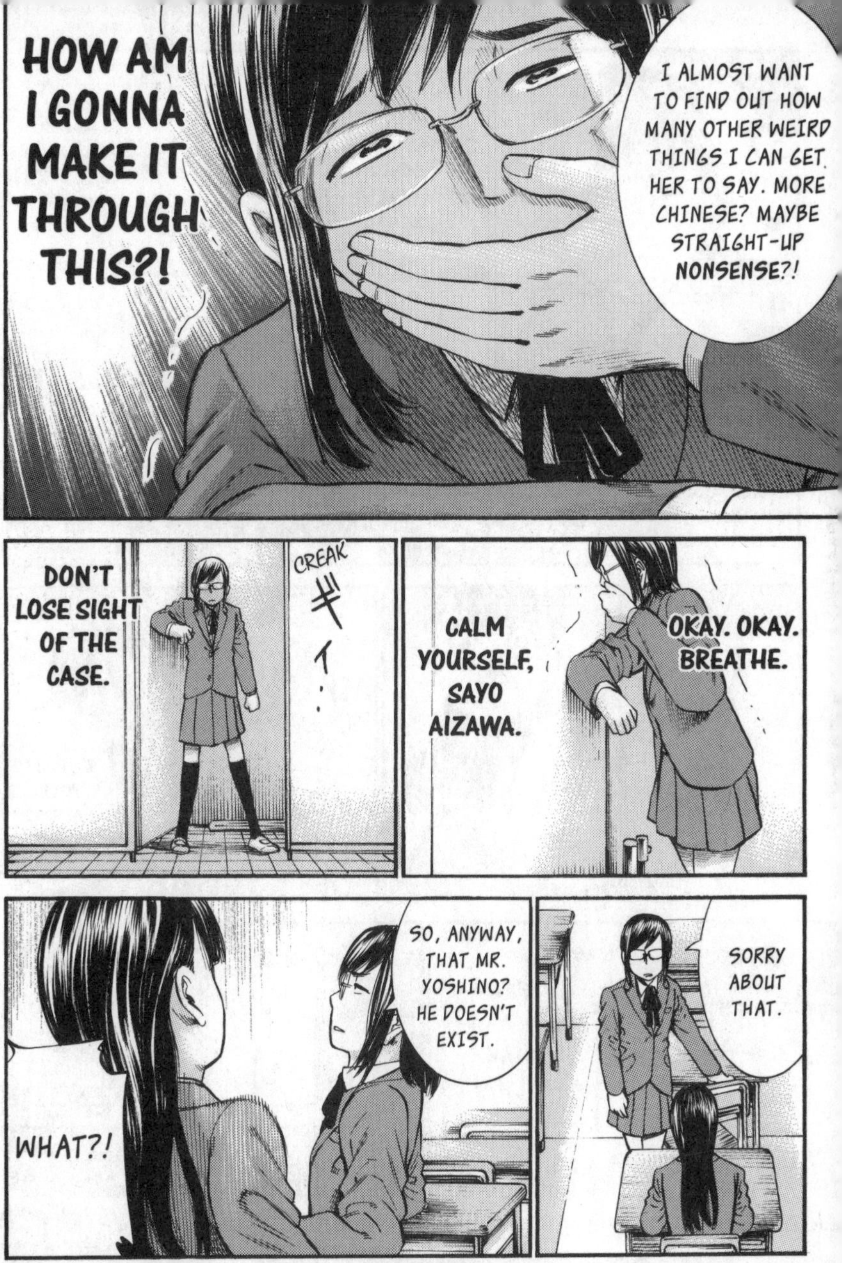
I ALMOST WANT TO FIND OUT HOW MANY OTHER WEIRD THINGS I CAN GET HER TO SAY. MORE CHINESE? MAYBE STRAIGHT-UP NONSENSE?!
HOW AM I GONNA MAKE IT THROUGH THIS?!
OKAY. OKAY. BREATHE.
CALM YOURSELF, SAYO AIZAWA.
CREAK
ギイ
DON'T LOSE SIGHT OF THE CASE.
SORRY ABOUT THAT.
SO, ANYWAY, THAT MR. YOSHINO? HE DOESN'T EXIST.
WHAT?!

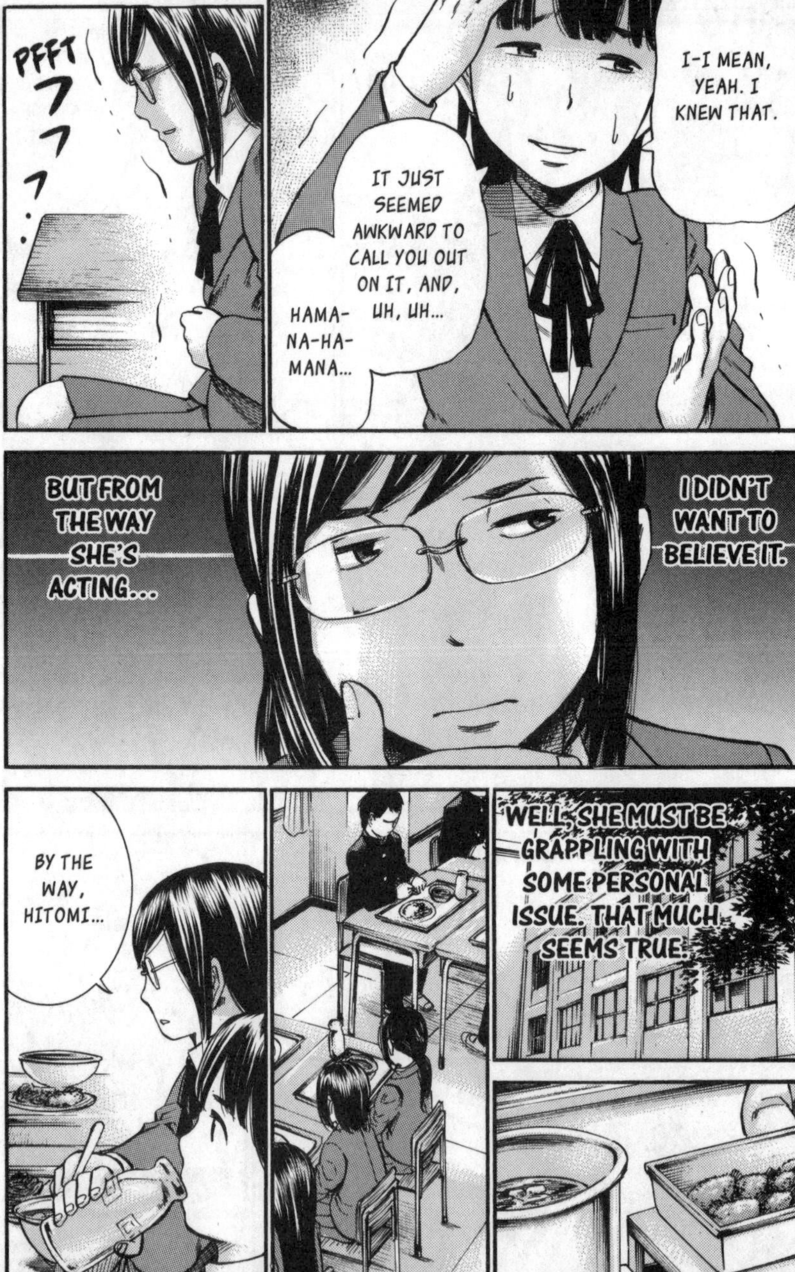
I-I MEAN, YEAH. I KNEW THAT.
IT JUST SEEMED AWKWARD TO CALL YOU OUT ON IT, AND, UH, UH...
HAMA-NA-HA-MANA...
PFFT
I DIDN'T WANT TO BELIEVE IT.
BUT FROM THE WAY SHE'S ACTING...
WELL, SHE MUST BE GRAPPLING WITH SOME PERSONAL ISSUE. THAT MUCH SEEMS TRUE.
BY THE WAY, HITOMI...

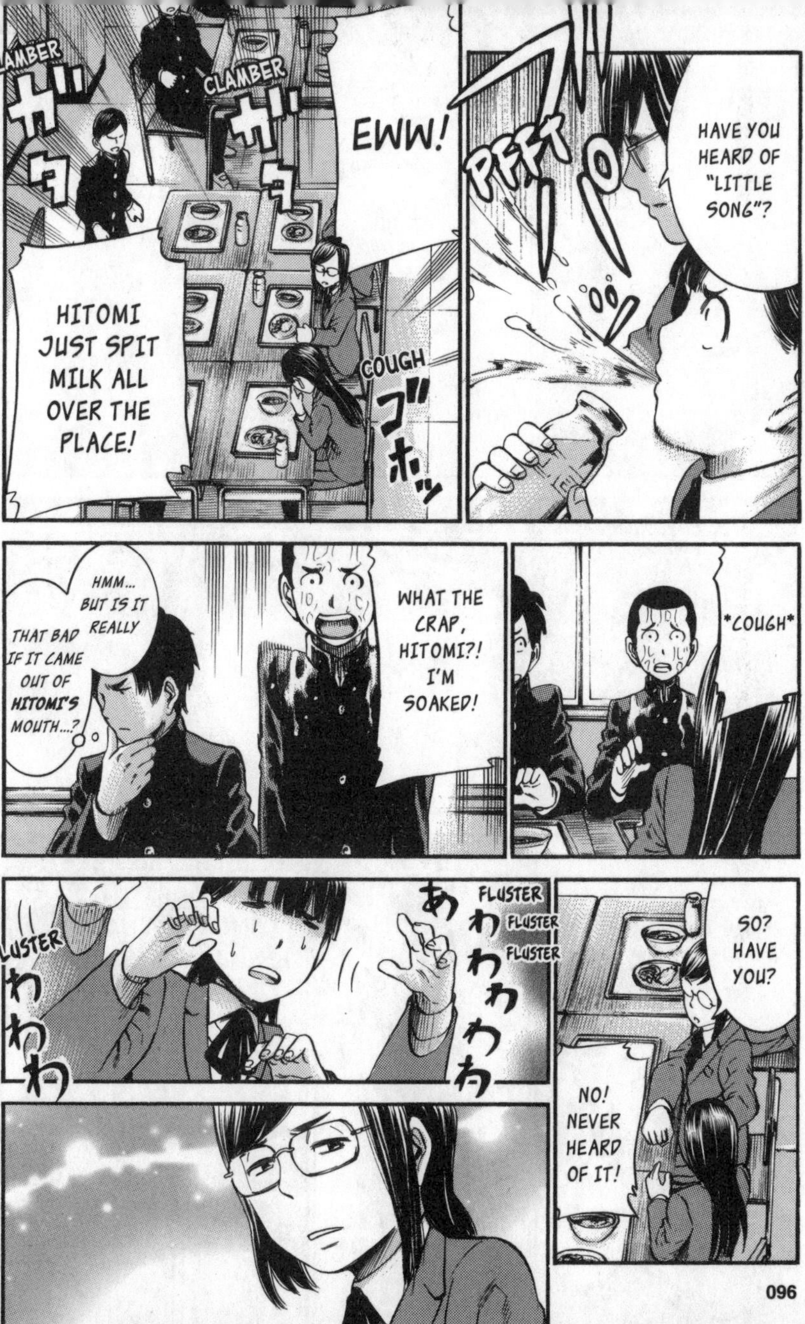
HAVE YOU HEARD OF "LITTLE SONG"?
PFFT
EWW!
CLAMBER
ガタ
CLAMBER
ガタ
HITOMI JUST SPIT MILK ALL OVER THE PLACE!
COUGH
ゴホッ
COUGH
WHAT THE CRAP, HITOMI?! I'M SOAKED!
HMM... BUT IS IT REALLY THAT BAD IF IT CAME OUT OF **HITOMI'S** MOUTH...?
SO? HAVE YOU?
NO! NEVER HEARD OF IT!
FLUSTER
FLUSTER
FLUSTER
あわわわわ
FLUSTER
わわわ

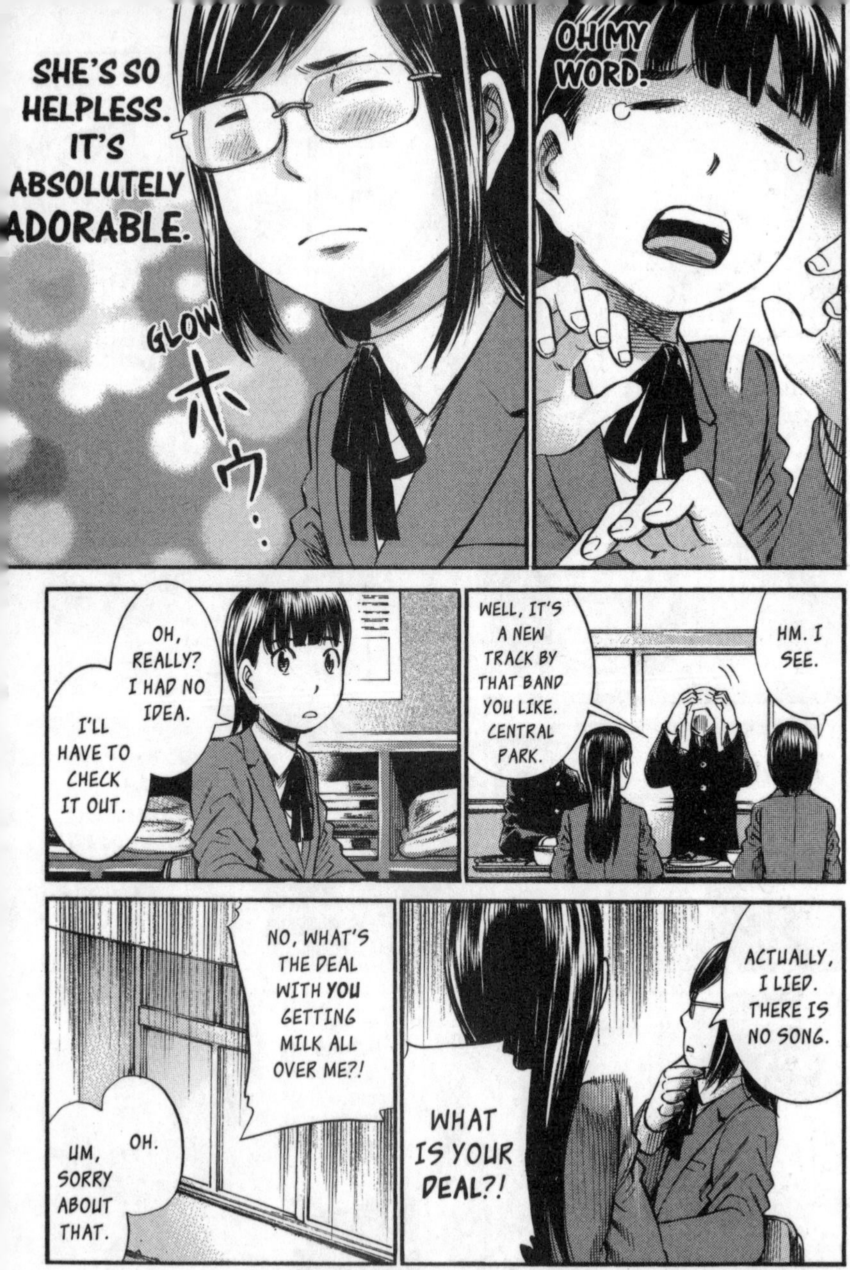
OH MY WORD.
SHE'S SO HELPLESS. IT'S ABSOLUTELY ADORABLE.
GLOW
ホウ…
HM. I SEE.
WELL, IT'S A NEW TRACK BY THAT BAND YOU LIKE. CENTRAL PARK.
OH, REALLY? I HAD NO IDEA.
I'LL HAVE TO CHECK IT OUT.
ACTUALLY, I LIED. THERE IS NO SONG.
WHAT IS YOUR DEAL?!
NO, WHAT'S THE DEAL WITH YOU GETTING MILK ALL OVER ME?!
OH.
UM, SORRY ABOUT THAT.

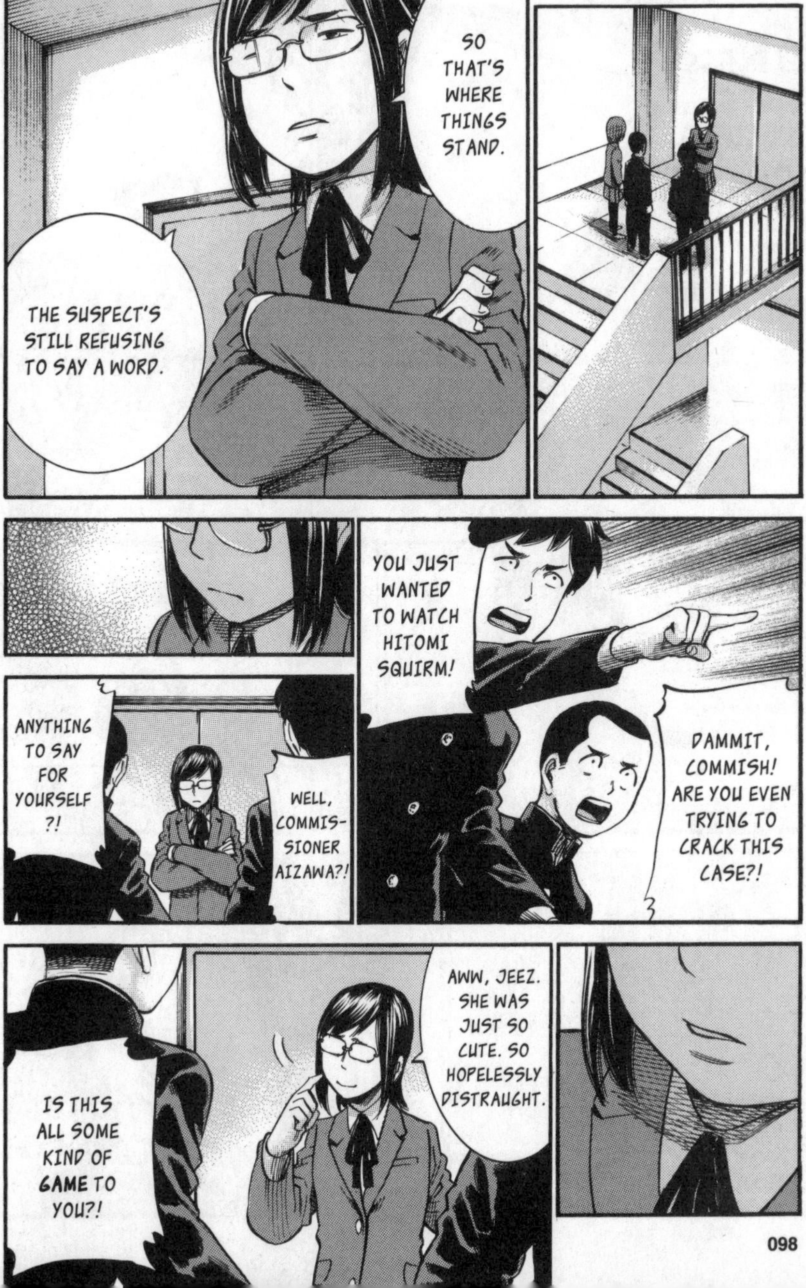

SO THAT'S WHERE THINGS STAND.
THE SUSPECT'S STILL REFUSING TO SAY A WORD.
YOU JUST WANTED TO WATCH HITOMI SQUIRM!
DAMMIT, COMMISH! ARE YOU EVEN TRYING TO CRACK THIS CASE?!
WELL, COMMISSIONER AIZAWA?!
ANYTHING TO SAY FOR YOURSELF?!
AWW, JEEZ. SHE WAS JUST SO CUTE. SO HOPELESSLY DISTRAUGHT.
IS THIS ALL SOME KIND OF **GAME** TO YOU?!

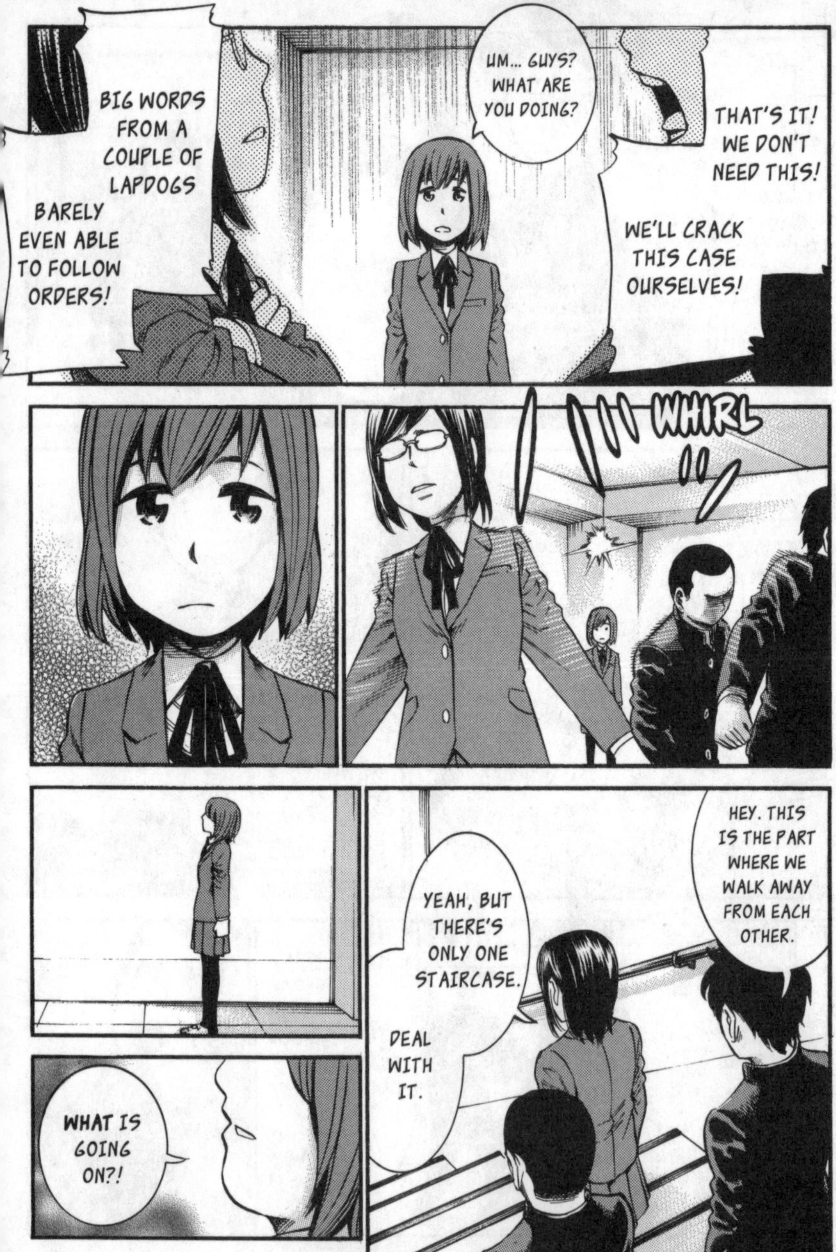
THAT'S IT! WE DON'T NEED THIS!
WE'LL CRACK THIS CASE OURSELVES!
UM... GUYS? WHAT ARE YOU DOING?
BIG WORDS FROM A COUPLE OF LAPDOGS
BARELY EVEN ABLE TO FOLLOW ORDERS!
WHIRL
HEY. THIS IS THE PART WHERE WE WALK AWAY FROM EACH OTHER.
YEAH, BUT THERE'S ONLY ONE STAIRCASE.
DEAL WITH IT.
WHAT IS GOING ON?!

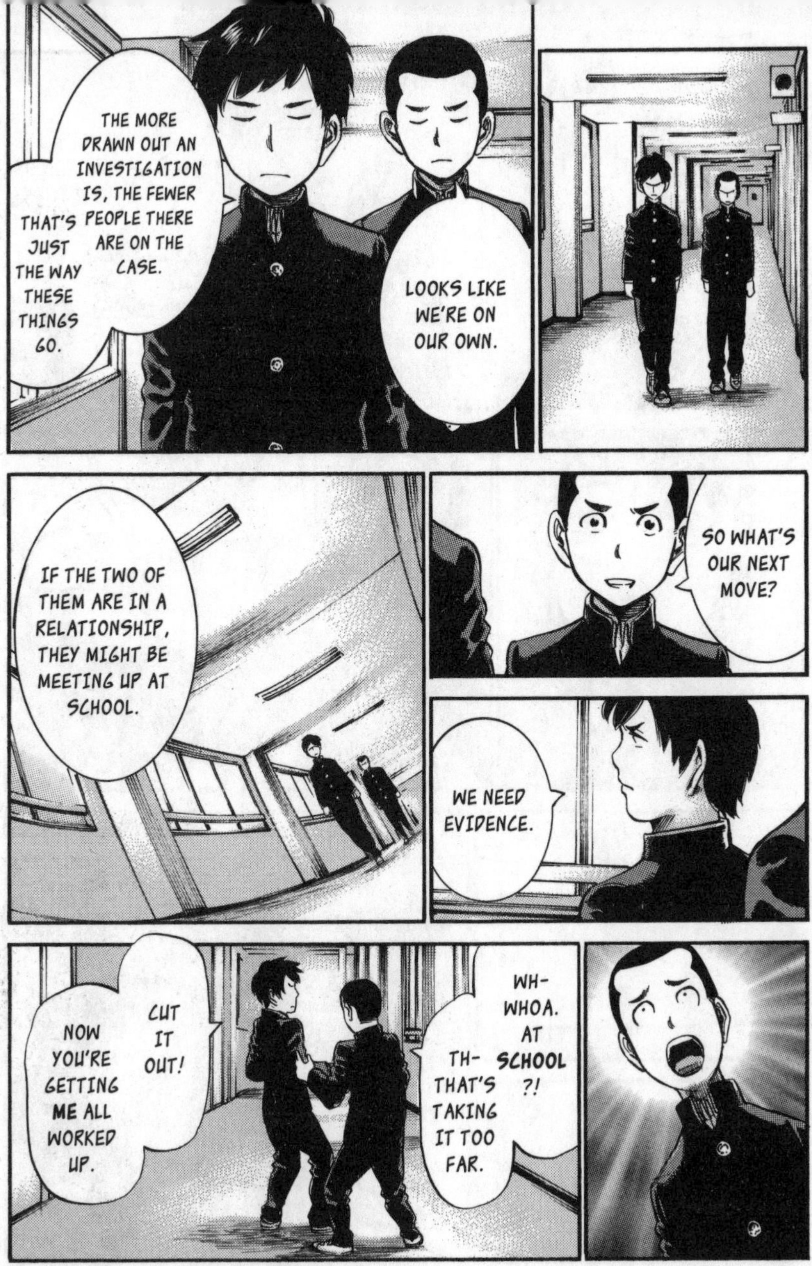
LOOKS LIKE WE'RE ON OUR OWN.
THE MORE DRAWN OUT AN INVESTIGATION IS, THE FEWER PEOPLE THERE ARE ON THE CASE.
THAT'S JUST THE WAY THESE THINGS GO.
SO WHAT'S OUR NEXT MOVE?
WE NEED EVIDENCE.
IF THE TWO OF THEM ARE IN A RELATIONSHIP, THEY MIGHT BE MEETING UP AT SCHOOL.
WH-WHOA. AT **SCHOOL** ?!
TH-THAT'S TAKING IT TOO FAR.
CUT IT OUT!
NOW YOU'RE GETTING ME ALL WORKED UP.

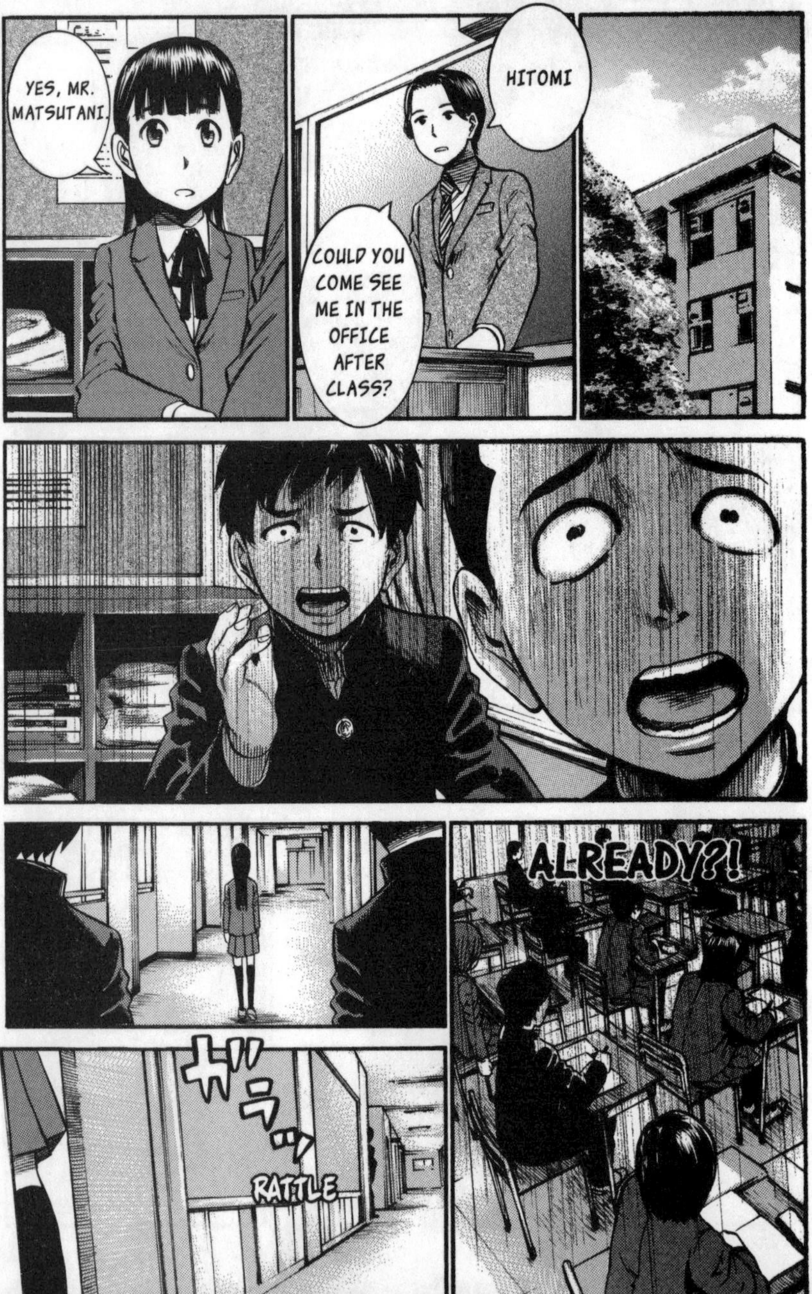
HITOMI
COULD YOU COME SEE ME IN THE OFFICE AFTER CLASS?
YES, MR. MATSUTANI.
ALREADY?!
ガラッ
RATTLE

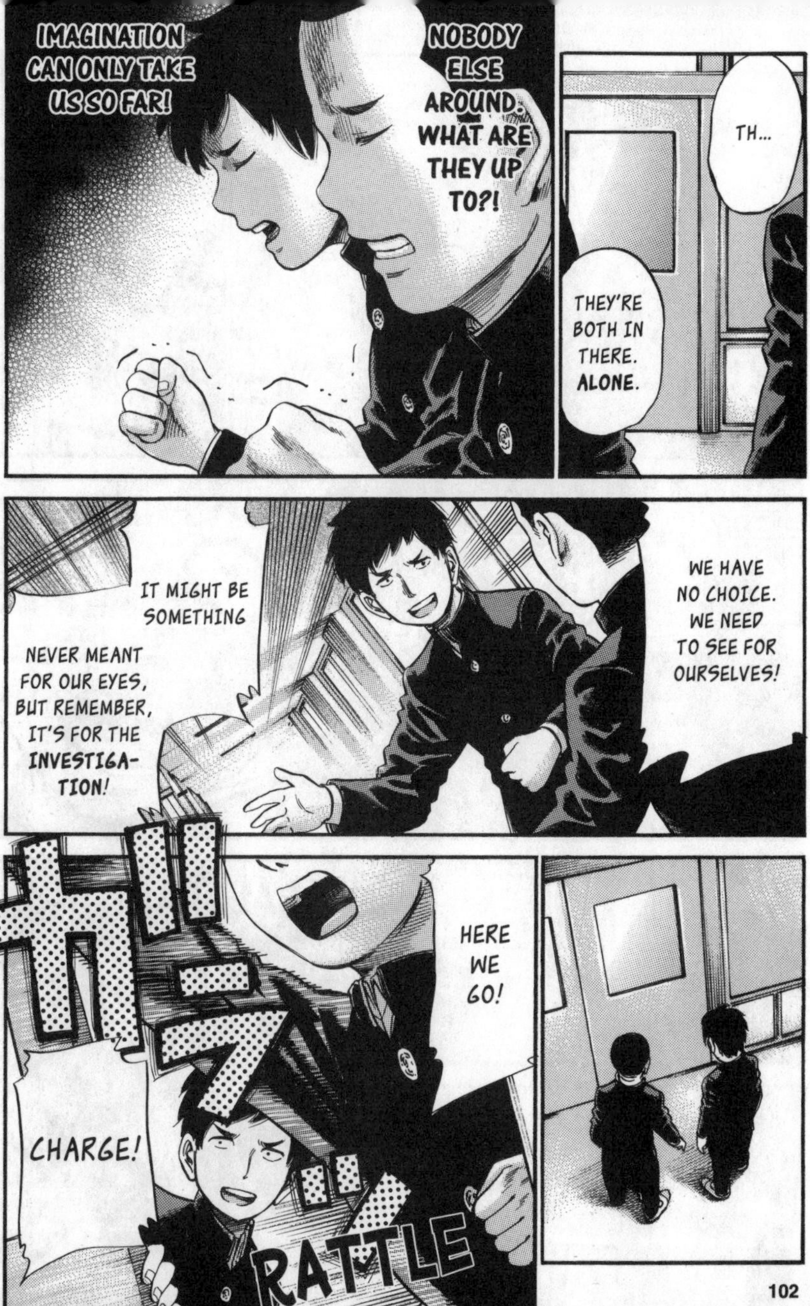
TH...
THEY'RE BOTH IN THERE. ALONE.
NOBODY ELSE AROUND. WHAT ARE THEY UP TO?!
IMAGINATION CAN ONLY TAKE US SO FAR!
WE HAVE NO CHOICE. WE NEED TO SEE FOR OURSELVES!
IT MIGHT BE SOMETHING
NEVER MEANT FOR OUR EYES, BUT REMEMBER, IT'S FOR THE INVESTIGA-TION!
HERE WE GO!
CHARGE!
RATTLE

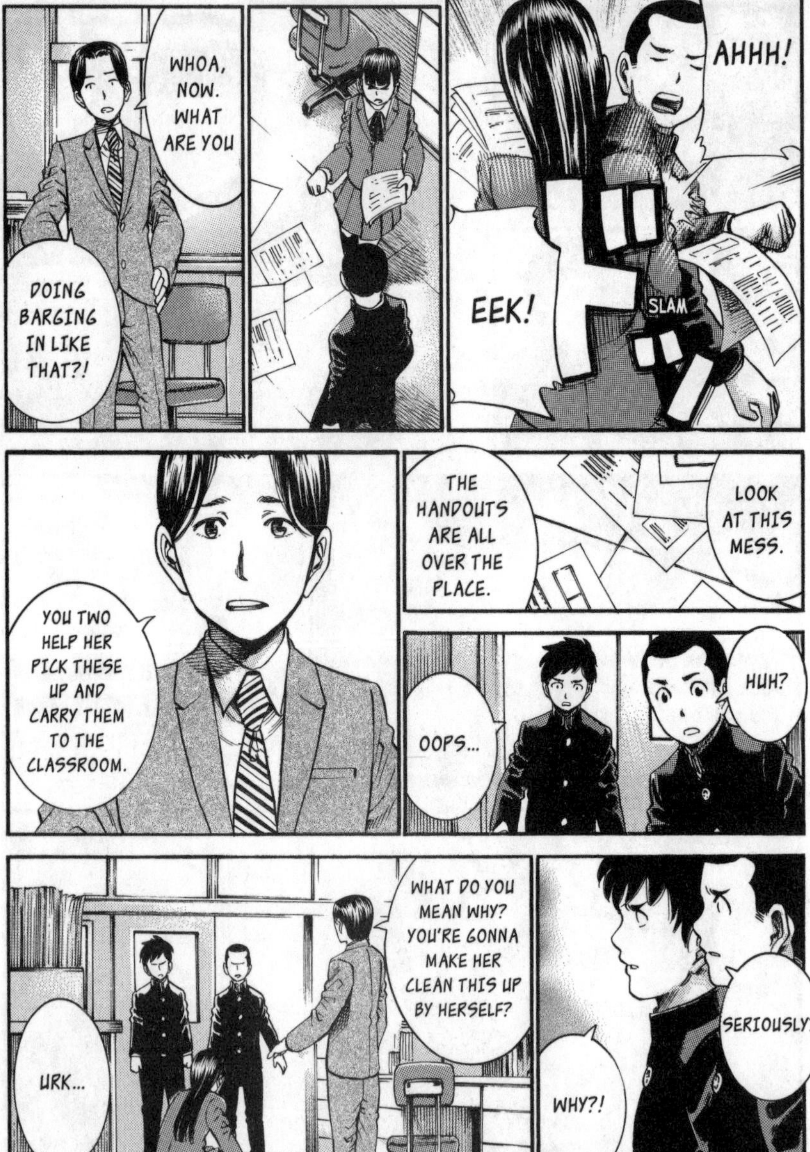
AHHH!
SLAM
EEK!
WHOA, NOW. WHAT ARE YOU
DOING BARGING IN LIKE THAT?!
LOOK AT THIS MESS.
THE HANDOUTS ARE ALL OVER THE PLACE.
HUH?
OOPS...
YOU TWO HELP HER PICK THESE UP AND CARRY THEM TO THE CLASSROOM.
SERIOUSLY?
WHY?!
WHAT DO YOU MEAN WHY? YOU'RE GONNA MAKE HER CLEAN THIS UP BY HERSELF?
URK...

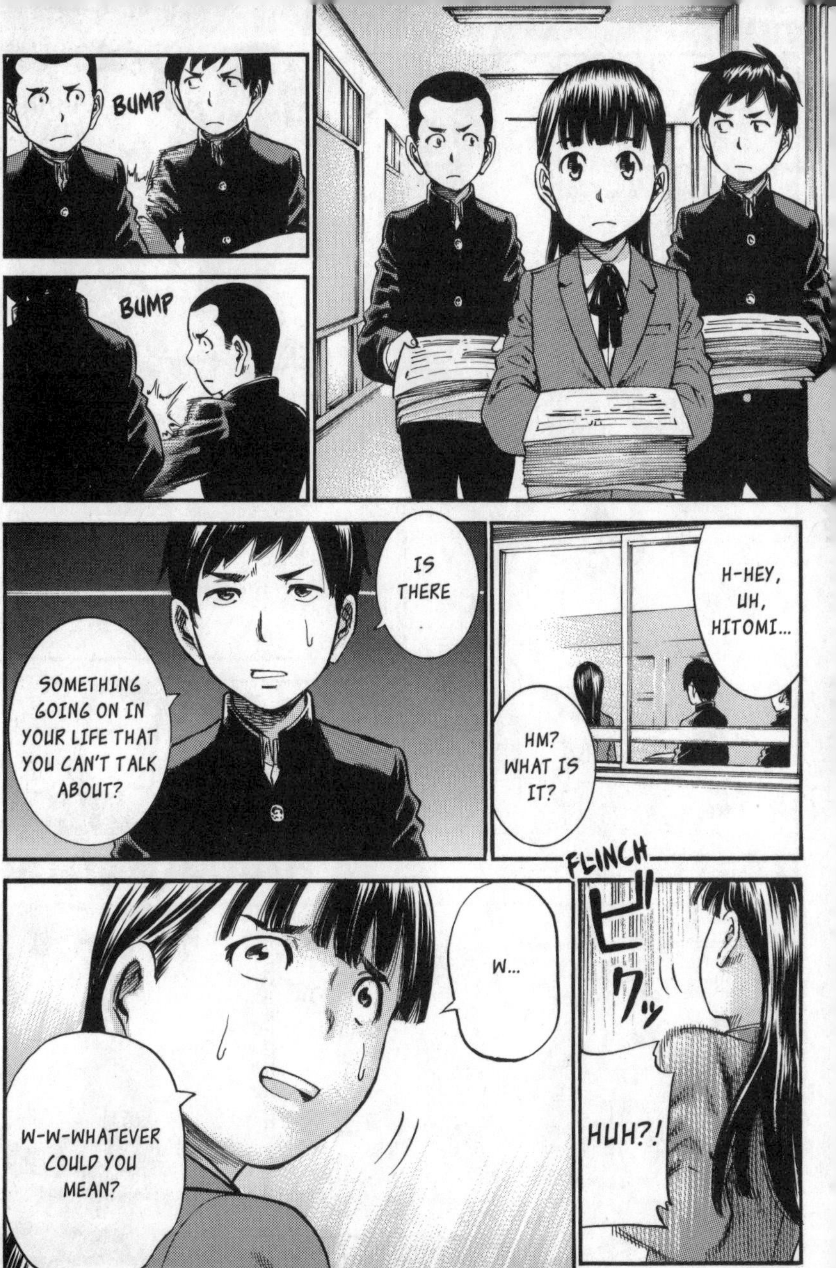
BUMP
BUMP
H-HEY, UH, HITOMI...
HM? WHAT IS IT?
IS THERE
SOMETHING GOING ON IN YOUR LIFE THAT YOU CAN'T TALK ABOUT?
FLINCH
ビクッ
HUH?!
W...
W-W-WHATEVER COULD YOU MEAN?

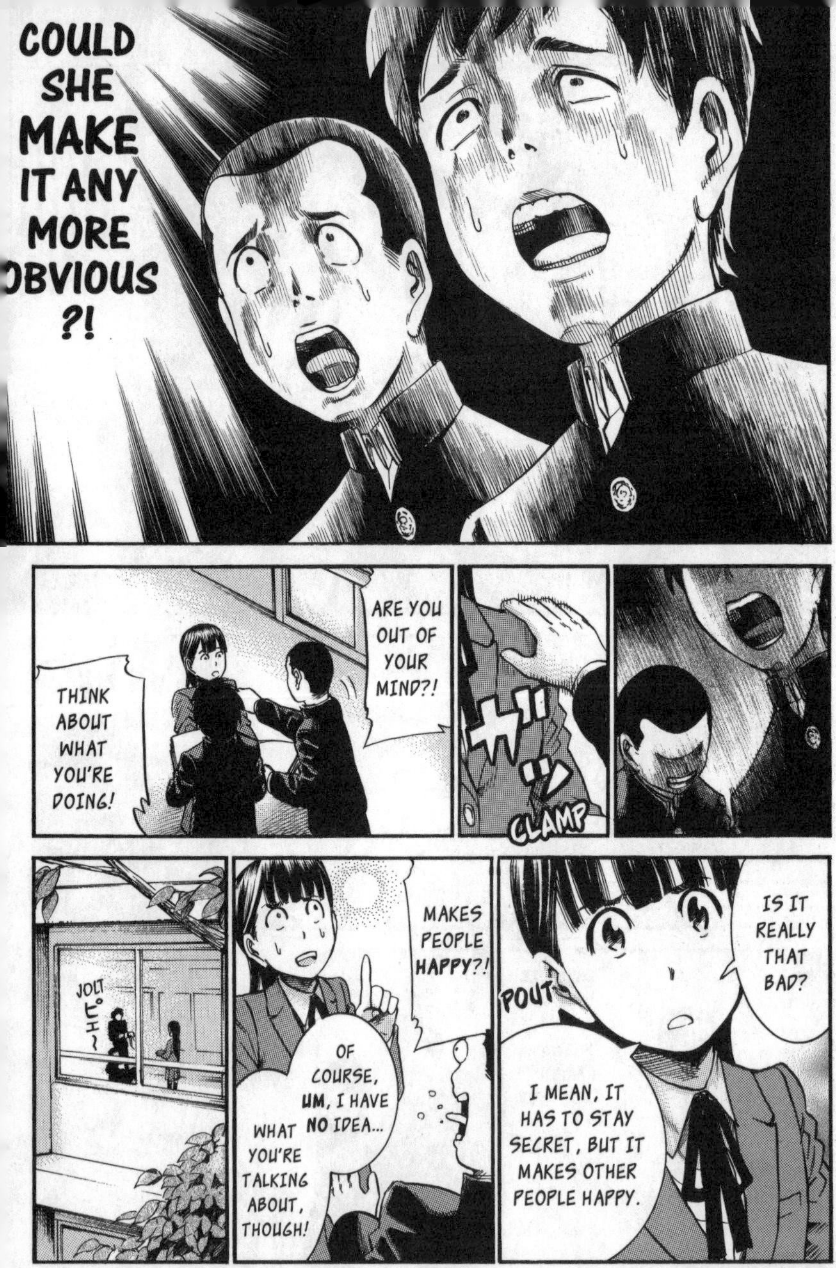
COULD SHE MAKE IT ANY MORE OBVIOUS ?!
CLAMP
ARE YOU OUT OF YOUR MIND?!
THINK ABOUT WHAT YOU'RE DOING!
IS IT REALLY THAT BAD?
POUT
I MEAN, IT HAS TO STAY SECRET, BUT IT MAKES OTHER PEOPLE HAPPY.
MAKES PEOPLE HAPPY?!
OF COURSE, UM, I HAVE NO IDEA...
WHAT YOU'RE TALKING ABOUT, THOUGH!
JOLT

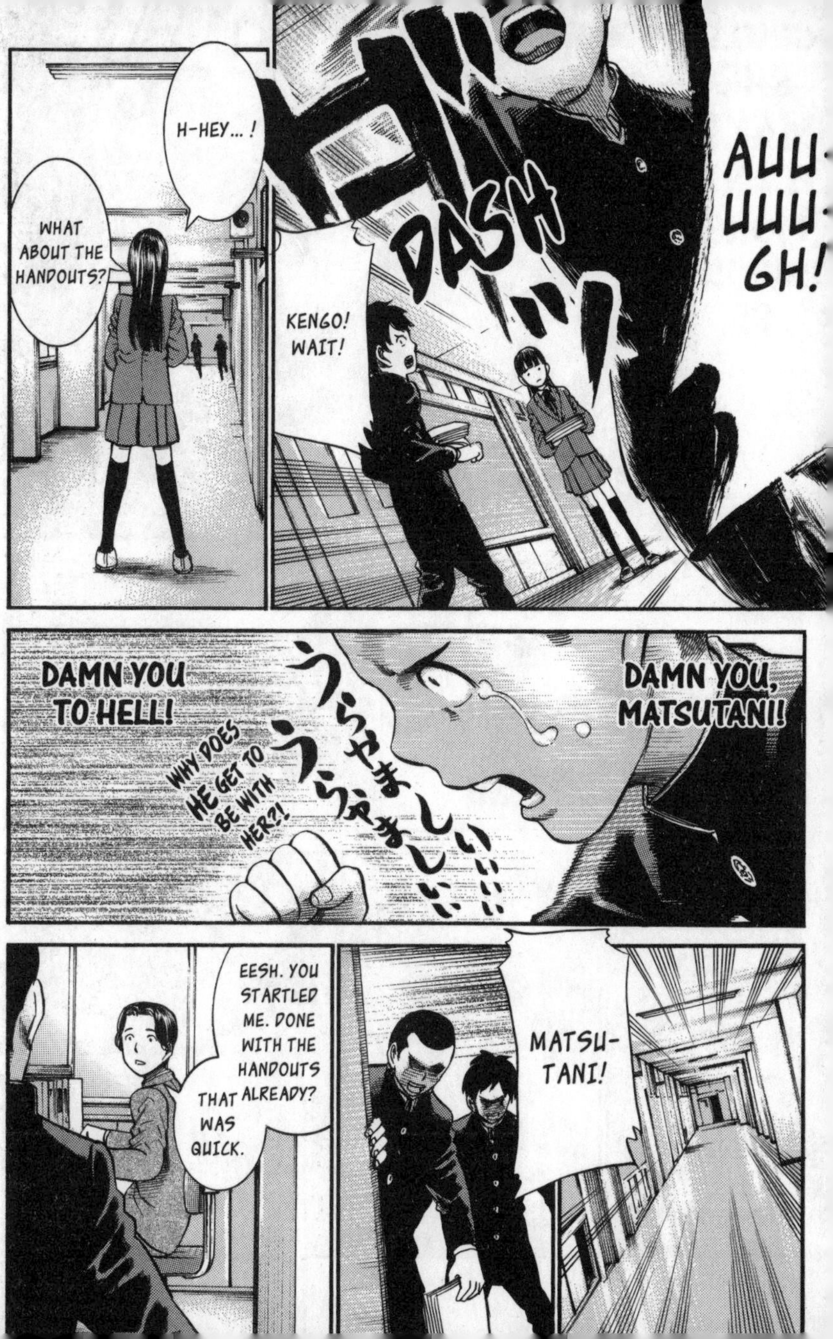
AUUU-UUUU-GH!
DASH
KENGO! WAIT!
H-HEY... !
WHAT ABOUT THE HANDOUTS?
DAMN YOU, MATSUTANI!
うらやましいい!!!
うらやましいい!!!
WHY DOES HE GET TO BE WITH HER?!
DAMN YOU TO HELL!
MATSU-TANI!
EESH. YOU STARTLED ME. DONE WITH THE HANDOUTS ALREADY?
THAT WAS QUICK.

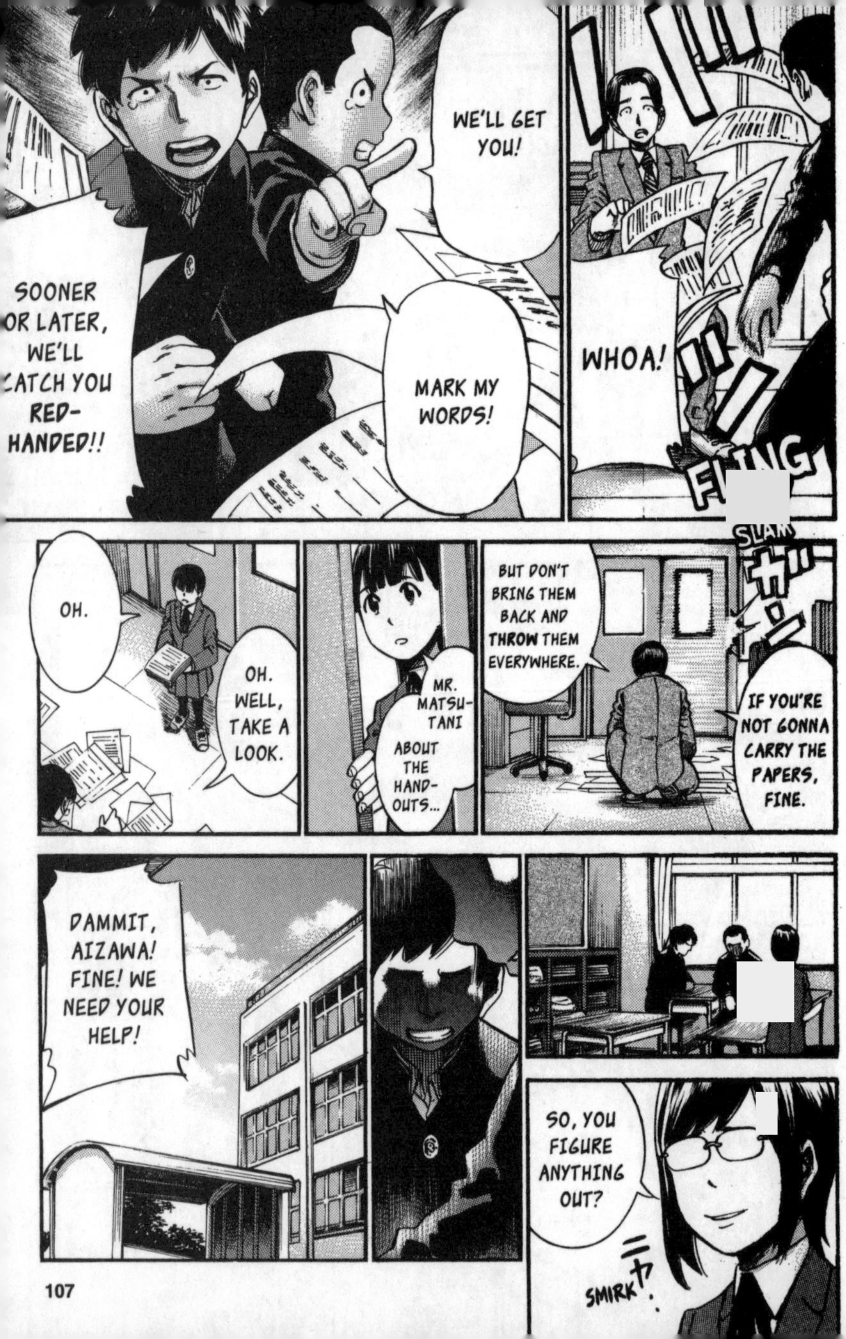
WHOA!
FLING
WE'LL GET YOU!
MARK MY WORDS!
SOONER OR LATER, WE'LL CATCH YOU RED-HANDED!!
SLAM
IF YOU'RE NOT GONNA CARRY THE PAPERS, FINE.
BUT DON'T BRING THEM BACK AND THROW THEM EVERYWHERE.
MR. MATSUTANI
ABOUT THE HANDOUTS...
OH.
OH. WELL, TAKE A LOOK.
SO, YOU FIGURE ANYTHING OUT?
SMIRK
DAMMIT, AIZAWA! FINE! WE NEED YOUR HELP!

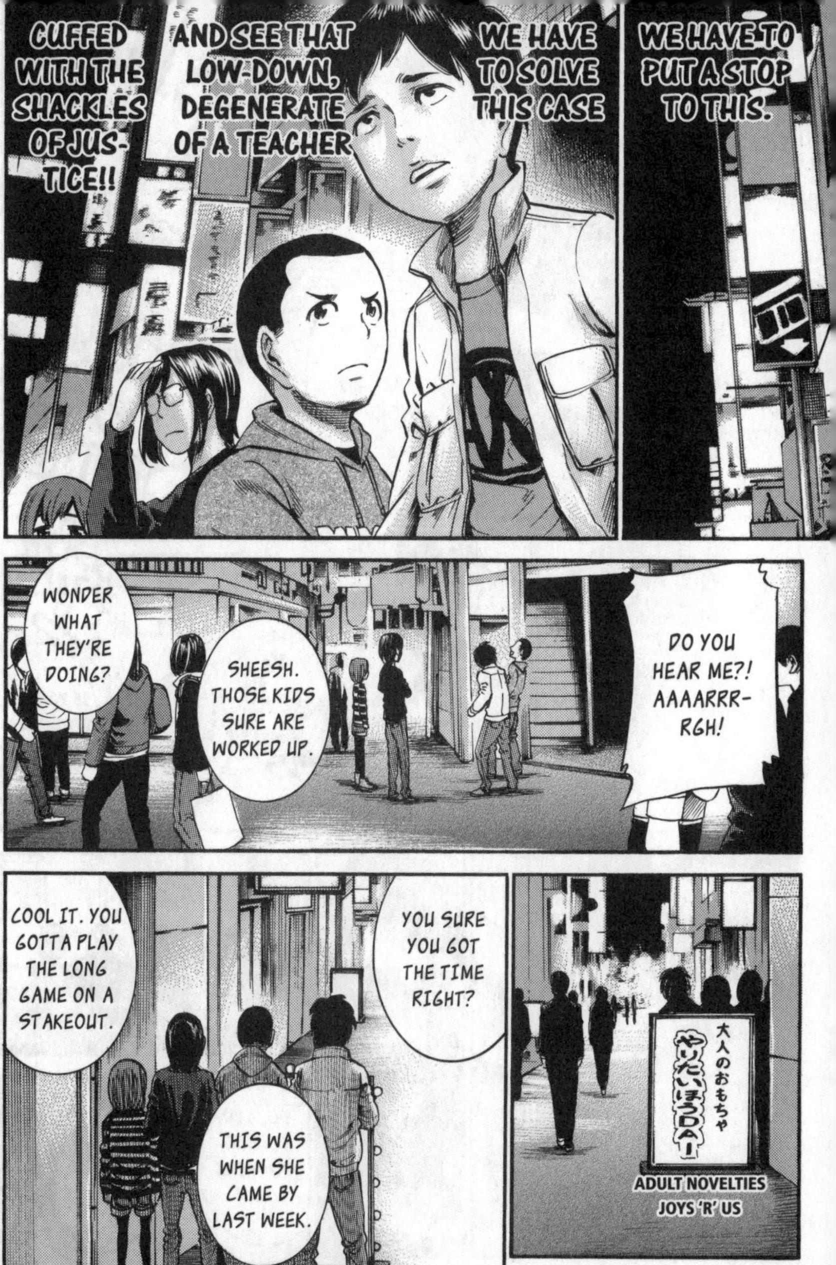
WE HAVE TO PUT A STOP TO THIS.
WE HAVE TO SOLVE THIS CASE
AND SEE THAT LOW-DOWN, DEGENERATE OF A TEACHER
CUFFED WITH THE SHACKLES OF JUS-TICE!!
DO YOU HEAR ME?! AAAARRR-RGH!
SHEESH. THOSE KIDS SURE ARE WORKED UP.
WONDER WHAT THEY'RE DOING?
大人のおもちゃ
やりたいほうDAI
ADULT NOVELTIES
JOYS 'R' US
YOU SURE YOU GOT THE TIME RIGHT?
COOL IT. YOU GOTTA PLAY THE LONG GAME ON A STAKEOUT.
THIS WAS WHEN SHE CAME BY LAST WEEK.

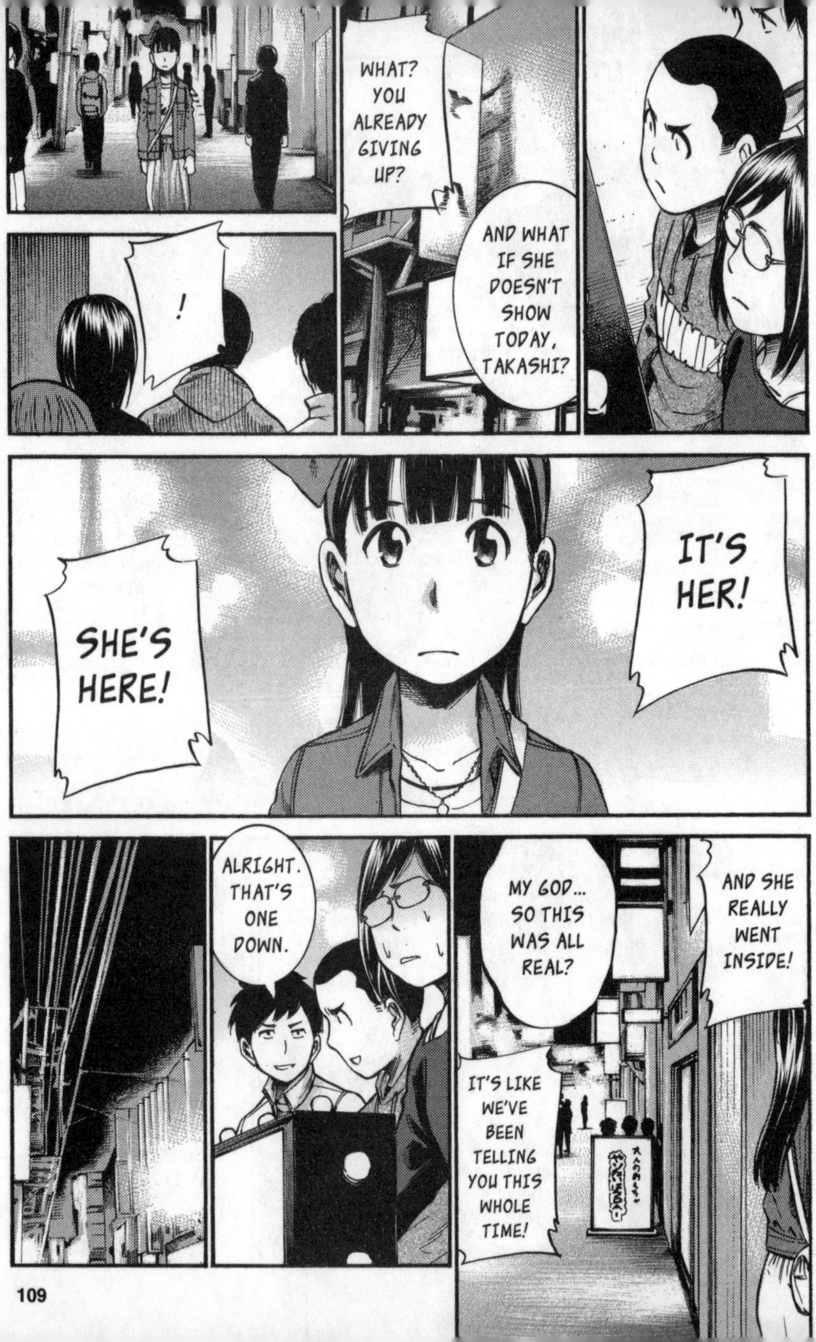
WHAT? YOU ALREADY GIVING UP?
AND WHAT IF SHE DOESN'T SHOW TODAY, TAKASHI?
!
IT'S HER!
SHE'S HERE!
AND SHE REALLY WENT INSIDE!
MY GOD... SO THIS WAS ALL REAL?
IT'S LIKE WE'VE BEEN TELLING YOU THIS WHOLE TIME!
ALRIGHT. THAT'S ONE DOWN.

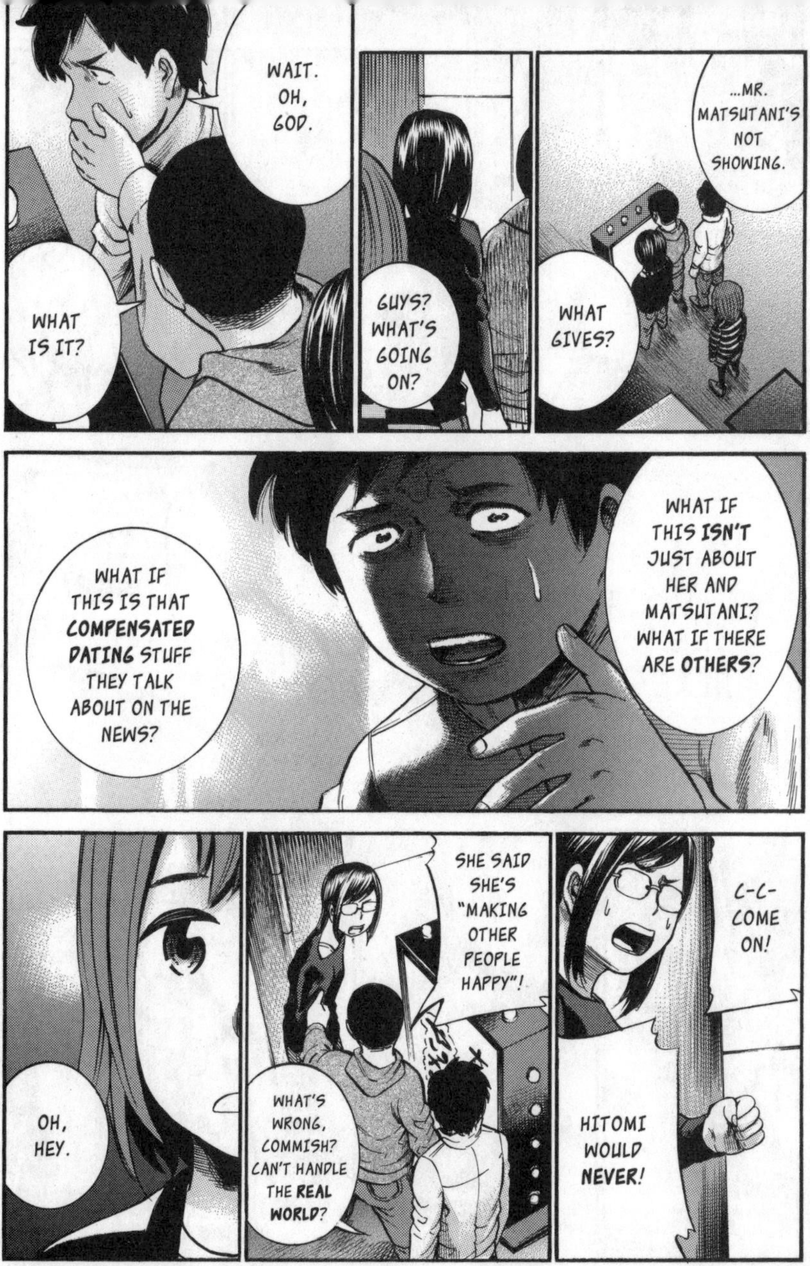
...MR. MATSUTANI'S NOT SHOWING.
WHAT GIVES?
GUYS? WHAT'S GOING ON?
WAIT. OH, GOD.
WHAT IS IT?
WHAT IF THIS **ISN'T** JUST ABOUT HER AND MATSUTANI? WHAT IF THERE ARE **OTHERS**?
WHAT IF THIS IS THAT **COMPENSATED DATING** STUFF THEY TALK ABOUT ON THE NEWS?
C-C-COME ON!
HITOMI WOULD **NEVER**!
SHE SAID SHE'S "MAKING OTHER PEOPLE HAPPY"!
WHAT'S WRONG, COMMISH? CAN'T HANDLE THE **REAL WORLD**?
OH, HEY.

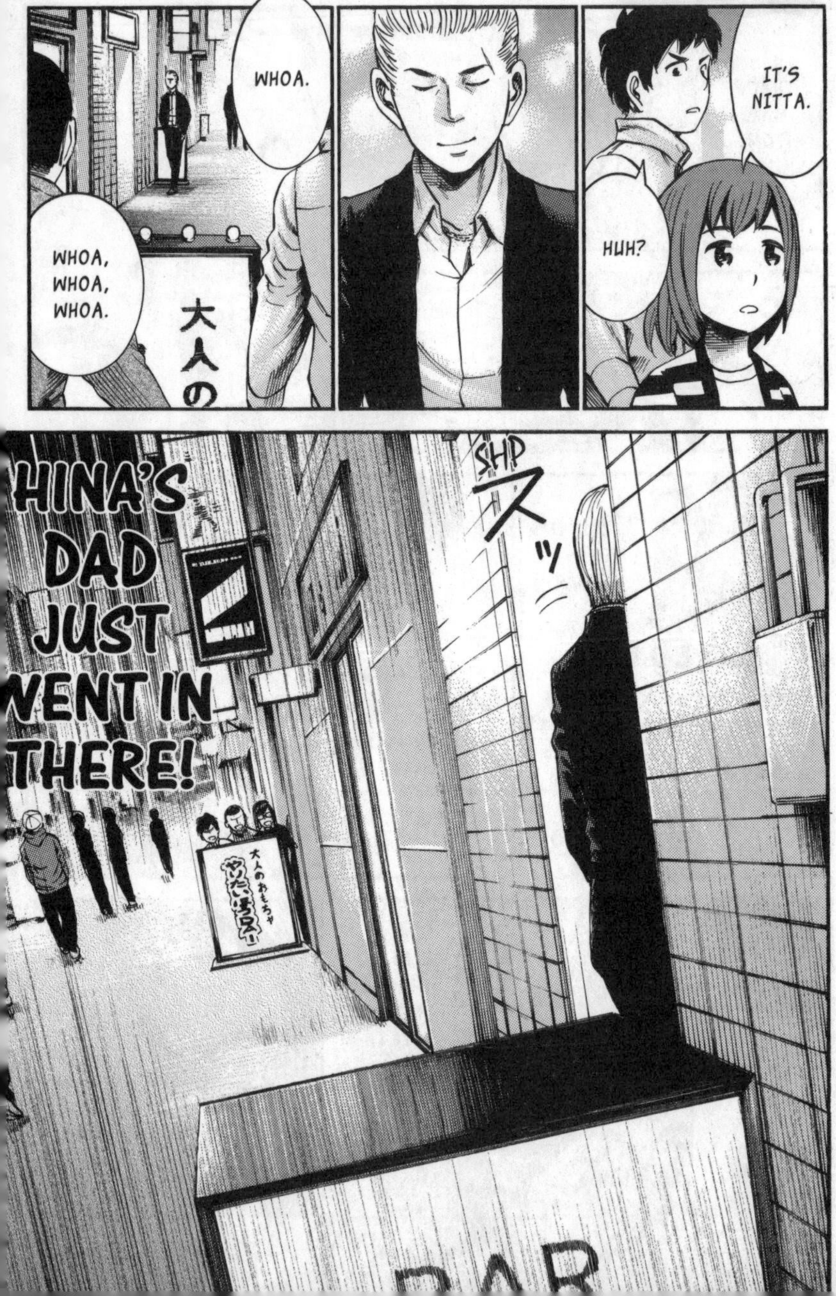
IT'S NITTA.
HUH?
WHOA.
WHOA, WHOA, WHOA.
大人の
SHP
スッ
HINA'S DAD JUST WENT IN THERE!

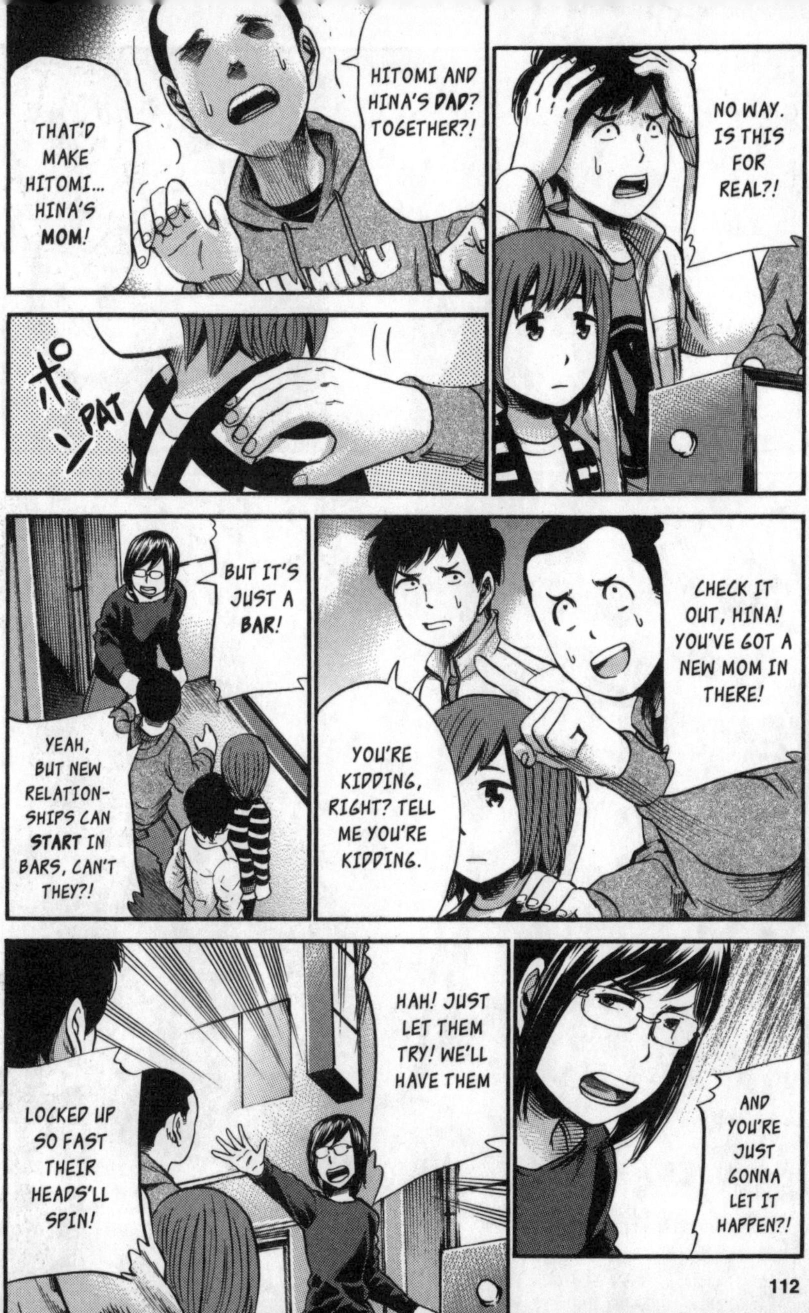
NO WAY. IS THIS FOR REAL?!
HITOMI AND HINA'S DAD? TOGETHER?!
THAT'D MAKE HITOMI... HINA'S MOM!
PAT
CHECK IT OUT, HINA! YOU'VE GOT A NEW MOM IN THERE!
YOU'RE KIDDING, RIGHT? TELL ME YOU'RE KIDDING.
BUT IT'S JUST A BAR!
YEAH, BUT NEW RELATION-SHIPS CAN START IN BARS, CAN'T THEY?!
AND YOU'RE JUST GONNA LET IT HAPPEN?!
HAH! JUST LET THEM TRY! WE'LL HAVE THEM
LOCKED UP SO FAST THEIR HEADS'LL SPIN!

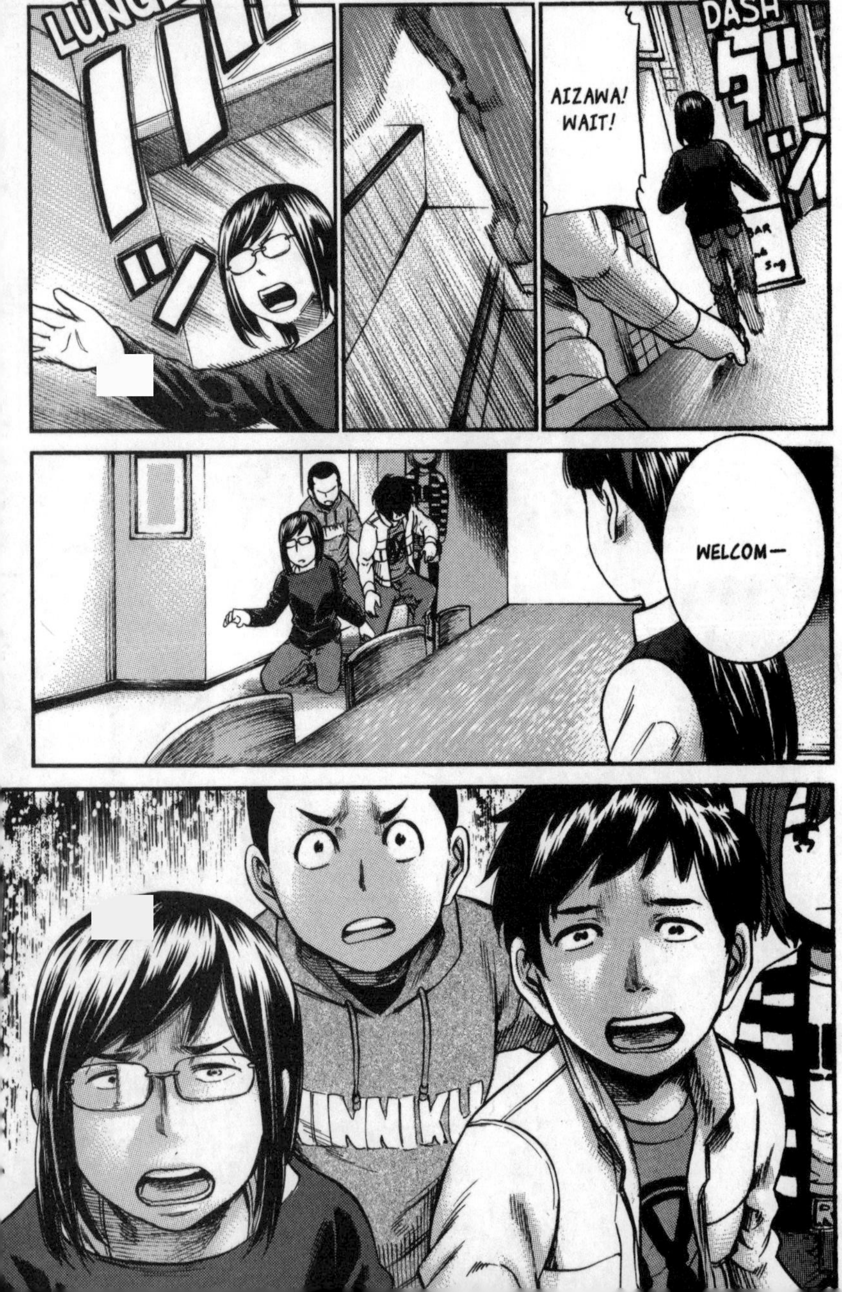
DASH
AIZAWA! WAIT!
LUNGE
WELCOM—

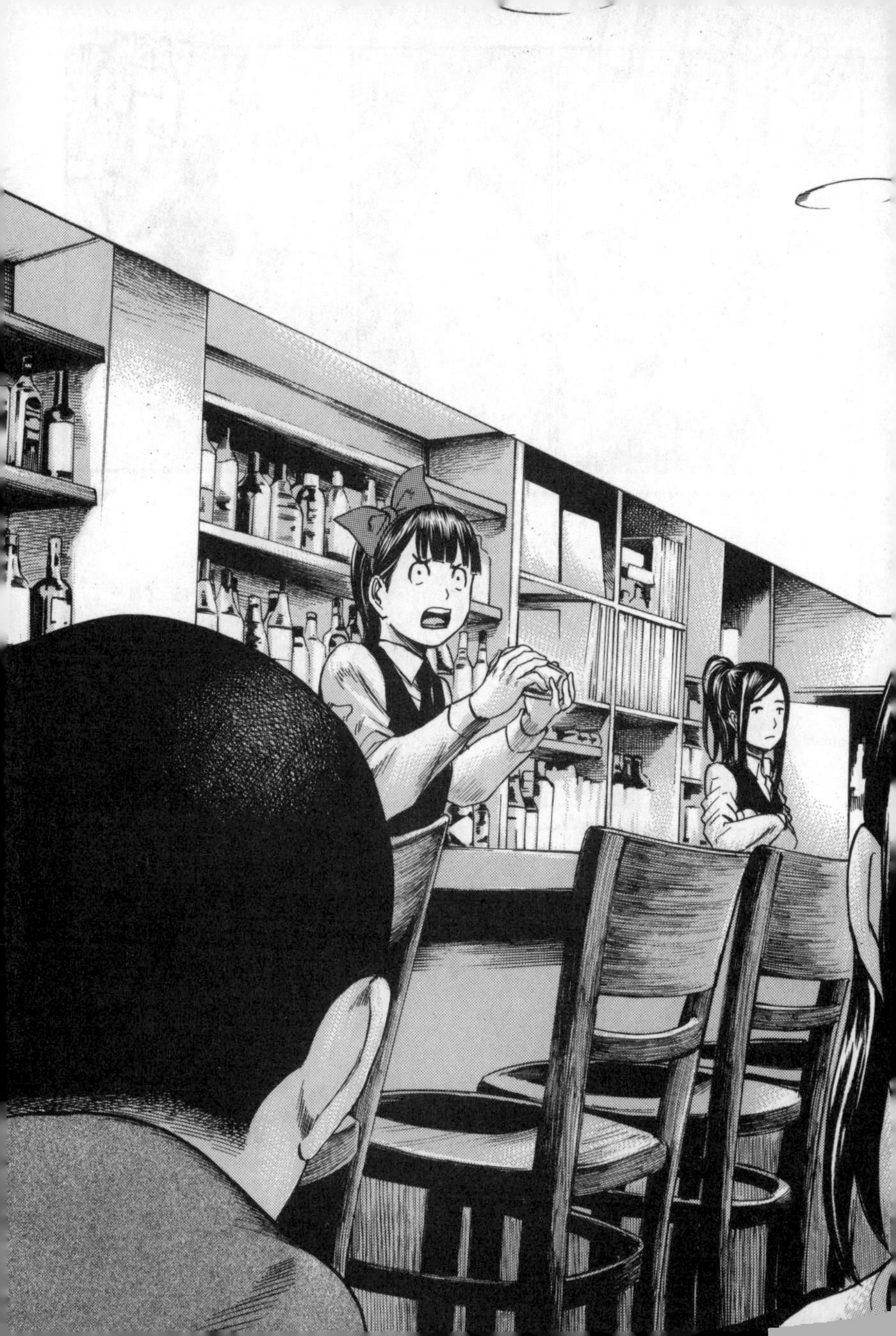

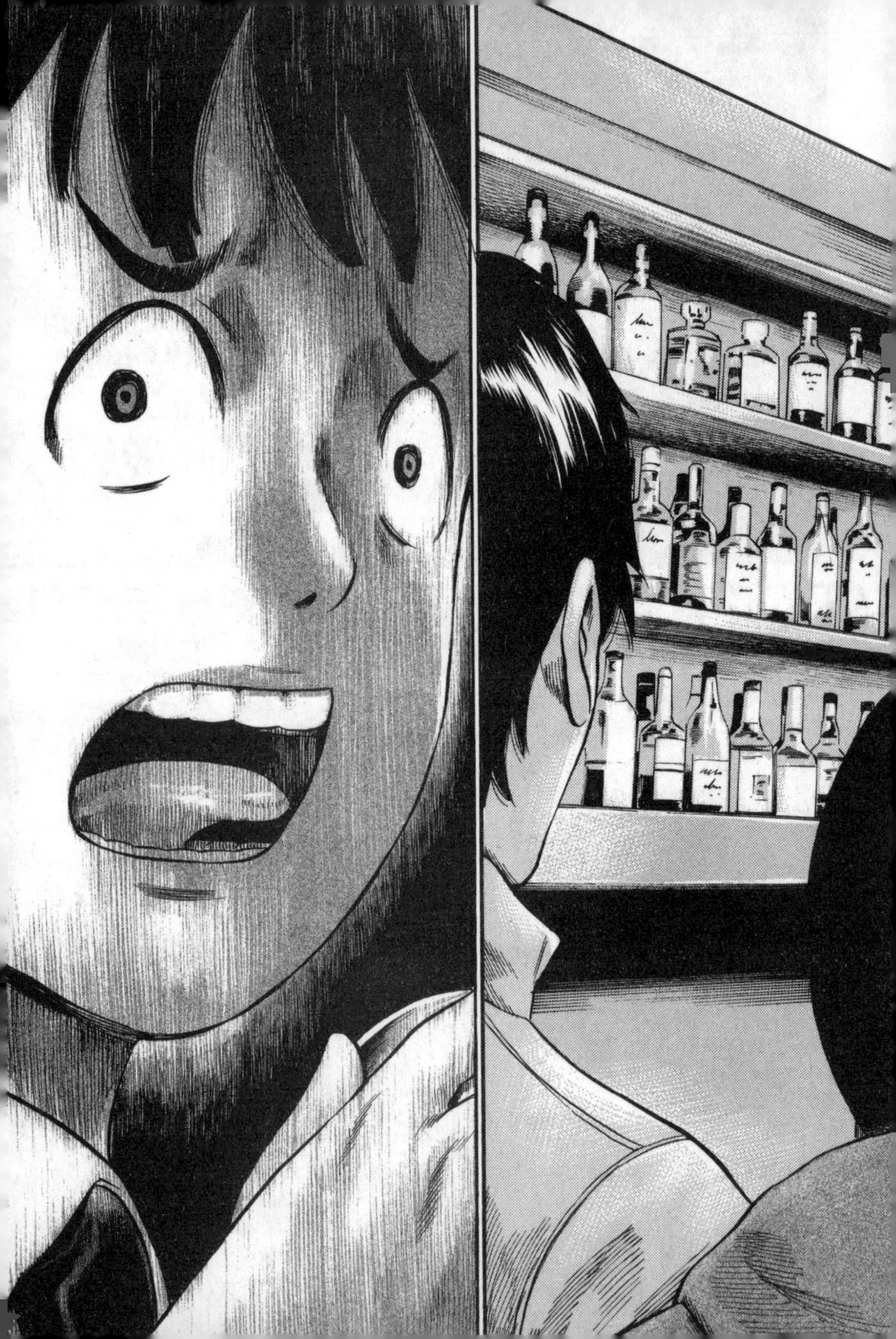

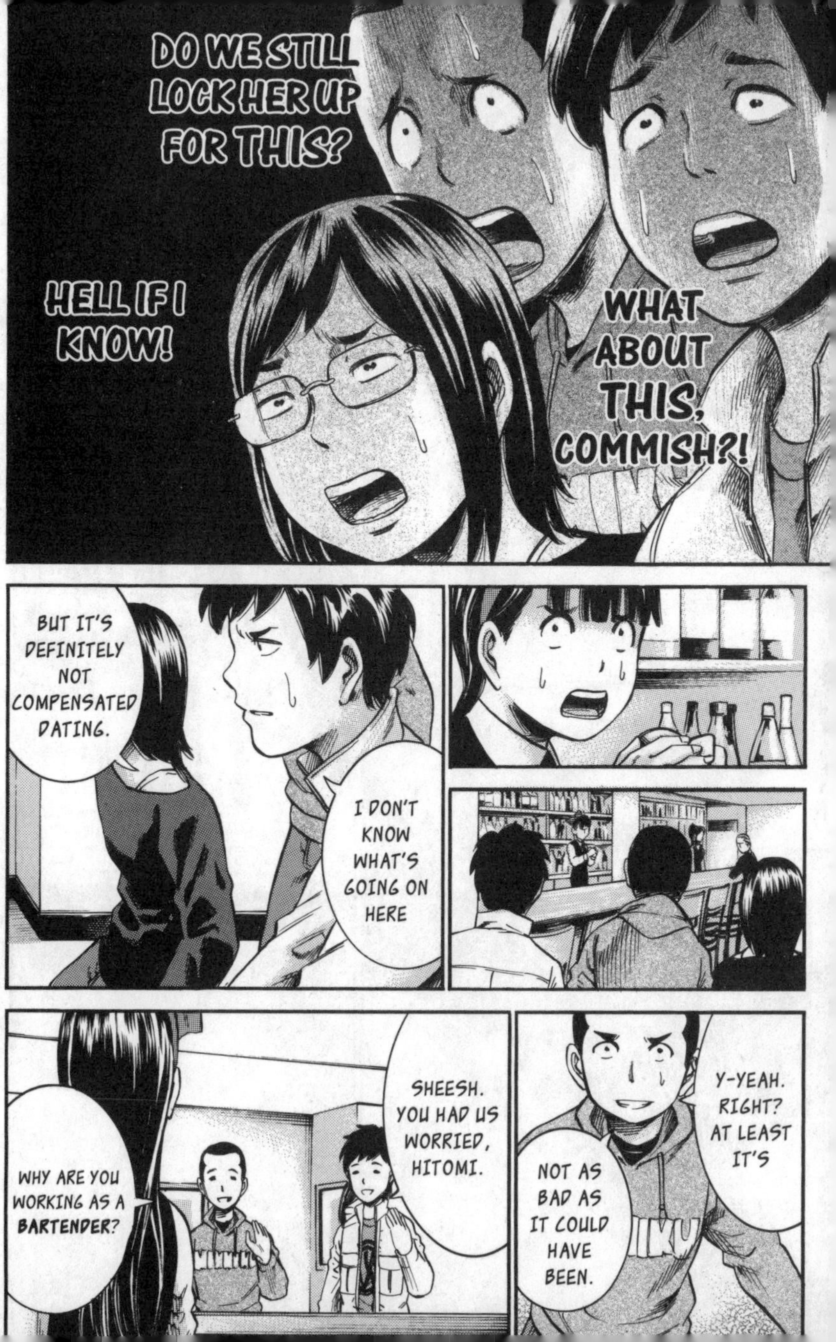
WHAT ABOUT THIS, COMMISH?!
DO WE STILL LOCK HER UP FOR THIS?
HELL IF I KNOW!
BUT IT'S DEFINITELY NOT COMPENSATED DATING.
I DON'T KNOW WHAT'S GOING ON HERE
Y-YEAH. RIGHT? AT LEAST IT'S
NOT AS BAD AS IT COULD HAVE BEEN.
SHEESH. YOU HAD US WORRIED, HITOMI.
WHY ARE YOU WORKING AS A BARTENDER?

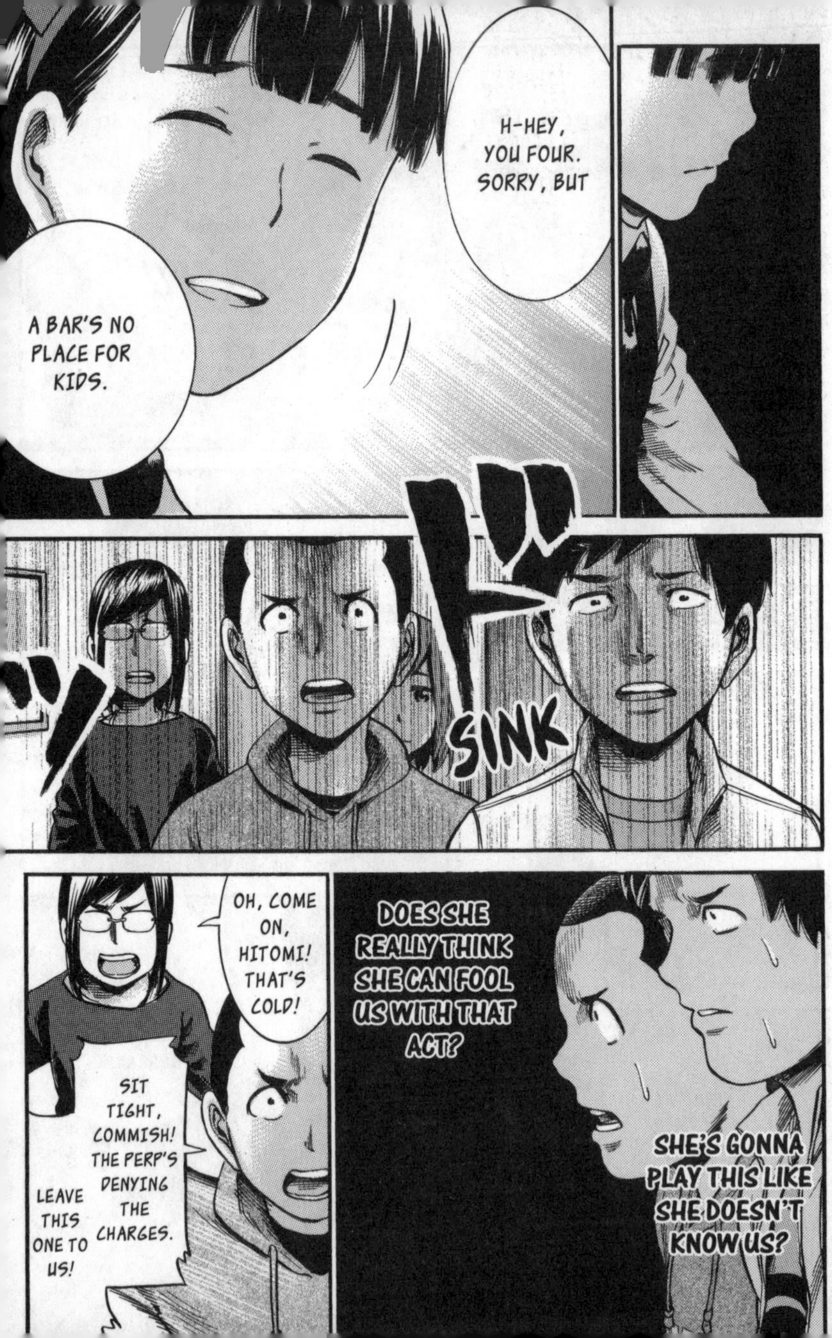
H-HEY, YOU FOUR. SORRY, BUT
A BAR'S NO PLACE FOR KIDS.
SINK
DOES SHE REALLY THINK SHE CAN FOOL US WITH THAT ACT?
SHE'S GONNA PLAY THIS LIKE SHE DOESN'T KNOW US?
OH, COME ON, HITOMI! THAT'S COLD!
SIT TIGHT, COMMISH! THE PERP'S DENYING THE CHARGES.
LEAVE THIS ONE TO US!

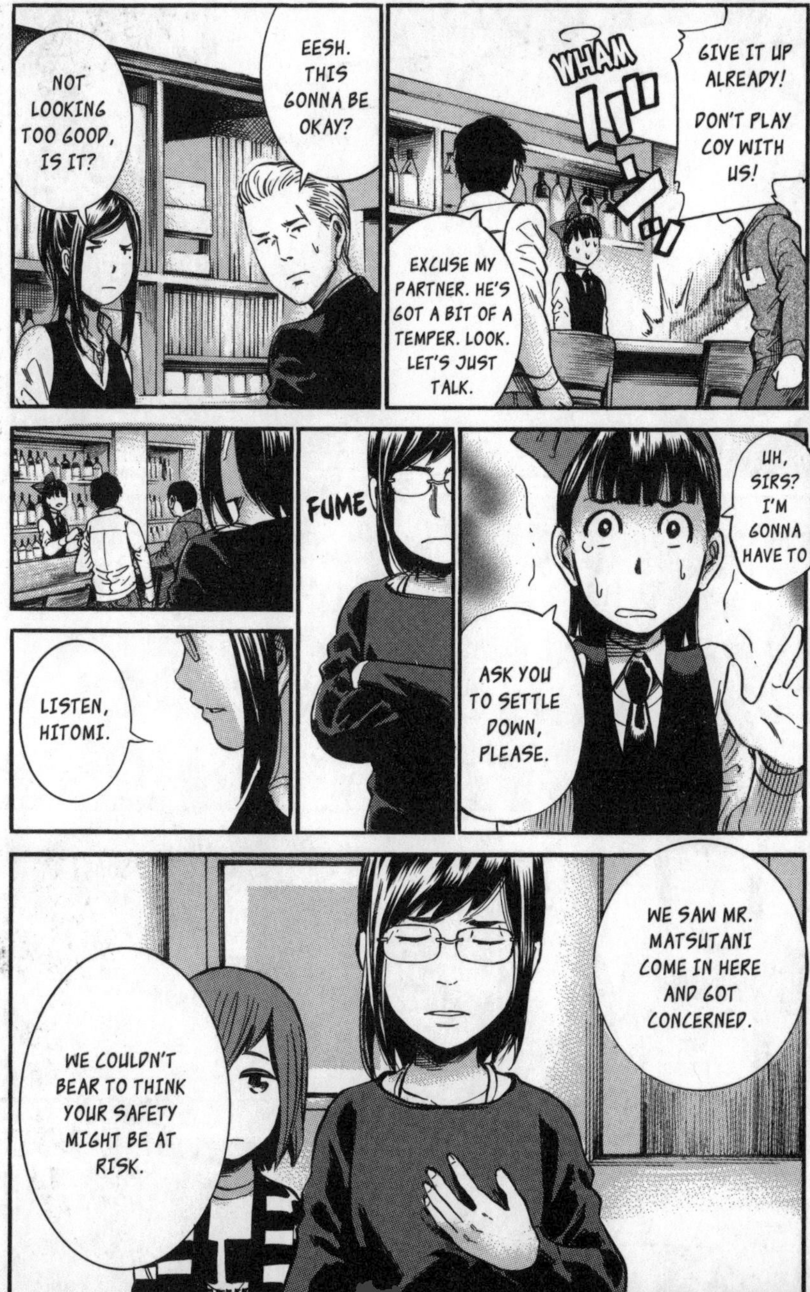
WHAM
GIVE IT UP ALREADY!
DON'T PLAY COY WITH US!
EXCUSE MY PARTNER. HE'S GOT A BIT OF A TEMPER. LOOK. LET'S JUST TALK.
EESH. THIS GONNA BE OKAY?
NOT LOOKING TOO GOOD, IS IT?
UH, SIRS? I'M GONNA HAVE TO
ASK YOU TO SETTLE DOWN, PLEASE.
FUME
LISTEN, HITOMI.
WE SAW MR. MATSUTANI COME IN HERE AND GOT CONCERNED.
WE COULDN'T BEAR TO THINK YOUR SAFETY MIGHT BE AT RISK.

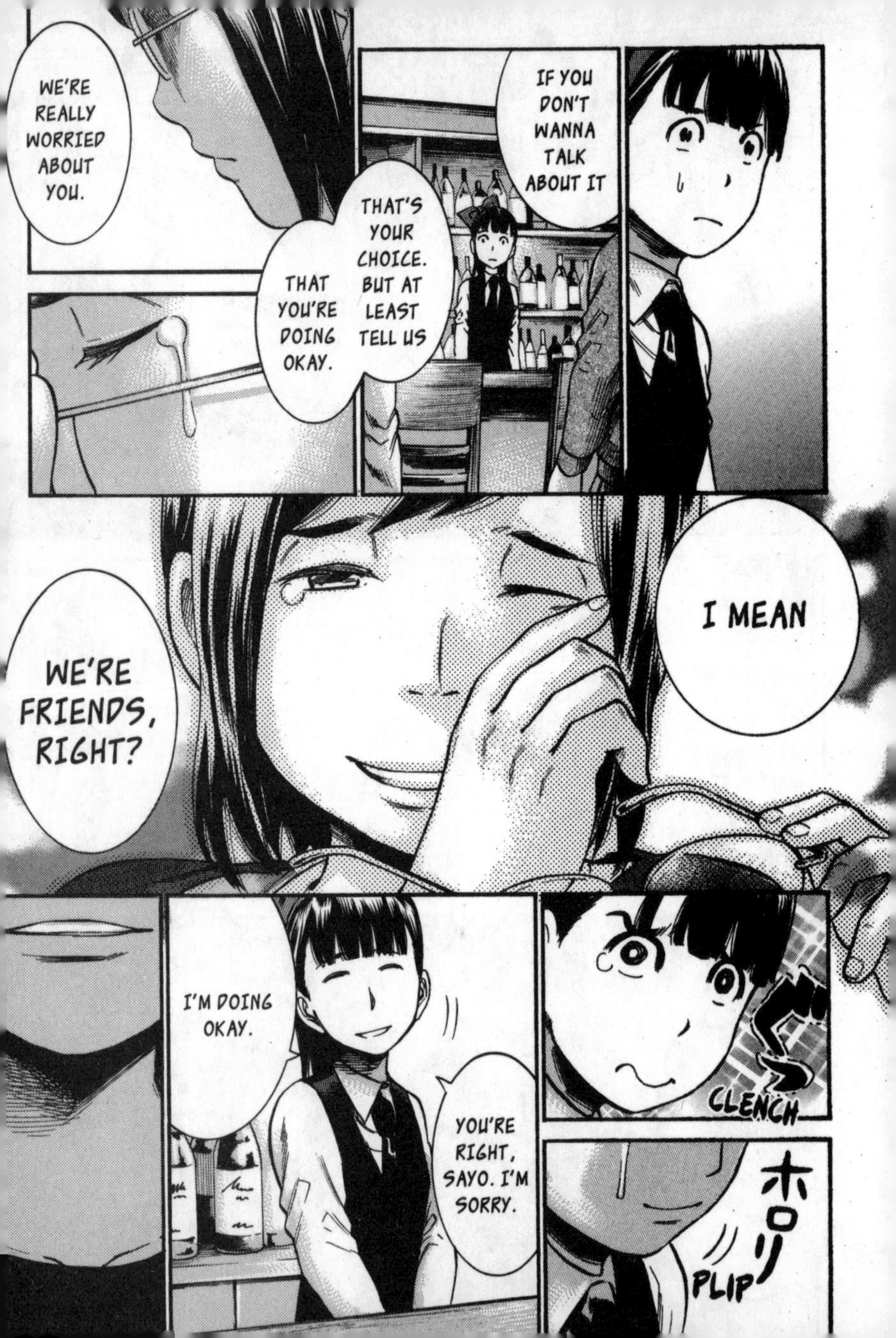
IF YOU DON'T WANNA TALK ABOUT IT
THAT'S YOUR CHOICE. BUT AT LEAST TELL US
THAT YOU'RE DOING OKAY.
WE'RE REALLY WORRIED ABOUT YOU.
I MEAN
WE'RE FRIENDS, RIGHT?
CLENCH
ホロリ
PLIP
I'M DOING OKAY.
YOU'RE RIGHT, SAYO. I'M SORRY.

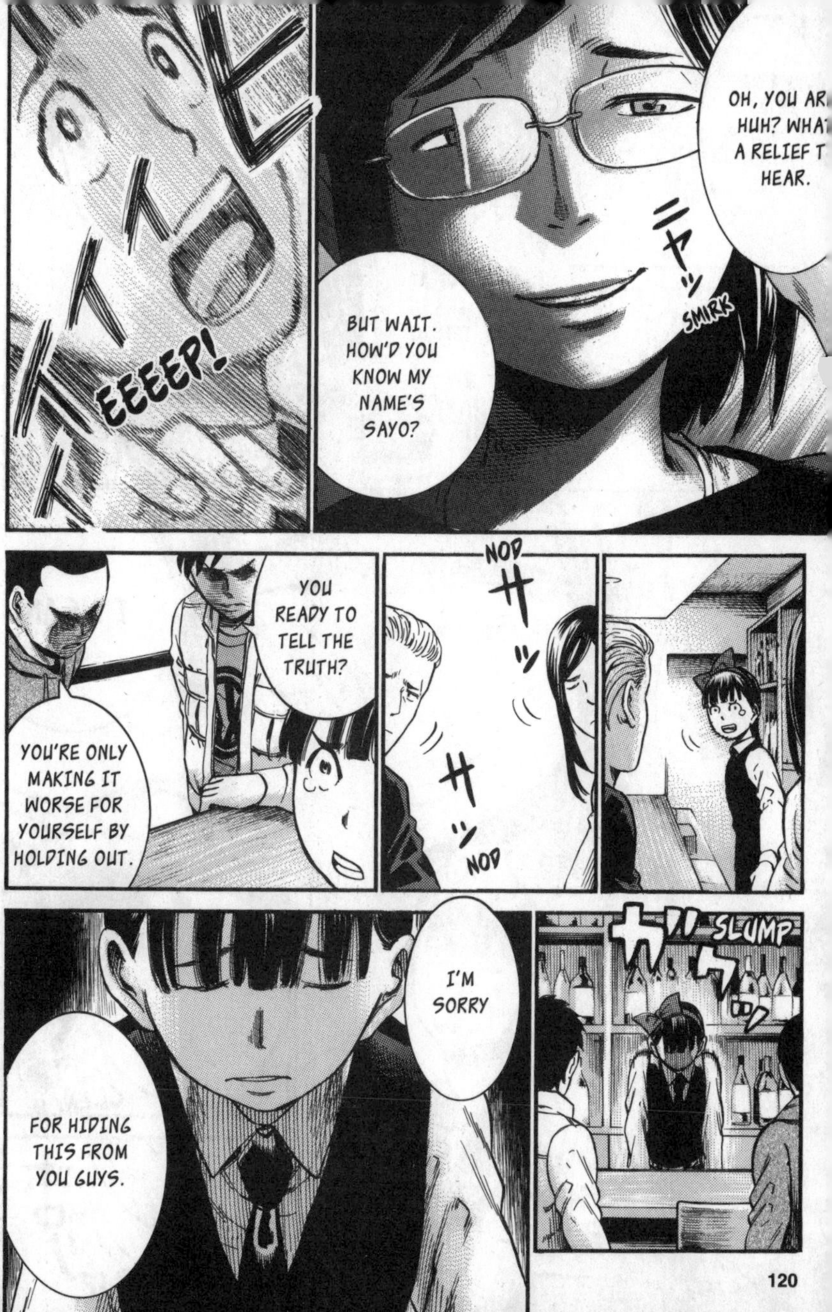
OH, YOU AR
HUH? WHA
A RELIEF T
HEAR.
ニヤッ
SMIRK
BUT WAIT. HOW'D YOU KNOW MY NAME'S SAYO?
EEEEP!
NOD
サッ
サッ
NOD
YOU READY TO TELL THE TRUTH?
YOU'RE ONLY MAKING IT WORSE FOR YOURSELF BY HOLDING OUT.
ガクッ
SLUMP
I'M SORRY
FOR HIDING THIS FROM YOU GUYS.

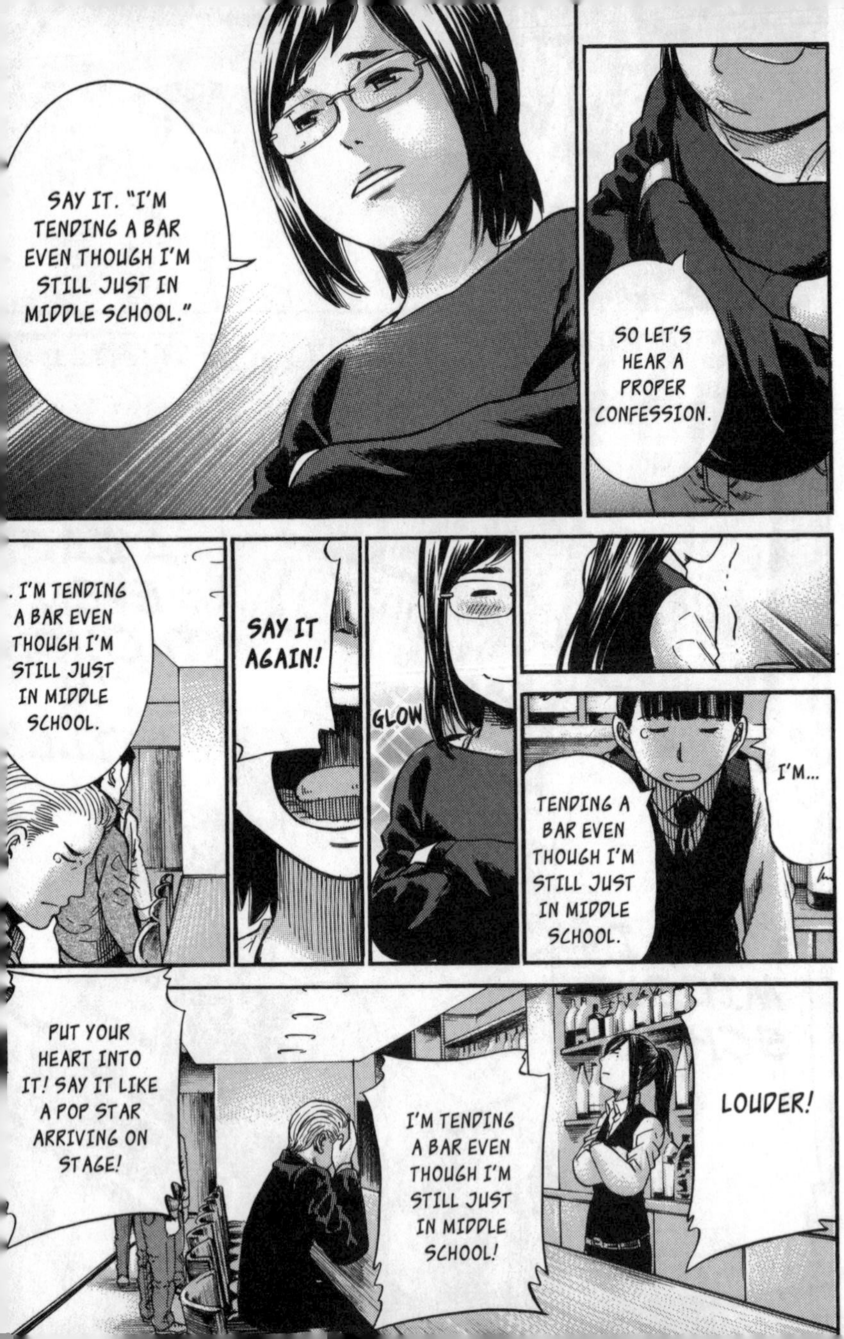
SO LET'S HEAR A PROPER CONFESSION.
SAY IT. "I'M TENDING A BAR EVEN THOUGH I'M STILL JUST IN MIDDLE SCHOOL."
I'M...
TENDING A BAR EVEN THOUGH I'M STILL JUST IN MIDDLE SCHOOL.
GLOW
SAY IT AGAIN!
. I'M TENDING A BAR EVEN THOUGH I'M STILL JUST IN MIDDLE SCHOOL.
LOUDER!
I'M TENDING A BAR EVEN THOUGH I'M STILL JUST IN MIDDLE SCHOOL!
PUT YOUR HEART INTO IT! SAY IT LIKE A POP STAR ARRIVING ON STAGE!

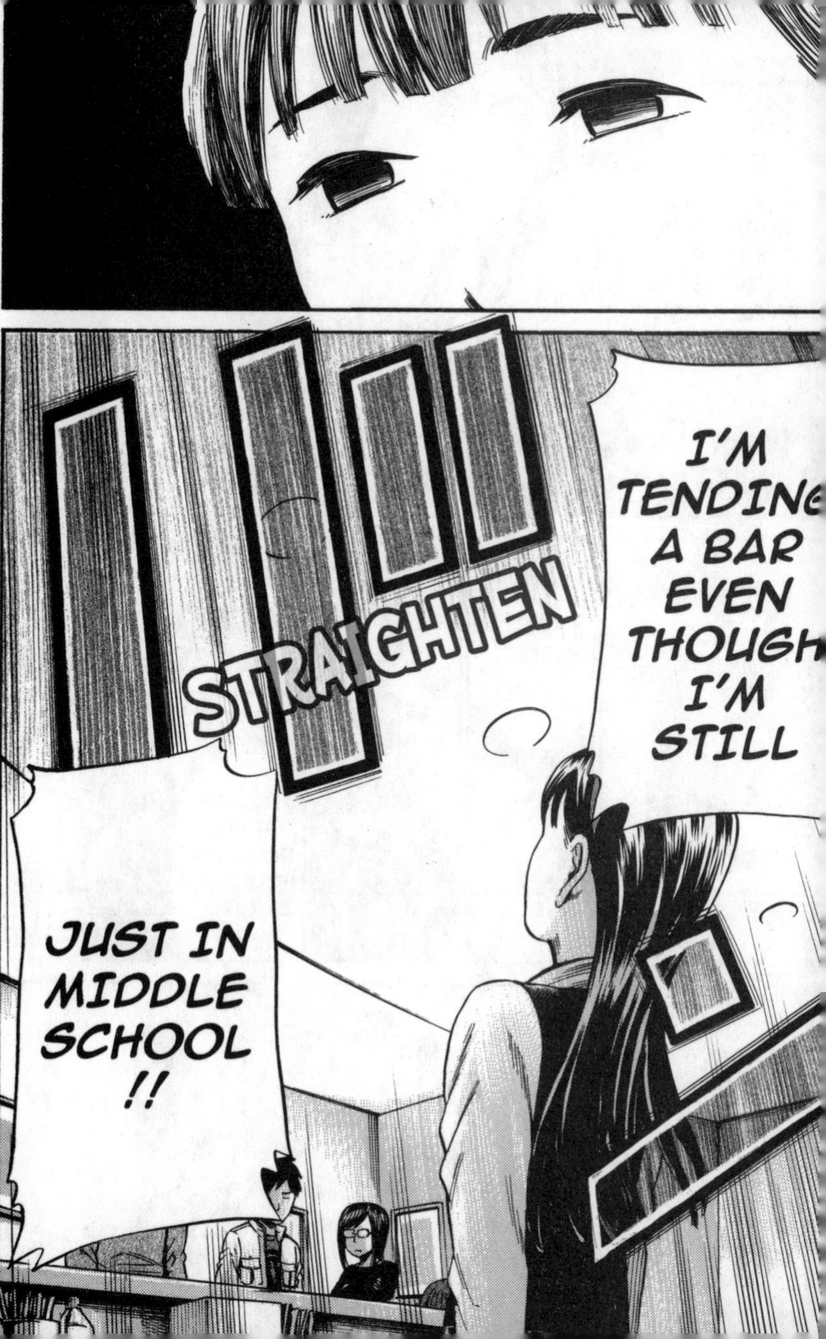
I'M TENDING A BAR EVEN THOUGH I'M STILL
STRAIGHTEN
JUST IN MIDDLE SCHOOL !!

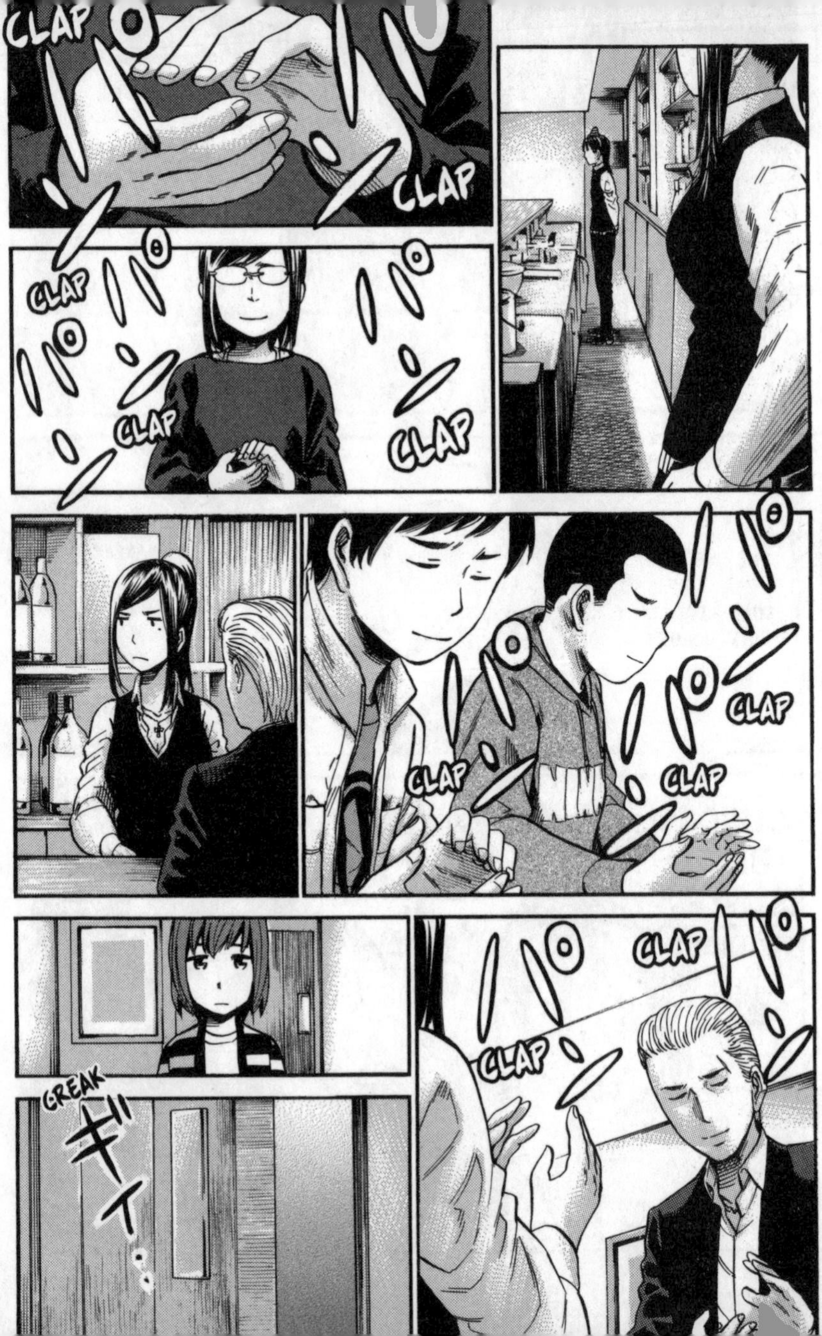
CLAP
CLAP
CLAP
CLAP
CLAP
CLAP
CLAP
CLAP
CLAP
CLAP
CREAK
ギイ...

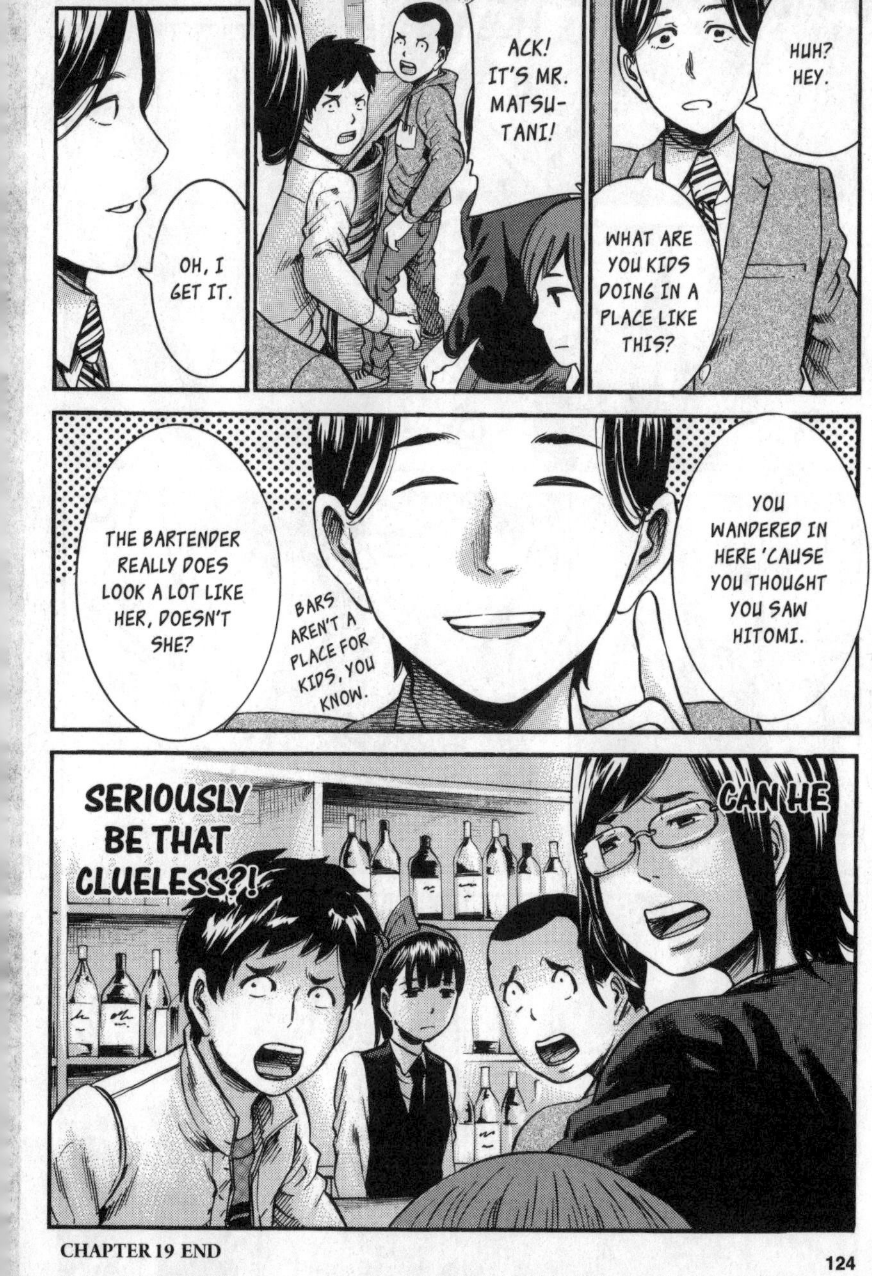
HUH? HEY.
WHAT ARE YOU KIDS DOING IN A PLACE LIKE THIS?
ACK! IT'S MR. MATSU-TANI!
OH, I GET IT.
YOU WANDERED IN HERE 'CAUSE YOU THOUGHT YOU SAW HITOMI.
BARS AREN'T A PLACE FOR KIDS, YOU KNOW.
THE BARTENDER REALLY DOES LOOK A LOT LIKE HER, DOESN'T SHE?
CAN HE
SERIOUSLY BE THAT CLUELESS?!

CHAPTER 19 END

ホウ··

GLOW

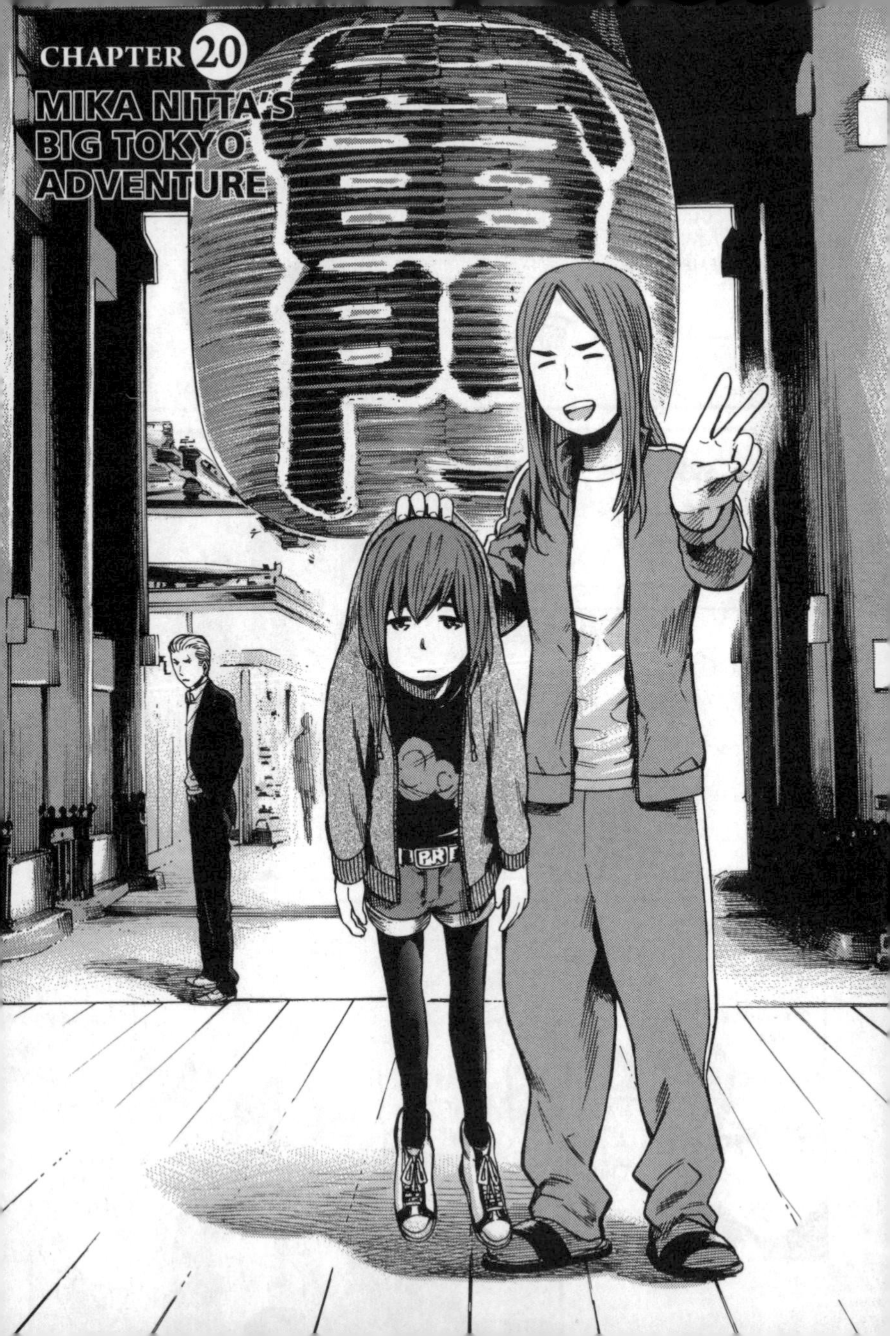
CHAPTER 20
MIKA NITTA'S BIG TOKYO ADVENTURE

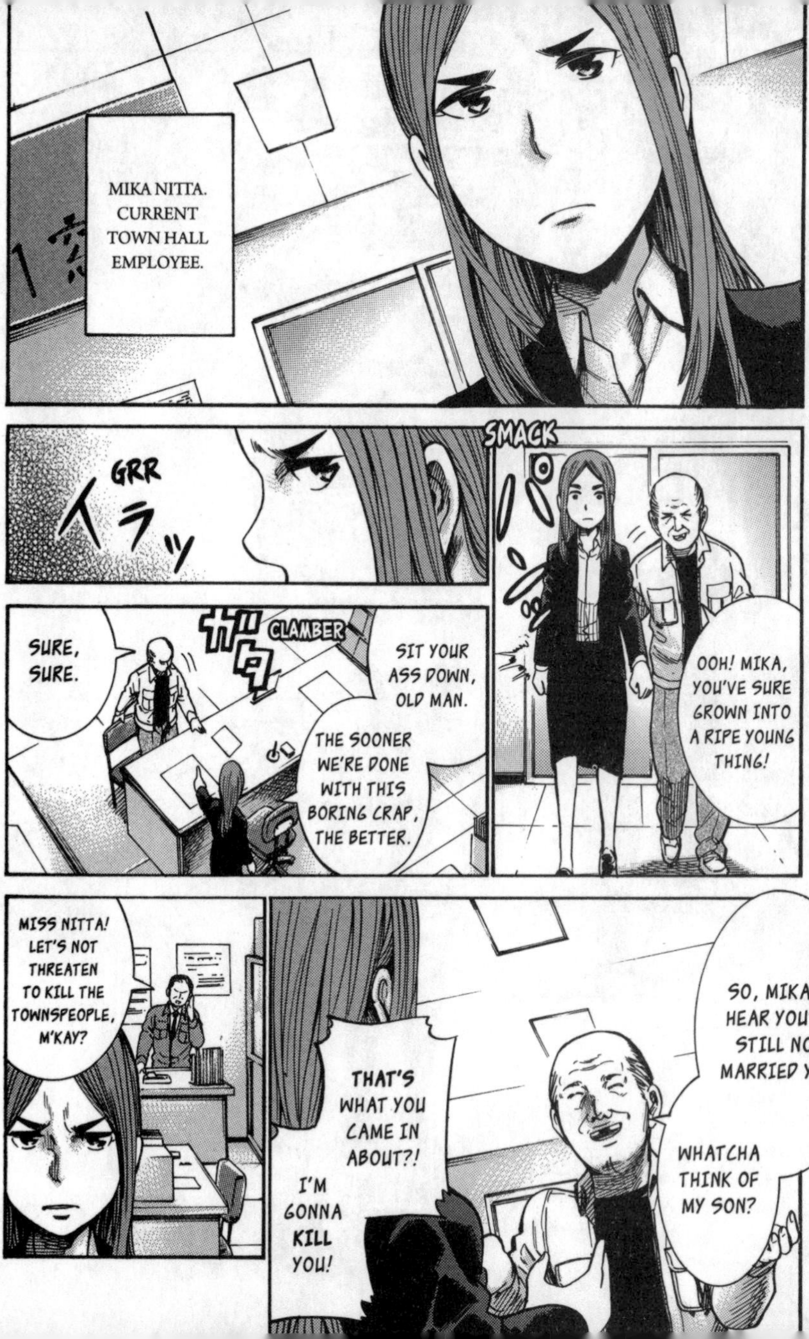
MIKA NITTA. CURRENT TOWN HALL EMPLOYEE.
SMACK
OOH! MIKA, YOU'VE SURE GROWN INTO A RIPE YOUNG THING!
GRR
イラッ
ガタ
CLAMBER
SIT YOUR ASS DOWN, OLD MAN.
THE SOONER WE'RE DONE WITH THIS BORING CRAP, THE BETTER.
SURE, SURE.
SO, MIKA, I HEAR YOU'RE STILL NOT MARRIED YET
WHATCHA THINK OF MY SON?
THAT'S WHAT YOU CAME IN ABOUT?!
I'M GONNA KILL YOU!
MISS NITTA! LET'S NOT THREATEN TO KILL THE TOWNSPEOPLE, M'KAY?

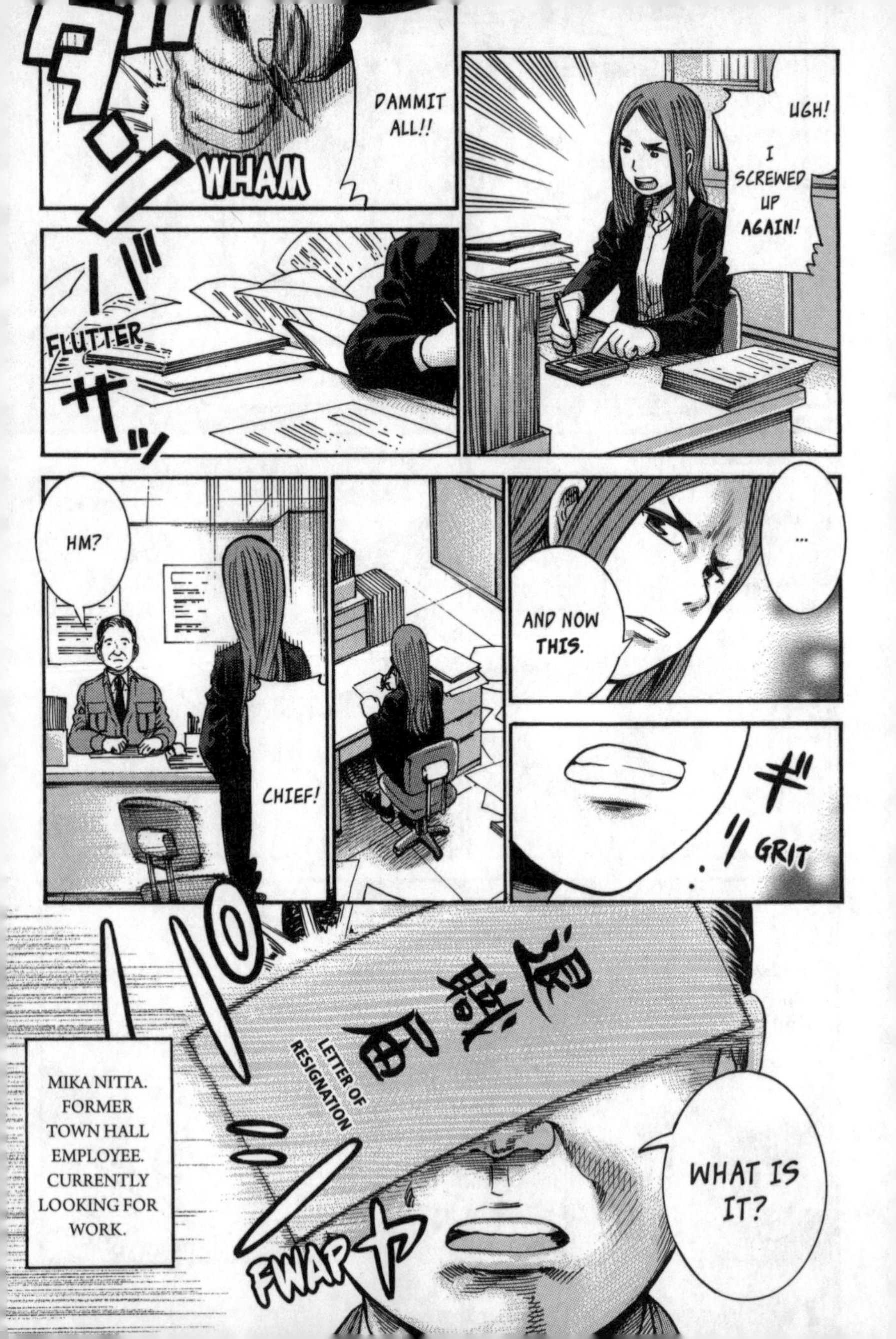
UGH!
I SCREWED UP AGAIN!
DAMMIT ALL!!
WHAM
FLUTTER
...
AND NOW THIS.
GRIT
CHIEF!
HM?
退職届
LETTER OF RESIGNATION
WHAT IS IT?
FWAP
MIKA NITTA. FORMER TOWN HALL EMPLOYEE. CURRENTLY LOOKING FOR WORK.

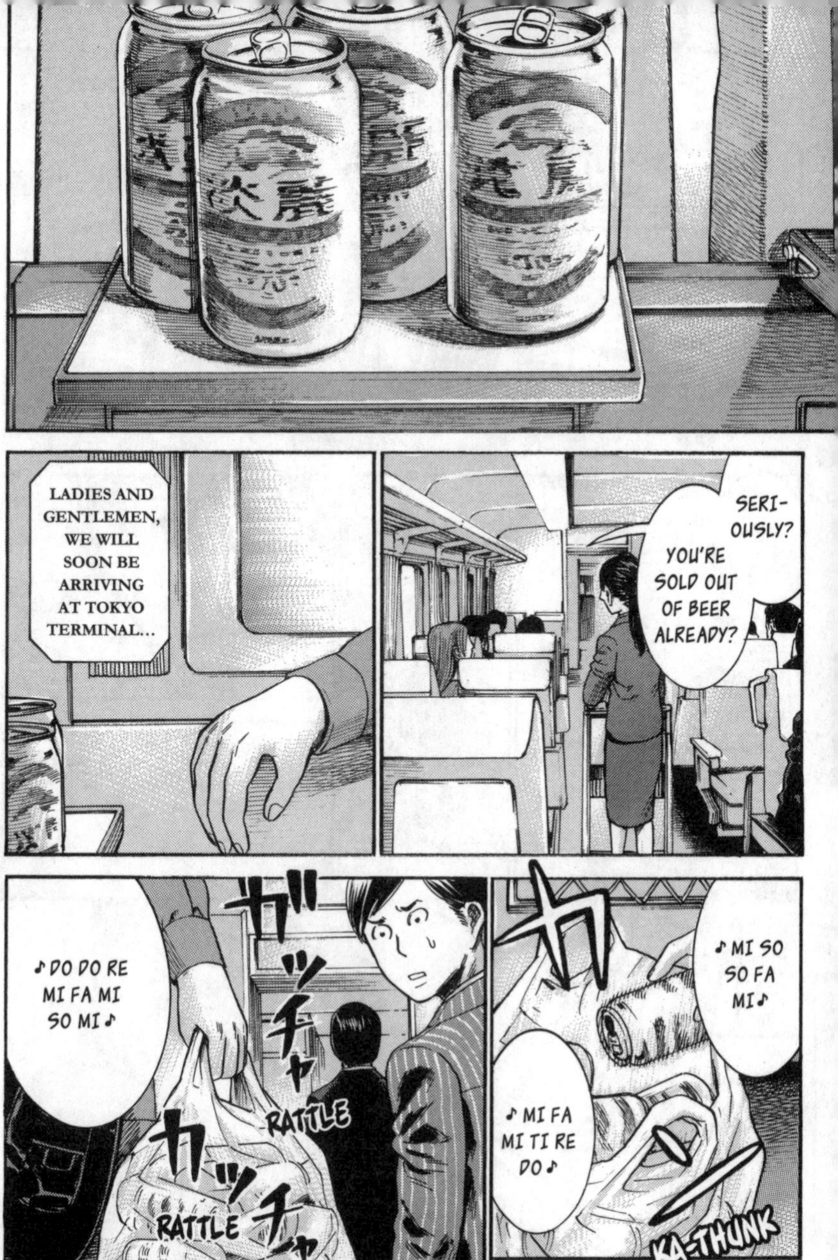
SERI-OUSLY? YOU'RE SOLD OUT OF BEER ALREADY?
LADIES AND GENTLEMEN, WE WILL SOON BE ARRIVING AT TOKYO TERMINAL…
♪ MI SO SO FA MI ♪
♪ MI FA MI TI RE DO ♪
KA-THUNK
♪ DO DO RE MI FA MI SO MI ♪
ガッチャ
RATTLE
カッチャ
RATTLE

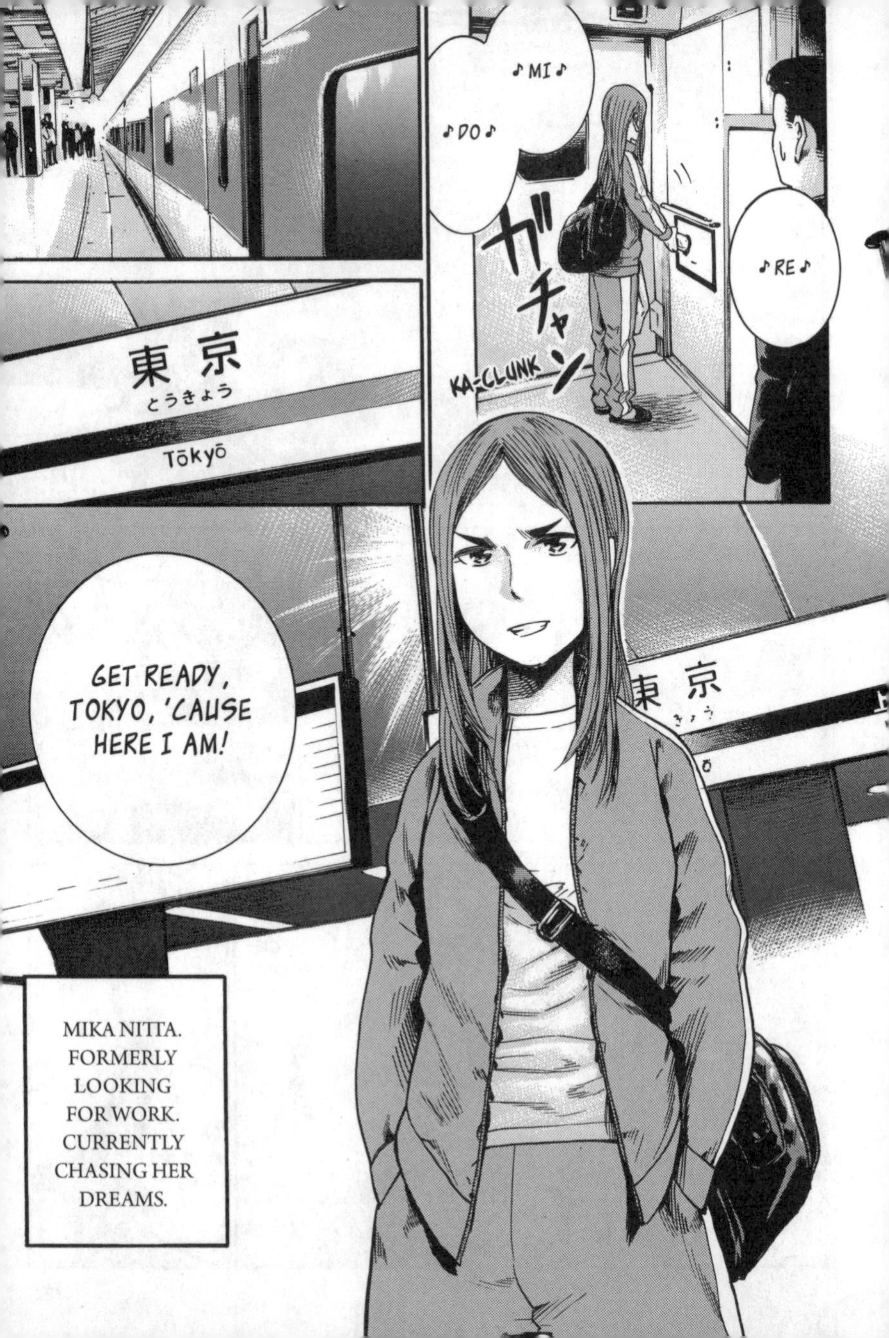

♪MI♪
♪DO♪
♪RE♪
ガチャン
KA-CLUNK
東京
とうきょう
Tōkyō
東京
GET READY, TOKYO, 'CAUSE HERE I AM!
MIKA NITTA. FORMERLY LOOKING FOR WORK. CURRENTLY CHASING HER DREAMS.

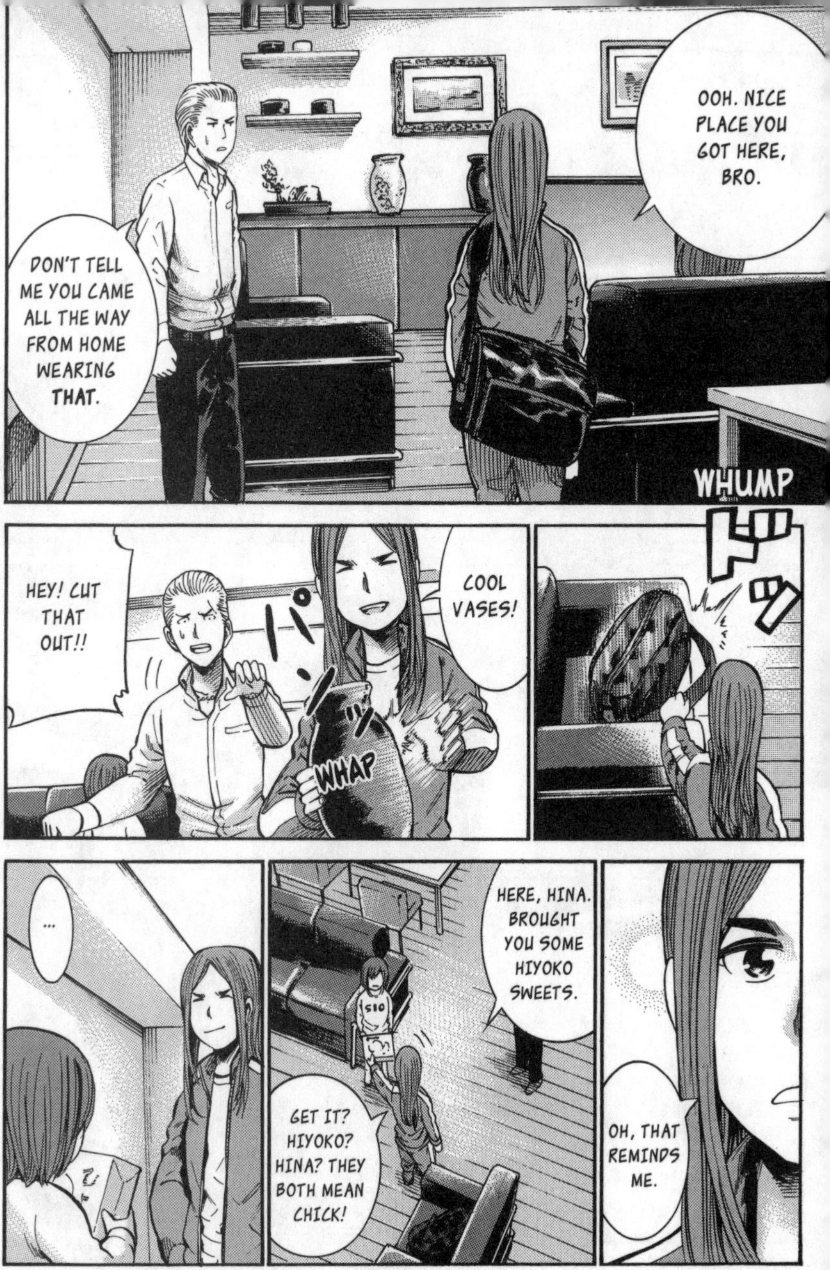
OOH. NICE PLACE YOU GOT HERE, BRO.
DON'T TELL ME YOU CAME ALL THE WAY FROM HOME WEARING **THAT**.
WHUMP
ドッ
COOL VASES!
パ
WHAP
HEY! CUT THAT OUT!!
OH, THAT REMINDS ME.
HERE, HINA. BROUGHT YOU SOME HIYOKO SWEETS.
GET IT? HIYOKO? HINA? THEY BOTH MEAN CHICK!
...

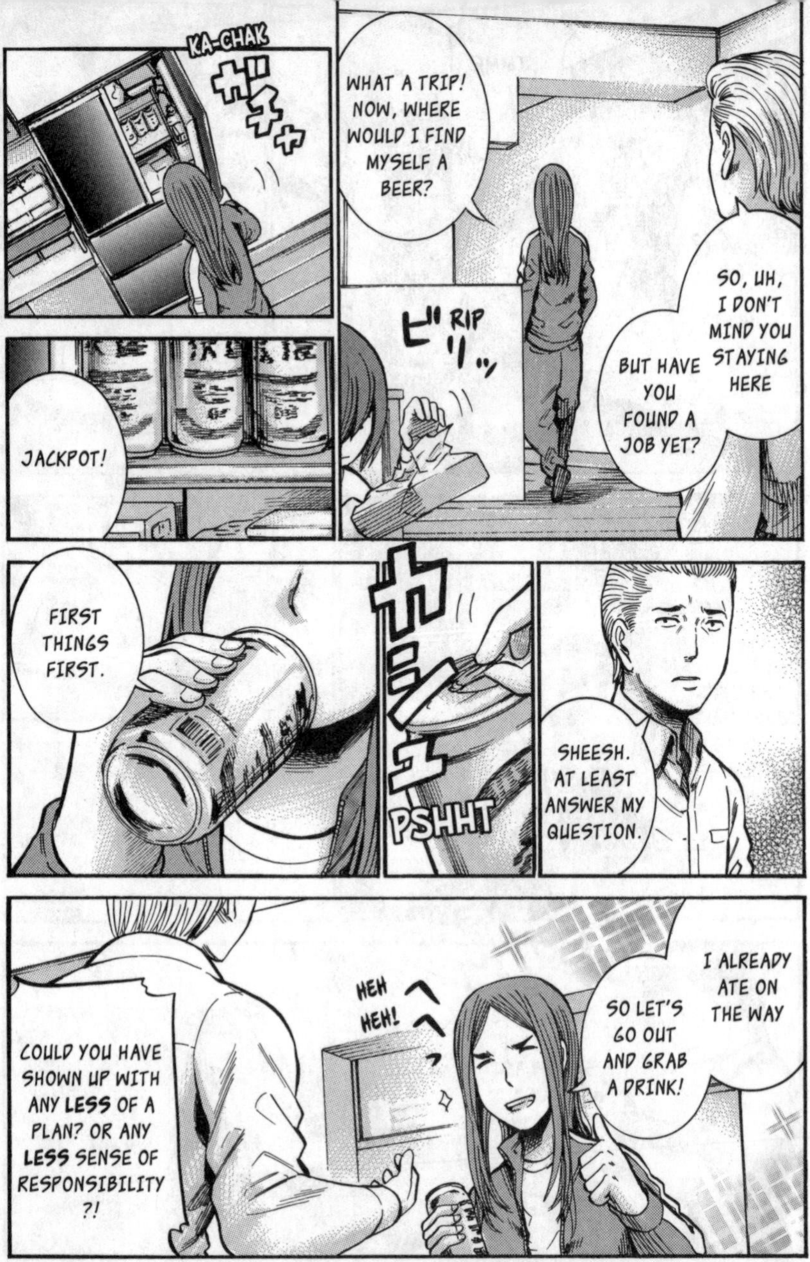

WHAT A TRIP! NOW, WHERE WOULD I FIND MYSELF A BEER?
SO, UH, I DON'T MIND YOU STAYING HERE
BUT HAVE YOU FOUND A JOB YET?
RIP
KA-CHAK
JACKPOT!
SHEESH. AT LEAST ANSWER MY QUESTION.
PSHHT
FIRST THINGS FIRST.
I ALREADY ATE ON THE WAY
SO LET'S GO OUT AND GRAB A DRINK!
HEH HEH!
COULD YOU HAVE SHOWN UP WITH ANY **LESS** OF A PLAN? OR ANY **LESS** SENSE OF RESPONSIBILITY ?!

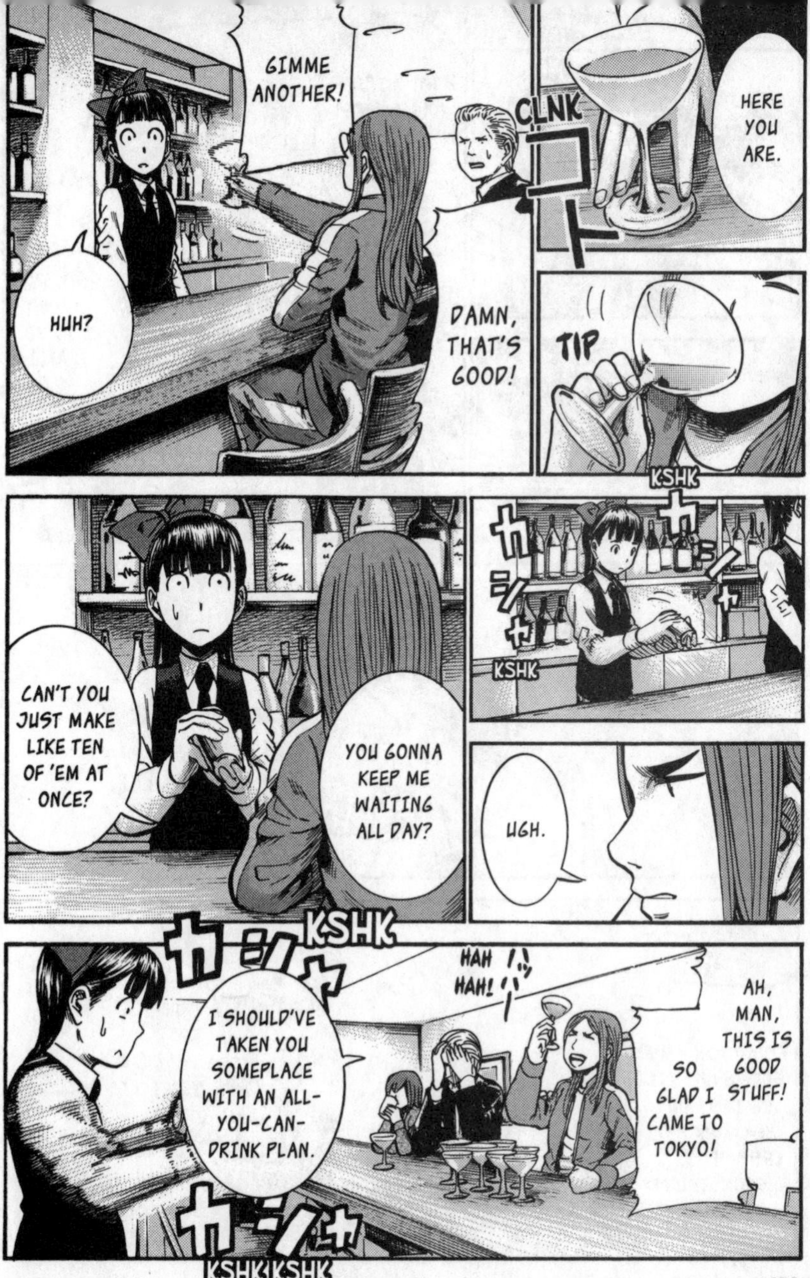
CLNK
HERE YOU ARE.
TIP
DAMN, THAT'S GOOD!
GIMME ANOTHER!
HUH?
KSHK
KSHK
UGH.
YOU GONNA KEEP ME WAITING ALL DAY?
CAN'T YOU JUST MAKE LIKE TEN OF 'EM AT ONCE?
AH, MAN, THIS IS GOOD STUFF!
SO GLAD I CAME TO TOKYO!
HAH HAH!
KSHK
I SHOULD'VE TAKEN YOU SOMEPLACE WITH AN ALL-YOU-CAN-DRINK PLAN.
KSHK KSHK

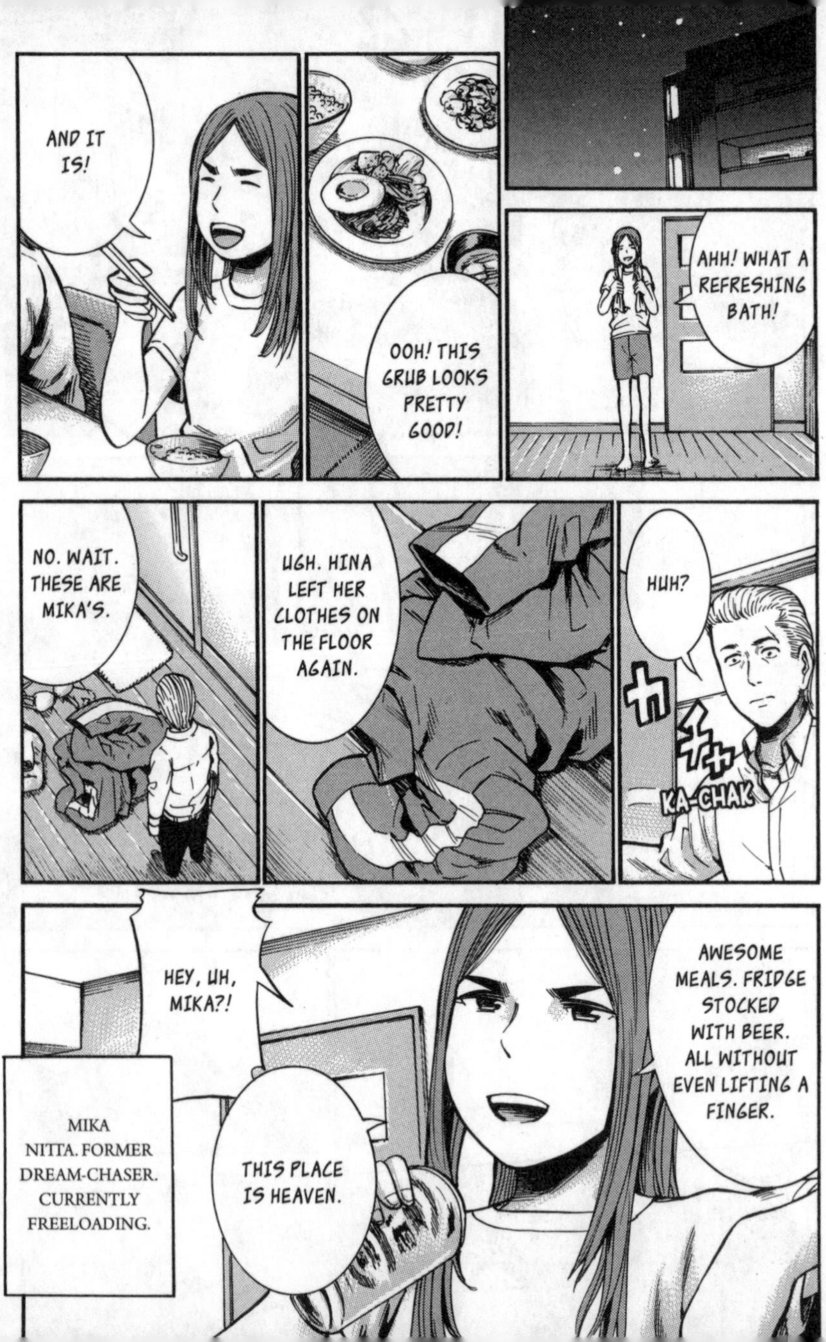
AHH! WHAT A REFRESHING BATH!
OOH! THIS GRUB LOOKS PRETTY GOOD!
AND IT IS!
HUH?
カチャ
KA-CHAK
UGH. HINA LEFT HER CLOTHES ON THE FLOOR AGAIN.
NO. WAIT. THESE ARE MIKA'S.
HEY, UH, MIKA?!
AWESOME MEALS. FRIDGE STOCKED WITH BEER. ALL WITHOUT EVEN LIFTING A FINGER.
THIS PLACE IS HEAVEN.
MIKA NITTA. FORMER DREAM-CHASER. CURRENTLY FREELOADING.

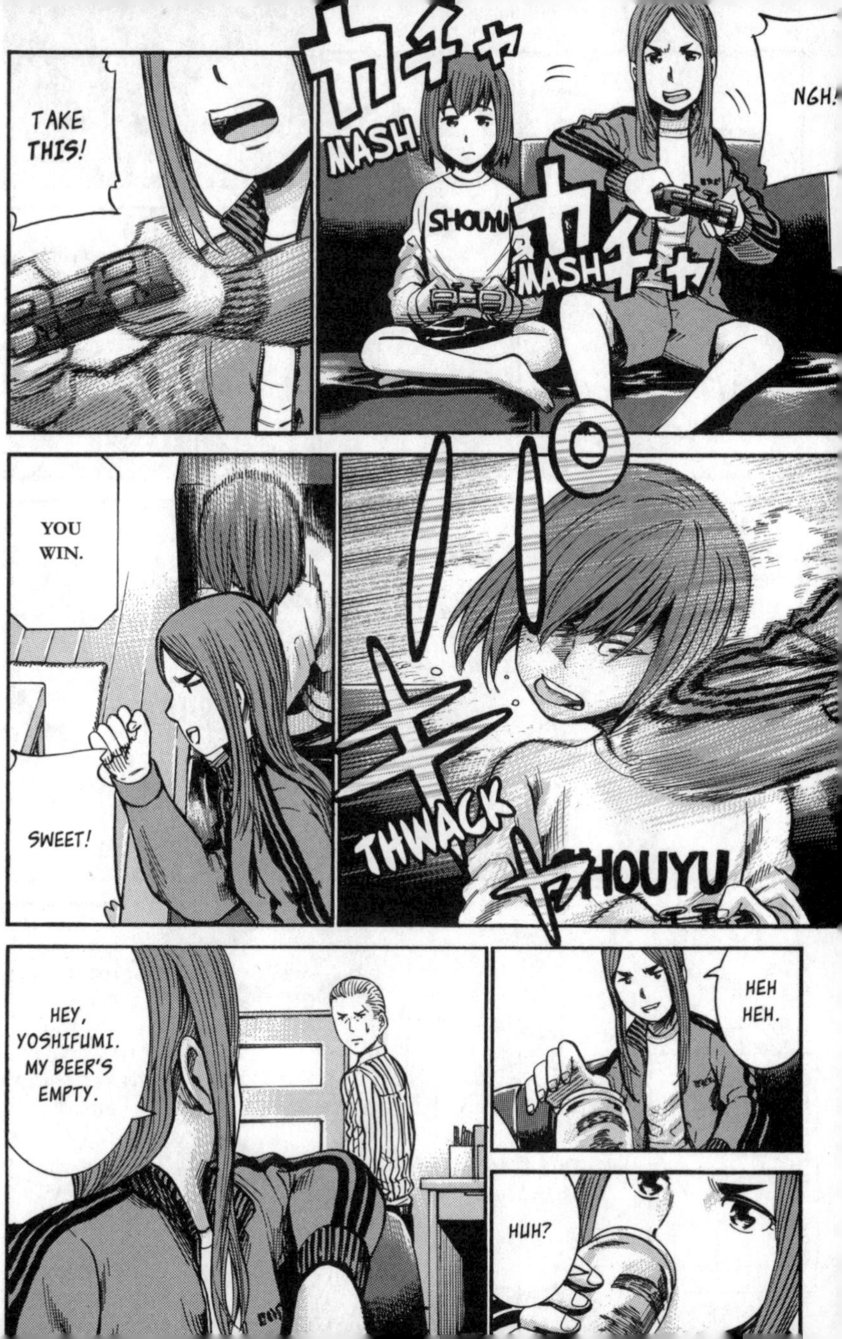
NGH!
カチャ
MASH
SHOUYU
カチャ
MASH
TAKE THIS!
THWACK
SHOUYU
YOU WIN.
SWEET!
HEH HEH.
HUH?
HEY, YOSHIFUMI. MY BEER'S EMPTY.

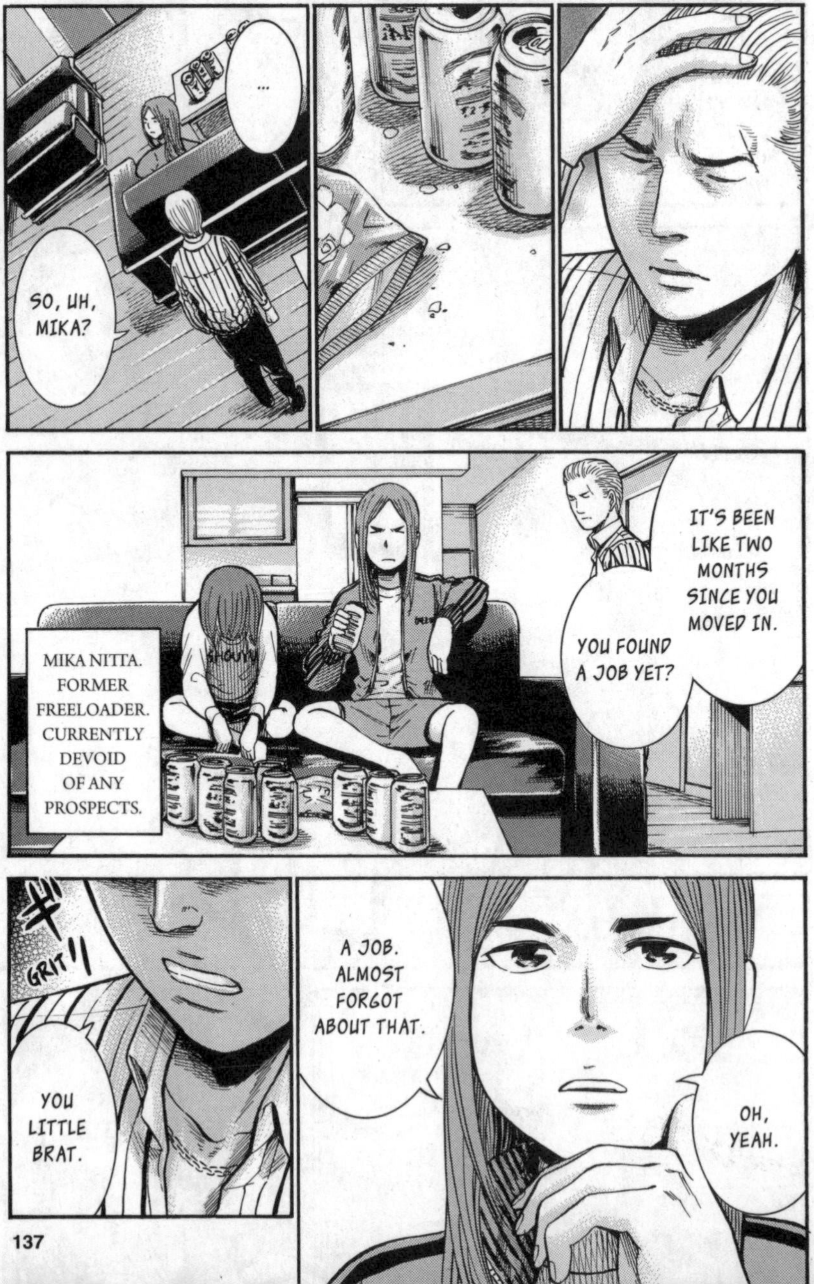
...
SO, UH, MIKA?
IT'S BEEN LIKE TWO MONTHS SINCE YOU MOVED IN.
YOU FOUND A JOB YET?
MIKA NITTA. FORMER FREELOADER. CURRENTLY DEVOID OF ANY PROSPECTS.
OH, YEAH.
A JOB. ALMOST FORGOT ABOUT THAT.
GRIT
YOU LITTLE BRAT.

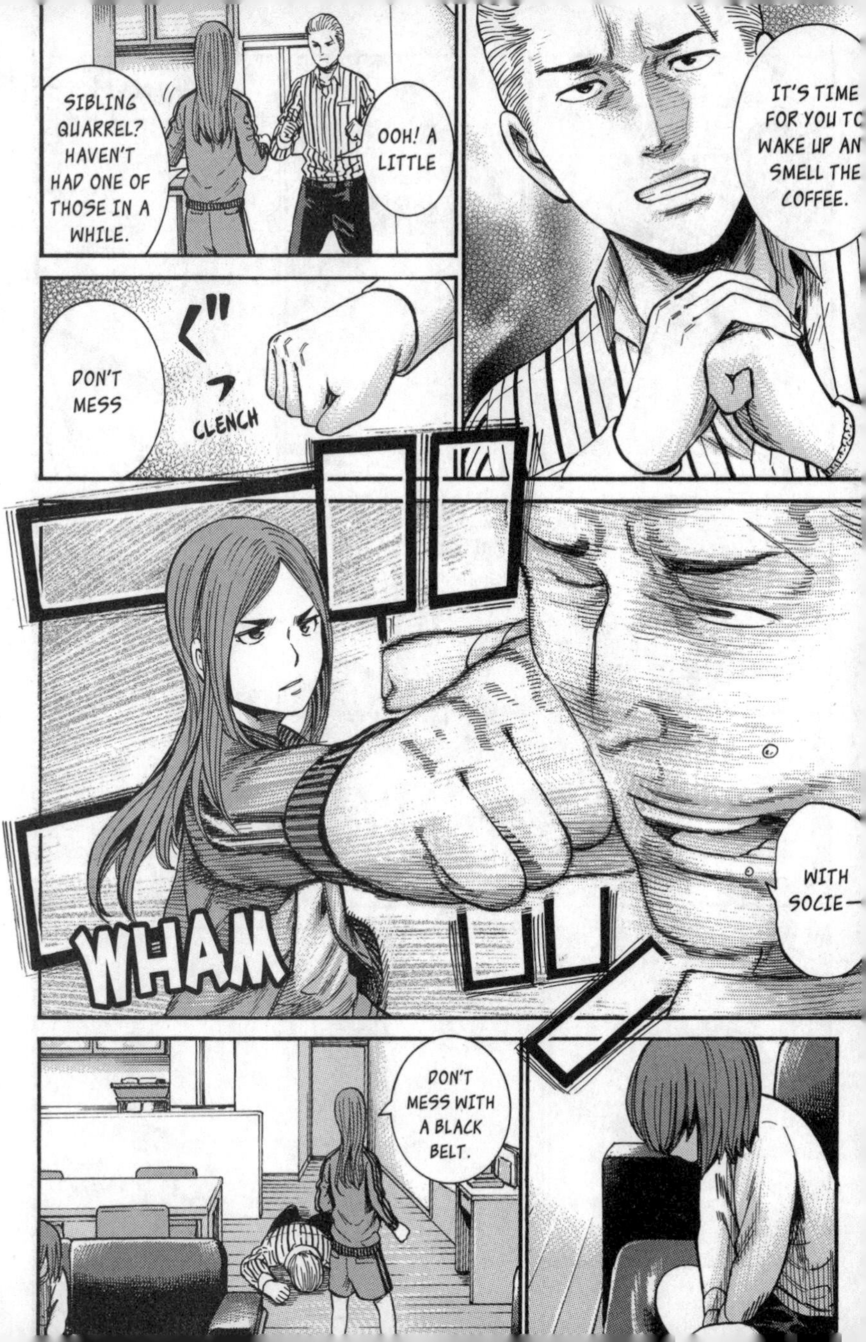

IT'S TIME FOR YOU TO WAKE UP AN SMELL THE COFFEE.
OOH! A LITTLE
SIBLING QUARREL? HAVEN'T HAD ONE OF THOSE IN A WHILE.
DON'T MESS
CLENCH
WITH SOCIE—
WHAM
DON'T MESS WITH A BLACK BELT.

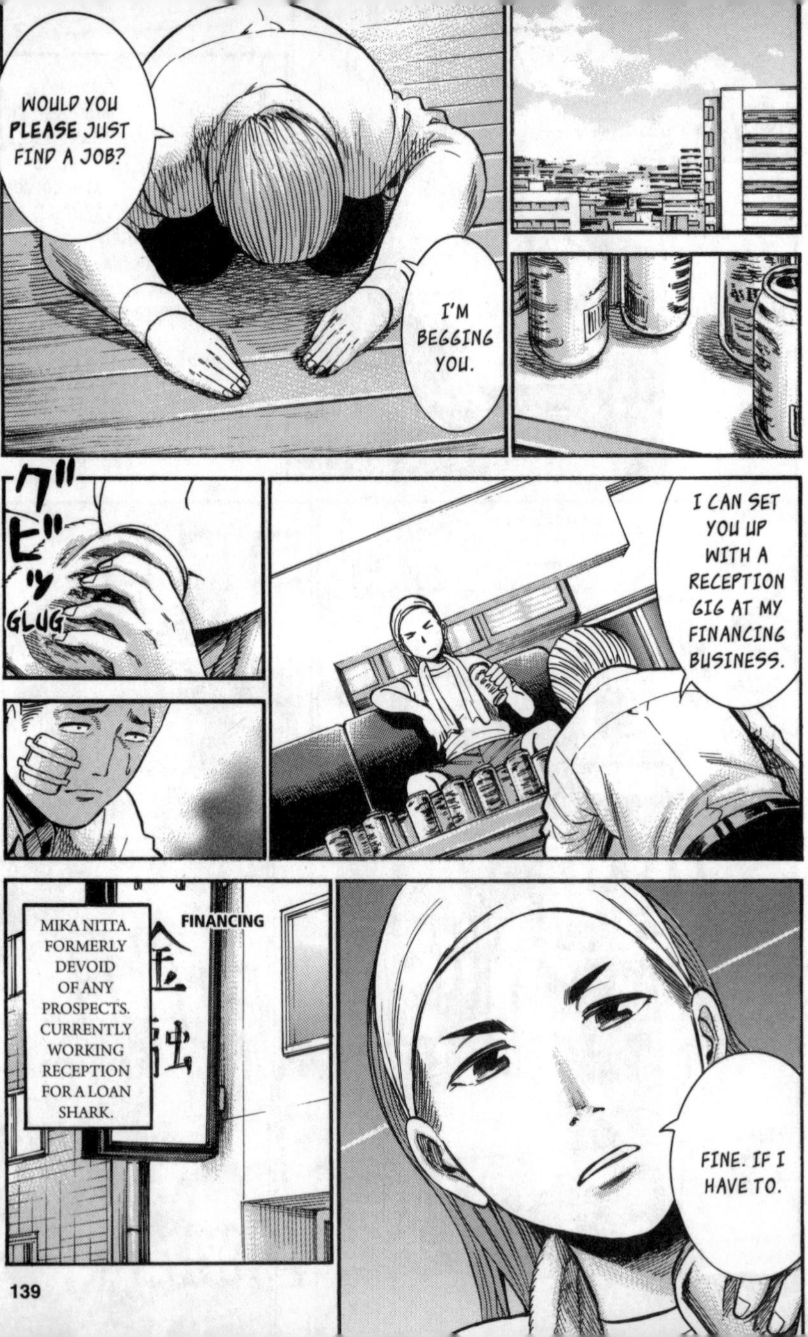
WOULD YOU PLEASE JUST FIND A JOB?
I'M BEGGING YOU.
I CAN SET YOU UP WITH A RECEPTION GIG AT MY FINANCING BUSINESS.
グビッ
GLUG
FINE. IF I HAVE TO.
FINANCING
MIKA NITTA. FORMERLY DEVOID OF ANY PROSPECTS. CURRENTLY WORKING RECEPTION FOR A LOAN SHARK.

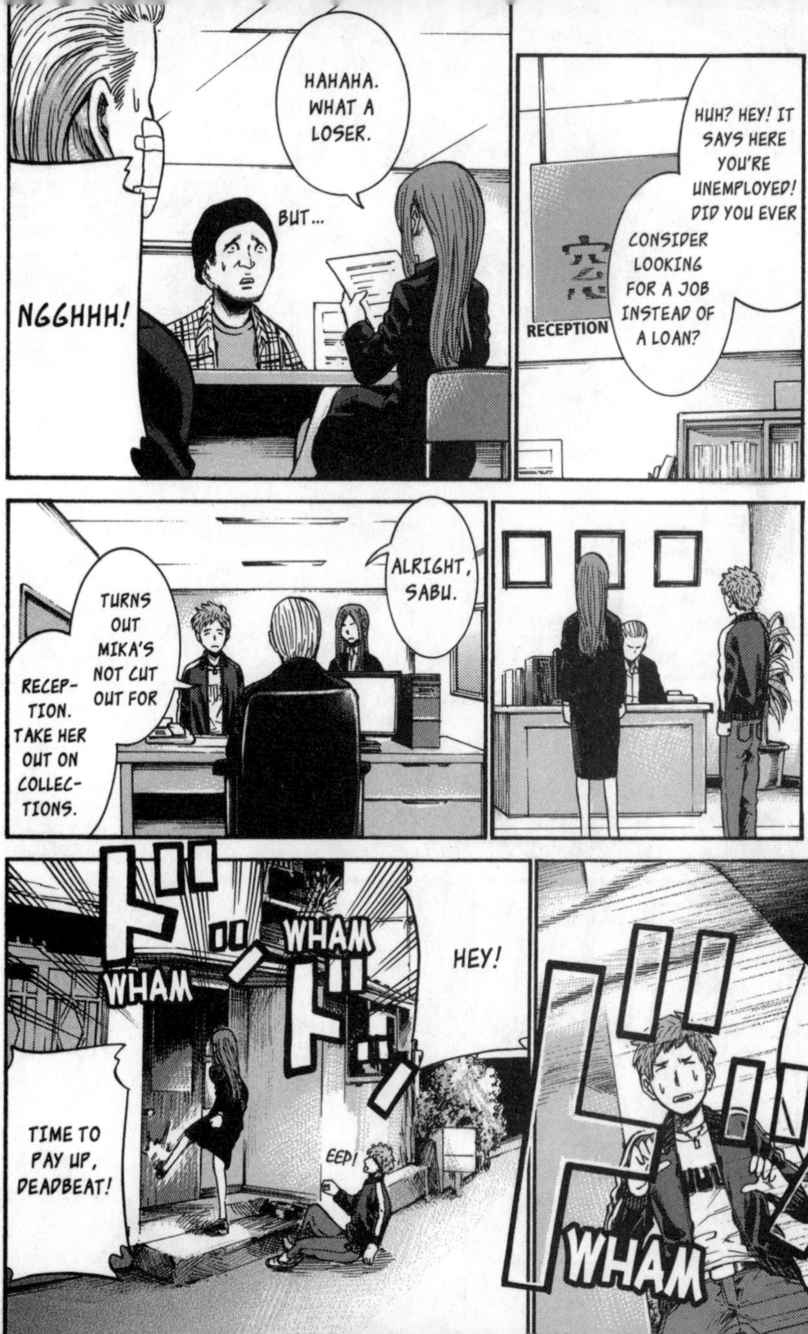

HUH? HEY! IT SAYS HERE YOU'RE UNEMPLOYED! DID YOU EVER CONSIDER LOOKING FOR A JOB INSTEAD OF A LOAN?
RECEPTION
HAHAHA. WHAT A LOSER.
BUT...
NGGHHH!
ALRIGHT, SABU.
TURNS OUT MIKA'S NOT CUT OUT FOR RECEPTION. TAKE HER OUT ON COLLECTIONS.
ドッ
WHAM
HEY!
ドッ
WHAM
ドッ
WHAM
TIME TO PAY UP, DEADBEAT!
EEP!

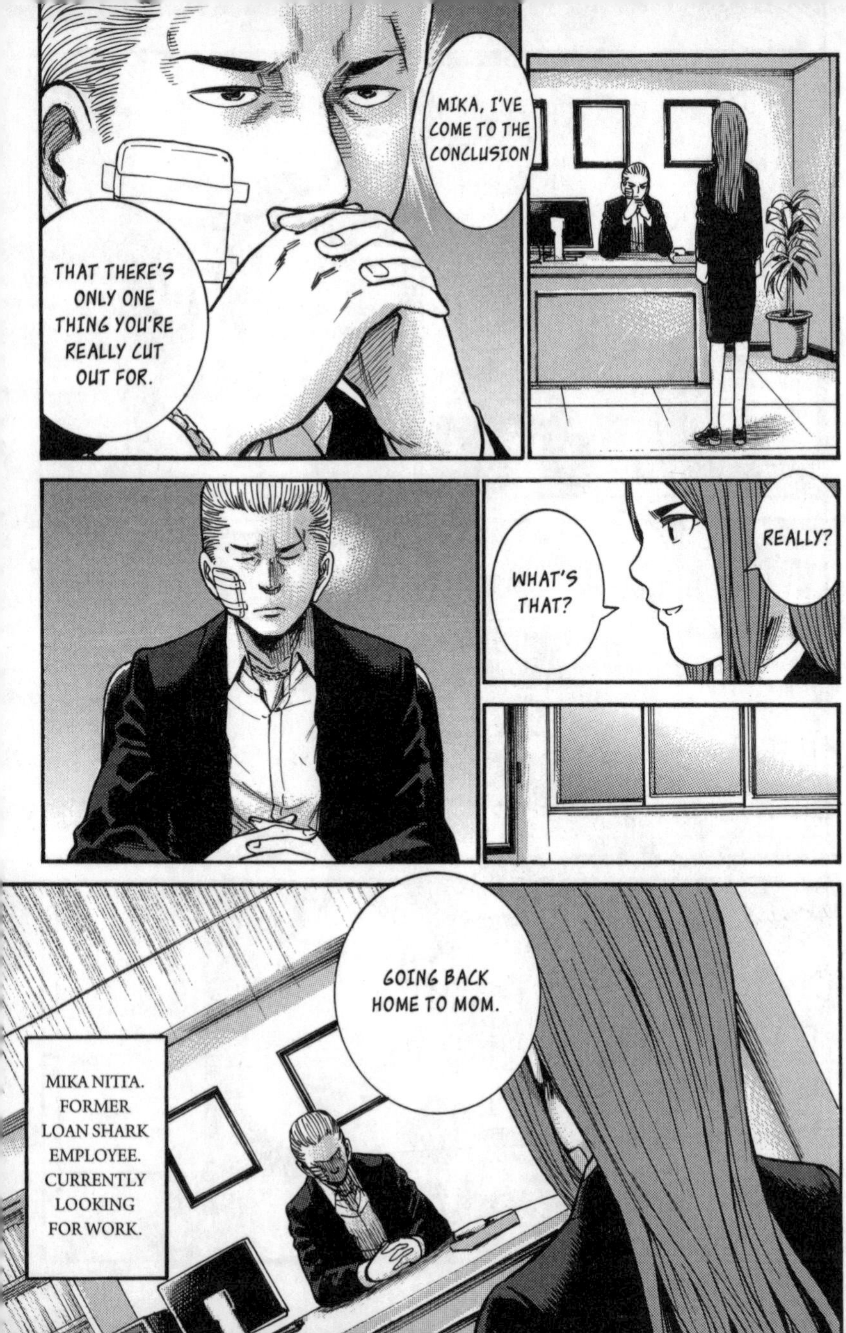
MIKA, I'VE COME TO THE CONCLUSION
THAT THERE'S ONLY ONE THING YOU'RE REALLY CUT OUT FOR.
REALLY?
WHAT'S THAT?
GOING BACK HOME TO MOM.
MIKA NITTA. FORMER LOAN SHARK EMPLOYEE. CURRENTLY LOOKING FOR WORK.

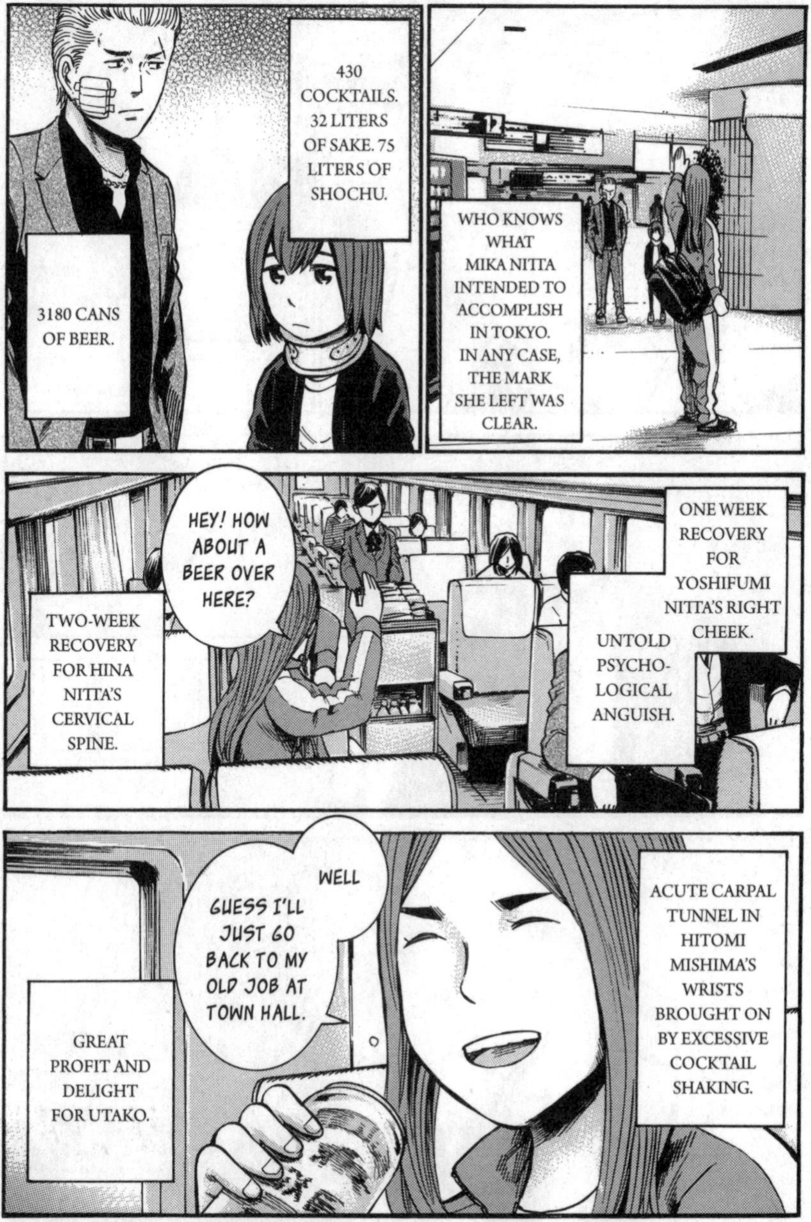
WHO KNOWS WHAT MIKA NITTA INTENDED TO ACCOMPLISH IN TOKYO. IN ANY CASE, THE MARK SHE LEFT WAS CLEAR.
430 COCKTAILS. 32 LITERS OF SAKE. 75 LITERS OF SHOCHU.
3180 CANS OF BEER.
ONE WEEK RECOVERY FOR YOSHIFUMI NITTA'S RIGHT CHEEK.
UNTOLD PSYCHO-LOGICAL ANGUISH.
HEY! HOW ABOUT A BEER OVER HERE?
TWO-WEEK RECOVERY FOR HINA NITTA'S CERVICAL SPINE.
ACUTE CARPAL TUNNEL IN HITOMI MISHIMA'S WRISTS BROUGHT ON BY EXCESSIVE COCKTAIL SHAKING.
WELL
GUESS I'LL JUST GO BACK TO MY OLD JOB AT TOWN HALL.
GREAT PROFIT AND DELIGHT FOR UTAKO.

CHAPTER 20 END

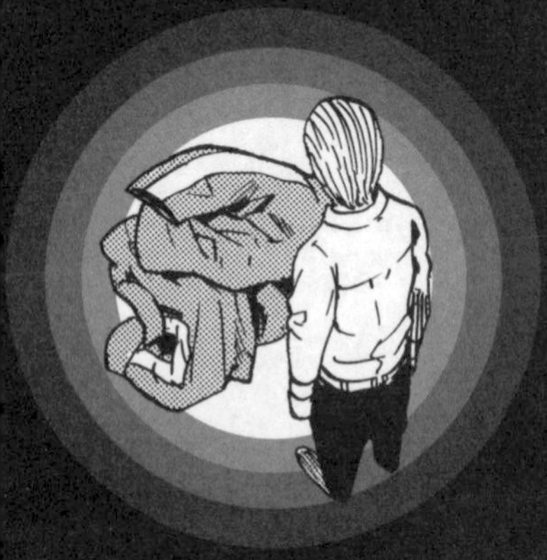

CHAPTER 21
A STUDY ON THE LIMITS AND ADVERSE EFFECTS OF EDUCATION

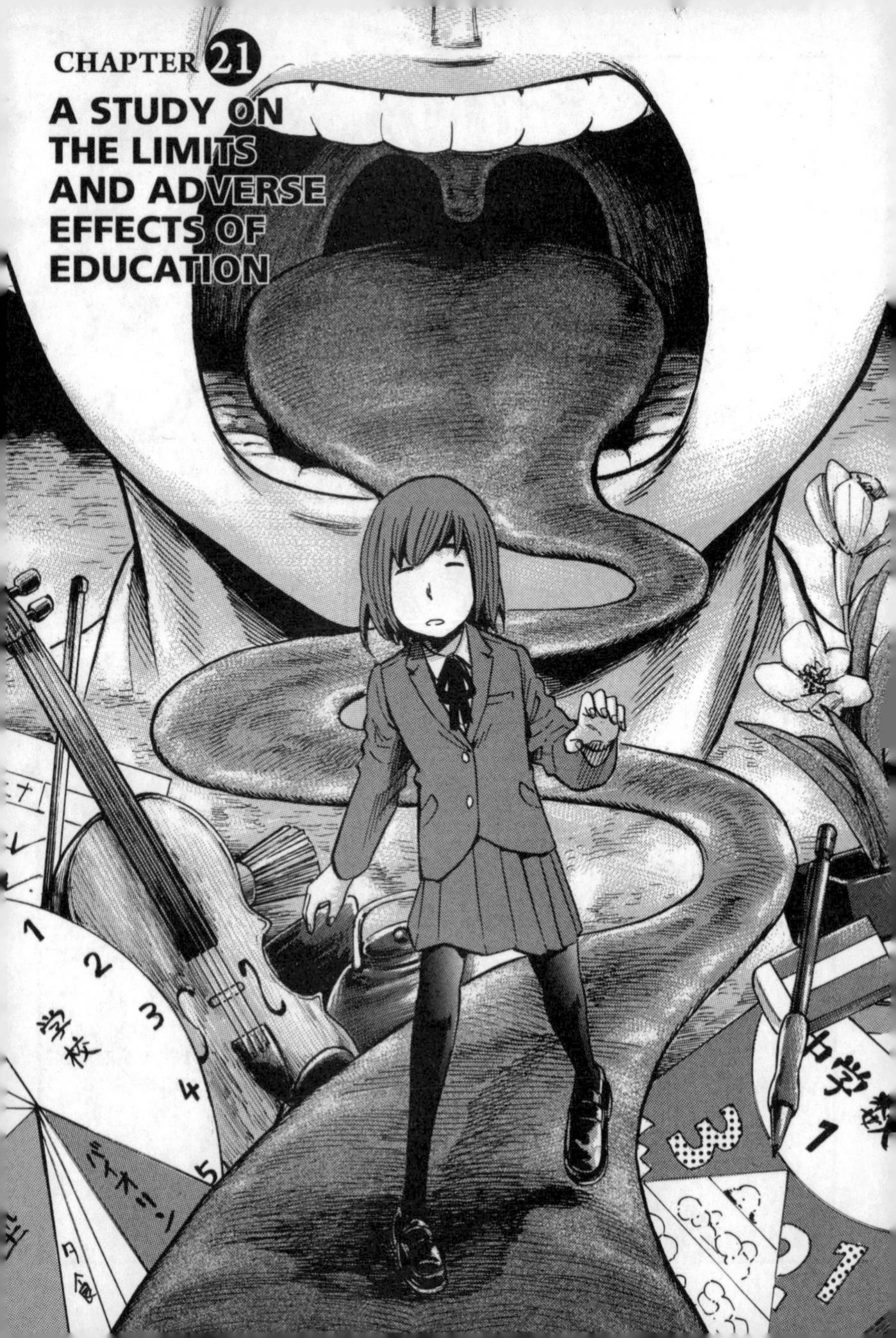

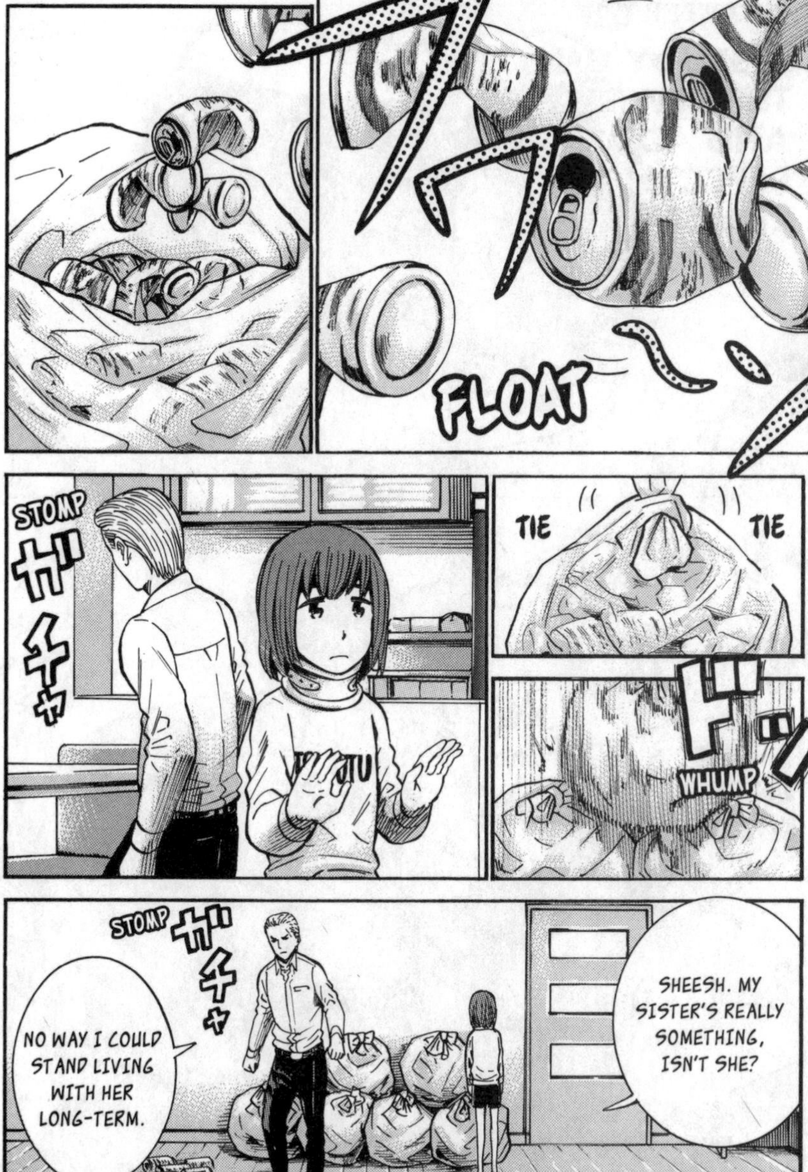
FLOAT
TIE
TIE
ドッ
WHUMP
STOMP
ガチャ
SHEESH. MY SISTER'S REALLY SOMETHING, ISN'T SHE?
STOMP
ガチャ
NO WAY I COULD STAND LIVING WITH HER LONG-TERM.

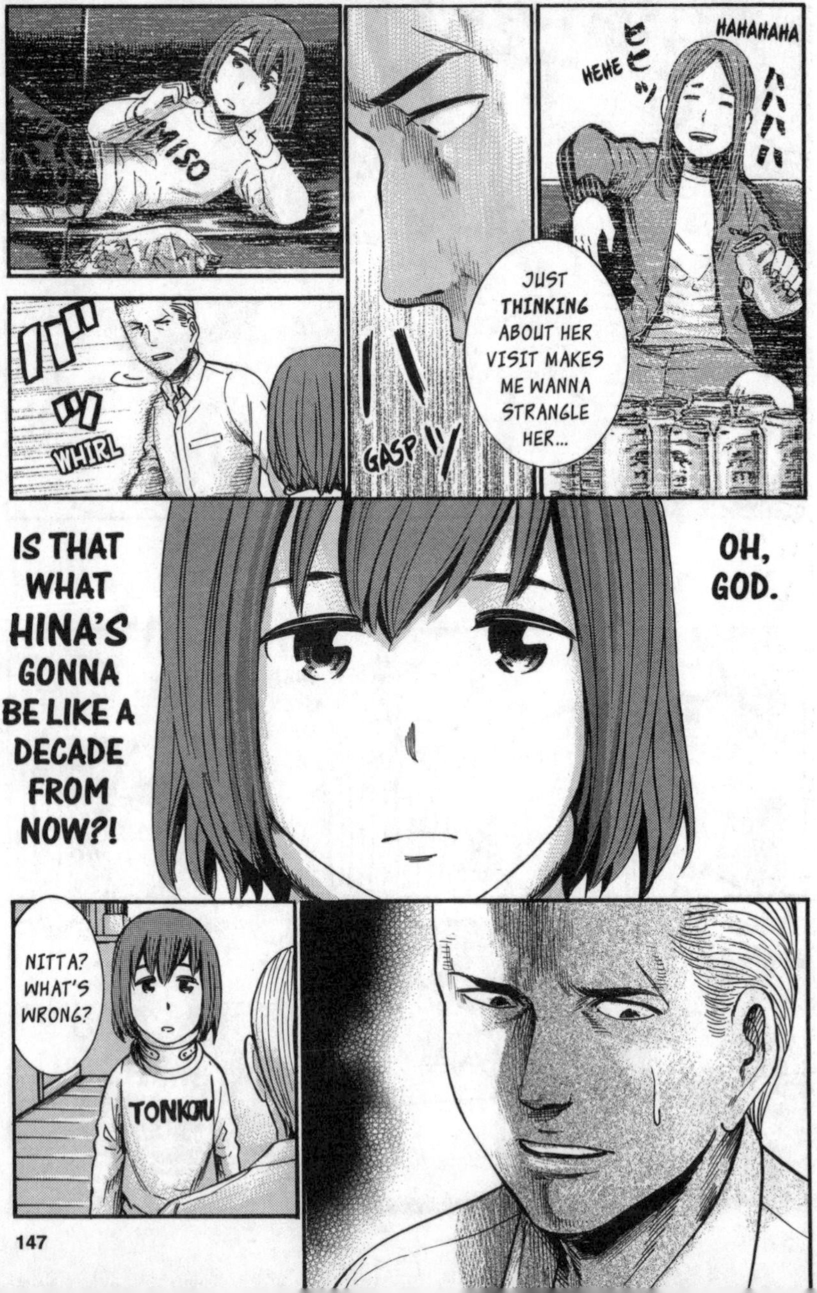
HEHE
ヒヒッ
HAHAHAHA
ハハハハ
JUST THINKING ABOUT HER VISIT MAKES ME WANNA STRANGLE HER...
GASP
MISO
WHIRL
OH, GOD.
IS THAT WHAT HINA'S GONNA BE LIKE A DECADE FROM NOW?!
NITTA? WHAT'S WRONG?

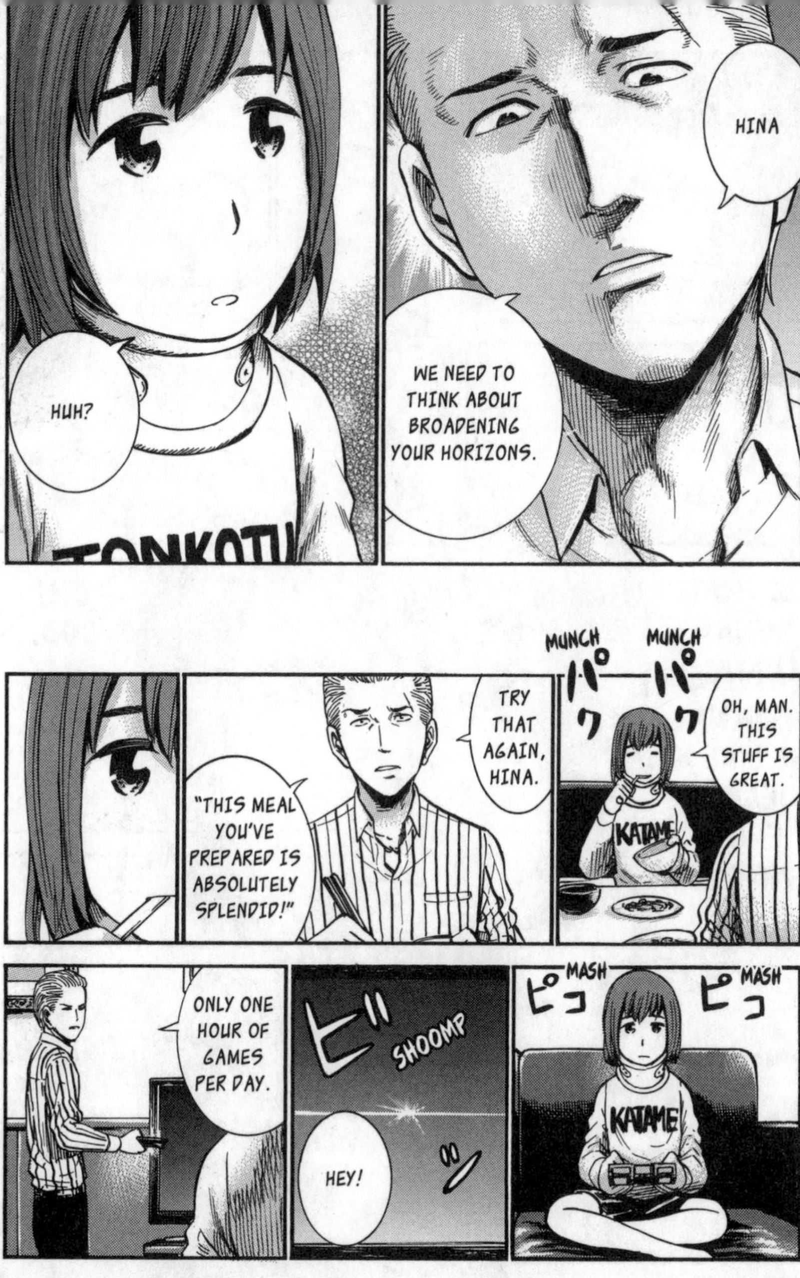
HINA
WE NEED TO THINK ABOUT BROADENING YOUR HORIZONS.
HUH?
MUNCH
パク
MUNCH
パク
OH, MAN. THIS STUFF IS GREAT.
KATAME
TRY THAT AGAIN, HINA.
"THIS MEAL YOU'VE PREPARED IS ABSOLUTELY SPLENDID!"
ピコ
MASH
ピコ
MASH
KATAME
ピッ
SHOOMP
HEY!
ONLY ONE HOUR OF GAMES PER DAY.

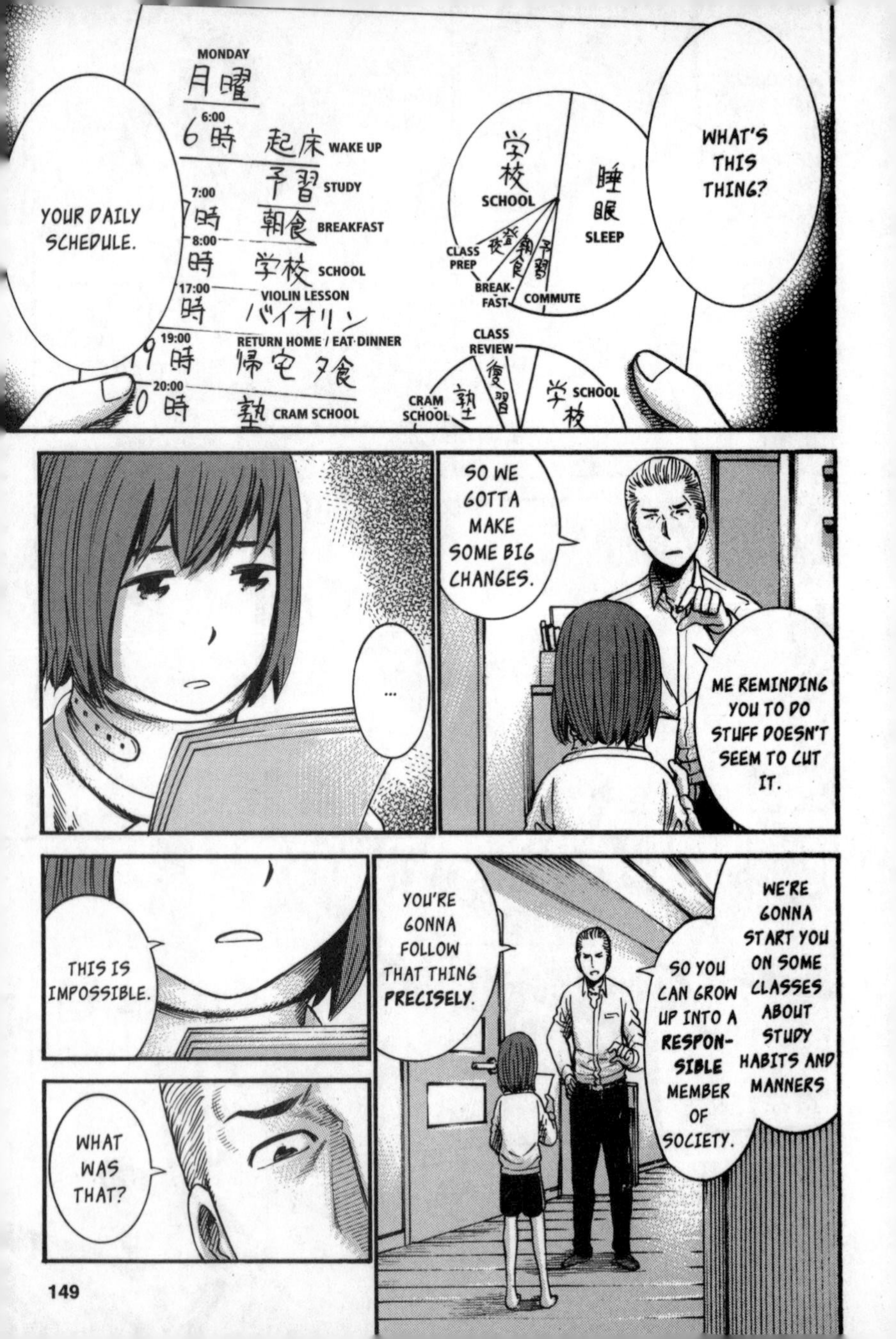
WHAT'S THIS THING?
YOUR DAILY SCHEDULE.
MONDAY
月曜
6:00 6時 起床 WAKE UP
予習 STUDY
7:00 時 朝食 BREAKFAST
8:00 時 学校 SCHOOL
17:00 時 VIOLIN LESSON バイオリン
19:00 19時 RETURN HOME / EAT·DINNER 帰宅 夕食
20:00 時 塾 CRAM SCHOOL
学校 SCHOOL
睡眠 SLEEP
CLASS PREP
BREAK-FAST
COMMUTE
CLASS REVIEW 復習
CRAM SCHOOL 塾
学校 SCHOOL
ME REMINDING YOU TO DO STUFF DOESN'T SEEM TO CUT IT.
SO WE GOTTA MAKE SOME BIG CHANGES.
...
WE'RE GONNA START YOU ON SOME CLASSES ABOUT STUDY HABITS AND MANNERS
SO YOU CAN GROW UP INTO A RESPONSIBLE MEMBER OF SOCIETY.
YOU'RE GONNA FOLLOW THAT THING PRECISELY.
THIS IS IMPOSSIBLE.
WHAT WAS THAT?

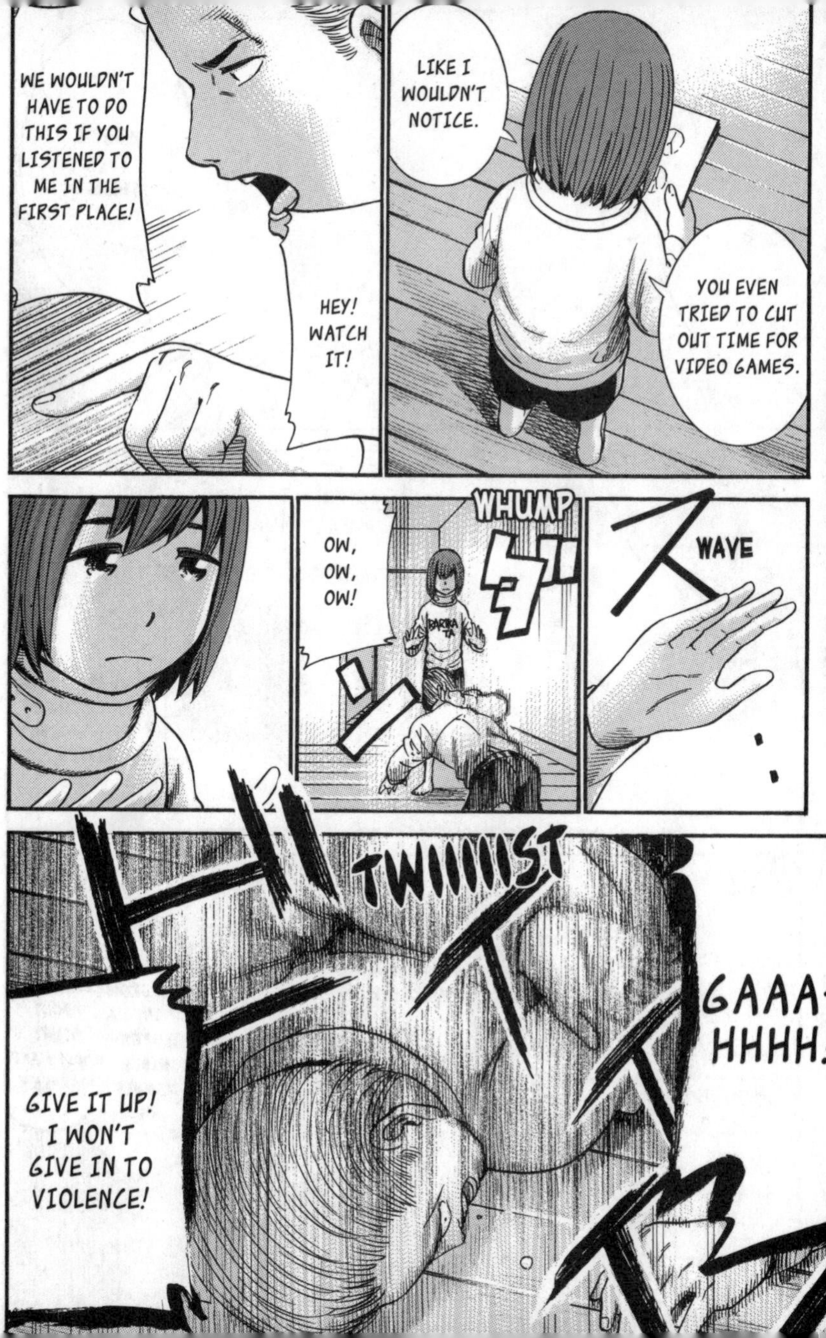
LIKE I WOULDN'T NOTICE.
YOU EVEN TRIED TO CUT OUT TIME FOR VIDEO GAMES.
WE WOULDN'T HAVE TO DO THIS IF YOU LISTENED TO ME IN THE FIRST PLACE!
HEY! WATCH IT!
WAVE
WHUMP
OW, OW, OW!
TWIIIIIST
GAAA-HHHH!
GIVE IT UP! I WON'T GIVE IN TO VIOLENCE!

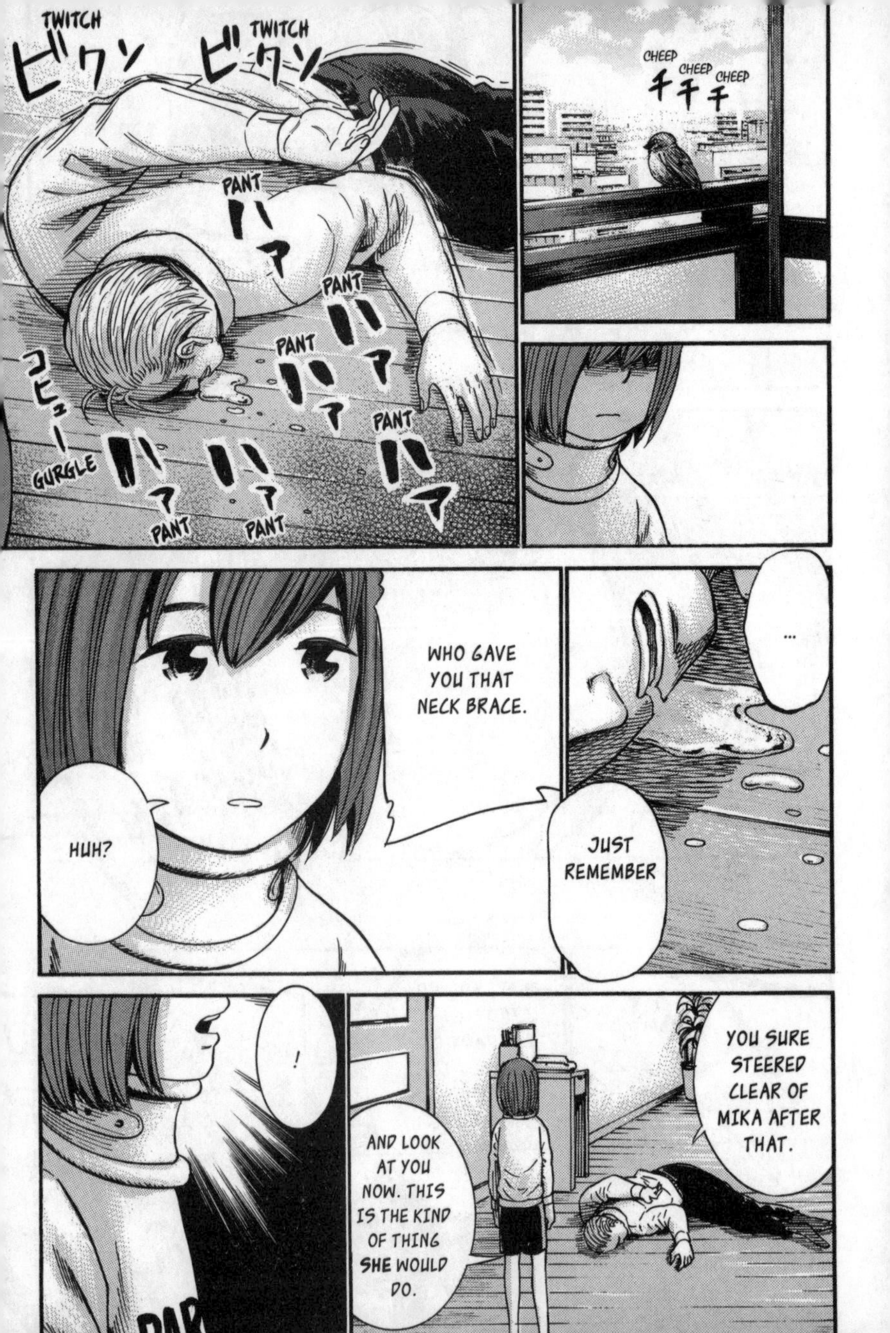
CHEEP CHEEP CHEEP
チチチ
TWITCH
ビクッ
TWITCH
ビクッ
PANT
ハァ
PANT
ハァ
PANT
ハァ
PANT
ハァ
ハァ
PANT
ハァ
PANT
コヒュー
GURGLE
...
JUST REMEMBER
WHO GAVE YOU THAT NECK BRACE.
HUH?
YOU SURE STEERED CLEAR OF MIKA AFTER THAT.
AND LOOK AT YOU NOW. THIS IS THE KIND OF THING SHE WOULD DO.
!

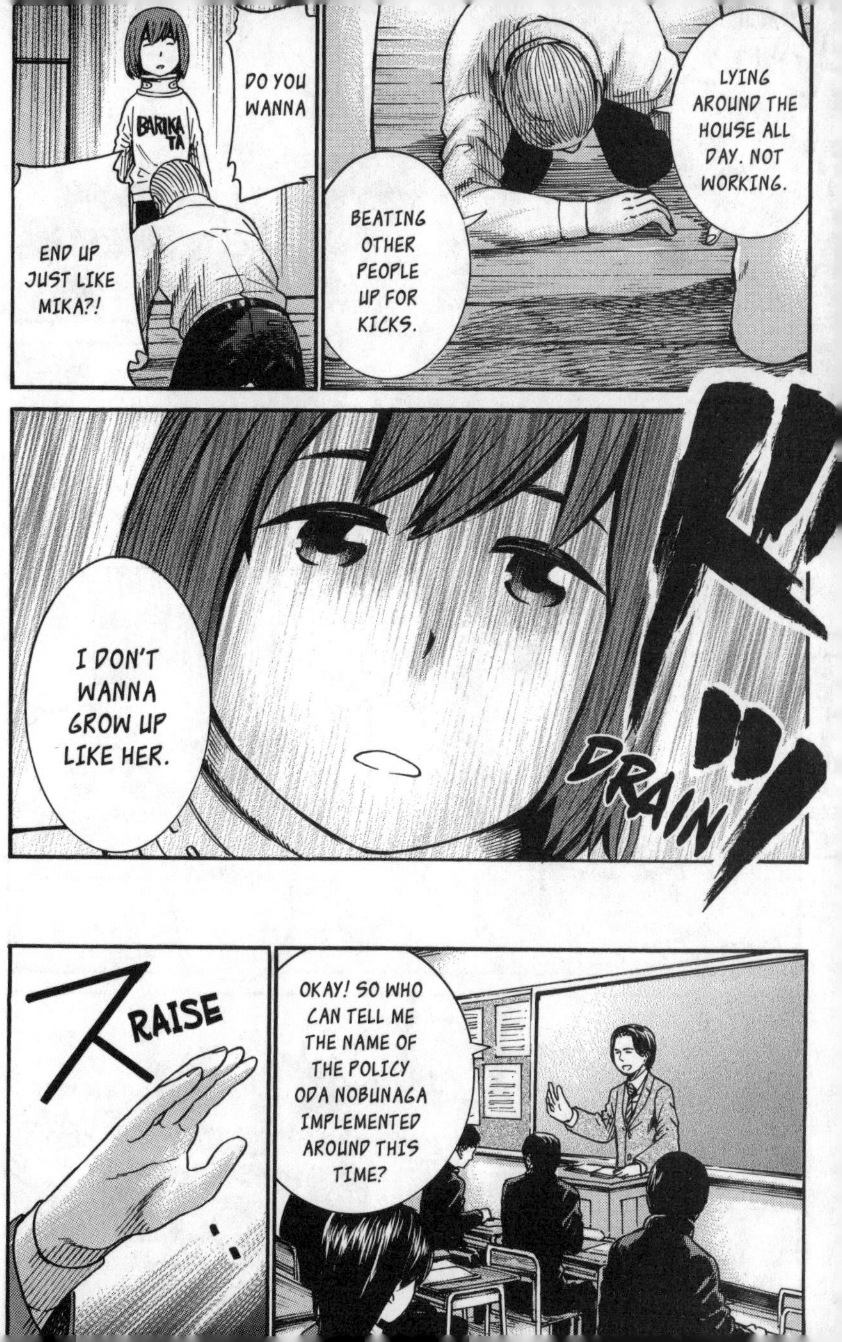
LYING AROUND THE HOUSE ALL DAY. NOT WORKING.
BEATING OTHER PEOPLE UP FOR KICKS.
DO YOU WANNA
BARIKA TA
END UP JUST LIKE MIKA?!
DRAIN
I DON'T WANNA GROW UP LIKE HER.
OKAY! SO WHO CAN TELL ME THE NAME OF THE POLICY ODA NOBUNAGA IMPLEMENTED AROUND THIS TIME?
RAISE

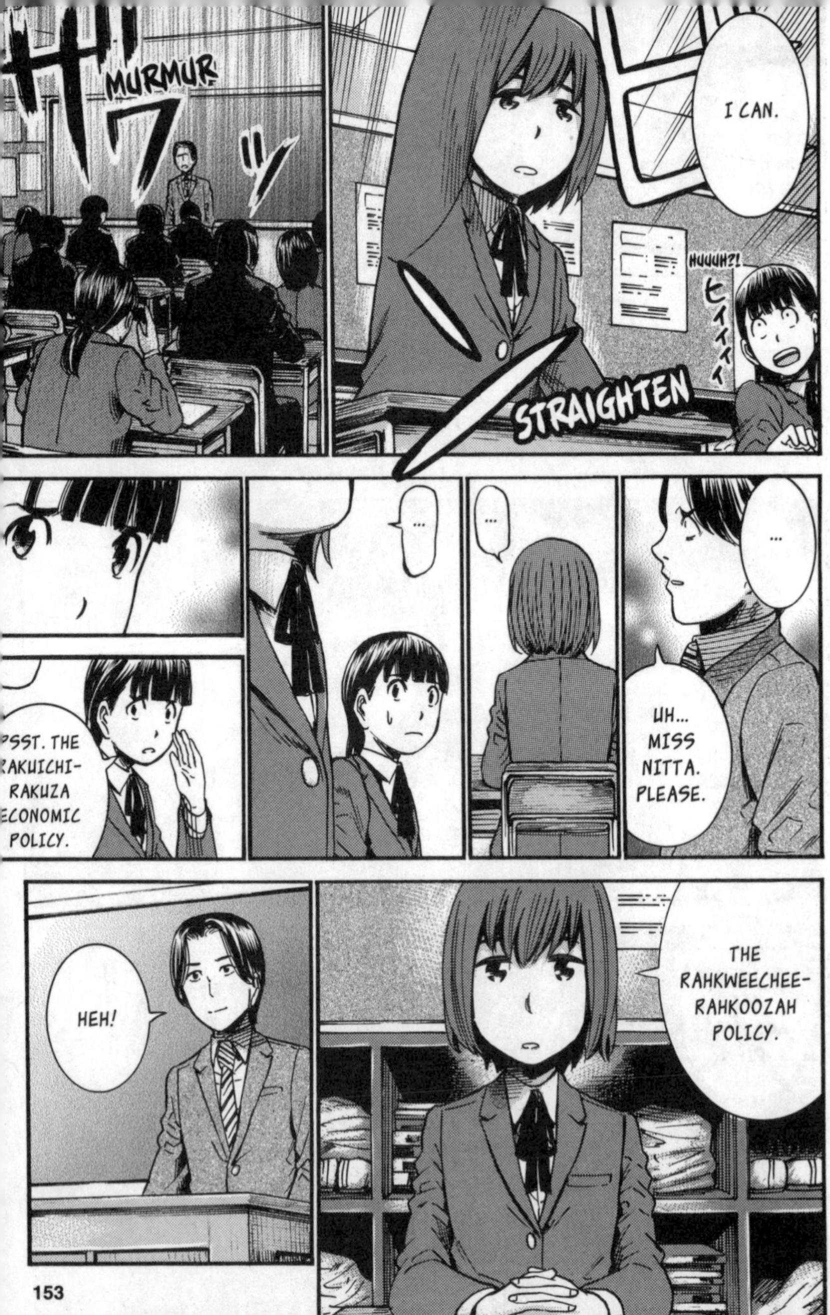
I CAN.
HUUUH?!
ヒィィィ
STRAIGHTEN
MURMUR
...
UH... MISS NITTA. PLEASE.
...
...
PSST. THE RAKUICHI-RAKUZA ECONOMIC POLICY.
THE RAHKWEECHEE-RAHKOOZAH POLICY.
HEH!

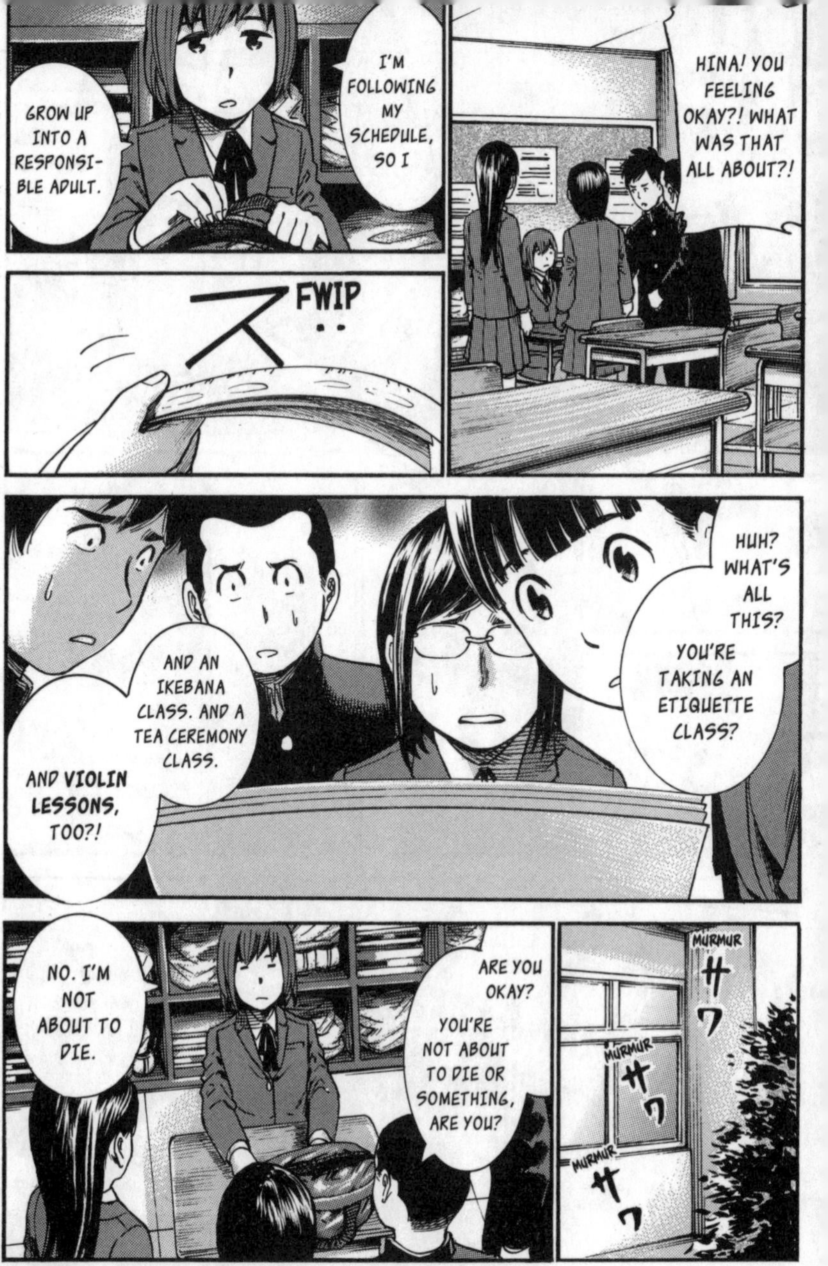
HINA! YOU FEELING OKAY?! WHAT WAS THAT ALL ABOUT?!
I'M FOLLOWING MY SCHEDULE, SO I
GROW UP INTO A RESPONSI-BLE ADULT.
FWIP
HUH? WHAT'S ALL THIS?
YOU'RE TAKING AN ETIQUETTE CLASS?
AND AN IKEBANA CLASS. AND A TEA CEREMONY CLASS.
AND VIOLIN LESSONS, TOO?!
MURMUR
サワ
MURMUR
サワ
MURMUR
サワ
ARE YOU OKAY?
YOU'RE NOT ABOUT TO DIE OR SOMETHING, ARE YOU?
NO. I'M NOT ABOUT TO DIE.

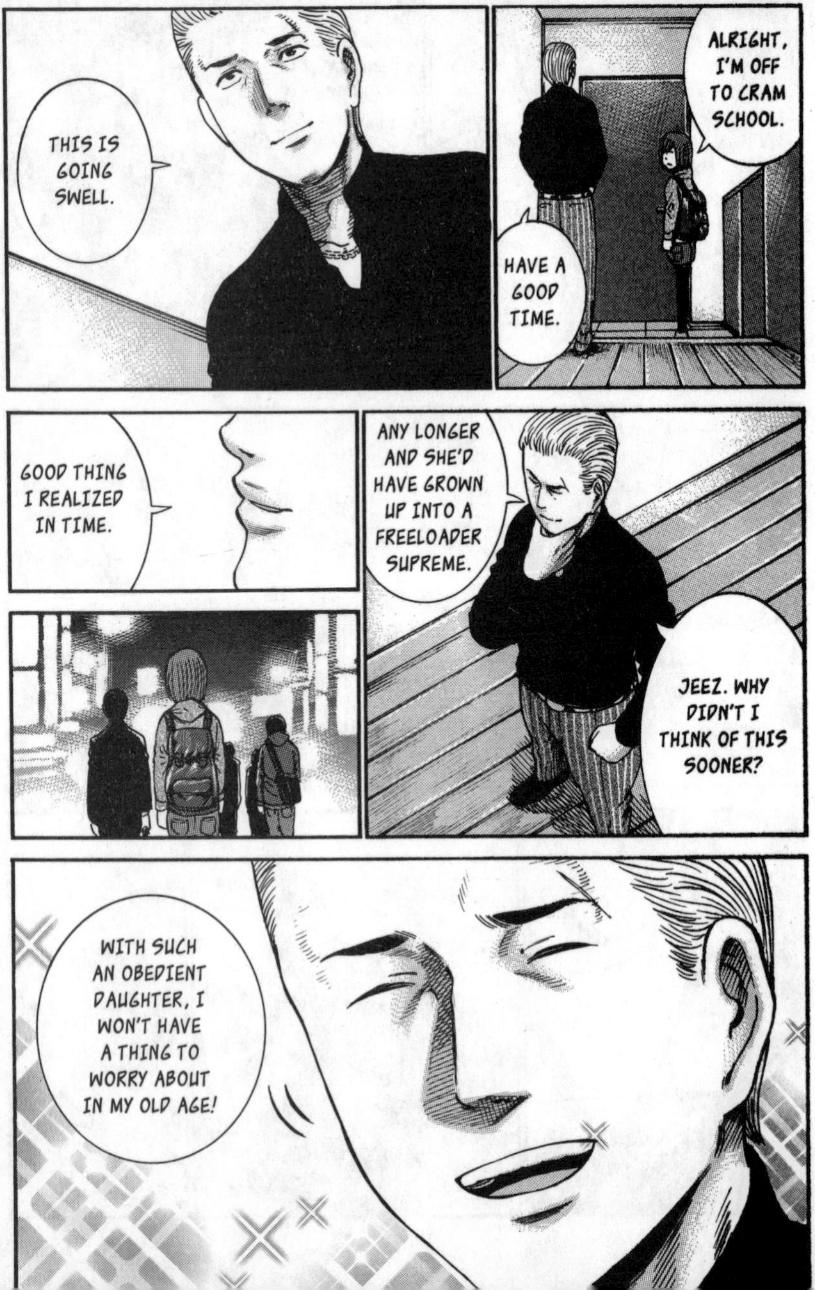
ALRIGHT, I'M OFF TO CRAM SCHOOL.
HAVE A GOOD TIME.
THIS IS GOING SWELL.
ANY LONGER AND SHE'D HAVE GROWN UP INTO A FREELOADER SUPREME.
JEEZ. WHY DIDN'T I THINK OF THIS SOONER?
GOOD THING I REALIZED IN TIME.
WITH SUCH AN OBEDIENT DAUGHTER, I WON'T HAVE A THING TO WORRY ABOUT IN MY OLD AGE!

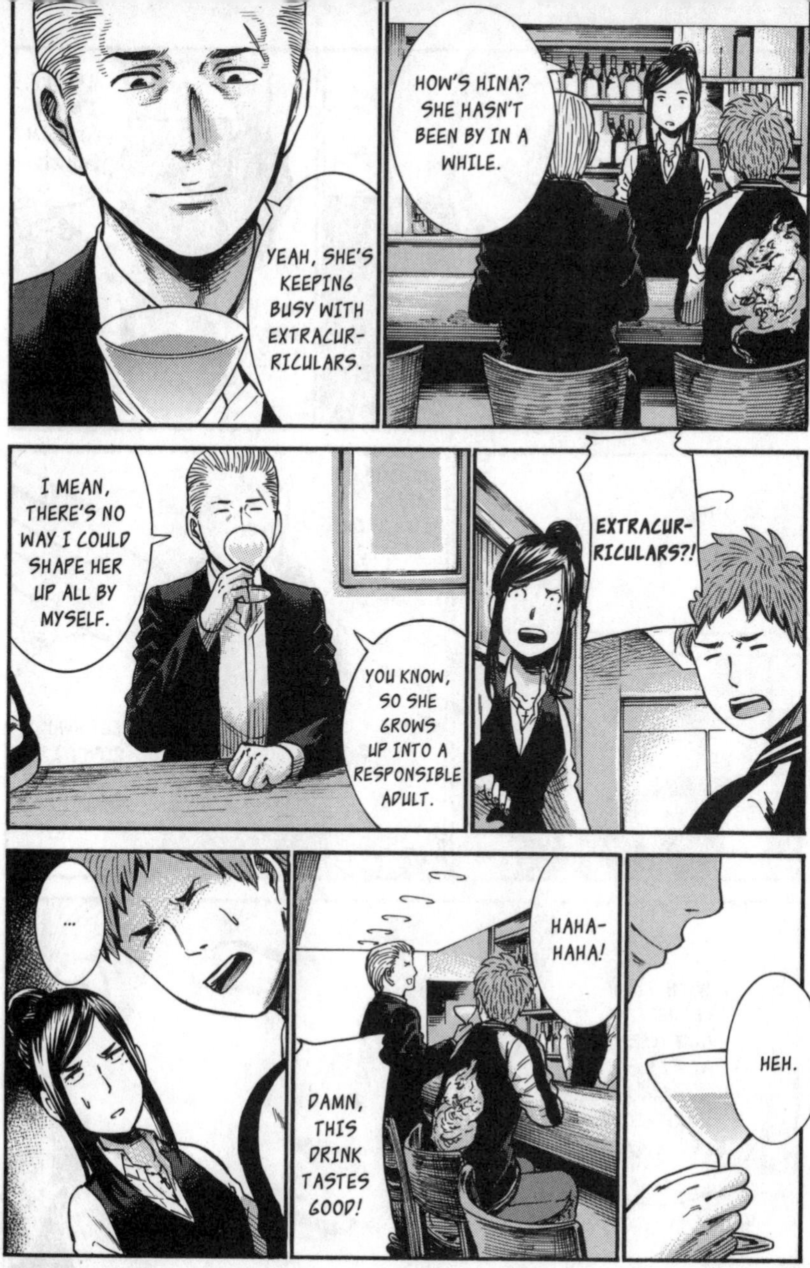
HOW'S HINA? SHE HASN'T BEEN BY IN A WHILE.
YEAH, SHE'S KEEPING BUSY WITH EXTRACUR-RICULARS.
EXTRACUR-RICULARS?!
I MEAN, THERE'S NO WAY I COULD SHAPE HER UP ALL BY MYSELF.
YOU KNOW, SO SHE GROWS UP INTO A RESPONSIBLE ADULT.
HEH.
HAHA-HAHA!
DAMN, THIS DRINK TASTES GOOD!
...

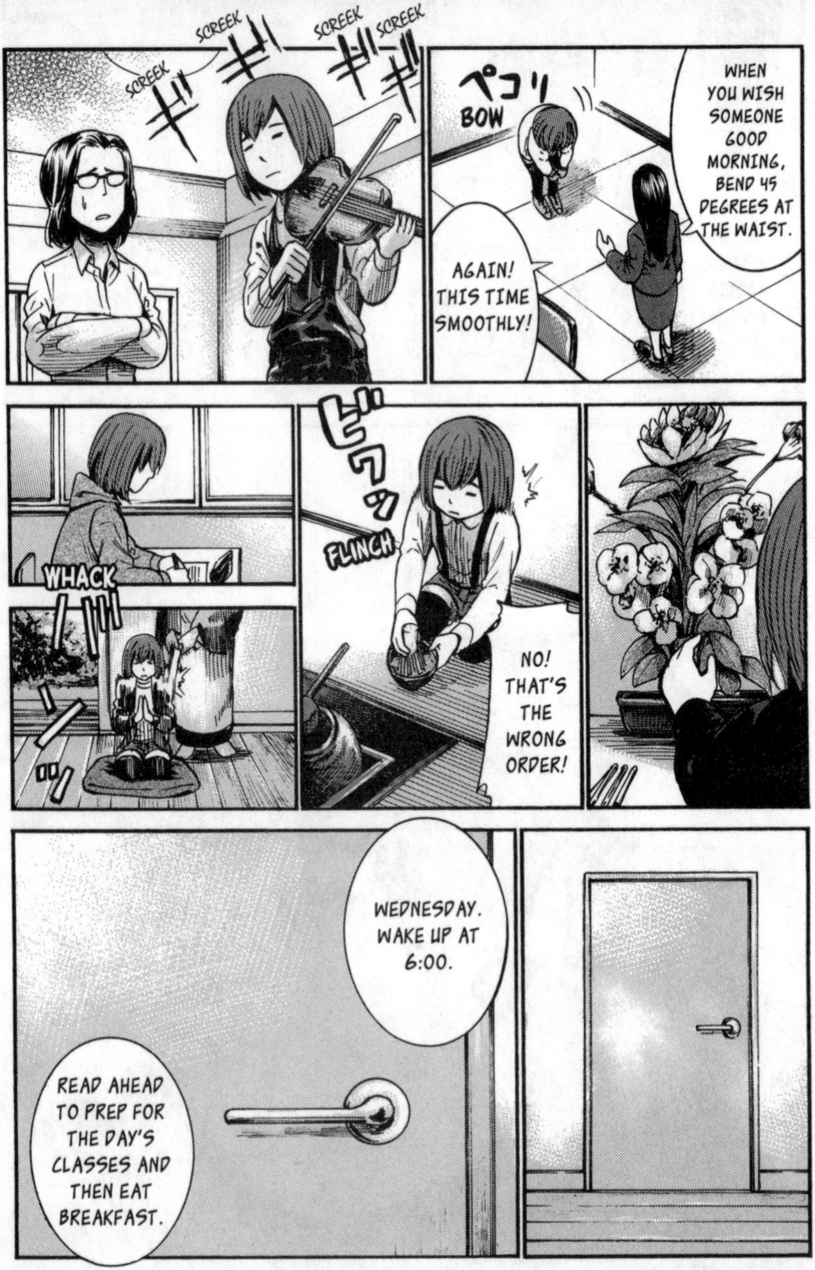
WHEN YOU WISH SOMEONE GOOD MORNING, BEND 45 DEGREES AT THE WAIST.
ペコリ
BOW
AGAIN! THIS TIME SMOOTHLY!
SCREEK
SCREEK
SCREEK
SCREEK
ビクッ
FLINCH
NO! THAT'S THE WRONG ORDER!
WHACK
WEDNESDAY. WAKE UP AT 6:00.
READ AHEAD TO PREP FOR THE DAY'S CLASSES AND THEN EAT BREAKFAST.

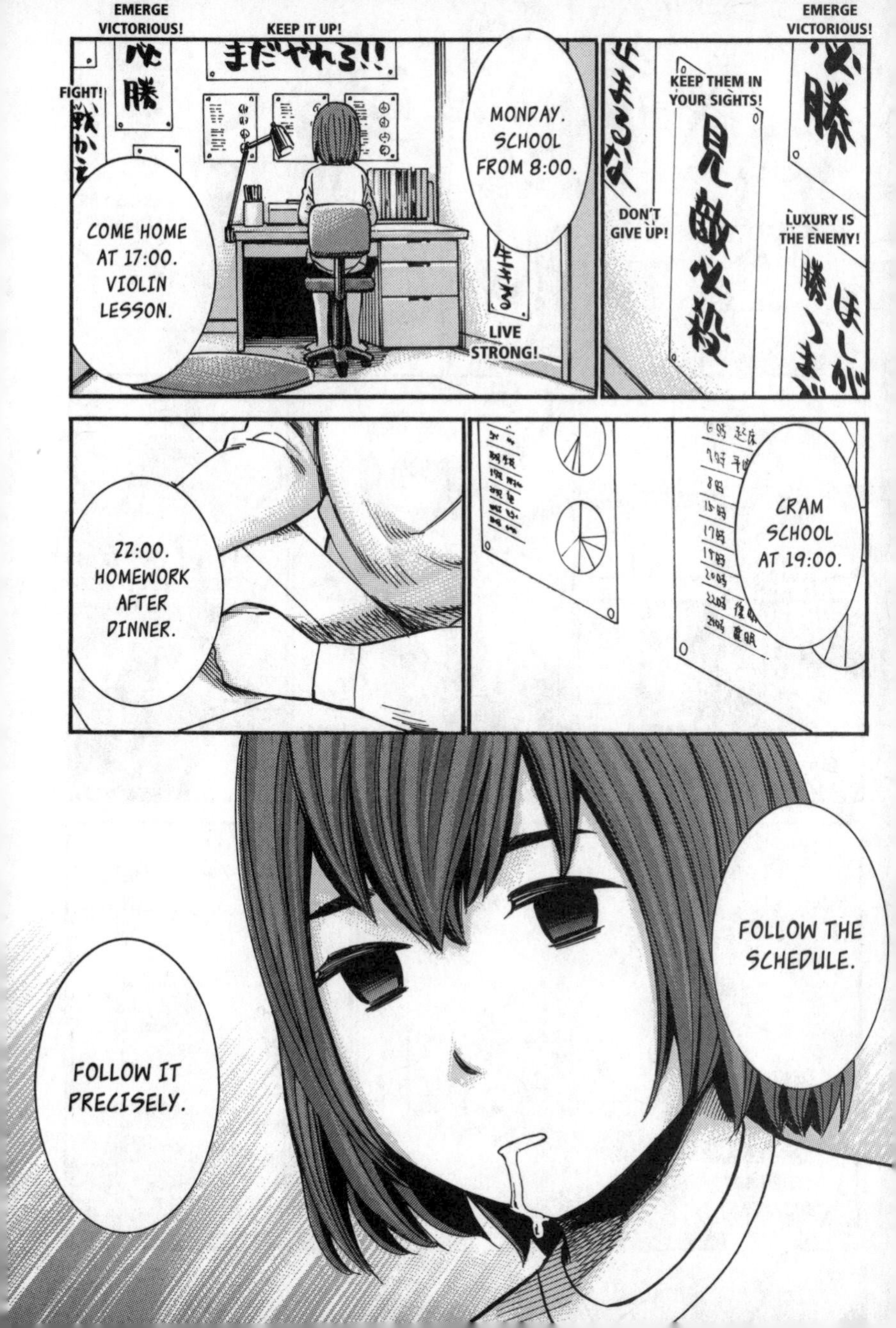
EMERGE VICTORIOUS!
KEEP THEM IN YOUR SIGHTS!
LUXURY IS THE ENEMY!
DON'T GIVE UP!
MONDAY. SCHOOL FROM 8:00.
LIVE STRONG!
KEEP IT UP!
EMERGE VICTORIOUS!
FIGHT!
COME HOME AT 17:00. VIOLIN LESSON.
CRAM SCHOOL AT 19:00.
22:00. HOMEWORK AFTER DINNER.
FOLLOW THE SCHEDULE.
FOLLOW IT PRECISELY.

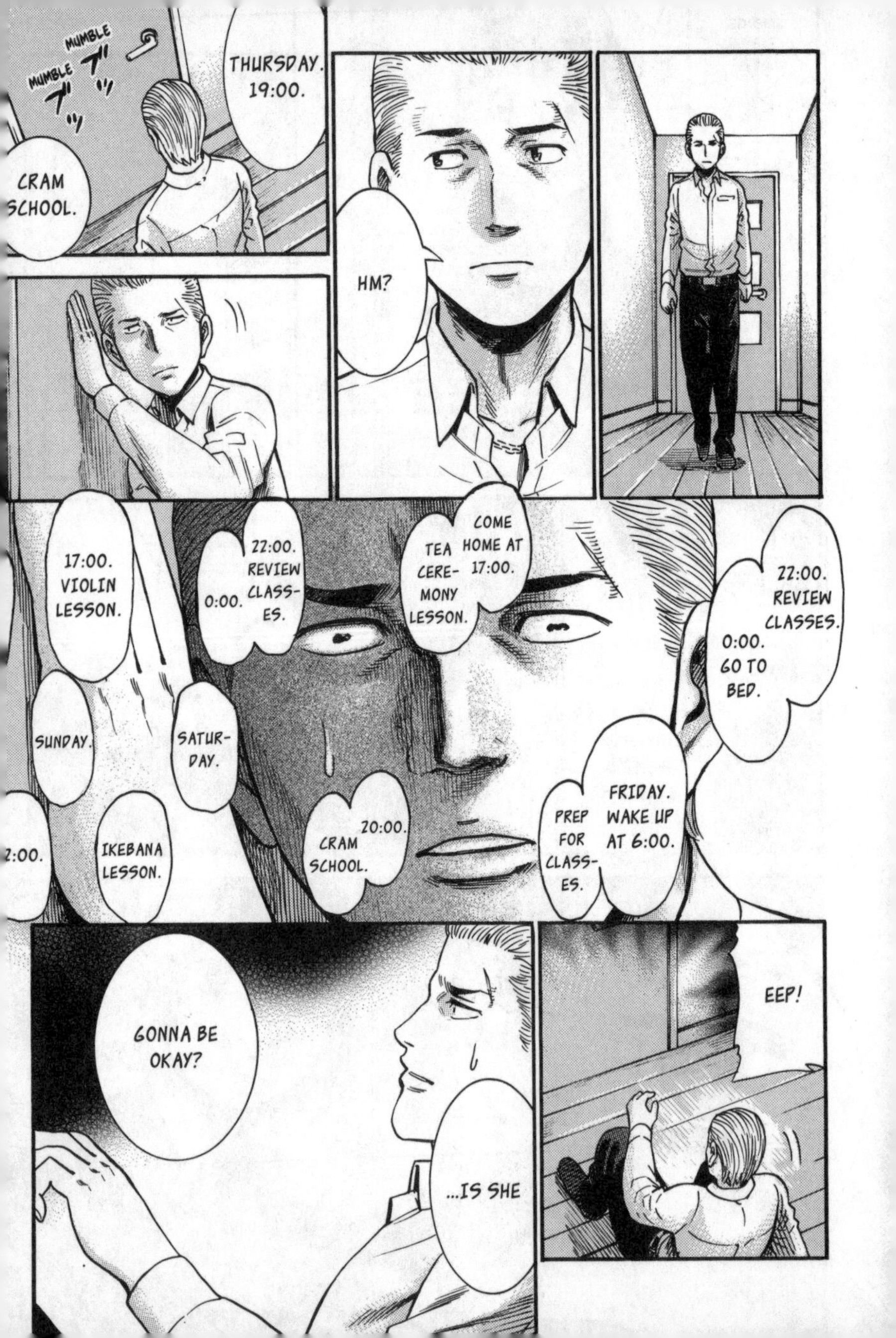
HM?
THURSDAY. 19:00.
CRAM SCHOOL.
MUMBLE
MUMBLE
22:00. REVIEW CLASSES.
0:00. GO TO BED.
FRIDAY. WAKE UP AT 6:00.
PREP FOR CLASSES.
COME HOME AT 17:00.
TEA CEREMONY LESSON.
20:00. CRAM SCHOOL.
22:00. REVIEW CLASSES.
0:00.
SATURDAY.
17:00. VIOLIN LESSON.
SUNDAY.
IKEBANA LESSON.
2:00.
EEP!
...IS SHE
GONNA BE OKAY?

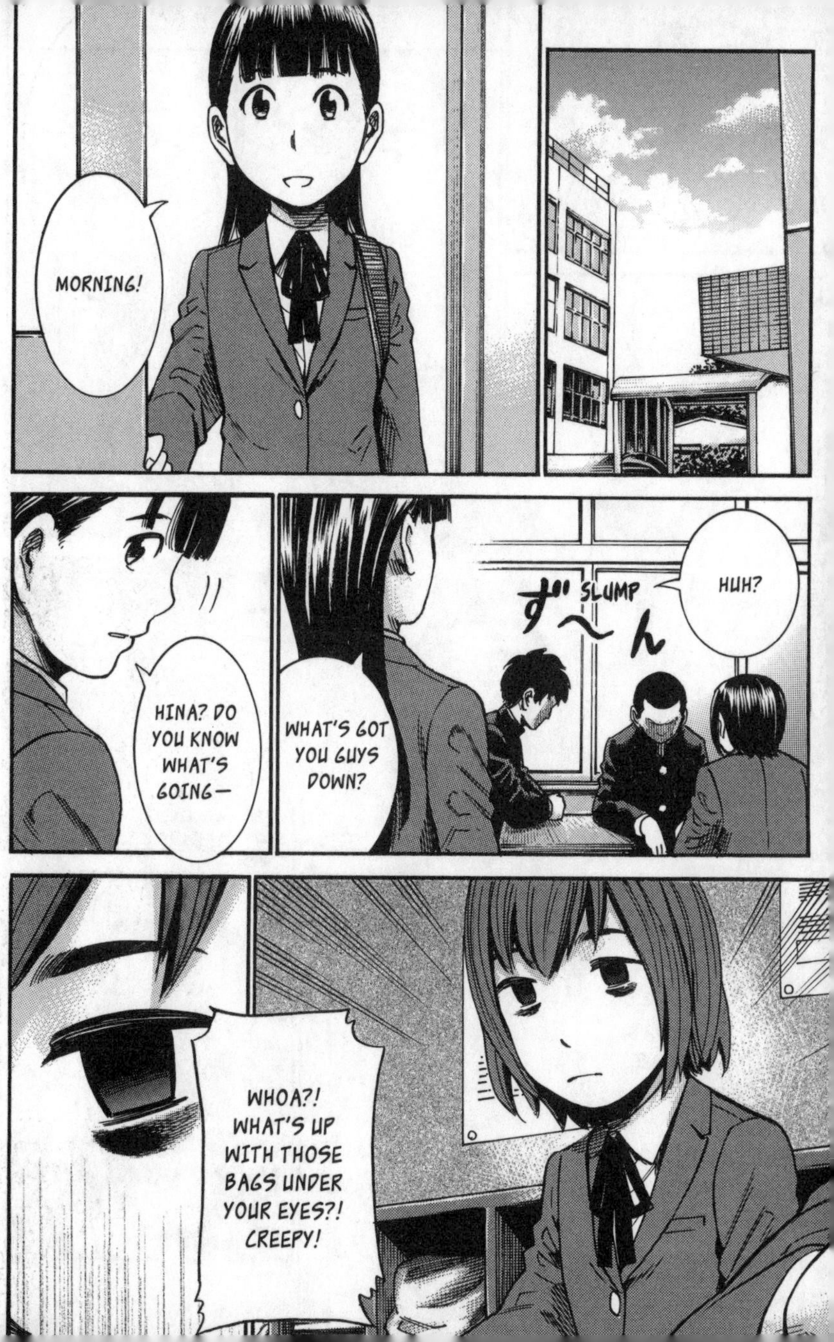
MORNING!
HUH?
ず〜ん SLUMP
WHAT'S GOT YOU GUYS DOWN?
HINA? DO YOU KNOW WHAT'S GOING—
WHOA?! WHAT'S UP WITH THOSE BAGS UNDER YOUR EYES?! CREEPY!

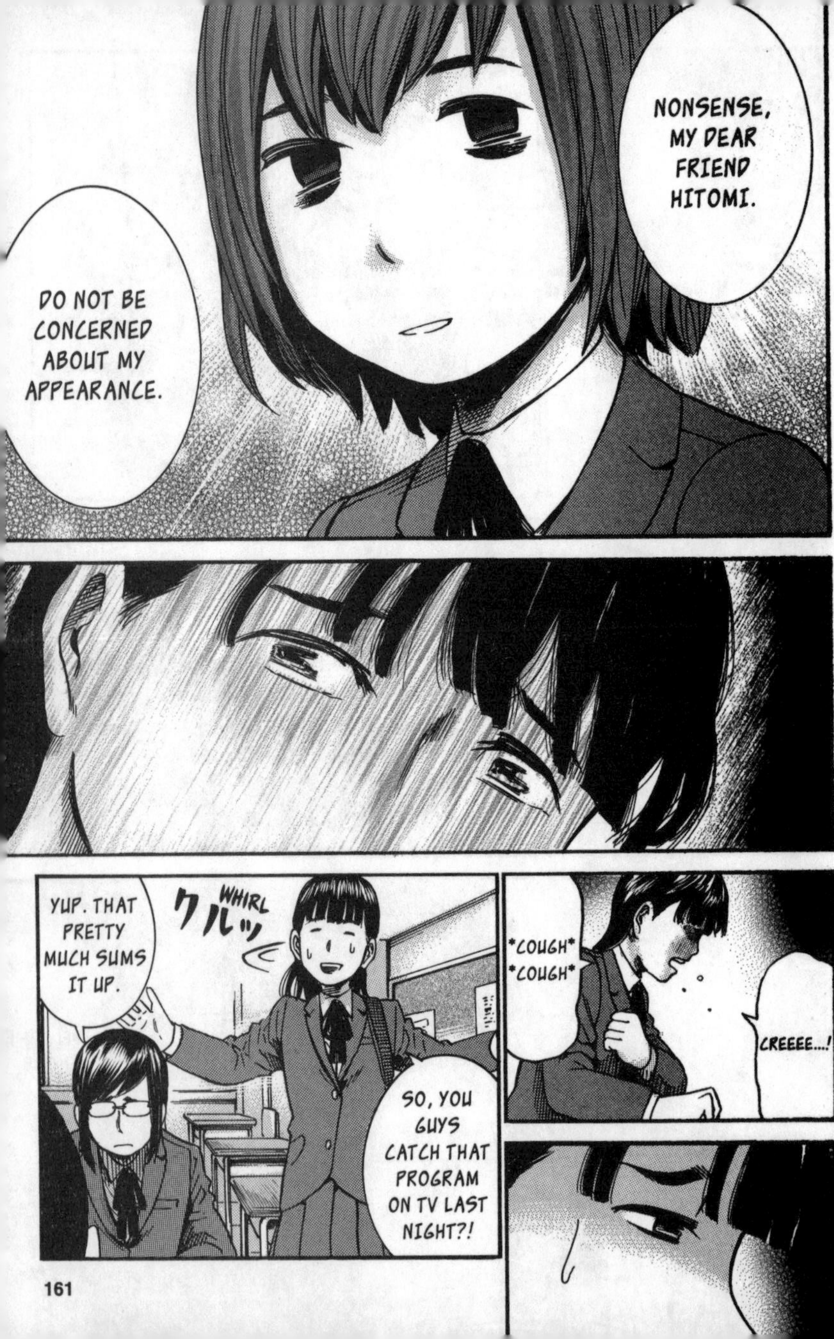
NONSENSE, MY DEAR FRIEND HITOMI.
DO NOT BE CONCERNED ABOUT MY APPEARANCE.
COUGH *COUGH*
CREEEE...!
クルッ
WHIRL
YUP. THAT PRETTY MUCH SUMS IT UP.
SO, YOU GUYS CATCH THAT PROGRAM ON TV LAST NIGHT?!

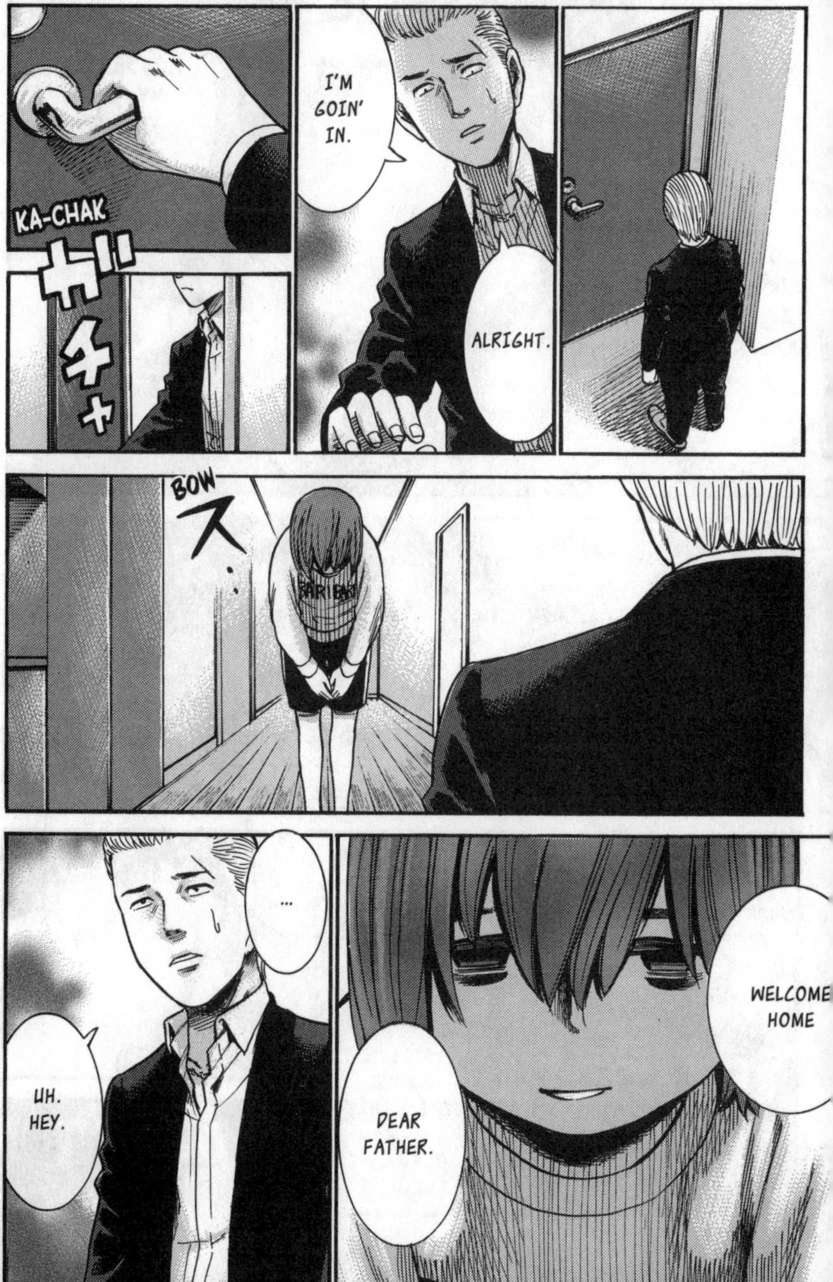
I'M GOIN' IN.
ALRIGHT.
KA-CHAK
ガチャ
BOW
ス
WELCOME HOME
DEAR FATHER.
...
UH. HEY.

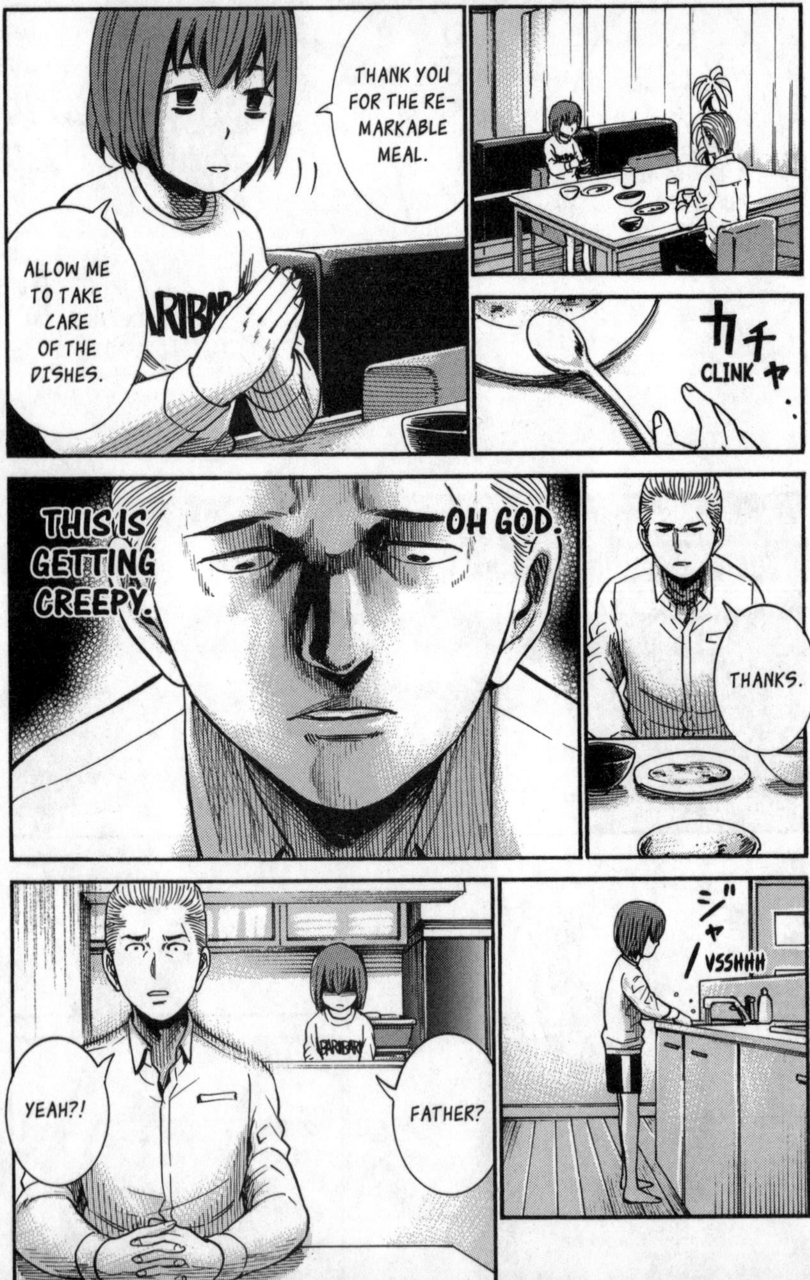
カチャ
CLINK
THANK YOU FOR THE RE-MARKABLE MEAL.
ALLOW ME TO TAKE CARE OF THE DISHES.
THANKS.
OH GOD.
THIS IS GETTING CREEPY.
ジャ
VSSHHH
FATHER?
YEAH?!

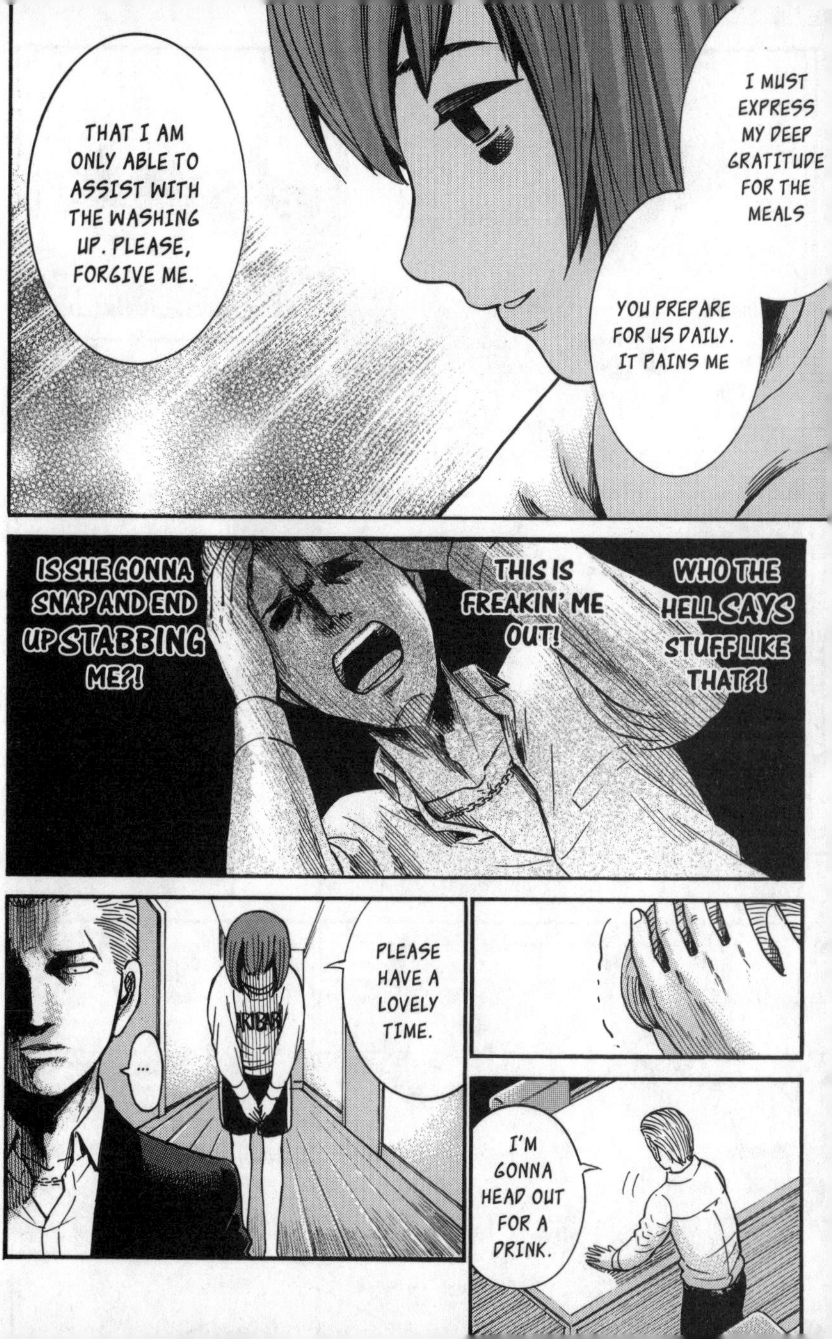
I MUST EXPRESS MY DEEP GRATITUDE FOR THE MEALS
YOU PREPARE FOR US DAILY. IT PAINS ME
THAT I AM ONLY ABLE TO ASSIST WITH THE WASHING UP. PLEASE, FORGIVE ME.
WHO THE HELL SAYS STUFF LIKE THAT?!
THIS IS FREAKIN' ME OUT!
IS SHE GONNA SNAP AND END UP STABBING ME?!
I'M GONNA HEAD OUT FOR A DRINK.
PLEASE HAVE A LOVELY TIME.
...

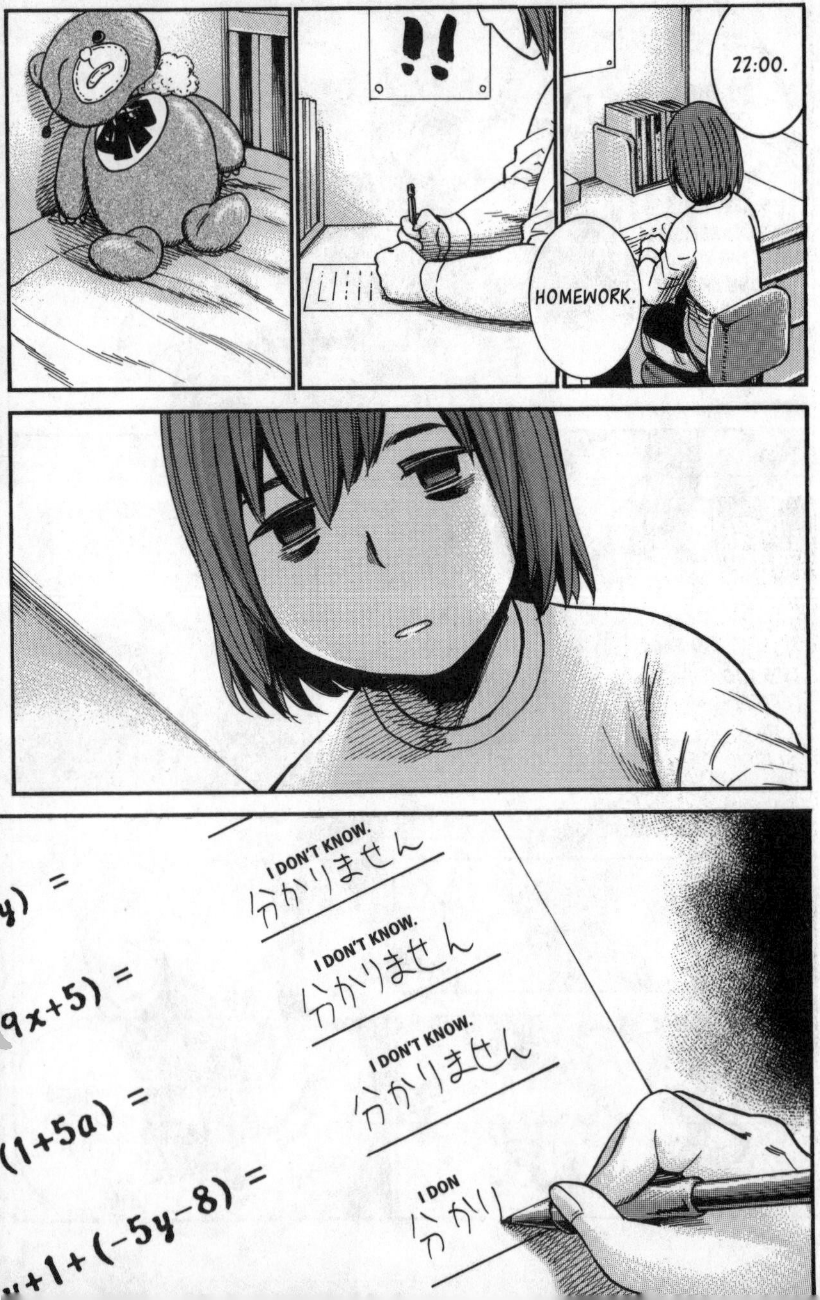
22:00.
HOMEWORK.
!!
y) =
I DON'T KNOW.
分かりません
9x+5) =
I DON'T KNOW.
分かりません
(1+5a) =
I DON'T KNOW.
分かりません
+1+(-5y-8) =
I DON
分かり

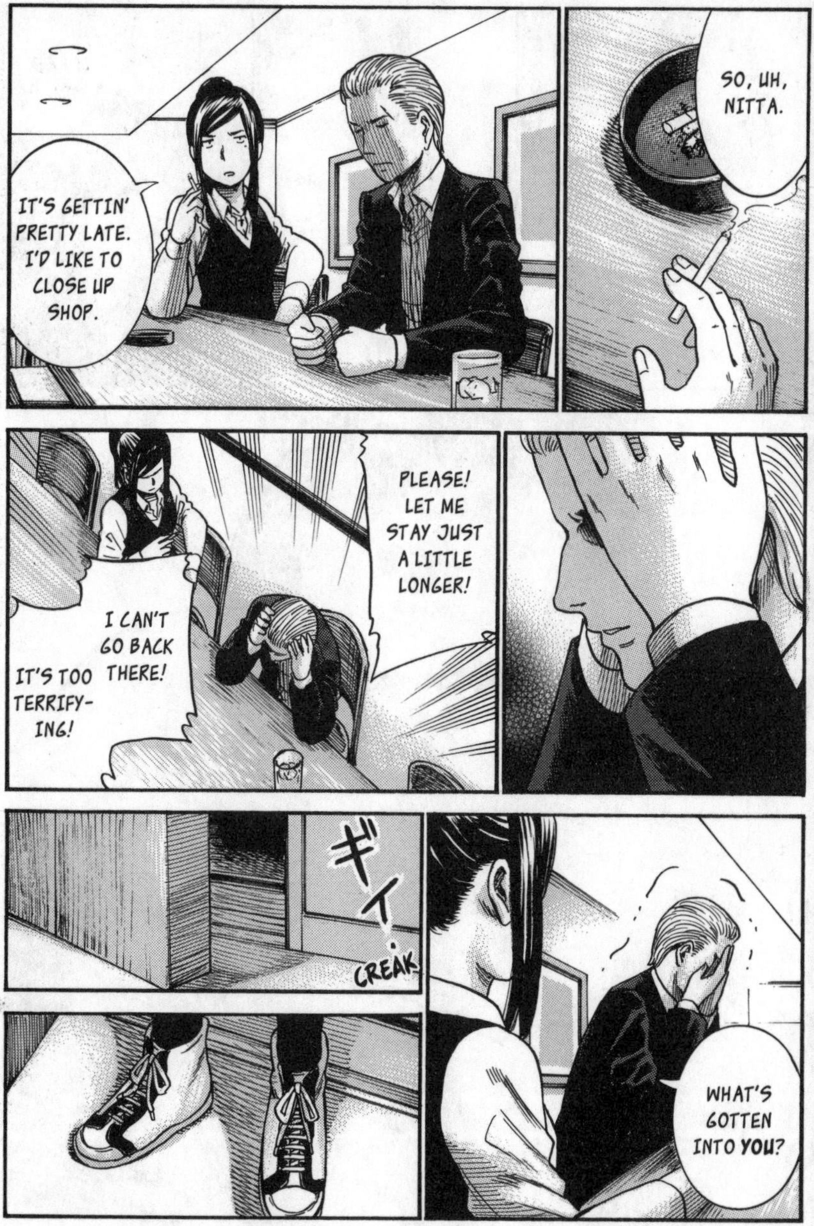
SO, UH, NITTA.
IT'S GETTIN' PRETTY LATE. I'D LIKE TO CLOSE UP SHOP.
PLEASE! LET ME STAY JUST A LITTLE LONGER!
I CAN'T GO BACK THERE!
IT'S TOO TERRIFY-ING!
WHAT'S GOTTEN INTO YOU?
ギイ
CREAK

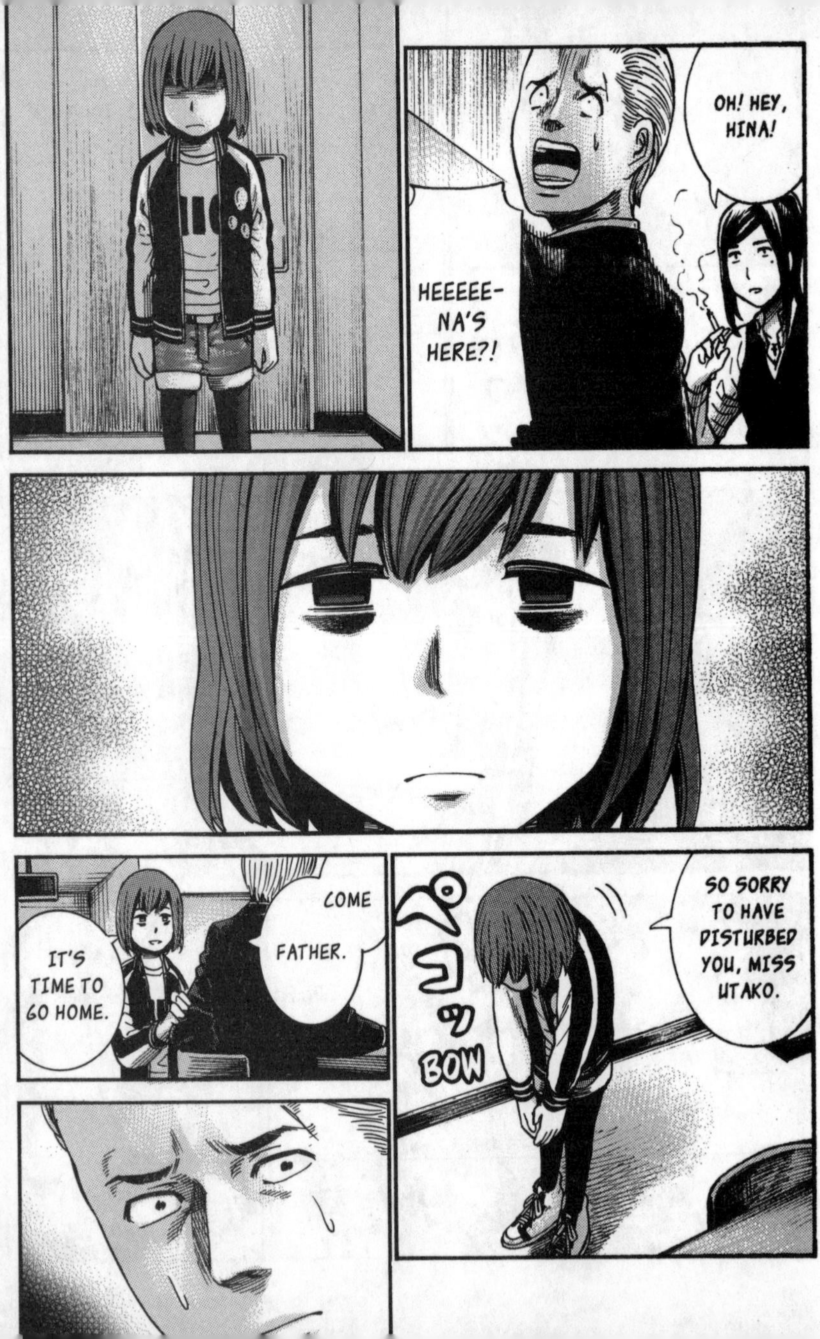
OH! HEY, HINA!
HEEEEE-NA'S HERE?!
SO SORRY TO HAVE DISTURBED YOU, MISS UTAKO.
ペコッ
BOW
COME FATHER.
IT'S TIME TO GO HOME.

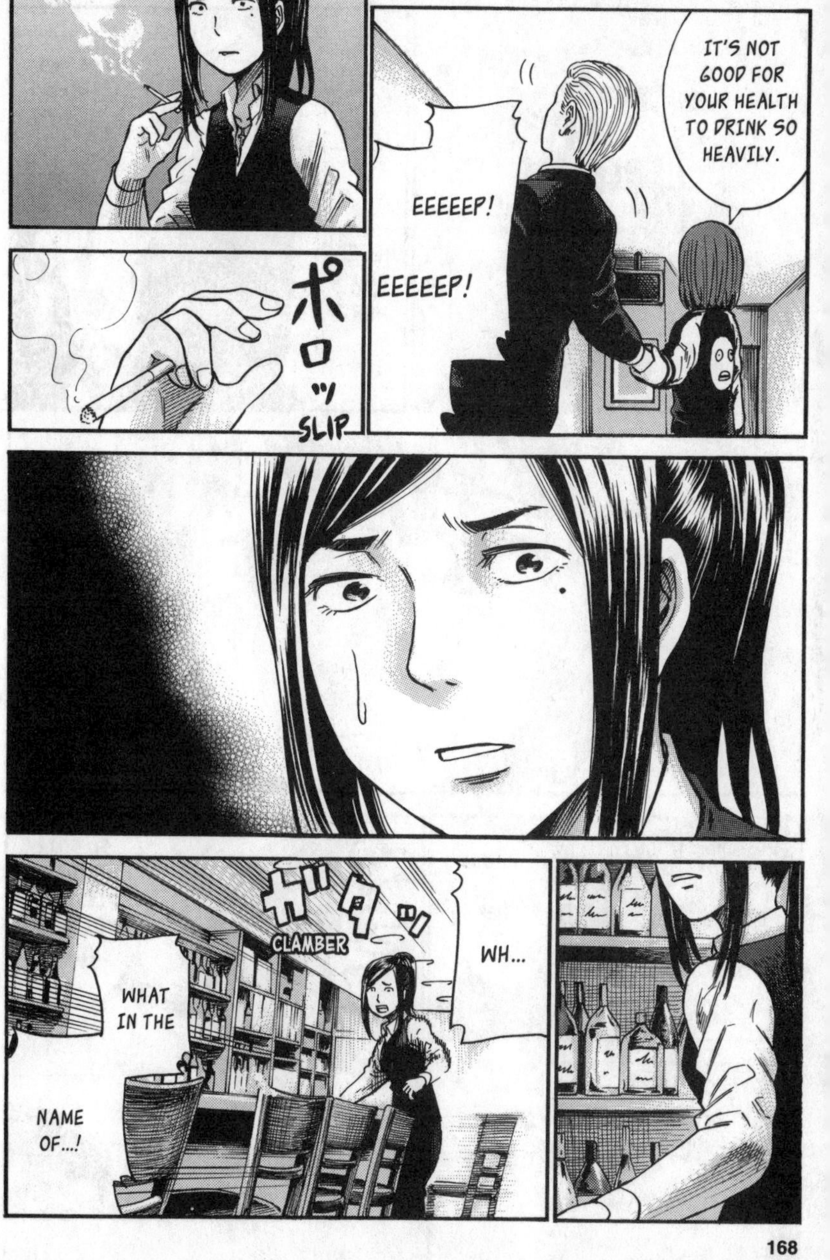
IT'S NOT GOOD FOR YOUR HEALTH TO DRINK SO HEAVILY.
EEEEEP!
EEEEEP!
ポロッ
SLIP
ガタッ
CLAMBER
WH...
WHAT IN THE
NAME OF...!

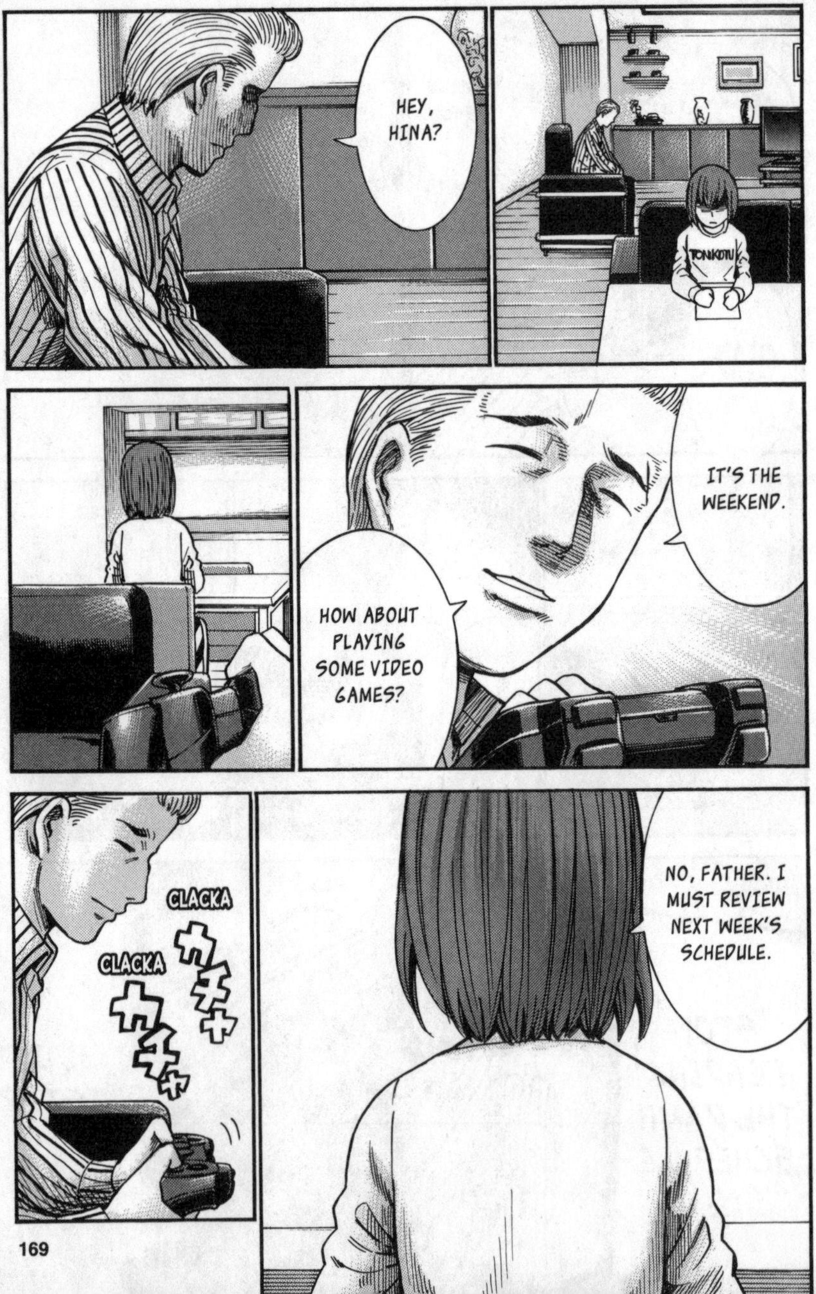
HEY, HINA?
IT'S THE WEEKEND.
HOW ABOUT PLAYING SOME VIDEO GAMES?
NO, FATHER. I MUST REVIEW NEXT WEEK'S SCHEDULE.
CLACKA
カチャ
CLACKA
カチャ

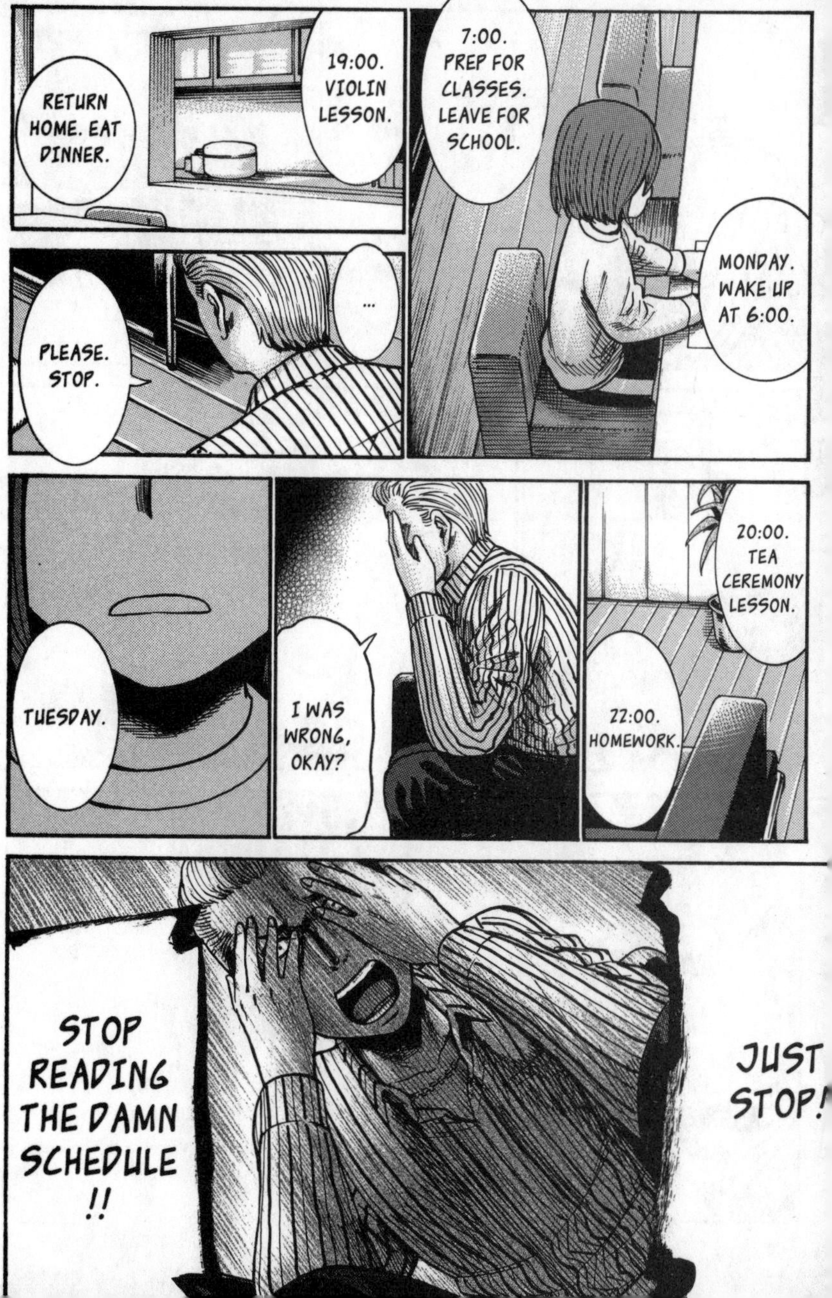
MONDAY. WAKE UP AT 6:00.
7:00. PREP FOR CLASSES. LEAVE FOR SCHOOL.
19:00. VIOLIN LESSON.
RETURN HOME. EAT DINNER.
...
PLEASE. STOP.
20:00. TEA CEREMONY LESSON.
22:00. HOMEWORK.
I WAS WRONG, OKAY?
TUESDAY.
JUST STOP!
STOP READING THE DAMN SCHEDULE !!

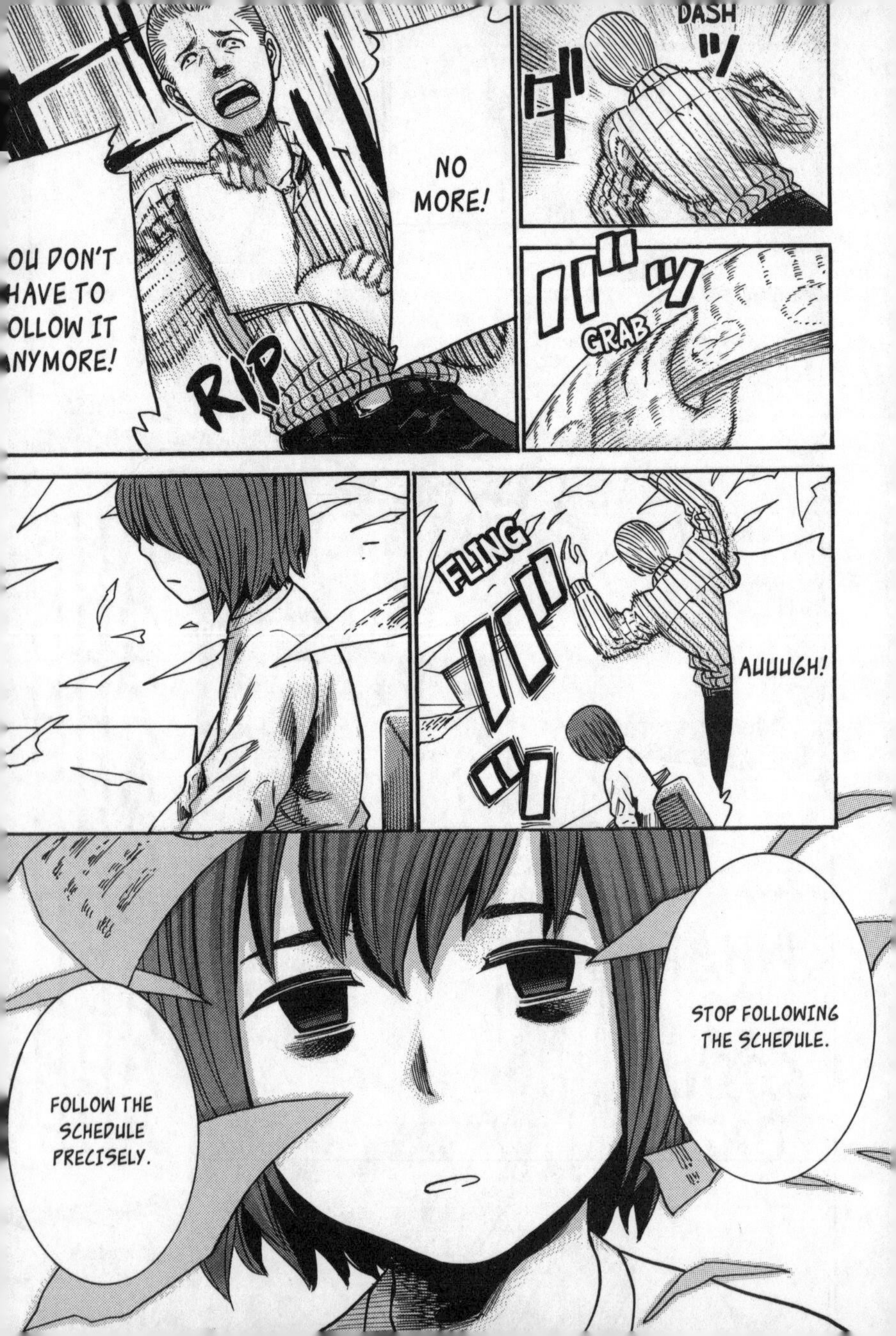
DASH
GRAB
NO MORE!
OU DON'T HAVE TO OLLOW IT NYMORE!
RIP
FLING
AUUUGH!
STOP FOLLOWING THE SCHEDULE.
FOLLOW THE SCHEDULE PRECISELY.

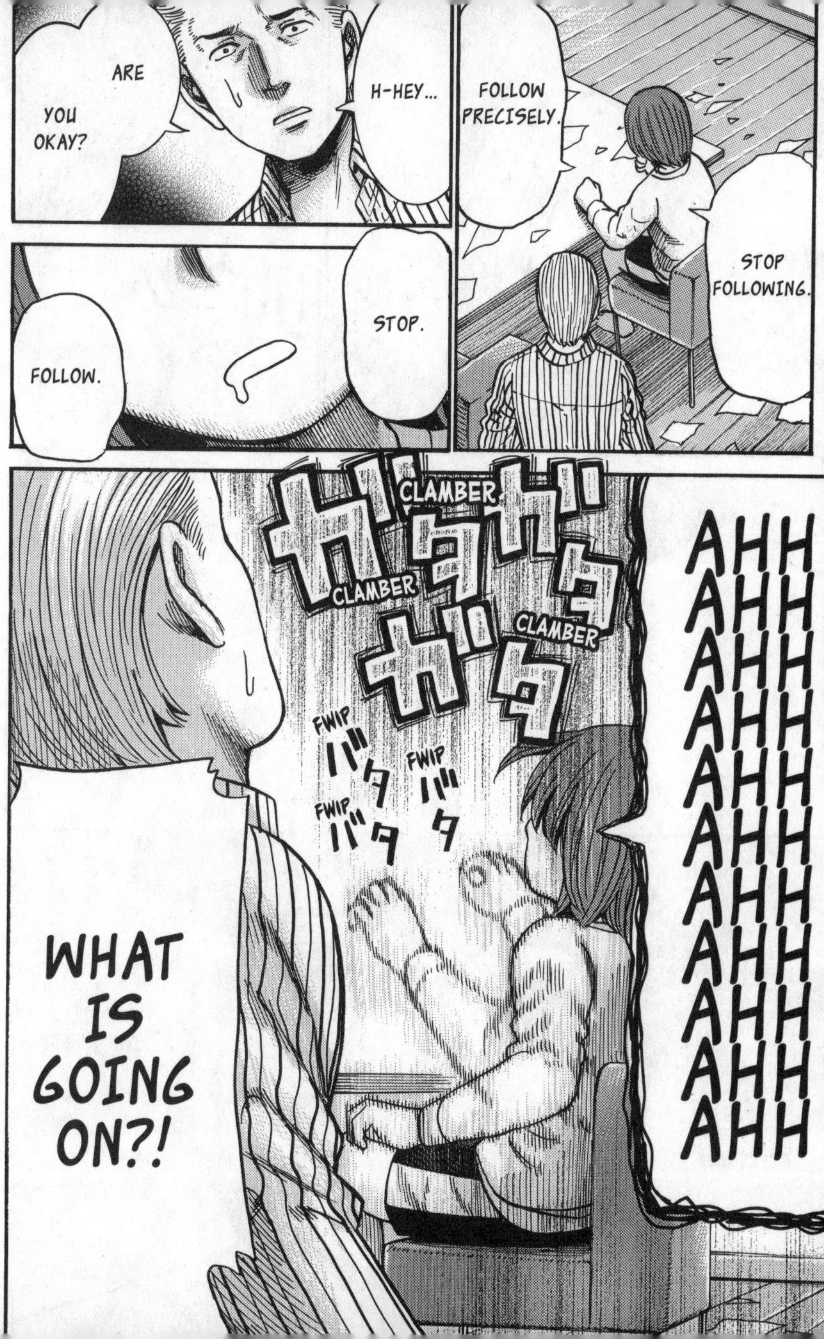
FOLLOW PRECISELY.
STOP FOLLOWING.
H-HEY...
ARE YOU OKAY?
STOP.
FOLLOW.
ガタガタ
CLAMBER
CLAMBER
CLAMBER
バタバタバタ
FWIP
FWIP
FWIP
AAAAAAAAAAAAAAAHHHHHHHHHHHHHHHHHHHHHHHHHHHHHH
WHAT IS GOING ON?!

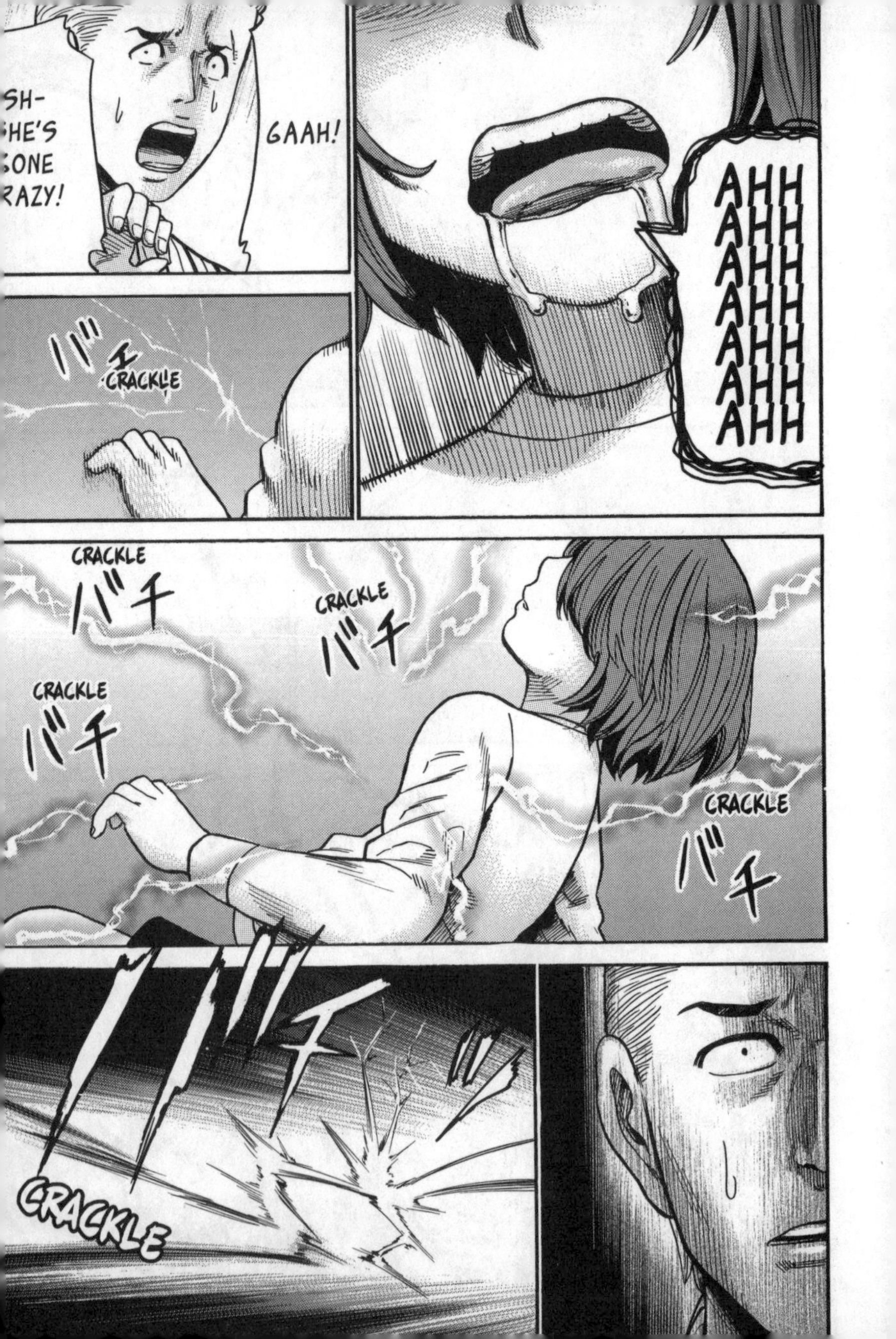
AHH AHH AHH AHH AHH AHH AHH AHH
GAAH!
SH- HE'S ONE RAZY!
バ
CRACKLE
CRACKLE
バチ
CRACKLE
バチ
CRACKLE
バチ
CRACKLE
バチ
バチ
CRACKLE

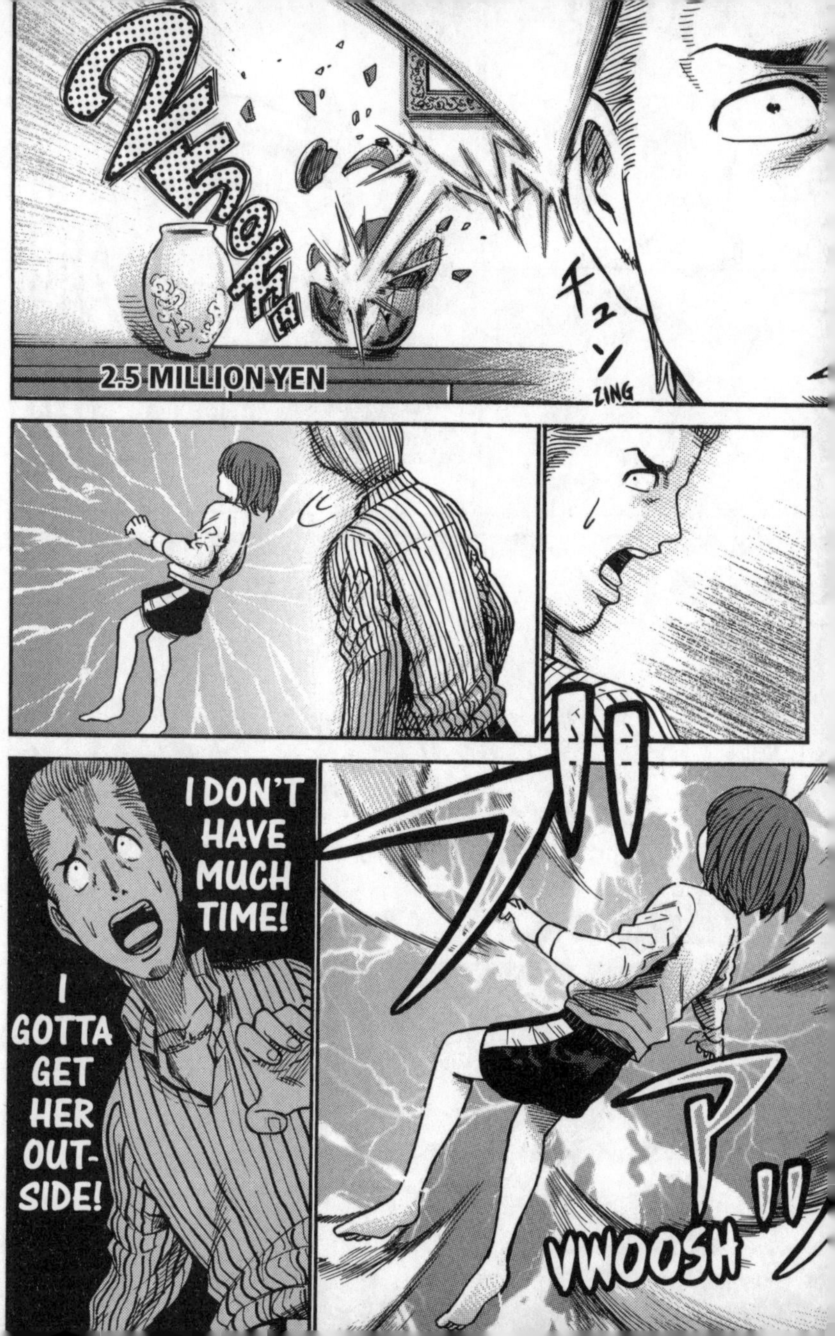

250万円
2.5 MILLION YEN
チュン
ZING
ブアッ
VWOOSH
I DON'T HAVE MUCH TIME!
I GOTTA GET HER OUT-SIDE!

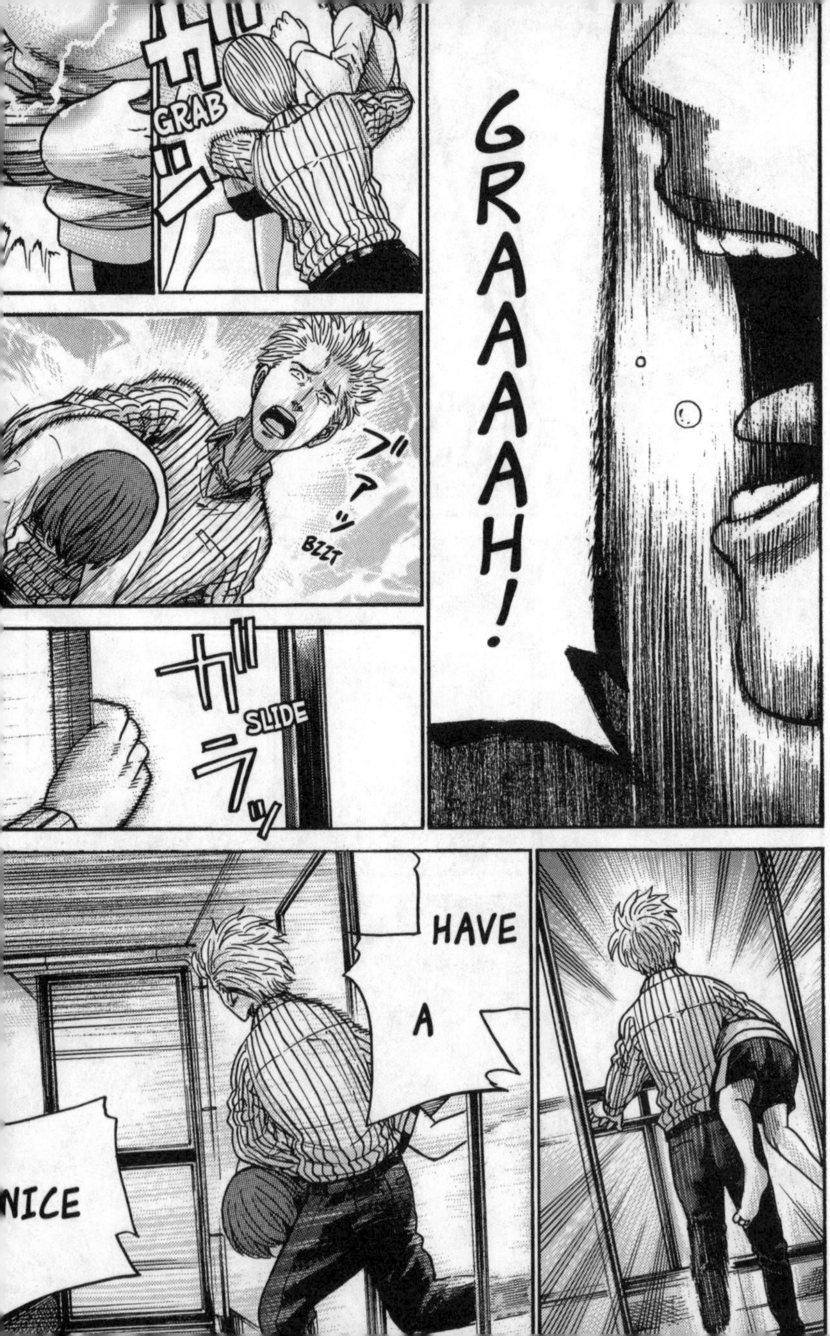
GRAAAAH!
ガッ
GRAB
ブアッ
BZZT
ガラッ
SLIDE
HAVE
A
NICE

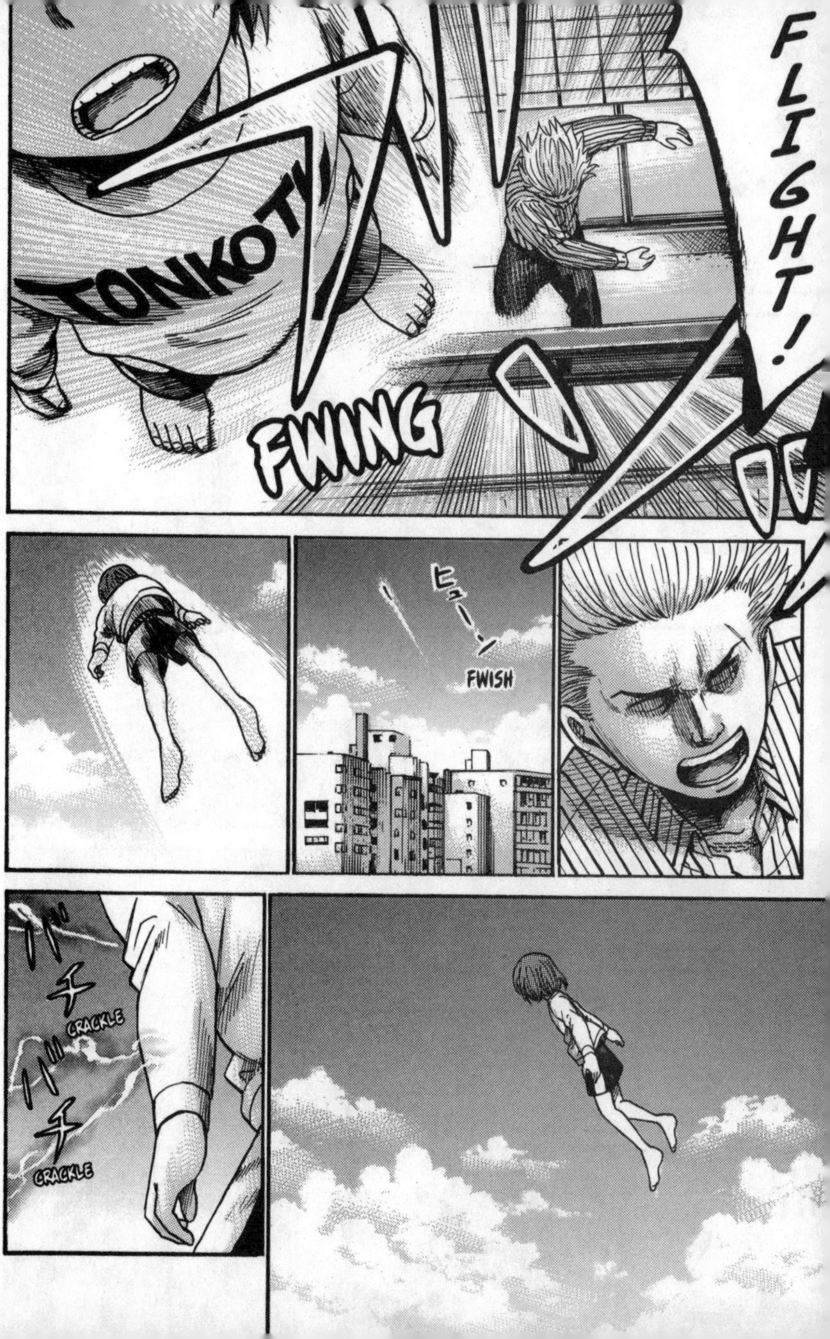
FLIGHT!
TONKOTI!
FWING
ヒューーン
FWISH
パチ
CRACKLE
パチ
CRACKLE

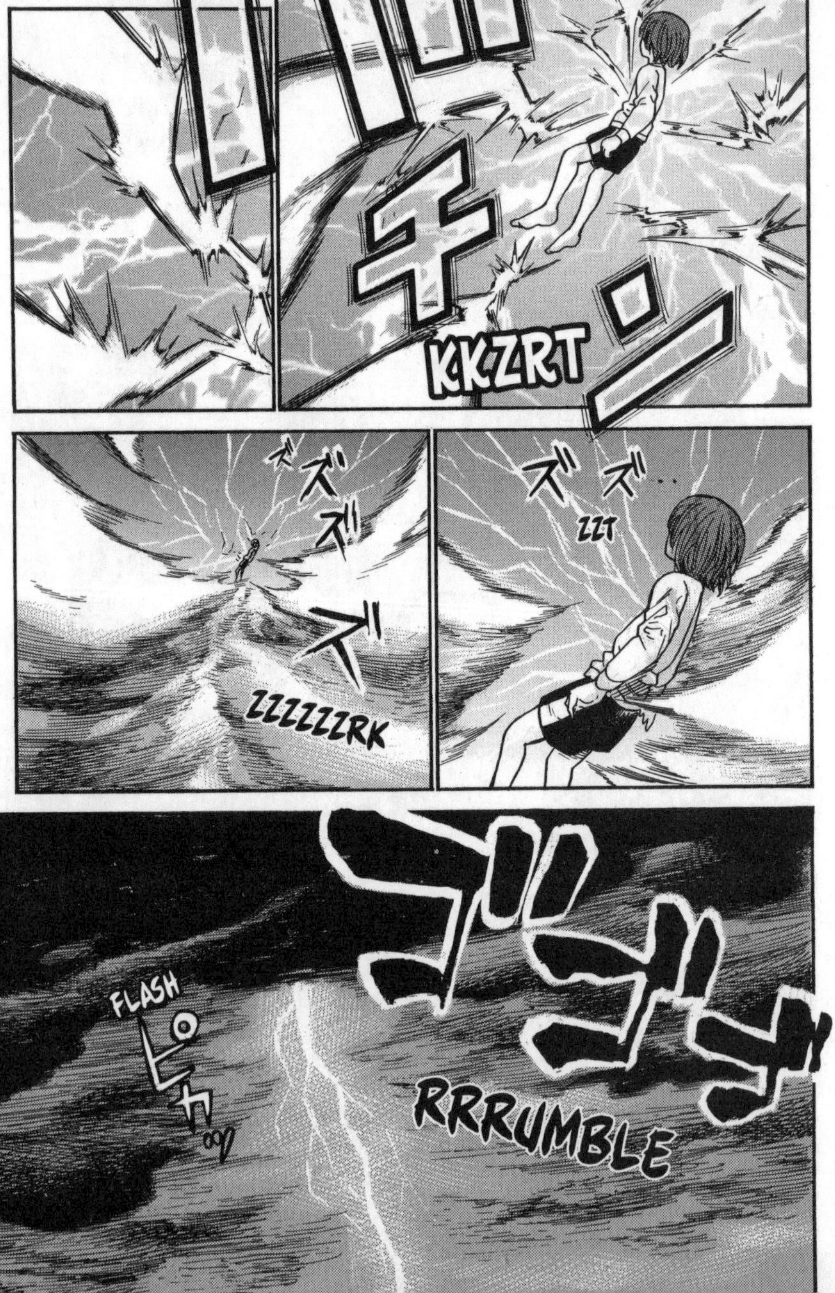

KKZRT
ZZT
ZZZZZZZRK
RRRUMBLE
FLASH

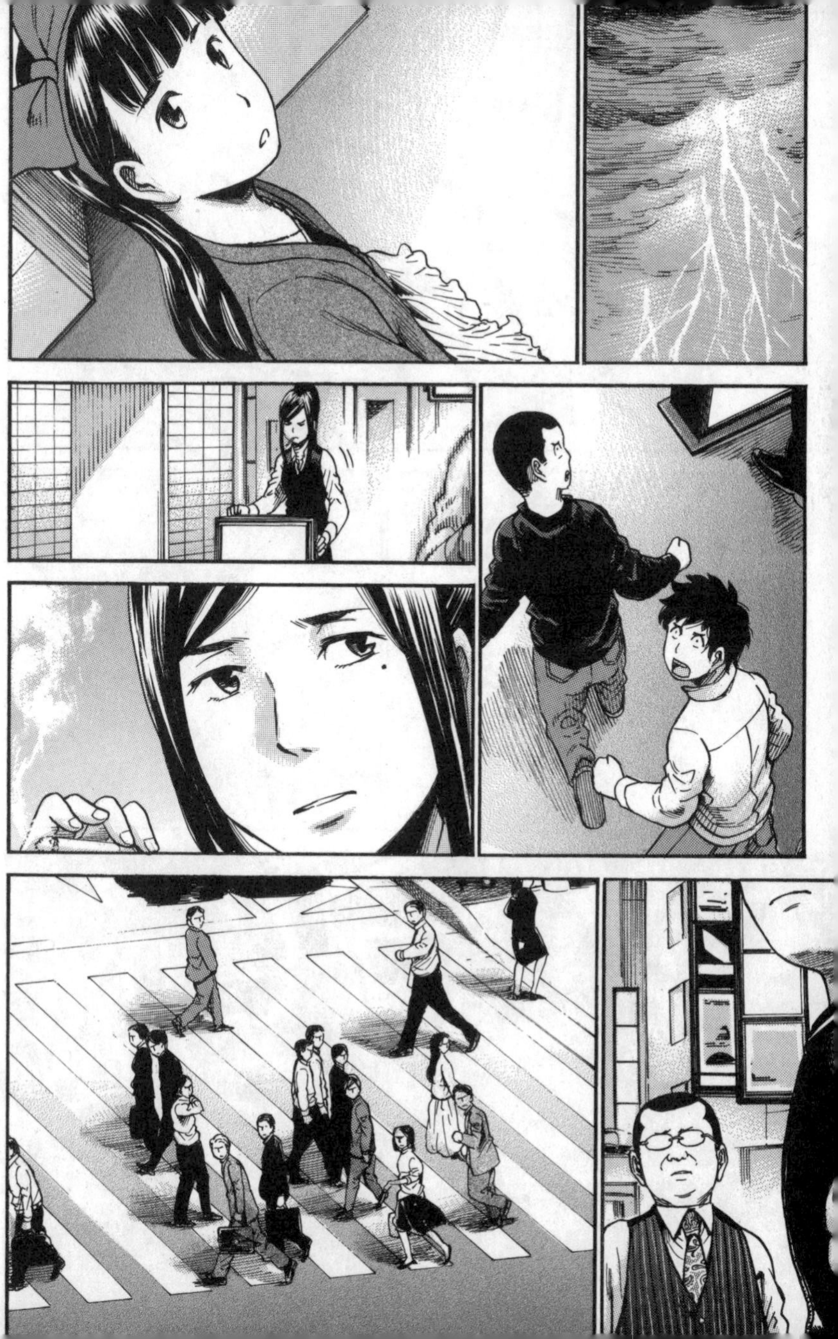

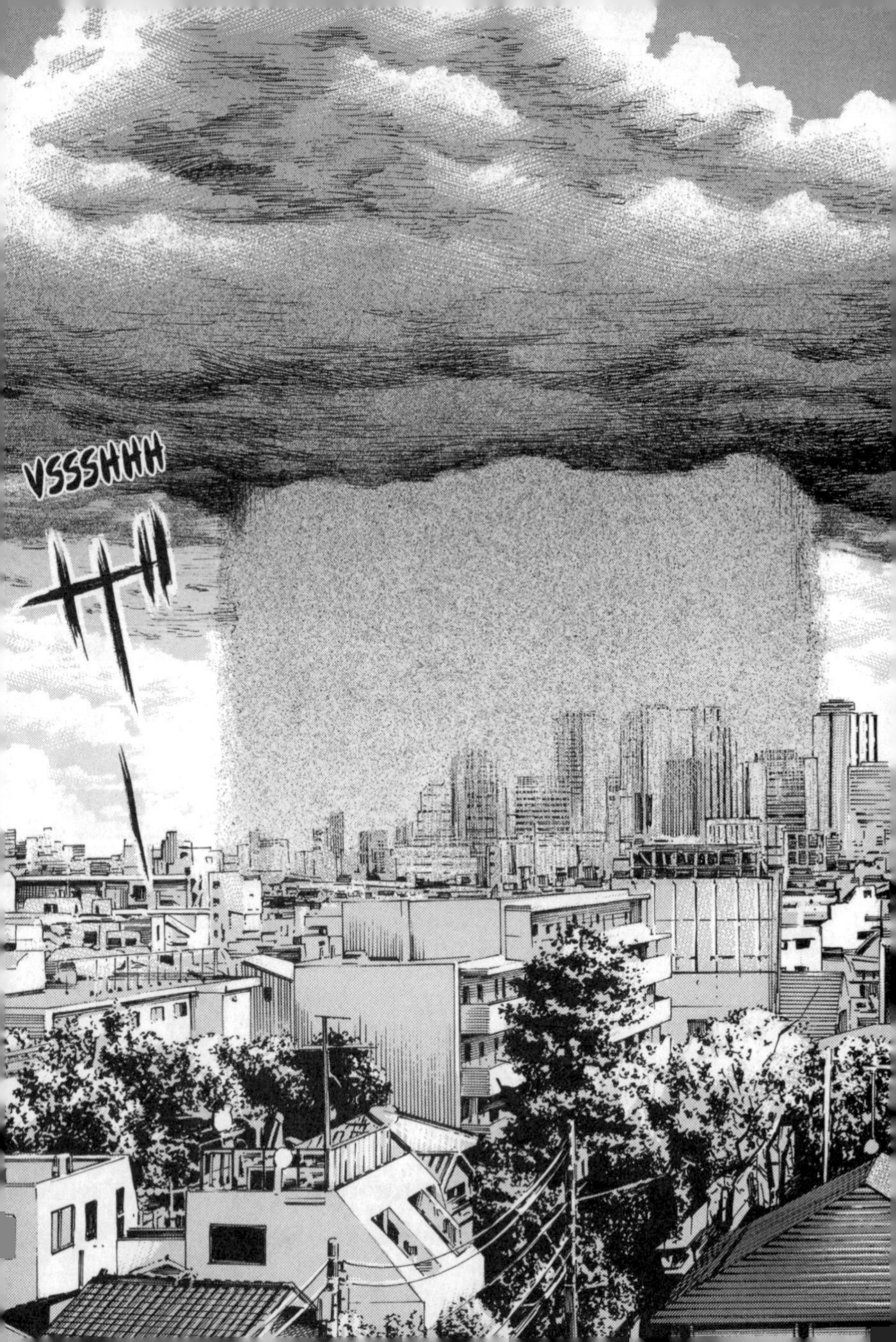
VSSSHHH

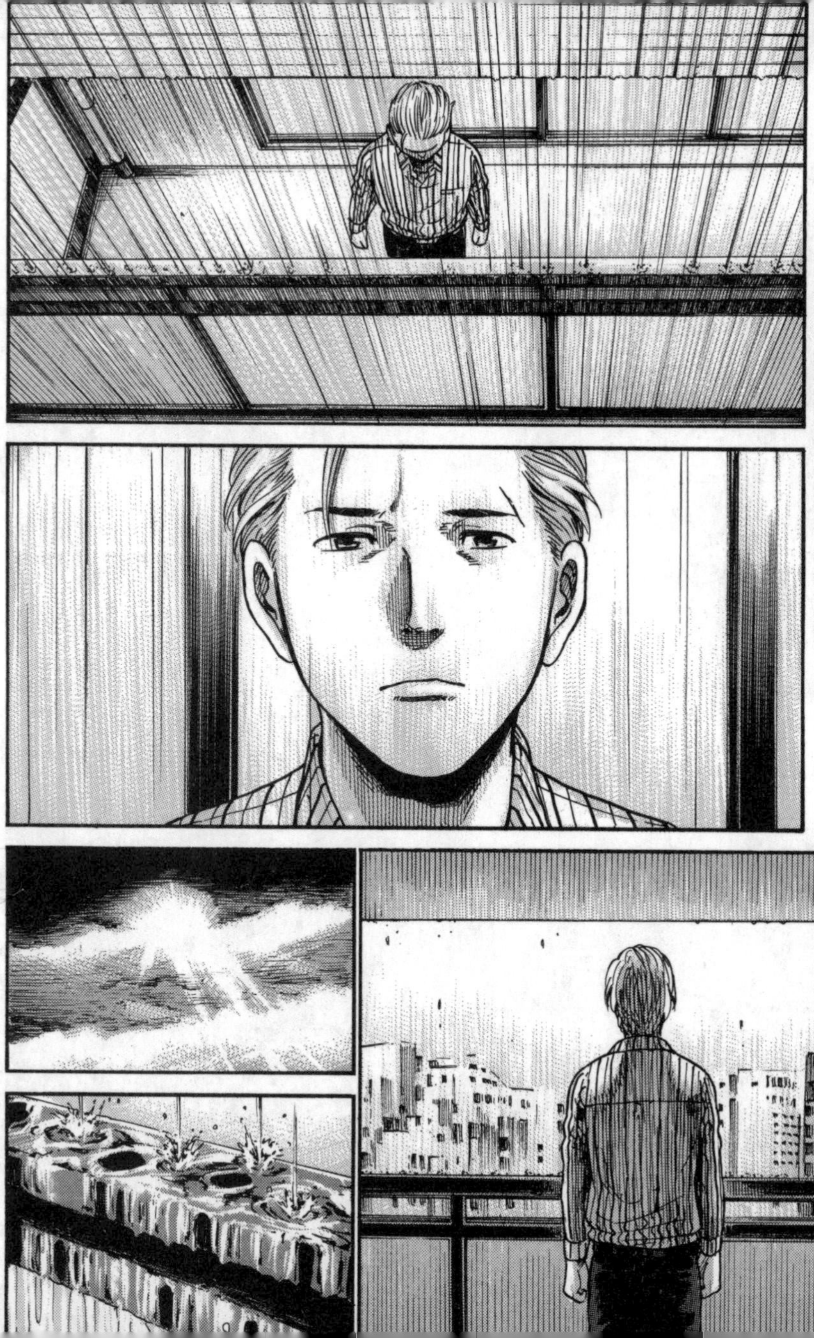

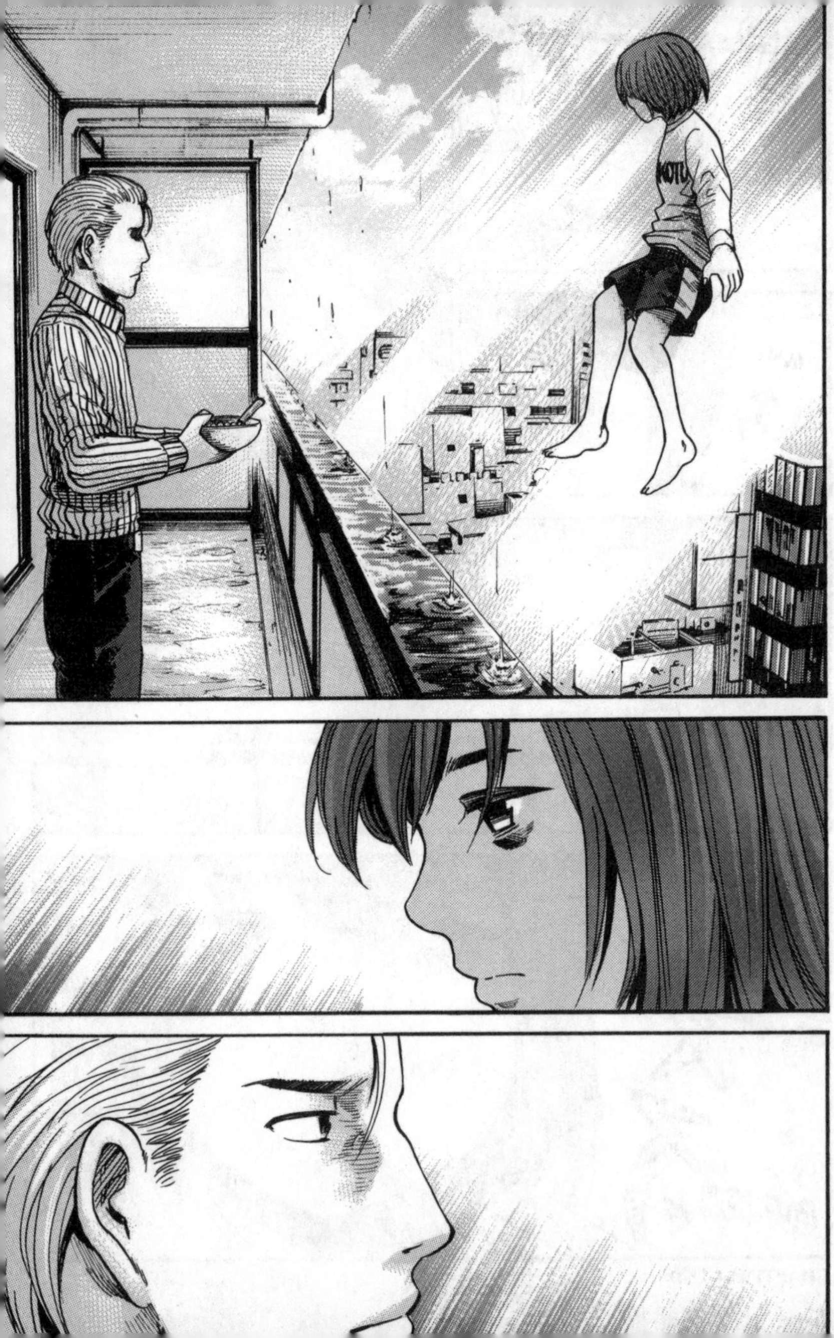

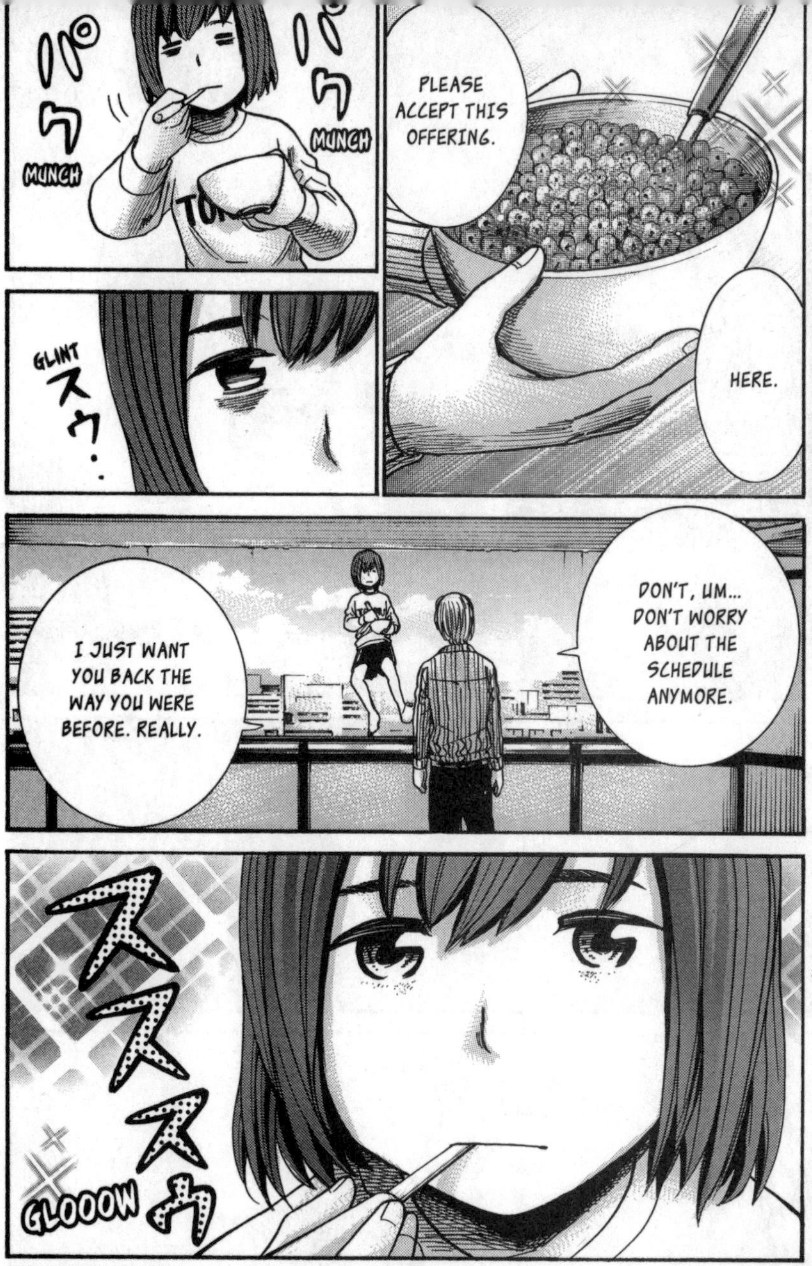
PLEASE ACCEPT THIS OFFERING.
HERE.
パク
MUNCH
パク
MUNCH
GLINT
スウ・・
DON'T, UM... DON'T WORRY ABOUT THE SCHEDULE ANYMORE.
I JUST WANT YOU BACK THE WAY YOU WERE BEFORE. REALLY.
スススウ
GLOOOW

CHAPTER 21 END

SCREEE
SCREEK
SCREEK
SCREEK

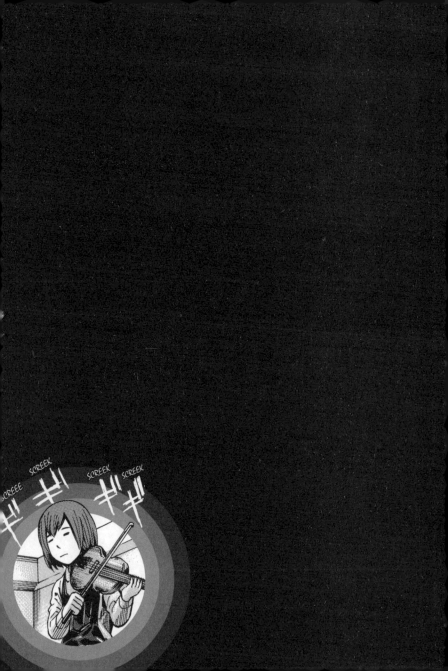

EXTRA 8 WHAT HAPPENS WHEN YOU LEAVE EVERYTHING UP TO A CAPABLE EMPLOYEE

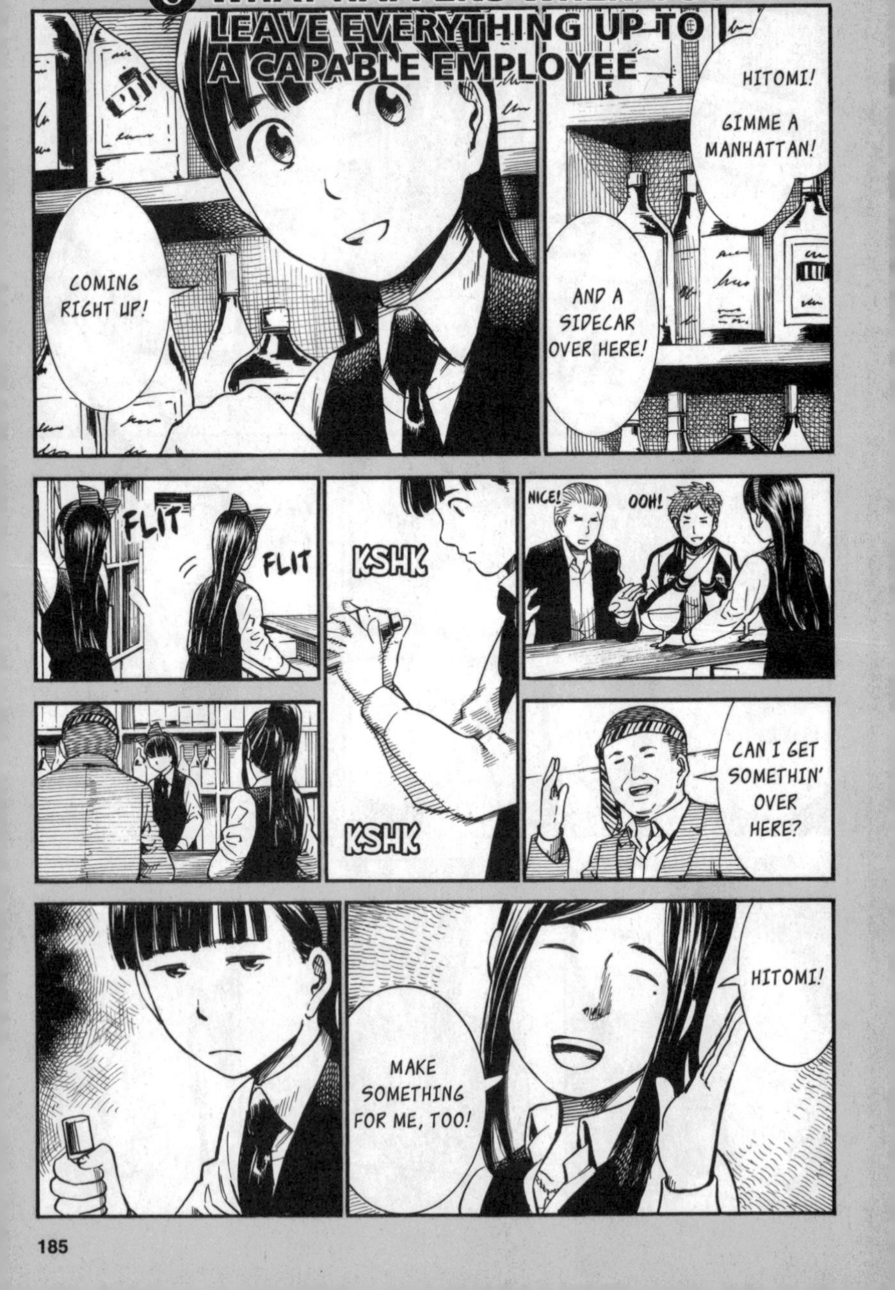
HITOMI!
GIMME A MANHATTAN!
AND A SIDECAR OVER HERE!
COMING RIGHT UP!
OOH!
NICE!
CAN I GET SOMETHIN' OVER HERE?
KSHK
KSHK
FLIT
FLIT
HITOMI!
MAKE SOMETHING FOR ME, TOO!

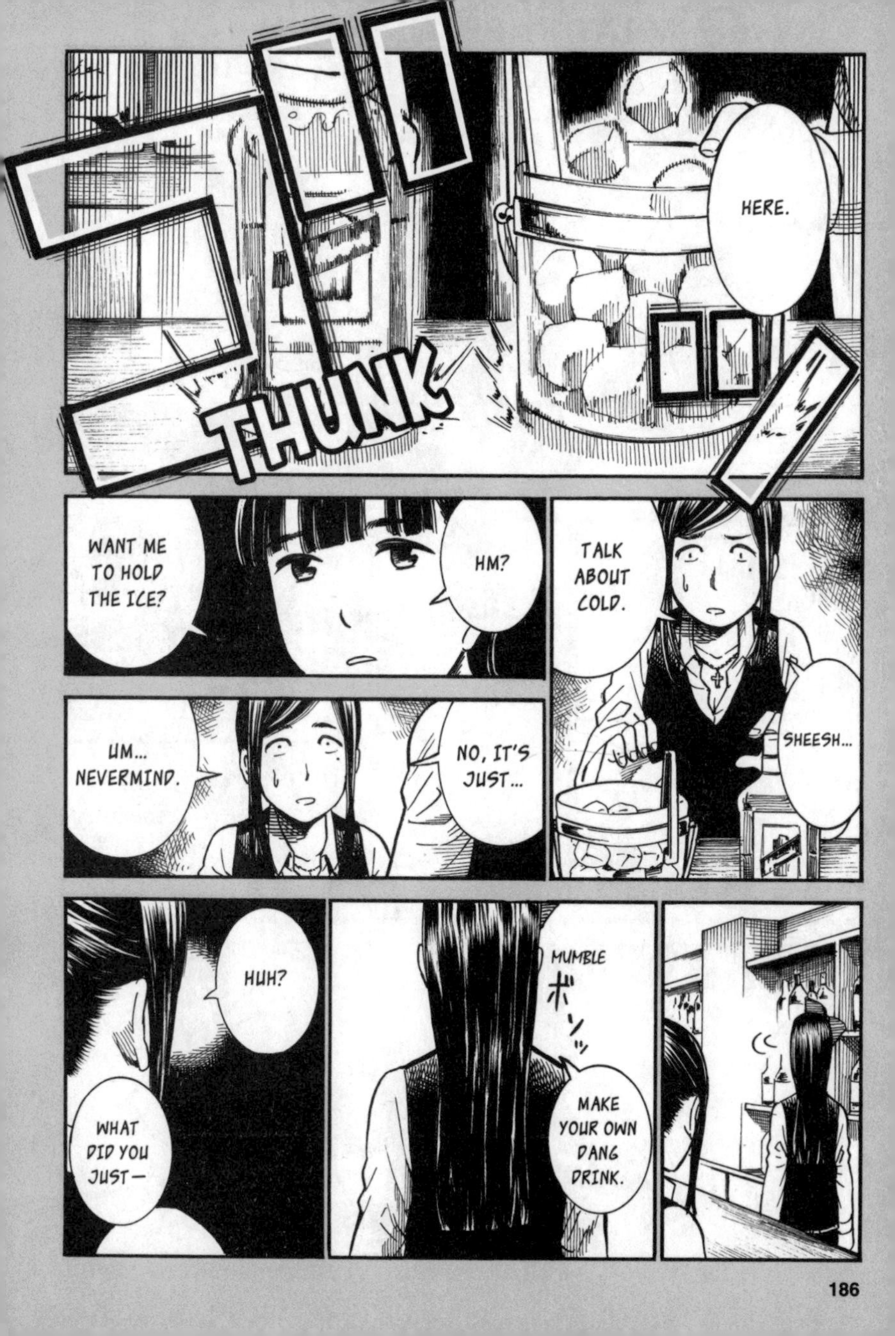
HERE.
THUNK
TALK ABOUT COLD.
SHEESH...
HM?
WANT ME TO HOLD THE ICE?
NO, IT'S JUST...
UM... NEVERMIND.
MUMBLE
ボソッ
MAKE YOUR OWN DANG DRINK.
HUH?
WHAT DID YOU JUST—

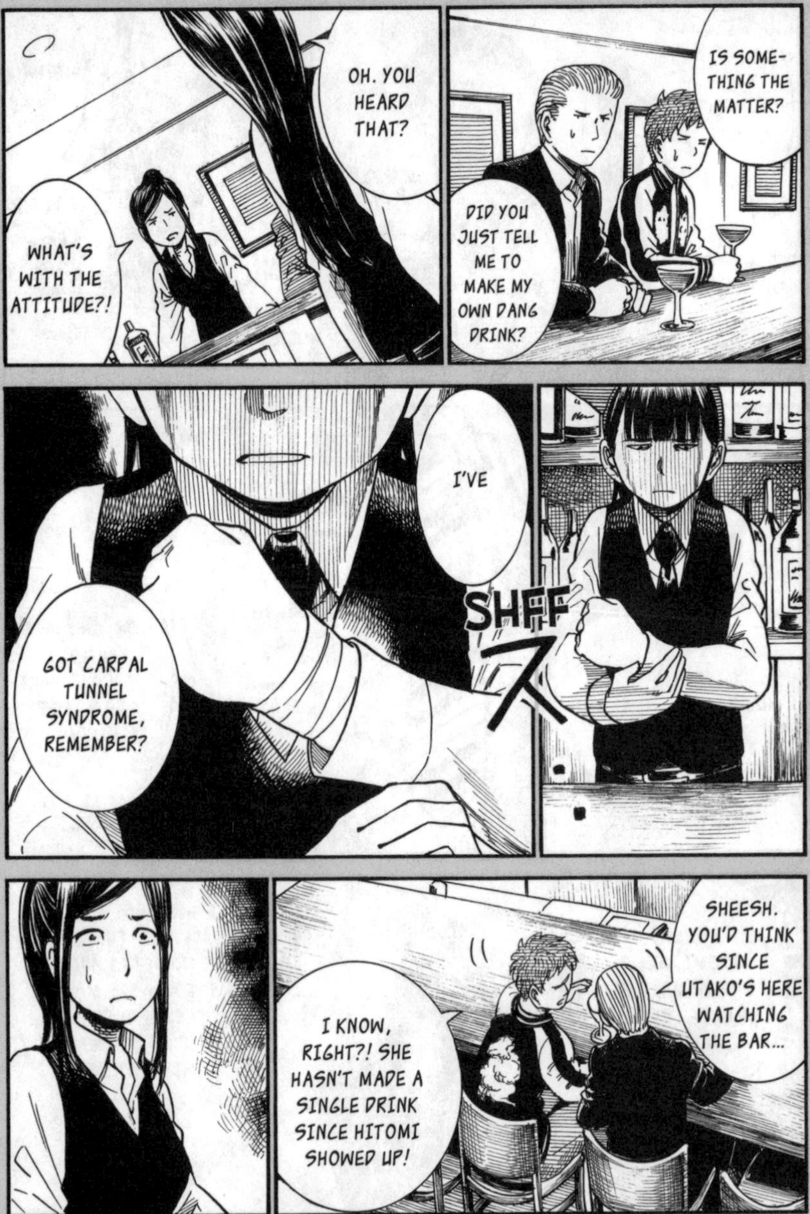
IS SOME-THING THE MATTER?
DID YOU JUST TELL ME TO MAKE MY OWN DANG DRINK?
OH. YOU HEARD THAT?
WHAT'S WITH THE ATTITUDE?!
SHFF
I'VE
GOT CARPAL TUNNEL SYNDROME, REMEMBER?
SHEESH. YOU'D THINK SINCE UTAKO'S HERE WATCHING THE BAR...
I KNOW, RIGHT?! SHE HASN'T MADE A SINGLE DRINK SINCE HITOMI SHOWED UP!

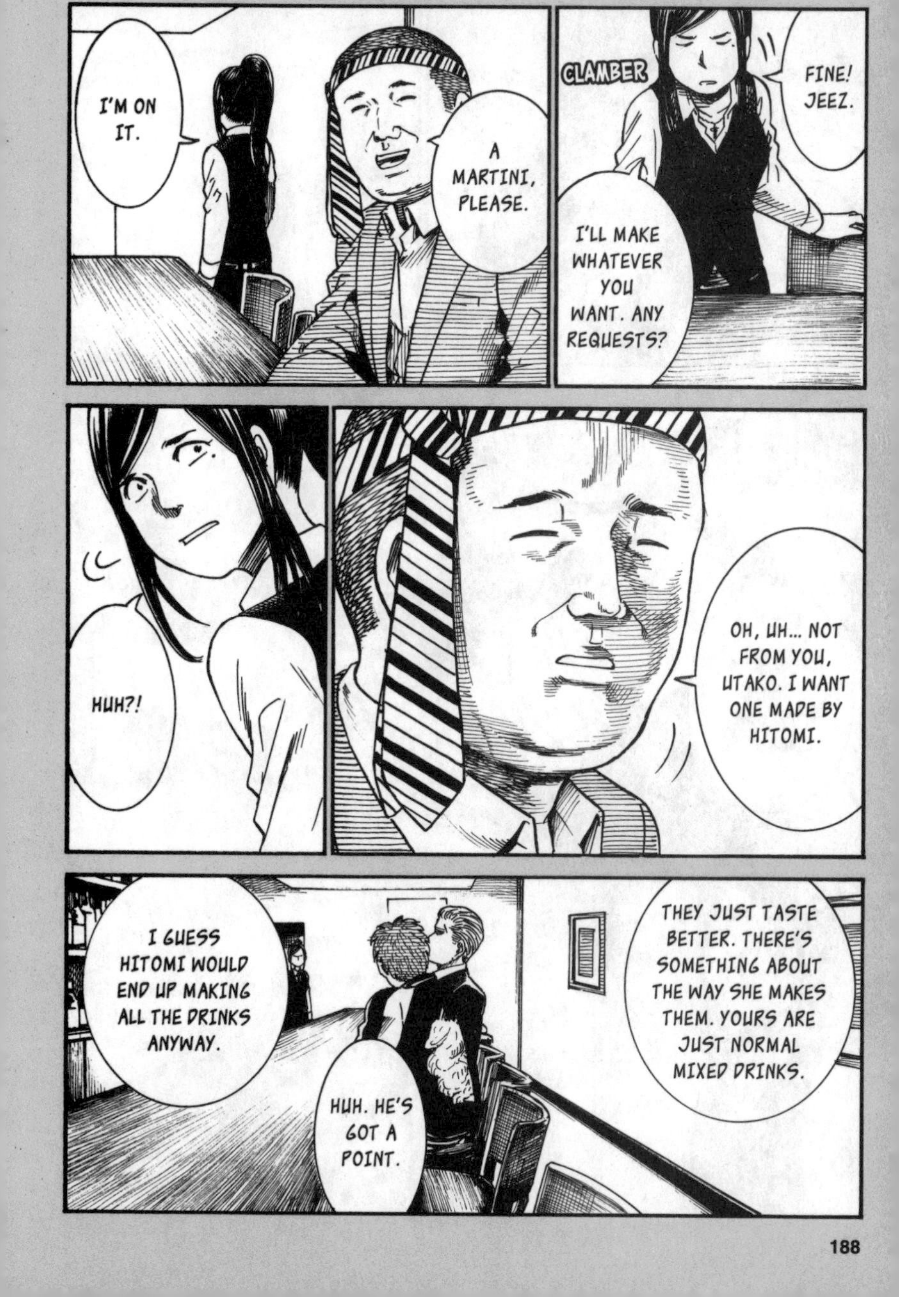
FINE! JEEZ.
CLAMBER
I'LL MAKE WHATEVER YOU WANT. ANY REQUESTS?
A MARTINI, PLEASE.
I'M ON IT.
OH, UH... NOT FROM YOU, UTAKO. I WANT ONE MADE BY HITOMI.
HUH?!
THEY JUST TASTE BETTER. THERE'S SOMETHING ABOUT THE WAY SHE MAKES THEM. YOURS ARE JUST NORMAL MIXED DRINKS.
I GUESS HITOMI WOULD END UP MAKING ALL THE DRINKS ANYWAY.
HUH. HE'S GOT A POINT.

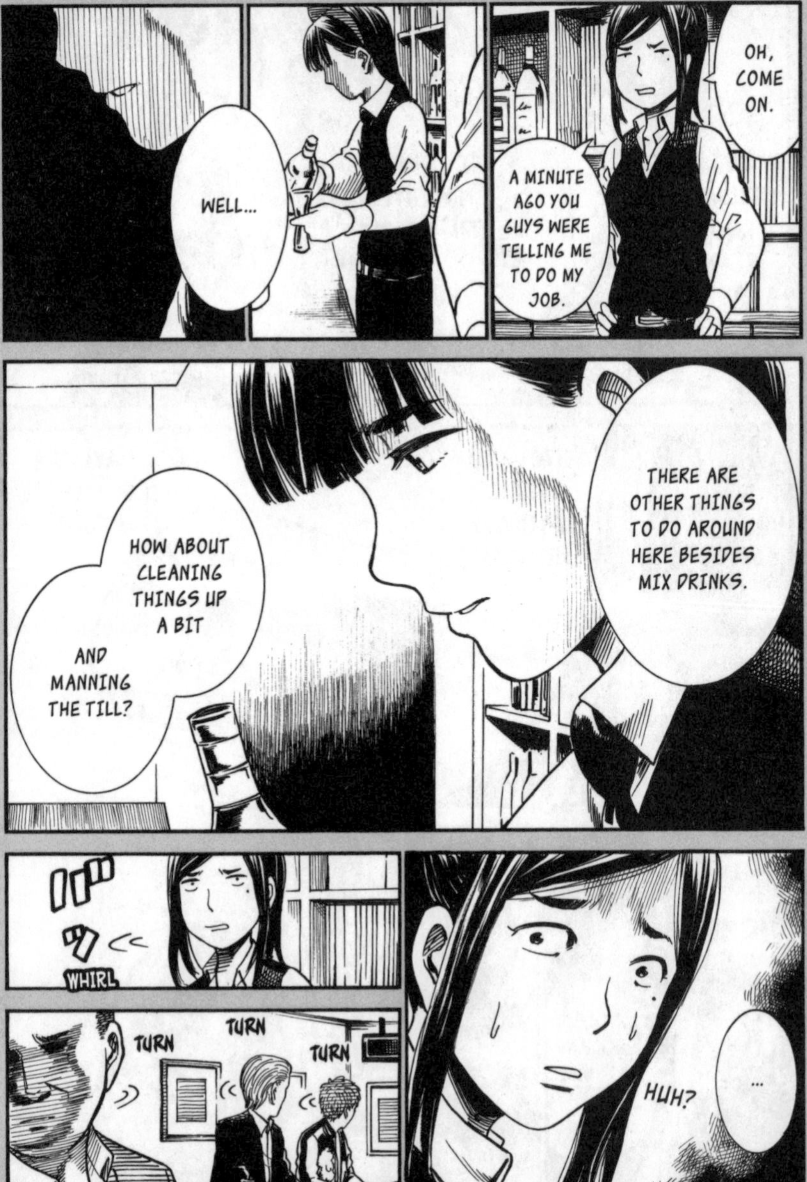
OH, COME ON.
A MINUTE AGO YOU GUYS WERE TELLING ME TO DO MY JOB.
WELL...
THERE ARE OTHER THINGS TO DO AROUND HERE BESIDES MIX DRINKS.
HOW ABOUT CLEANING THINGS UP A BIT
AND MANNING THE TILL?
...
HUH?
WHIRL
TURN
TURN
TURN

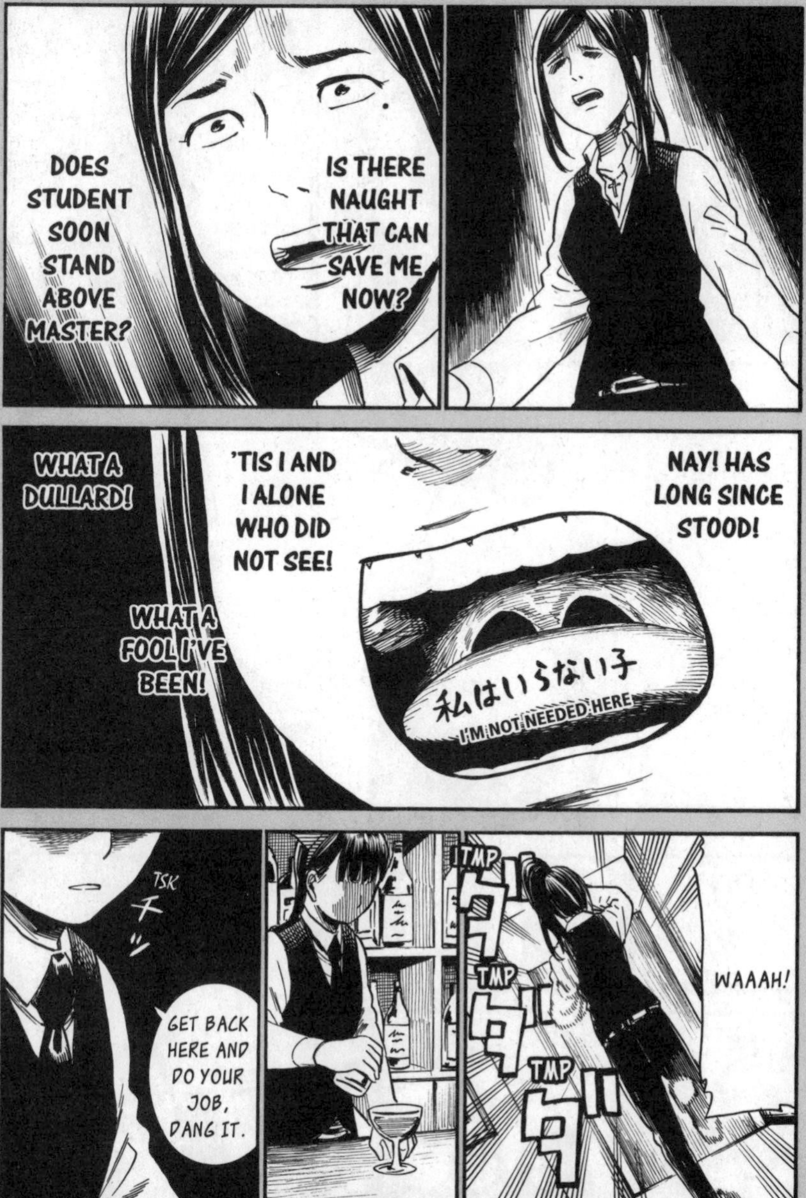
IS THERE NAUGHT THAT CAN SAVE ME NOW?
DOES STUDENT SOON STAND ABOVE MASTER?
NAY! HAS LONG SINCE STOOD!
'TIS I AND I ALONE WHO DID NOT SEE!
WHAT A DULLARD!
WHAT A FOOL I'VE BEEN!
私はいらない子
I'M NOT NEEDED HERE
TMP
タッ
TMP
タッ
TMP
タッ
WAAAH!
TSK
チッ
GET BACK HERE AND DO YOUR JOB, DANG IT.

EXTRA 8 END

HINAMATSURI.
TO BE CONTINUED
IN VOLUME 5.

ONE PEACE BOOKS

HINAMATSURI Volume 4
© Masao Ohtake 2012
First published in Japan in 2012 by KADOKAWA CORPORATION, Tokyo
English translation rights arranged with KADOKAWA CORPORATION, Tokyo

ISBN: 978-1-64273-030-2

Written and illustrated by Masao Ohtake
Translated by Stephen Kohler
English Edition Published by One Peace Books 2019

Printed in Canada
3 4 5 6 7 8 9 10

One Peace Books
43-32 22nd Street STE 204 Long Island City New York 11101
www.onepeacebooks.com